# On Geography

*Selected Writings of*

## PRESTON E. JAMES

SYRACUSE GEOGRAPHICAL SERIES, 3

PRESTON E. JAMES

# On Geography

## Selected Writings of
## PRESTON E. JAMES

*Edited by*
**D.W. MEINIG**

*Introduction by*
RICHARD HARTSHORNE

SYRACUSE UNIVERSITY PRESS

Library of Congress Catalog Card Number: 77-170097
ISBN: 0-8156-0084-4

G
59
J34

## SYRACUSE GEOGRAPHICAL SERIES

No. 1 Theodore Oberlander, *The Zagros Streams: A New Interpretation of Transverse Drainage in an Orogenic Zone,* 1965.

No. 2 Edward W. Soja, *The Geography of Modernization in Kenya: A Spatial Analysis of Social, Economic, and Political Change,* 1968.

No. 3 D. W. Meinig, Editor, *On Geography: Selected Writings of Preston E. James,* 1971.

Library of Congress Cataloging in Publication Data

James, Preston Everett, 1899–
    On geography.
    (Syracuse geographical series, 3)
    "A chronological list of the writings and major addresses
of Preston E. James, 1922–1970": p.
    Includes bibliographical references.
    1. Geography—Addresses, essays, lectures.
I. Title.  II. Series.
G59.J34            910.01            77-170097
ISBN 0-8156-0084-4

*Manufactured in the United States of America*

# CONTENTS

# PREFACE

This volume presents a series of interrelated essays which very well express the dominant American view of the history, nature, and significance of geography around the middle decades of the twentieth century. It also offers a good sampling of the work of an internationally known scholar who has been widely acclaimed as one of the most capable writers and one of the most influential geographers during that time.

The very attempt to combine these objectives of course makes it impossible to be complete or balanced in either. Although Preston James has been aware of the full breadth of and the shifting emphases within the field of geography, his interpretation cannot but reflect something of his particular career. On the other hand, while these selections, together with the Introduction, Commentaries by the Editor, and Bibliography, offer much information about the man's career, they by no means constitute a full professional biography.

Nevertheless, this volume is offered with confidence that it will be welcomed by many as very useful; for these writings, grouped by topic rather than by time, provide not only a series of efficient statements and examples of the geographical thought of their time but in most cases deal quite explicitly with fundamental matters of enduring significance.

While the quality of James's work carries its own justification for republication, and the intent is not so much to honor a geographer as to serve the field of geography, publication of this collection in this series is one of the means by which his colleagues wish to recognize "Jimmy" James for his fifty years of service to his profession, his twenty-five years on the faculty of Syracuse University, and his seventeen years as chairman of the Department of Geography.

*Syracuse, Summer 1971*                    D. W. MEINIG

# INTRODUCTION

Looking back over the record of American geography, during the years in which we have been involved together in the profession, I am struck by the number of different aspects in which Preston James has made outstanding contributions to the field. He has been a leader in teaching both students and teachers; in supplying materials to aid others to teach more effectively; in scholarly research and publication; in clarifying the objectives and methods of the discipline; in applying geography in government service; in promoting geographic education; and in organizing cooperation among geographers and with students of other disciplines.

All these varied activities are recorded, though some in lesser part, in the list of his publications, of which relatively few can be included in this volume. For James has been a prolific writer, recognizing, as every teacher should, that what is taught in class or presented orally at a meeting but remains unpublished will in very short time perish. In addition to numerous books, his bibliography is a record of publication of two or three articles practically every year for nearly fifty years, not to mention a large number of reviews and short geographical notes. That these vary greatly in level of consideration is a reflection of the variety of professional purposes indicated above.

Preston James's career as a teacher of undergraduates began over fifty years ago, in 1919 when he was a senior at Harvard. He served as a teaching assistant there and continued to do so through his graduate work at Harvard, where he received the M.A. in 1921, majoring in climatology, and at Clark University, where he earned a Ph.D. in geography in 1923. He has been a member of the Geography Department at the University of Michigan and, after 1945, at Syracuse, following four years of war service supplying geographic intelligence in the Research and Analysis Branch of the Office of Strategic Services. In addition he has been visiting professor at six or more American universities and at Edinburgh and in Brazil.

ix

It is of course in his published textbooks that James has been able to teach the greatest number of students—and, no doubt, their teachers. The complaint of some of the latter, that his texts were "not easy to teach," may reflect the fact that they are not conventional compilations of well-known materials, but rather are structured on sophisticated concepts and enriched with no small amount of original research. The teacher therefore must learn before he can teach.

Teaching the teachers has been a continuous concern of James. More than a score of addresses given at teachers' meetings, and other papers discussing the purpose and methods of geography, have been published in the journals of teachers of geography and the social sciences. In addition, as by-products of field research, he has provided teachers with more than a dozen substantive articles useful for teaching. Throughout the history of American geography, few have contributed so much to understanding of the subject on the part of those who teach it in the schools.

The same may well apply to those of us who teach geography at the university level, for James has taught, and been taught by, his peers. If at times the teaching took on a hortatory tone, we recognized that he was exhorting himself as well as us. Likewise for James, the purpose of discussions about geography was not to win arguments but to reach mutual understanding. This is demonstrated in the sixteen or more papers that developed from such discussions, some of the more recent of which are included in this volume. If much of this is re-statement of what others have written before—as indeed must be true of nearly all that is written in this field—I find, so far as anything of mine is involved, that the meaning has always been understood correctly, its statement frequently improved in clarity, and the source commonly acknowledged—attributes by no means common in this form of writing.

Particularly significant in relation to his own substantive work are the discussions of the regional concept and the regional method, beginning with the paper published in 1934 on "The Terminology of Regional Description," and culminating perhaps in the presidential address of 1952 (Article 3). More clearly than most, James has recognized the region as a form of generalization and has shown that the concept is involved in all aspects of geography —systematic as well as regional.

In his research work, James had demonstrated in practice what he repeatedly urged in precept, the need for regional specialists and the importance of field work. His teaching of field techniques, to be sure, led to studies of three scattered areas in the United States of which two are included in this volume (articles 5 and 6). Otherwise, however, almost all his research has been concerned with countries of Latin America, where he went repeatedly to carry out field studies, both intensive and extensive.

A number of his publications on Latin America are in a sense "systematic" studies, dealing with such varied topics as surface configuration, air masses, city patterns, economic development, and geopolitical structures. But all are treated as necessary to the purpose of regional geography, to establish the character of areas as formed from the interrelated associations of diverse elements. This is demonstrated most effectively in the part of Latin America where his detailed field study has been particularly focused, having spent three seasons in intensive field study. In these, as well as in the regional analyses in his volume on Latin America, he has presented original studies lifted above the level of simple description through the effective utilization of concepts and generalizations which have been developed by specialists in the systematic fields of geography.

For Preston James, intellectual pursuits, including research as well as teaching, are promoted by social interchange. At Michigan he was stimulated by discussions with Robert Hall and Stanley Dodge. It was primarily at his instigation that a group of us then junior members of geography departments in the Midwest (following a pattern set by a group of older colleagues) met in the field in the spring of 1926 and following years to examine and try out techniques of field investigation. In the free-wheeling discussions which ensued, James was a leading participant, learning as well as teaching.

James was for many years a regular and active participant in the annual meetings of the Association of American Geographers —the AAG. In 1934, he became involved in the direction of its affairs, first as member of the council, then for six years as secretary, later as president, in 1952. During the 1930s the AAG had no staff, and its operations were necessarily very largely in the hands of the secretary. The capacity thus demonstrated to promote and organize was called upon later, in 1949, when the AAG undertook to prepare the cooperative volume on *American Geography: Inventory and Prospect.* Those of us who took part in this enterprise remember how often it seemed the plan could never be carried out; to maintain collaboration of ten committees, each expected to secure participation of proponents of diverse views, would prove impossible. Without James's leadership in organizing and persistent drive on carrying through, no such volume would even have appeared. No doubt much the same is true of the volume on *New Viewpoints in Geography,* the 1959 Yearbook of the National Council for the Social Studies.

Promotion of geography has always been avocation as well as vocation for James—promotion, that is in the sense of bringing to workers in related fields understanding of what geography has to contribute to common purposes of knowledge. James has represented American geography on a variety of interdisciplinary or international organizations, including the National Research Council, the Research and Development Board, and especially the Pan-American Institute of Geography and History, in which he headed the United States delegation to meetings in Latin America in 1949, 1952, 1954, and 1956, and the National Council of Geography of Brazil.

This is not the time nor should I be the one to evaluate the importance of the work of Preston James for the future development of American geography. As one who has experienced with him a half-century in the profession, I can testify that during that period his role has been outstanding, his total impact second to none. It is also true that he has mirrored his time: in his view of geography, in his methods of investigation and his objectives, he has reflected continuously the changing viewpoints of the second quarter of the century.

Like all of us who had our graduate training before 1925, James was taught the environmentalist concept of geography (by which, of course, I do not mean a "deterministic environmentalism"). In the papers published from his dissertation he wrote in terms of "Geographic Factors," and in mimeographed text materials and two short papers on purpose and methods, published in 1924, he expressed the traditional American view of geography as he had learned it from W. M. Davis, Atwood, and Semple—the study of the influence of the natural environment on man. But in carrying out his first post-doctoral field study, in Trinidad, he found this viewpoint unsatisfactory, and became one of the first to adopt the concepts which Carl Sauer introduced from German and French geography. In discussions at meetings, which Sauer rarely attended, James was one of his followers who most effectively presented the challenge to the traditional American viewpoint, compelling others of us to study not only what Sauer had written but his European sources. (Unquestionably this was one of the stimuli leading me to the writing of *The Nature of Geography*.)

At the start, James adopted not only the ideas but the terminology that Sauer had introduced from German sources. The concept of landscape as region appears in his Trinidad paper of 1926 (article 8); indeed he used it in the oral presentation at 1925 meetings only two months after the publication of "Morphology of Landscape." He used the term even more in the Blackstone Valley study (article 5) and stressed its importance in textual materials mimeographed for students in 1929. But in subsequent research publications the term disappears almost entirely, though still considered as essential in his textbook published in 1935 (article 13a), a work for which the basic structure is taken from Passarge's "Landschaftsgürtel." Ultimately, however, the term "landscape" has been omitted.

On the other hand, James has adhered to the basic theme established for geography in that period—namely the focus on the study of areas. Although he has recognized the need for systematic, or topical, studies, his own writings, whether of research or for teaching, have been almost exclusively regional. His concern has been to present explanatory descriptions of specific—that is, individual—regions, rather than to establish general principles or laws.

James did not follow Sauer into historical geography; his concern is with the living present, but the present seen as the result of historical development, continuing into a somewhat predictable future. He has said that it was O. E. Baker who first taught him to view human geography in terms of successive stages in man's adjustment to his environment, an approach followed in his study of Trinidad (article 8). The influence of Sauer's emphasis on the development of the cultural landscape and the theme which Whittlesey later called "sequent occupance" are clearly reflected in the Blackstone Valley study (article 5). Throughout the work on Latin America the interrelations of man and the land are presented as the product of historical development.

In the 1930s, the Depression and the New Deal led to a new objective in American geography, namely the search for solutions of practical problems of areas. This purpose, which James was later to call "remedial," appears in his 1938 analysis of the "hollow frontier" of land settlement in Brazil. In the decades after World War II, as the United States came to be concerned with economic and political problems of other lands, his studies in Latin America, while still distinctly regional in nature, have focused particularly on problems of agricultural settlement, poverty, and economic development, and on problems of political organization internally and in relation to the United States.

In sum, James has been a skilled craftsman in utilizing the work of many students to provide scientific knowledge necessary for understanding and appreciating the total character of the interrelated complex of elements which forms the environment of man at any place. By precept and example, he has been the most effective exponent of the chorographic method in American geography.

*Madison, Wisconsin* RICHARD HARTSHORNE

# PART I

# *On History and Theory*

# COMMENTARY

The three papers in this opening section offer a succinct review of the historical development and some fundamental characteristics of the field of geography. Each represents James's distillation of a large body of thought, and together they well display his characteristic stance with reference to the field.

As will be readily apparent from the first two papers, geography is an unusually broad field, one which, in James's words, "cannot be defined by its subject matter." While that very feature has been a special attraction to some, others inevitably have found it uncomfortable and have sought to bring it into narrower focus. Such attempts have recurred through the long history of geography, and several can be identified even during the span of James's career to date. At the time of his own graduate training, American geography was still strongly marked by a movement to define it as the study of the "influences of the geographic environment" on man. By the 1930s the reaction to this rather crude "environmentalism" seemed to be limiting geography to a rather narrow and innocuous range of topics within the geographers' "landscape," while in the 1960s there have been some powerful movements which by their stress upon the special significance of certain objectives and/or methods would also in effect greatly narrow the historic breadth of the field.

These papers mirror something of these controversies. The article "Geography" was originally written for the 1956 edition of the *Encyclopaedia Britannica*. Parts II–IV, dealing with the progress of exploration and problems of measurement, written by H. R. Mill and revised by James, have been omitted, as has a final subsection on subdivisions of geography. It is a skillful summation of the dominant view at mid-century: a Kantian definition of geography's place in the over-all framework of organized knowledge, with chorographic science as the "main stream" of geographic thought, and the regional concept as the basic

2

tool. It is a presentation strongly grounded upon the interpretations of Richard Hartshorne and, directly and indirectly, of Alfred Hettner. "Environmentalism" and "landscape" are described as having been "deviants" from the central traditions of the field. Since this article was first written another strong challenge has emerged which insists that such "orthodoxy" of mid-century represented an undue emphasis upon "areal differentiation" and the study of "the characteristics of particular places," with too little attention to the geometrical tradition and too little concern for the need for a much larger body of spatial theory. In Section VII, the only part revised for the 1970 edition of the *Britannica*, James gives some recognition to these new emphases and methods. While those few paragraphs are not likely to be considered a very satisfactory summation by either James or his critics, they do have the merit of insisting that such recent movements are not so new as some may assume but, rather, are modern versions of an old debate within the field.

A number of the topics directly related to that recurrent debate are dealt with in article 2. This presidential address (that it was his second such address was made possible by a change in the structure of the AAG; that he was selected for a second presidency was one more measure of his stature in the field), given in 1966, is a creative and stimulating paper written with typical Jamesian flair. The issues dealt with are fundamental, and James, characteristically, places them in historical context and shows throughout a concern for preserving the balance and wholeness of the field. If, as one hopes, it would be read for generations to come, it might itself serve to mitigate the "persistence" of at least some kinds of "error."

Article 3 is widely regarded as a classic statement, a succinct formulation of the regional concept in terms of definitions, classification, scale, and methods. That James would choose this topic for his presidential address to his fellow professional geographers in 1952 is not surprising in view of the nature of his research and writing up to that time. He had by then produced a long list of studies on specific regions, working at every scale from the topographic to the global; moreover, he had shown a good deal of concern for methodology, as, for example, in his 1934 paper on "The Terminology of Regional Description" where he dealt with some of the same ideas and terms as appear in the address. That paper was part of a special session devoted to "Conventionalizing Geographic Investigation and Presentation," at an annual meeting of the Association of American Geographers. In 1949 the AAG initiated much wider ranging discussions toward the preparation of a volume to mark its fiftieth anniversary in 1954. James became a co-editor of that book, *American Geography: Inventory and Prospect,* and the principal author of two chapters. Thus his 1952 address was also a logical manifestation of very current concerns; the opening line—"The regional concept constitutes the core of geography"—asserts the centrality of his theme, and it is not surprising to find whole sections of that address incorporated in his opening chapter on "The Field of Geography" in that landmark volume. This item is thus a natural complement to his *Britannica* article, for it is an extended exposition on geography as "chorographic science," and it stands as an important exhibit of interpretations at mid-century. But it is also more than that, for though the recent emergence of an array of new techniques makes his discussion of specific methods of regional analysis seem dated, this address as a whole still merits close attention because the substance of the argument is timeless and the clarity of the thought and language is unusual.

# 1

## GEOGRAPHY

### INTRODUCTION

Geography is that field of learning in which the characteristics of particular places on the earth's surface are examined. It is concerned with the arrangement of things and with the associations of things that distinguish one area from another. It is concerned with the connections and movements between areas. The face of the earth is made up of many different kinds of features, each the momentary result of an ongoing process. A process is a sequence of changes, systematically related as in a chain of cause and effect. There are physical and chemical processes developing the forms of the land surface, the shapes of the ocean basins, the differing characteristics of water and climate. There are biotic processes by which plants and animals spread over the earth in complex areal relation to the physical features and to each other. And there are economic, social, and political processes by which mankind occupies the world's lands. As a result of all these processes the face of the earth is marked off into distinctive areas; geography seeks to interpret the significance of likenesses and differences among places in terms of causes and consequences.

In ancient and medieval times geographers could do no more than identify and describe the features that gave distinctive character to different countries. Writers of geography, to be sure, speculated regarding cause and effect processes, sometimes with amazing insight. They made the first attempts to measure things and to place them on maps. During the great age of exploration which began about 1500, the methods of mapping were greatly developed: the continental outlines were plotted with ever increasing accuracy; the rivers appeared in more and more detail; the positions of mountain ranges were established by survey rather than guesswork. Furnished with all these new data, geographers about the middle of the eighteenth century started to define broadly homogeneous regions in terms of physical make-up, or in what were conceived to be the major characteristic associations of plants and animals, or in terms of the economic life, or in terms of the political organization of national territories.

As man's understanding of the world increased, more and more attention was given to systematic studies; that is, to those features that were systematically related to each other because they were the result of a single process. Geography has sometimes been called the mother of sciences, since many fields of learning that started with observations of the actual face of the earth turned to the study of specific processes wherever they might be located. These new disciplines were defined by the subjects they investigated. Some of the processes at work on the surface of the earth, notably the physical and chemical ones, were reproduced under laboratory conditions where they could be examined in isolation from the environments of particular places. From these studies there resulted a great increase in the understanding of cause and effect relations, and numerous fundamental principles were formulated to describe the ideal or theoretical sequences of change. In a similar way the biotic processes were examined under controlled conditions, and such important concepts were developed as those of evolution and natural selection. The social sciences, too, have sought to understand the theoretical sequences of economic, social, and political change as these sequences were presumed to go on when isolated from the disturbing circumstances of actual places. Since the so-called cultural processes could not be isolated in laboratories, they were isolated symbolically by such phrases as "other things being equal."

Modern geography starts with the understandings provided by the systematic sciences. Unlike these other fields, geography cannot be defined by its subject matter, for anything that is unevenly distributed over the surface of the earth can be examined profitably by geographical methods. Rather geography is a point of view, a system of procedures. It makes three kinds of contribution to understanding: (1) it extends the findings of the systematic sciences by observing the differences between the theoretical operation of a process and the actual operation as modified by the conditions of the total environment of a particular place; (2) it provides a method of testing the validity of concepts developed by the systematic sciences; and (3) it provides a realistic analysis of the conditions of particular places and so aids in the clarification of the issues involved in all kinds of policy decisions.

Obviously a large amount of geographic work is done by persons not identified professionally as geographers. Scholars in the various systematic fields do not fail to concern themselves with the applications of their theoretical understandings to the study of conditions in particular situations, and such applications usually involve geographic work. When an economist examines the economic conditions of a country and prescribes remedial measures designed to provide for more production, he is involved in part with the geographic point of view. When a businessman studies the advantages or disadvantages of a specific location for his factory or his retail store, or when he plans for the more efficient operation of a system of transportation or of a marketing organization, he is working in part with geographic data.

Professional geographers can offer certain concepts and methods derived from experience in the analysis of the significance of areal differences on the earth. They play a role similar to that of the professional historian. Many persons who are not historians write accounts of the sequences of events that are called history, but such persons would be severely criticized if they failed to make expert use of historical method. Professional geographers encourage nongeographers to apply geographic concepts and to make use of acceptable geographic method, but they condemn the inexpert use of concepts or method. Unfortunately much work of a geographic nature is done by scholars in other fields, by businessmen and engineers, in a way that reveals an ignorance of the concepts of modern geography and that makes crude and imprecise use of geographic method. . . .

## DEVELOPMENT OF GEOGRAPHIC CONCEPTS

During all the centuries when geography was chiefly concerned
with the exploration of unknown areas and with the plotting of
continental outlines, geography as a field of scholarship was developing slowly. In the course of its development many concepts regarding the purposes and methods of geography have been formulated, tested, reformulated, or abandoned.

1. *Geographic Ideas of the Greeks.* The stream of geographic
ideas that permeates the Western world had its origin in the writings
of the early Greeks. The Homeric poems include a strange mixture
of fact and fancy concerning the lands and peoples of the Aegean
area. However, it is Thales of Miletus (*c.* 624–*c.* 545 B.C.) who is
commonly recognized as the first Greek geographer. During a visit
to Egypt, Thales became acquainted with the practices of abstract
geometry as developed in that country for the measurement of
land, and he introduced the geometry of lines to Greek thought.
His disciple Anaximander (fl. 6th century B.C.) made a map of the
world based on information obtained from sailors in Miletus.

One of the fundamental problems with which the Greek geographers wrestled was the form and size of the earth. Before the time
of Homer (900 B.C.) the earth had been conceived as a flat disk
surrounded by the river Oceanus. Anaximander offered the concept
of the earth as a cylindrical mass suspended in a spherical universe.
It was Aristotle, however, who first demonstrated the sphericity of
the earth by noting: (1) that all matter tended to fall together toward a common center; (2) that the earth threw a circular shadow
on the moon during an eclipse; and (3) that as one traveled from
north to south familiar stars disappeared and new ones came above
the horizon.

Eratosthenes of Alexandria (*c.* 276–*c.* 192 B.C.) calculated the
circumference of the earth. He learned of a deep well located at
Syene (now Aswan) in Egypt which was completely illuminated by
the sun at the summer solstice. Assuming this place to be on the
tropic, and assuming Alexandria to be directly north of Syene, he
measured the zenith distance of the sun at the latter place at the

solstice. Reckoning the distance between the two places to be about five hundred geographical miles, he arrived at a figure for the whole circumference of the earth which was within 16 percent of the figure which is known to be correct.

The Greek geographers, like most of the Greek philosophers, were great believers in the concept of symmetry. Herodotus (c. 484–425 B.C.), who was both a geographer and a historian, held to the view that the inhabitable lands were not circular but were longer from east to west than they were broad from north to south, from which is derived the modern designation of longitude and latitude. He followed the principle of symmetry to fill in the arrangement of lands and the courses of rivers beyond the limits reached by explorers. He insisted that the Nile must flow from west to east before turning north in order to balance the Danube, which flows from west to east before turning south. He also named the three continents that border the eastern Mediterranean: on the northern side, Europe; on the eastern side, Asia; and on the southern side, Africa. The geographical and historical ideas that Herodotus accumulated were derived from the critical examination of a vast number of documents and also from extensive and arduous travels and field observations.

The first geographer to divide the surface of the earth into zones based on latitude (known as *klimata*) was Parmenides (c. 450 B.C.). He conceived of a torrid zone that was too hot to be inhabitable, two frigid zones that were too cold, and two intermediate temperate zones that constituted the inhabitable earth. Aristotle developed the idea of zones of climate and defined the temperate zone as extending from the tropics to the polar circle. Purely on the basis of theory he assumed the existence of a south-temperate zone corresponding to the known world of the Greeks. He, too, believed that the torrid zone was too hot to be inhabitable and that people who lived too close to the equator had been burned black by the sun.

The word *geography* was probably first used by Eratosthenes. The writing of geography, under whatever name, was greatly stimulated by the expansion of Greek culture, partly through the establishment of colonies of Greeks around the coasts of the Mediterranean and the Black Sea, and partly through the conquests of

Alexander the Great, who extended Greek horizons eastward to India.

2. *Ideas of the Romans*. Unlike the Greeks, the Romans were primarily concerned with practical questions. The first of the encyclopaedic descriptive works dealing with the geography of countries came from the Roman geographers. The one whose works are best known is Strabo (*c*. 64 B.C.–A.D. 20). His seventeen volumes describing the whole of the known world, and supported in considerable part by his own field observations, are like a handbook for the guidance of military commanders or public administrators. This work set a pattern for encyclopaedic geographic writing which has been followed ever since.

Claudius Ptolemaus, known as Ptolemy, was a mathematician, astronomer, and geographer who lived in Alexandria between A.D. 127 and 141 or 151. In his great work on geography (*c*. A.D. 150–160) he brought together the results of Greek geographical learning. He attempted to provide the data on latitude and longitude by which maps might be constructed, but unfortunately he discarded the estimate of the earth's circumference made by Eratosthenes in favor of a much less accurate one offered by another Greek geographer. He adopted a suggestion of Hipparchus that the equator be divided into 360 parts (later known as degrees). Ptolemy recognized the difference between treatments of the world as a whole, of parts of the world or regions, and of localities; for these different kinds of writings he used the terms "geography," the treatment of the world as a whole; "chorography," the treatment of parts of the earth; and "topography," the treatment of small localities in detail.

3. *Muslim Geographers*. The dark age of geography began before the fall of the Roman Empire. It resulted in part from the completion of Roman conquests and in part from the rise of Christianity. A narrow interpretation of the Scriptures led certain ecclesiastics to deny the sphericity of the earth and any of the geographical concepts based on it. Greek science gave way to widespread ignorance and bigotry.

Many of the Greek writings, and especially the works of Ptolemy, were translated into Arabic and tested by new observations over a wide area. Such traveling merchants as Ibn Kaukal in the tenth century, and Ibn Batutah in the fourteenth century journeyed far beyond the limits reached by the Greeks. Ibn Batutah (1304–68) went far to the south along the east coast of Africa to a place nearly 10° S. of the equator. He found the temperatures on the equator more moderate than those farther to the north. The idea of uninhabitable torrid zones which appears in the book by Aristotle was thrown in doubt. Yet so simple and persuasive is the idea that the world's climates can be properly grouped in just three zones and that these zones have some effect on the way people live in them that even in the mid-twentieth century it was still being taught in the schools. This oversimplification has been the cause of much obscurity regarding the relation of man to climate.

The Muslim scholars did much not only to preserve and criticize Greek learning but also to add new knowledge and new concepts of their own. The works in historical geography of al-Biruni, al-Baladhuri, and especially of Ibn Khaldun (1332–1406) reach new standards in accuracy of observation and in interpretation of the relations of people to the land. It is apparent, too, that the Muslim geographers had started to formulate ideas concerning the uplift of mountains by folding and the erosion of slopes by running water, and also of the great amounts of time which these processes require. Such advanced ideas were developed by field men, by great travelers; for example, Ibn Batutah, during thirty years of travel, is estimated to have covered seventy-five thousand miles, ranging as far east as India and the Malay archipelago. The Muslims, however, contributed nothing to the progress of cartography.

4. *Revival of Sixteenth–Eighteenth Centuries.* While the Muslim geographers were making their contributions to the development of geographic thought, the geographic horizons in Christian Europe remained narrow. Roger Bacon, writing in the thirteenth century and generally credited with originating the modern scientific method, described Ethiopia in terms which Ptolemy would have considered naive and careless and which were based on information as much as fifteen hundred years old. Geographic horizons were re-opened in Europe first as a result of the crusades and then of the discoveries of the Portuguese and Spanish expeditions.

The revival of geographic thought is recorded in the works of several scholars during the sixteenth, seventeenth, and eighteenth centuries. The first of these was Petrus Apianus (Peter Bienewitz), whose book published in 1524 went back to Ptolemy for its inspiration. Gerardus Mercator (Gerhard Kremer) (1512–94) was a student of Apianus and later established a geographical institute at Louvain, where he worked on the development of his well-known projection. Sebastian Münster in 1544 published a descriptive book that followed the example of Strabo. But not until Philipp Clüver (1580–1622) and Bernhardus Varenius (Bernhard Varen) (1622–50) wrote their monumental geographical treatises was the revival of geographic learning well started. Varenius divided the field into general geography (dealing with the earth as a whole) and special geography (dealing with parts of the earth on a chorographic or topographic scale). His early death at the age of twenty-eight prevented him from undertaking his proposed work on special geography, but a century later his general geography was still the accepted standard authority. In 1625 Nathanael Carpenter published the first geographical work in English, in which he showed a remarkable degree of scientific objectivity in his interpretations of observed phenomena. He foreshadowed the point of view of geographers of later centuries by focusing attention on the areal relationships of things on the surface of the earth. In 1686 Edmund Halley produced the first wind chart and presented his theory of the trade winds which related them to the distribution of heat on the earth. In the second half of the eighteenth century and the early nineteenth century there was a large amount of geographical writing, bringing together a vast number of new observations concerning physical geography. Some of this was summarized in the works of Philippe Buache (1756), the first geographer to make use of contour lines (1737), and in writings by Torbern Bergman (1766) and J. R. Forster (1783). At the same time Jedidiah Morse of Charlestown, Massachusetts, published his *American Universal Geography* in 1793; in Britain John Pinkerton's *Modern Geography* appeared in 1802; and on the Continent Conrad Malte-Brun started the publication of the first *Géographie universelle* in 1810. This was the period in which there was a wave of new scientific writing, including works by such masters as J. B. de Lamarck, P. S. de Laplace, A. G. Werner, James Hutton, Charles Lyell, Georges Cuvier, William

Smith, and J. F. Blumenbach. This was the intellectual environment in which Immanuel Kant lived.

5. *Kant.* Kant, the great German master of logical thought, gave geography its place in the over-all framework of organized, objective knowledge (science). For a number of years after 1765 he lectured at the University of Königsberg on physical geography, and these lectures were subsequently published. It is possible, according to Kant, to classify all knowledge gained from observation in either of two ways: a classification of things perceived in accordance with some logical system, a logical classification; or a classification of things perceived in terms of the time and space where they occur, a physical classification. From the former method a systematic classification of nature is gained, as when plants or animals are placed in a system of species and genera regardless of where they occur. From the latter a geographic description of nature is gained, as when the plants and animals that occur together in the same area are identified. Description according to time is history; description according to place is geography. History is a report of phenomena that follow one another; geography is a report of phenomena that are beside one another. Geography and history together fill up the entire circumference of our perceptions. This is essentially the concept of the place of geography among the sciences that has guided the mainstream of geographic thought since Kant.

Kant regarded physical geography as the summary of nature, the basis not only of history but also of "all other possible geographies." Of the latter he enumerates five: (1) mathematical geography, the measurement of the form, size, and movements of the earth and its place in the solar system; (2) moral geography (in the sense of mores), an account of the different customs and characteristics of mankind; (3) political geography, the study of areas according to their governmental organization; (4) commercial geography, dealing with trade in surplus products of countries; and (5) theological geography, the study of the distribution of religions.

6. *Humboldt and Ritter.* Until the latter part of the eighteenth century there were essentially two main purposes of geographic study: there was the study of the shape and size of the earth, represented by Ptolemy and Apianus-Mercator; and there was the com-

pilation of informative descriptions of countries and regions, represented by Strabo and Münster. Kant provided a place in the broad
framework of geography for both. Since Kant, the mathematical
tradition has been carried on by the cartographers, on the border-
line between geography and geodesy; the tradition of descriptive
writings about places has become the mainstream of geographic
work.

With Alexander von Humboldt (1769–1859) and Carl Ritter
(1779–1859), however, the nature of the mainstream itself was
changed. When Strabo was writing, and even when Münster was re-
viving the descriptive tradition, geographers were seeking to identify the phenomena and the associations of phenomena that gave
distinctive character to particular places. Understanding of process
had not advanced far enough to permit a recognition of phenomena that were systematically related to each other in that they had
been produced by the same process. The purpose of descriptive
writing had been an essentially practical one: that of providing geographically organized information either for the use of military
commanders or public administrators or as a basis for the understanding of history. No scientific principle (that is, no concept of
systematically related phenomena) guided the selection of what information to include, what classifications of phenomena to adopt.
Such writings have been described as encyclopaedic in that the information included was not necessarily tied together by its relevance to a problem.

By the beginning of the nineteenth century the systematic sciences, each discipline being devoted to the examination of a
particular process (as defined in the introduction to this article),
had so far advanced the understanding of physical and chemical
processes that no longer could such knowledge be disregarded in
the study of particular places. Since the beginning of the nineteenth
century the selection of phenomena to include in a study of the
physical aspects of geography and the definition of categories of
phenomena to be included in a system of classification have been
guided by systematic knowledge of the processes involved. This advance in geographic theory was the result of the work of numerous
geographers in the late eighteenth century who made the first applications of the new knowledge; yet it remained for two men to make

the first effective use of these ideas and so to stand out as giants in the development of geographic thought.

It is remarkable that geography all over the world should owe so great a debt to two scholars—Humboldt and Ritter—who worked at the same time, both in Germany, and both for thirty years in the same city, Berlin. They were in many ways quite different in their backgrounds and in their approach to the common subject. Humboldt began his education with the purpose of becoming a diplomat, but stimulating contacts with teachers of science developed the passion and capacity for careful, direct field observations of natural phenomena. During his early twenties he traveled in England and in 1795 he made a geological and botanical tour of Switzerland and Italy. Then for five years (1799–1804) he traveled in South and Central America, amassing a vast amount of recorded and measured data regarding the countries he visited. Later, in 1829, at the age of sixty, Humboldt traveled into central Asia. For most of the later years of his life, however, he was engaged in the writing of his great works: the account of his travels in America and his description of the physical geography of the earth in the *Kosmos*. He lived alternately in Paris and Berlin.

Humboldt's great contributions to geographic procedure were two. First, he applied his knowledge of physical and biological processes to the systematic classification and comparative description of the phenomena he and others had observed; second, he devised methods of measuring the phenomena he observed. For example, in his field studies of tropical mountains in America he measured the temperature at different elevations and for the first time showed temperature differences on a map by drawing lines to connect points of equal temperature (isotherms). He made use of census data where they were available, but in the absence of such data he carefully checked estimates of the population of various regions and countries of America. The step from qualitative, encyclopaedic description to quantitative, systematic description was a major one in the history of geography.

Carl Ritter was Humboldt's junior by ten years. He always regarded Humboldt as his master and in many ways based his geographical writings on the ideas of the elder scholar. Perhaps no man had a broader background of preparation for geographic

study than did Ritter. He was taught by men who insisted that
knowledge of the world could be gained only by the direct observation of nature. Like Humboldt, Ritter was a persistent and careful
field observer; unlike Humboldt, he never made long journeys to
distant places, but rather confined his field observations to Europe.
He received a fine training in the natural sciences, and he was also
a student of history and theology. In many of his writings he was
more historian than geographer, and opposition to his ideas that
developed after his death arose in part from the accusation that he
had made geography a handmaiden of history. He wrote what has
come to be known as geographical history (a geographical interpretation of history) rather than historical geography (the reconstruction of past geographies and the tracing of geographical changes
through time). Ritter emphasized the importance of comparative
studies of different parts of the world and the danger of drawing
conclusions or formulating generalizations on the basis of knowledge of one area alone. In his studies he always attempted to show
how things existed together in the same areas in mutual interrelationship. He thought of geography as a kind of physiology and
comparative anatomy of the features of the earth's surface. Yet his
deeply religious attitude led him to adopt a strongly teleological
point of view. His monumental work, *Die Erdkunde im Verhältnis
zur Natur und zur Geschichte des Menschen,* two volumes
(1817–18; 2nd ed., 1822–59), covered only Asia and a part of Africa.

Ritter also made two contributions to geographic method.
First, he insisted that one should proceed from observation to observation, not from opinion to hypothesis to observation. He was
among the first, for example, to show that Buache's idea of continuous mountain systems separating the drainage basins of the great
rivers was contrary to observed facts. In gathering together impres-
sive arrays of data from the reports of others, Ritter's purpose was to
let these data speak for themselves in bringing out the coherent
relations among things. He was the first to provide a system of subdivisions of the continents based on surface features as a framework
for his detailed regional descriptions. Second, Ritter's approach was
regional rather than systematic; that is, he focused his attention on
particular places and on the phenomena unsystematically associated

there rather than on systematically related phenomena wherever they might occur. Yet Ritter himself acknowledged that without the systematic studies of Humboldt his own work could never have been carried out.

### GEOGRAPHY AFTER HUMBOLDT AND RITTER

Humboldt and Ritter had gathered together the geographical ideas of the past, and from their writings there emerged a new and unified concept of the nature of geography. The mainstream of geographic scholarship since Humboldt and Ritter has been devoted to an understanding of the significance of likenesses and differences from place to place on the earth and of the meaning of the associations and interconnections among phenomena in particular places. Armchair geography, based on the spinning of elaborate theories in advance of precise observation, is no longer acceptable; in contrast geography has become essentially an out-of-door subject, based in large measure on the direct observation of phenomena in the field. One technical problem has been the method of recording such direct observations. At first such data were recorded only in the form of notes (written or sketched); since 1915 the recording of field data on maps in the field has become standard practice, and since about 1930 the recording of observations on vertical aerial photographs has given a precision to geographical study that it never could have possessed before.

The idea that Humboldt represented a systematic or topical approach to geographic study in contrast with Ritter's regional approach has been overemphasized by some geographers. Clearly both these scholars used both approaches, perhaps with varying emphasis. The modern concept does not recognize the topical and the regional approach as different aspects of geography, but rather recognizes the need for combining them.

In the period since the middle of the nineteenth century chorographic study (that is, study of areal differentiation and its meaning) has been moving steadily away from the encyclopaedic description of the Strabo-Münster tradition toward an organization of material relevant to a specified purpose or objective. Modern geographic writing starts with a problem and applies the geographic method to the search for answers or for clarification of the issues involved in the formulation of policy.

Meanwhile, however, a number of deviations from the mainstream of geographic scholarship have appeared. One such deviation conceived of geography as a science of relationships, specifically those between man and his physical environment. Another conceived of geography as devoted solely to the interpretation of the visible features of the landscape. Still another and widely popular deviation identified geography with geopolitics. Others, such as the identification of geography with geophysics, need not be discussed in this article since they have few if any adherents in the modern period.

### *The Mainstream: Geography as Chorographic Science*

Chorographic science is that aspect of learning which treats of the areal arrangements and associations of things on the face of the earth and seeks to understand the causes and consequences of such areal differentiation. As already stated, geography cannot be defined by its subject matter, for anything that is unevenly distributed over the earth can be examined by the methods of geographic study. The continued development of the chorographic approach has led to greater and greater attention to procedures for selecting features to be studied and for rejecting other features as irrelevant. It has also led to great increase in precision of field observation. Both these developments were adumbrated in the writings of Humboldt and Ritter.

Clearly the mainstream of geographic scholarship was defined in Germany by two late nineteenth- and early twentieth-century figures. These were Ferdinand von Richthofen and Alfred Hettner. In the modern period the geographers whose contributions have been of the utmost importance, and who have set forth their philosophical ideas regarding the content of geography, are too numerous to permit mention of more than a few. The ideas of Richthofen and Hettner and of many others were discussed and critically analyzed in English in the monumental work of Richard Hartshorne, *The Nature of Geography* (1940).

1. *French Tradition of Regional Studies.* No country has contributed more to the development of geography than France. In proportion to the size of the country and the financial resources of its universities the quantity and quality of French geographic work has been outstanding. But France has achieved this status largely during the twentieth century.

During most of the nineteenth century geography was widely taught, and geographic writings were in demand. The first chair of geography was established at the Sorbonne in 1809, and in 1821 one of the oldest geographical societies in the world was established at Paris. But the geographical writings of that century were in the encyclopaedic tradition, and the teaching was aimed chiefly at a geographic interpretation of history. Two comprehensive series were published under the title *Géographie universelle:* the eight-volume series (1810–29) by Conrad Malte-Brun, and the nineteen-volume series (1875–94) by Élisée Reclus. The series by Reclus represented in its day the most scholarly kind of descriptive geography; yet it represented no conceptual advance over the work of Ritter since the genetic approach had not yet been applied to the study of population.

French geography was raised to a new level of accomplishment by the great master Paul Vidal de la Blache (1845–1918). In 1899 Vidal de la Blache set the new tone for French geographical studies in his inaugural address at the Sorbonne. He expressed himself as opposed to any strict determinism with regard to the relation of human activities to the physical environment; rather he recognized man as the active agent, operating in a setting that offered both possibilities and obstacles to man's wishes. But he was convinced that the way to go forward in geographical studies was to focus attention on relatively small areas in which to examine in detail the areal differentiation resulting from physical and human processes. Vidal's influence was great, and most of the French geographers after his time were either his pupils or pupils of his pupils.

Perhaps Vidal's greatest disciple was Jean Brunhes (1869–1930), whose *Human Geography* is a widely read book in English as well as in the original French.

The French geographers who developed under the influence of Vidal showed a remarkable unity of purpose and achieved a high

standard of performance. The French regional monographs, some
dealing with parts of France, others dealing with other parts of the
world, are a famous and distinctive part of geographic literature.
Vidal was responsible for formulating the original plans for another
great *Géographie universelle,* and after his death the direction of
the project was carried on by his successor Lucien Gallois. The first
of these volumes to appear were the ones on the Netherlands
(1927) and Great Britain (1928) by Albert Demangeon. The whole
series was completed in 1946–48 with the publication of the three
volumes on France by Emmanuel de Martonne and Demangeon.
No finer books bringing together material on the geography of the
whole world had ever been published.

Although all the volumes are of a high standard of accuracy
and literary quality, the outstanding volumes by de Martonne and
Demangeon on *La France,* by de Martonne on *Europe Centrale,*
by Henri Baulig on *L'Amérique septentrionale* and by Pierre Denis
on *Amérique du Sud* should be given special mention. In these the
regional descriptions are given focus through the inspired identification of central themes around which the descriptive material is
organized.

The French regional tradition was passed, also, to workers in
other countries. In Germany Friedrich Ratzel initiated a series of
regional monographs dealing with different parts of Germany
under the general title of *Forschungen zur deutschen Landeskunde.*
The Pan American Institute of Geography and History, a specialized agency of the Organization of American States, undertook to
plan and coordinate the preparation of a series of volumes dealing
with the countries of the western hemisphere. Brazilian geographers
were especially active in the writing of regional monographs in the
French tradition. They were stimulated, in part, by the presence of
several outstanding French scholars, notably Pierre Deffontaines
and Pierre Monbeig. The Brazilians were also influenced by the
German-American geographer Leo Waibel and by several geographers from the United States who introduced techniques of field
mapping and resource inventory.

The French and German chorographic tradition was extended,
also, to other parts of the world, where a number of outstanding
scholars made contributions to geographic thought. Major geo-

graphic work has been done in Australia, New Zealand and South Africa, in Italy, Czechoslovakia, Poland, and the Russian S.F.S.R. The Russians were especially important during the nineteenth century for introducing new concepts in the study of soil geography. Geographical work has also been important in China, Japan, and India.

2. *Twentieth-Century Developments.* By the middle of the twentieth century the chorographic tradition had been notably advanced by new concepts regarding the focus of geographic objectives and by new techniques of observation and analysis. These changes had their roots in the nineteenth century, but appeared strongly after World War I. France, Germany, Great Britain, and the United States shared in the return to the mainstream of geography.

In the first place the need for a central theme or problem around which to organize geographic material became more widely recognized. The encyclopaedic coverage of areas was recognized as important, but it became more and more clearly demonstrated that even an encyclopaedia must be written for a specific purpose or to fill a specific kind of need. This involves, then, a certain amount of selection in the kinds of data to be treated. If the encyclopaedia is to provide background information for the planning of a military campaign, this determines the kind of information required. If the encyclopaedia is to be used as a reference work in schools or colleges, a different selection is required. But there are also many kinds of questions concerning origins and antecedents that may be asked regarding the geographic features of an area, and these questions are problems which in turn provide a means for distinguishing between relevant and irrelevant items. Or there may be an economic, social, or political situation which needs to be changed or remedied, and this also provides a problem around which to organize the materials and analyses of geography. By mid-twentieth century leaders in professional geography were critical of research undertakings not specifically directed toward stated ends.

This trend away from the uncritically encyclopaedic kind of writing gave additional emphasis to direct field observation, again in the tradition of Humboldt. Direct field observation must of necessity be carried out in small areas, for the range of human vision on the curved surface of the earth is small. When the features of the

earth are mapped on small-scale maps they must be highly generalized, as when a pattern of specific fields and farms is generalized
into a kind of agricultural region. But the agricultural region cannot be seen directly, for it is too big; the details that make it up are
the specific features of human settlement, the specific slopes and
soils, and these must be mapped on large-scale maps. Geographers
still use the adjective *topographic* to define that scale of field mapping which permits the plotting of specific fields and farms or specific blocks and even buildings in a city; a topographic map is one
with a scale large enough to permit such specific features to be
mapped.

Topographic studies, using the word in this sense, were common in Great Britain even during the nineteenth century. As early
as 1895 Hugh Robert Mill wrote an essay in which he described in
detail the characteristics of a small part of Sussex. He urged similar
treatment for the area of each of the sheets of the British topographic maps (inch-to-the-mile scale). The numerous essays
brought together under the editorship of Alan Grant Ogilvie in
1928 (*Great Britain: Essays in Regional Geography*) dealt with
specific kinds of problems or features in relatively small areas. In
few of these studies, however, were the physical, biotic, and human
features of an area treated with the same degree of detail. It was
commoner to treat the physical characteristics of an area in detail
and then to sketch in the human aspects superficially.

The development of geographic thought and method were
greatly advanced when geographers in the United States first developed the procedures for treating all the relevant features of a small
agricultural area with the same degree of detail. One of the first geographers to insist on the need for such balance was Wellington D.
Jones. With Carl O. Sauer he published an outline for the detailed
field study of an agricultural area in 1915. In the summer of 1915
graduate students at the University of Chicago were offered the first
field course in which such a balanced approach was taught. Shortly
thereafter Sauer made field study a basic part of graduate training
at the University of Michigan at Ann Arbor. Thereafter it became
standard procedure to examine geographic problems in the field in
small areas.

3. *Surveys and Inventories.* In the period since 1920 the

methods of detailed field study have been applied, with increasing success, to the practical problems of land planning. By mid-twentieth century it was widely appreciated that an inventory of land quality and existing land use was an essential basis for formulating land-use policy. The first survey with the purpose of providing such background information was the Michigan Land Economic survey undertaken during the 1920s and 1930s to tell the policy makers what actually existed in the cutover lands of the northern part of the state. During the 1930s similar field methods were used by geographers to survey the area of the Tennessee Valley Authority. There, for the first time in connection with a large survey, mapping was done on aerial photographs.

At this same time, L. Dudley Stamp introduced the idea of the detailed field survey to Great Britain. In 1930 the British Land Utilisation survey was started with the objective of recording on maps of suitable scale the facts of land use and land quality for every acre of England, Scotland, and Wales. The survey was carried out by unpaid volunteers from the universities, colleges, and schools under the guidance of professional geographers, using maps of a scale of 1:10, 560 (six inches to the mile). This survey proved of inestimable value during World War II, when Britain was forced to make use of every available acre of land for agricultural production. It is not too much to say that the survey was a most important factor in helping Britain to survive the war years. It also provided the material for Stamp's book, *The Land of Britain: Its Use and Misuse.*

Two other surveys made use of geographic field methods for resource inventory and land-use mapping as a basis for the formulation of public policy. One was the Puerto Rico Rural Land Classification program (1948–52), done for the government of Puerto Rico, in which the island was mapped on a scale of 1:10,000. From these maps effective plans for the better use of the limited agricultural base were drawn up. Another survey was directed broadly at the resources of tropical Africa under the direction of George H. T. Kimble. It was widely recognized that at mid-twentieth century there were not enough adequately trained field men to carry on surveys fast enough, even in the world's critical areas. Geographers and others were seeking to perfect the methods of resource inventory through the interpretation of aerial photographs with a minimum of direct field contact. In this development professional geographers in the universities were handicapped by lack of financial support; meanwhile government agencies and private organizations were in some cases proceeding without the benefit of the experience gathered by the geographic profession over centuries of field study.

4. *Spatial Interchange.* The study of the movements and communications that connect one area with another has long been an essential aspect of chorographic work. To treat areal differentiation as a purely static phenomenon is insufficient. During the nineteenth century, especially in Germany and France, there was much interest in transportation as a geographic phenomenon. The study of spatial interchange deals not only with the volumes of movement but also with the facilities, such as railroad equipment, or the capacities of ports and ships to move different kinds of goods. At mid-twentieth century a tendency had appeared to apply mathematical formulas from the field of physics to the description of the volume and velocity of movements in relation to the factors of location and distance.

### Deviants From the Mainstream

During the nineteenth and twentieth centuries there were a number of deviant developments in the field of geography. Some of these died out early; for example, the proposal that geography should concern itself wholly with geophysics, abandoning studies of human geography as "unscientific." Other deviants were proposed by individual scholars but attracted few followers; for example, that geography should be defined as human ecology, a field already claimed, if not developed, by sociology. Among the various deviant currents that have appeared, three may be given special attention: (1) geography as the science of relationships; (2) geography as the study of landscape; and (3) geography as geopolitics.

1. *Science of Relationships.* The idea of defining geography as the study of relationships appeared during the second half of the nineteenth century. At that time the understanding of the physical

and biotic processes at work on the earth had been much farther advanced than the understanding of the economic, social, and political processes. Few geographers have at any time thought of their field as covering only the physical and biotic aspects of the earth or of omitting study of the human or cultural aspects; yet the concepts of causal relationship as developed in nineteenth-century physical geography and biogeography were quite out of harmony with those of human geography. The theory of evolution applied to the changes in plants and animals had a tremendous influence on the intellectual world. It was reflected in physical geography, especially, by attempts to define ideal sequences of change, such as the cycle of youth, maturity and old age of land forms. These attempts were notably successful. William Morris Davis, professor of geography at Harvard University, was an outstanding leader in this development.

But when the new concepts appeared in physical geography and biogeography, no similar principles were immediately forthcoming to organize the treatment of man and his works. It was in this situation that an attempt was made to relate the human aspects of geography to the better-understood physical aspects and to define geography as the study of the interrelationships between man and his physical environment.

In Germany, Friedrich Ratzel attempted to bring the treatment of man into line with the treatment of physical features. In the first volume of his *Anthropogeographie* (1882 and 1899), he organized his material in terms of the natural conditions of the earth, in relation to which he examined various cultural features. In the second volume (1891 and 1912) he did the opposite, organizing his material in terms of human culture, in relation to which he examined the physical features of the earth. Ratzel, however, was thoroughly in sympathy with the tradition of Humboldt and Ritter; he never lost sight of the need for direct observation of all relevant elements of a situation. Thus in his classic volume on *Deutschland* he pointed out that two physically similar areas, the Black Forest and the Vosges mountains, had developed in quite different ways because of the differences in economy and historical tradition.

Some of Ratzel's disciples were not so careful to observe all the relevant interrelated phenomena. Especially those who were trained chiefly in physical geography insisted that a geographic analysis must show a relationship that crossed the border between physical and human phenomena, thus neglecting the relationships on the same side of the border. Few geographers ever subscribed to such extreme forms of environmental determinism as suggested by the historian H. T. Buckle and others; but many went forth deliberately to seek examples of environmental influence on human activities, and many remained blind to contrary evidence. As a result geography was divided into physical geography (a well-developed field of science) and human geography (a relatively superficial treatment of man's relations to the physical earth). The adjective *geographic* came to refer to the physical character of an area. Thus a "geographic factor" was some condition of the physical environment to which human activities were to be related as "responses" or "adjustments."

Geography as the science of relationships persisted longer in the English-speaking world than elsewhere. It found few adherents in Germany, where Alfred Hettner was developing the ideas associated with the mainstream of geography. It was effectively attacked by the French geographers under the leadership of Paul Vidal de la Blache. But it was given persuasive support in the United States by such scholars as William Morris Davis, Ellen C. Semple, Wallace W. Atwood, Ellsworth Huntington, Robert De-Courcy Ward, and R. H. Whitbeck. Yet this approach to geographic study proved to be a dead end. As Griffith Taylor, an eloquent supporter of the ideas of environmental determinism, wrote, such relationships between man and his environment are nowhere more clearly seen than when one looks at the world as a whole. Yet when one looks at the world as a whole all the aspects of the face of the earth, physical as well as human, are highly generalized. Only when the earth is examined in topographic detail—that is, on maps large enough to permit the plotting of specific features of human occupance—can generalization be kept to such limits that results can be checked. At mid-twentieth century detailed field studies had yet to demonstrate through proper historical and comparative methods the validity of the concept of environmental determinism. Modern geographers, on the contrary, insist on the principle that the significance to man of the features of the physical earth is a function of the attitudes, objectives, and technical abilities of man himself. In other words, the physical and biotic environment has different meaning for different persons; and further, geography examines the relationships not only between man and the physical or biotic aspects of the environment but also between man and the variety of cultural features resulting from economic, social, and political processes. Only thus can the relative significance of areal differences be weighed and evaluated. Geography can no longer be divided neatly into physical and human geography, and a geographic factor is any factor of location or areal association that is relevant to a problem.

2. *Study of Landscape.* The idea that geography should be restricted to an examination of the visible character of the landscape appeared as another deviant in nineteenth-century Germany, especially in the works of Otto Schlüter. In the United States this approach to geography was introduced by Carl O. Sauer in a paper entitled "The Morphology of Landscape" (1925). The immediate popularity of this point of view among the younger geographers of that period represented a reaction against the idea that geography was restricted to a study of the relationships between man and his physical environment. Sauer's paper shows the results of experience in detailed field mapping and field study, the influence of ideas from German geographic literature and the challenge of concepts presented by the rapidly developing field of anthropology. Sauer was concerned with the significance to man of the physical and biotic conditions of a small area or site, and also with man's transformation of the site. Perhaps it was the followers of Sauer rather than Sauer himself who tried to restrict geographic attention to form and structure alone to the neglect of function—in other words, to the anatomy of the visible landscape rather than to its physiology.

As in other attempts to provide a limited definition of the field of geography, this proved to be a dead end. Geography, according to the concepts developed by Kant and restated by Sauer, is one aspect (along with history) of the whole range of perception; Sauer called it a "naively-given sector of reality." Geography, then, is not subject to definition or limitation; geography is not what geographers do, for much work in this sector of reality is done by persons who are not professional geographers and who are not especially competent in the use of geographic methods.

3. *Geopolitics.* Another deviant from the mainstream of geographic science is that known by the popular term "geopolitics." The great popularity of geopolitics as a practical field of study in which human geography and applied political science are used for the examination of certain problems in international relations had its great development as a result of World War II. Karl Haushofer, a German geographer, was credited with the formulation of ideas that had a profound effect on the strategic policy of Adolf Hitler. Whether Haushofer's ideas had the greater influence on Hitler or Hitler's on Haushofer has not been established. The fact is, however, that the German school of geopolitics was used to provide a pseudoscientific rationalization of Nazi policy. In the United States and Great Britain another school of geopolitics was developed which sought to go back to H. J. Mackinder and A. T. Mahan rather than to Haushofer.

Geopolitics, as distinguished from political geography, combines the concepts and techniques of a variety of disciplines for the purpose of formulating strategic policy in international relations. But strategic policy as formulated by the leaders of any one state has the basic purpose of advancing the interests of that state; every state has a somewhat different set of purposes and these are often in conflict with the purposes of other states. Geopolitics, then, is an applied field which would seem inevitably to be divided into as many schools as there are independent states. Geography may be used, along with other disciplines, in working out the plans of geopolitics; but geography is not the same as geopolitics, nor is geopolitics a field of scholarship by itself.

GEOGRAPHY IN THE TWENTIETH CENTURY

*Scope*

Geography, like other fields of learning, continues to debate basic questions about scope and method. Is geography purely descriptive, seeking to provide a more and more useful and accurate picture of the face of the earth as the home of man, or is its chief mission to formulate general concepts or theories? In other words, is geography an idiographic or a nomothetic subject? Unfortunately for clarity of thought, many people think of these two objectives as incompatible. Perhaps the more advanced a field of study becomes the easier it is to accept the notion that all science can do is describe. But is description restricted to the reproduction of unique things, or is description to be in terms of theoretical models?

In the 1960s most geographers agreed that the chief purpose was nomothetic, that is, to formulate laws. Formulating and testing general concepts became more effective through the increased use of mathematical procedures. Instead of seeking deterministic concepts of strict cause and effect, geographers discovered that the theory of probability could be applied to the formulation of concepts and forecasts.

These discussions brought out ideas that were not really so new as some thought. A review of the history of geography and of other fields of learning shows how much of this discussion about scope had been argued before. Richard Hartshorne, in *The Nature of Geography* (1939) and *Perspective on the Nature of Geography* (1959), presented a discussion of the scope of the field as reflected in the writings of geographers, chiefly in the United States and Europe. In 1954 the Association of American Geographers published *American Geography, Inventory and Prospect* (edited by Preston E. James and Clarence F. Jones), in which the record of geography in the United States was set forth. Two other important contributions to discussions of scope and method were *The Science of Geography,* by a committee of the National Research Council in 1965, and *Locational Analysis in Human Geography,* by Peter Haggett in 1966.

Geography is seen as a single discipline, unified by its general concepts and the kinds of questions it asks about the face of the earth. Geographers ask questions about location and about the interconnections among things that are associated in segments of earth space. The region, as geographers define this term, is still a basic device for identifying the areal spread of spatial systems, that is, systems of interconnected parts occupying specific parts of the earth's surface. Popularly, the word *region* denotes a relatively large area having some general quality of homogeneity, but with boundaries not precisely defined. Geographers define a region as an

area of any size that is homogeneous in terms of specific criteria
and that is distinguished from bordering areas by a particular kind
of association of areally related features. The old distinction between topical (or systematic) geography and regional geography is
not considered valid. Topical geography is defined as the study of a
particular group of features produced by one kind of process wherever these features may occur in the world (Varenius' general geography); regional geography is defined as the study of many different
kinds of features as they occur in particular areas (Varenius' special
geography). Insofar as all regions must be defined in terms of specific
criteria the approach to regions is a topical one; and since the study
of any topic involves the definition of homogeneous areas, all topical
study must make use of the regional method.

The new concept of the region stemmed from experience in detailed field studies. It is clear that no two points on the face of the
earth are identical. On the other hand, if the complexity of the face
of the earth is to be brought within manageable limits for the purpose of examining the causes and consequences of areal differentiation, to examine each spot separately would defeat the endeavor.
Geographers must always generalize; they must define categories of
phenomena that are meaningful in that they are associated in area
with other phenomena; they must seek associations of phenomena,
defined as regions, that are significant in that they are related to a
particular process or group of processes. In all science, as formulated by Kant, there are two kinds of generalizations: one that deals
with the classification of phenomena into categories of greater or
lesser degree of generalization; and another that describes the ideal
operation of a process, or a sequence of events. Geography traditionally deals with the former; but modern geography classifies phenomena on the basis of systematic knowledge of process.

Conceived in this way the region is a device for illuminating
the factors of a problem that otherwise would be less clearly understood. It is not an objective fact; rather it is an intellectual concept.
A region is justified if it illuminates the elements of a problem; it is
not justified if it obscures these elements. There is no such thing as
a "true region"; there are, in fact, as many regional systems as
there are problems worth studying by geographic method.

Two important developments after 1954 permitted a much

greater precision in the definition of regions, and in the identification of regularities in the location of things on the face of the earth. First was the improvement of remote sensing, that is, deriving a picture of the earth's surface from photographic or electronic images. Satellite images reveal details on the earth's surface never before available for study. In the late 1960s much attention was being given to working out new techniques for the analysis of satellite images. Furthermore, pictures derived from remote sensing could be fed into computers for the analysis of areal associations, and for the preparation of complex maps.

The other development in geographic study was the use of mathematical procedures. Statistical procedures make possible the formulation and testing of hypotheses with much greater precision than could be done with word symbols. In the fields of experimental science, the scholar can retreat to his laboratory and set up an experiment in which outside, disturbing effects are one by one eliminated until the operation of a process in isolation can be observed. The economist does this symbolically by the use of the phrase "other things being equal." But hitherto the geographer, for whom other things are never equal, lacked the procedures for probing complex interconnections among things of diverse origin. By the use of statistical procedures he can identify the elements of spatial systems and discard those elements which are irrelevant to any particular process. By using probability theory he can take account of those "chance" interconnections that are purposely left out of studies in most other disciplines. With the aid of computers it became possible to carry out computations that are far beyond the capacity of the man with a pencil and paper.

But computers and mathematical procedures are not foolproof. Clearly, if one asks a computer to reply to a silly question the answer will be silly. A basic problem in the use of quantitative data is the enumeration area to which the data apply. For example, the population of a city is commonly given by adding the number of individuals within the city limits. But city limits are made for political purposes, and are important for those purposes. In terms of the size of the urban population functionally related to the central city, the political city limits are irrelevant. It is impossible to make a comparative study of urban sizes by using the numbers within political city limits. If data are to be plotted within a grid of rectangles to be fed into a computer, the dimensions of the screen become a very important matter. Too coarse a screen, that is, one with rectangles that are too large, gives less precise information than a fine screen. How fine must the screen be for a particular kind of problem? Mathematical procedures can be of the greatest aid in reaching more precise and useful answers to geographical problems, but they are no substitute for careful observation and logical thinking.

The interconnections among the elements of a spatial system must be traced through time. If two or more phenomena are found to occupy exactly the same segment of earth space, that is no evidence that they are interconnected. Interconnection involves processes, or sequences of events that run through time.

This means that geography cannot be strictly contemporary. All geographic study must be approached historically if it is to be complete. Historical geography is understood to be concerned with the re-creation of past geographies and with geographical changes through time. A full understanding of contemporary geographic phenomena requires the full perspective of past geographies, for the operation of any one process at a particular place and time is to a certain extent modified by the total environment with which the process is involved. The systematic sciences work to unravel all these disturbing connections with the environment and to describe the ideal operation of the process in isolation; geography seeks to put the process back in its earthly setting and to see its connections both in space and time. . . .

# 2

## ON THE ORIGIN AND PERSISTENCE
## OF ERROR IN GEOGRAPHY

This essay offers some thoughts on the origin and persistence of error in geography.[1] Not that geographers have contributed more than their share of error to the unfolding of man's comprehension of the universe. In all fields of learning, as Joseph Jastrow pointed out, the rare flashes of intuitive judgment illuminate man's slow progress through "quagmires of ignorance, thickets of superstition, obstructions of dogma, ineptitudes of reason. . . ." [2] In the long story of man's efforts to gain a more useful comprehension of the face of the earth as the human habitat, and of the man-land systems that characterize different parts of his habitat, error has played an essential role. One may even insist that the present conceptual structure of geography has been built on the errors of those who preceded us. The students of geography in past generations, even as far back as Homer, should be honored for certain kinds of useful error, even as we may hope to be honored by future generations of geographers for what we may confidently assume will some day be recognized as error.

What is important is that useless error be minimized, that the same errors should not be repeated, and that error, once identified, should not be allowed to persist. Yet in the course of the great adventure of the human mind during which men of learning gradually developed more and more illuminating mental images of the face of the earth as the home of man numerous errors have persisted, and some continue even now to impede man's efforts to place human problems and events in meaningful spatial context. One major

Reprinted from *Annals of the Association of American Geographers,* 57, 1 (March 1967), 1–24.

source of error that impedes geographic scholarship is the persistent failure of too many geographers to read what other geographers, past and present, have written. The common ignorance of the flow of geographic thought is a surprising characteristic not only of contemporary geography, but also of the geography of centuries past. As a result the same errors are repeated over and over again, and the theoretical models that seem to illuminate the problems of one generation become the obstacles to the continued development of geographic ideas by the next generation.

This essay has four chief parts: (1) an examination of some of the pitfalls in the geographer's universe; (2) some examples of avoidable error; (3) some examples of the important part played by error in the progress of geographic understanding; and (4) some examples of the persistence of error.

## PITFALLS IN THE GEOGRAPHER'S UNIVERSE

Some of the distinctive kinds of error that appear in the course of geographic scholarship result from the nature of the geographer's field of study.[3] Geographers deal with things and events of unlike origin that occur together and in mutual interaction on the face of the earth. Some geographers are curious about the association of things and events that give special character to particular places, and about the interconnections that tie different areas together. Some geographers are especially concerned to identify regularities among the patterns of things and events, and to throw new light on the working of the systems that occupy segments of earth-space.[4] Furthermore, some geographers seek to define their problems and gather their data out-of-doors within the areas they are investigating, whereas others prefer to work with data collected by others. Some are especially skilled in the use of word symbols, some in the construction and use of map symbols, and some in the new application of mathematics. But in any case geographers deal with things and events of unlike origin, ranging across physical, biotic, and cultural processes, and they deal with things and events within that zone on the surface of the earth which is the habitat of man. Geographic study, from whatever point of view and by whatever kind of method, is concerned with areas, or segments of earth-space.

### The Nature of Earth-Space

The argument about the nature of space has gone on since the earliest times of which there are records. The man-like creatures of *genus homo* that preceded *homo sapiens* had learned how to communicate by language, and those who possess language are inevitably puzzled by some of the abstract ideas that only language can formulate. One persistent abstraction has to do with the question of whether space is a receptacle for things or an attribute of them. Aristotle thought of space as the logical condition for the existence of things. Newton decided that space is an objective reality, but intrinsically void. Descartes insisted that space is the essence of bodily substance. Spinoza thought of space as an attribute of substance. Berkeley developed the idea that space is a mental construct based on the coordination of sight and motion.

Kant is credited with the recognition that space offers one of the "naively-given" frames of reference within which human knowledge can be organized. When things and events of like origin are grouped together, regardless of the time and place of their occurrence, this is what Kant described as a logical classification. When things and events of unlike origin are grouped together in time or space, this is what he called a physical classification.[5] Geography has to do with spatially organized knowledge.[6] Hartshorne has traced the reappearance of this classification of knowledge among nineteenth-century European scholars.[7] More recently this same division has been incorporated in a discussion of symbolic logic.[8]

Three words that geographers frequently use, sometimes inexactly, are *space, area,* and *region.*[9] Space is boundless and extends in all directions. When geographers use this word they usually refer to earth-space, which is the three-dimensional zone forming the surface of the earth including its atmosphere.[10] Area, on the other hand, is a segment of earth-space, and is bounded. As abstracted on a map, area is a two-dimensional geometric surface, but it is usually conceived by geographers as three-dimensional. A region, as defined by geographers, is an area identified by specified criteria.

Because geographers deal with things that occupy segments of earth-space, and with events that occur in earth-space, they must come to grips with three basic facts about their universe. First, it is a curved surface, and very much larger than the observer. It has never been possible for the individual geographer to observe closely any large part of the earth. Even today with the new techniques of remote sensing, the individual geographer will not be able to see for himself any large part of the earth during a normal lifetime. The geographers are forced, therefore, to gather much of their knowledge about the earth at second hand.

The second fact about their universe is that no two pinpoints on the face of the earth are identical. Every smallest point of earth-space differs from every other one. Yet in all this diversity there are regularities that can be identified by geographic methods. Geographers define regions for the purpose of demonstrating regularities,[11] but each region so defined, whatever its size, contains many elements of diversity. Each region is a generalization which is based on certain degrees of homogeneity, and which disregards many elements of diversity that are not relevant to the purpose of the study. For this reason any kind of geographic study (whether developed in terms of verbal symbols, map symbols, or mathematical symbols) must start with a very careful and critical selection of criteria for defining areas of homogeneity or patterns of regularity. The criteria are well selected, and the resulting regions are justified if the result is to illuminate the problem under investigation: the work is judged unsatisfactory if the result is to obscure the relationships being sought.

The third fact about the geographer's universe is that it is constantly changing, and the processes of change are infinitely complex. There are many different kinds of processes, or sequences of events, that are taking place on the face of the earth. Furthermore the tempo of change varies with each kind of process. Although geography is focused on the examination of spatially organized knowledge, the fact remains that space and time cannot be separated, and the time dimension remains an essential part of spatial analysis.[12] In simple language, inherited from the past, "all geography must be treated historically."

## Percepts and Concepts

A major pitfall hidden in the geographer's universe, and only recently identified, has to do with the interrelationship between percepts and concepts. A percept is a direct observation of a thing or event, made by an individual through his senses. This is what geographers used to speak of as reality. A concept, on the other hand, is a mental image of a thing or event. The idea is that if one looks at a specific hill, this is a percept, but the mental image one forms of hills in general is a concept.

The relationship between percept and concept, however, is not so simple as this. It is now quite clear that different people develop different mental images of reality, and what they perceive is the reflection of these preconceptions.[13] We see things as we are, not as they are. It is the function of an artist to make us see things we never saw before. When several artists are set to painting the same scene, or even the same person, it is amazing to note the very different ways the same real object is perceived. Similarly the direct observation of things and events on the face of the earth is so clearly a function of the mental images in the mind of the observer that the whole idea of reality must be reconsidered. Note how the observers of landforms once saw only cataclysms or floods, where —since Hutton and Playfair—they see the results of processes now going on. Note how glacial landforms took shape before our eyes when the mental concept of glaciation had been formulated. And then Agassiz even perceived the evidence of glaciation in the Amazon Valley. How many peneplains were identified after Davis had presented the concept! And where peneplains were once identified we now see clearly the formation of pediplains. Wright's recent book offers example after example of the collection of data from the direct observation of reality that were regarded as evidence in support of the preconceived mental images of reality.[14]

Nevertheless, someone must collect data from direct observation. There are some geographers who, when they become aware of the interrelationship between percept and concept, fall back on the comfortable reality of census data, already prequantified. But most of the gatherers of statistical data also face the same problem of relating concept to percept, and they must do so without the benefit of geographical training. In spite of the existence of this pitfall, geographers must learn to observe carefully in the field, even if only to understand the mental process involved in the initial transfer of what is directly observed to the symbol that represents it. If we let the symbol become reality it is because we have dropped headfirst into this trap.

### The Search for Significance

It is the geographer's quest to search for significance among all the complexities of the face of the earth. What is significance? To the geographer significance means the identification of regularities and functional interconnections within spatial systems. Because of the trained interplay between concept and percept, the geographer can discover meaning among the things and events that differentiate the face of the earth, much as the artist can lead people to see beauty where beauty was not perceived before.

The geographers, however, should not make too much of the supposed distinction between description and explanation. The most sophisticated scientists are perhaps the first to accept the fact that all they can do is describe the things and events with which they deal. Explanation in any ultimate sense is beyond the range of the human mind. If explanation in geography consists in describing a previous condition and noting the processes of change that lead to the present condition, we may then say that explanation is only adding the time dimension to mere description. It might seem advisable to avoid the intellectual arrogance suggested by too much emphasis on explanation, and recognize that all geography must include the time dimension in its descriptions of the things and events that form significant regularities and interconnections on the face of the earth.

The search for significance involves the formulation of concepts, or mental images. Geographers must deal with two quite different kinds of concepts. First, and simplest, there are concepts regarding the arrangement of things in earth-space. These concepts have to do with the areal associations among functionally interconnected elements, or of covariance among two or more elements. Since the range of vision is restricted by the size of man and by the curved surface of his universe, only relatively small areas can be observed directly at any one time. It is possible to observe the areal association of a forty-acre field of wheat with soil types or slope or the occurrence of water. It is possible to observe the associations of lines of travel with hills and valleys, or of a factory in relation to a highway. But when these things are extended beyond the range of vision, the problem is changed. We cannot similarly observe a type-of-farming region, or a hilly upland, or a manufacturing region. We, or someone else, must travel widely over an area, storing up images of the direct observation of topographic-scale features and then generalizing these images into composites of the larger areas. There is, in fact, no more flexible and potentially productive computer than the one enclosed in the human head.

Second, there are concepts regarding the operation of processes, or sequences of events. The search for significance involves not only the identification of regularities of association or pattern, but also—and especially—the events that extend through the time dimension from which the regularities of pattern are derived. These concepts are what we describe as theoretical models, that is, mental images of ideal sequences of events by which we visualize the processes of change, the movements and interconnections, and the functional relationships among things. This is not the same as providing an explanation, or as tracing events back to causes. This, in reality, is a description of the processes of change acting through time. One of the great advances in geographic methodology in recent years has been the use of the theory of probability. The physicists many decades ago discovered that the identification of strict causal relationships was beyond reach; but by using the stochastic approach, recognizing the existence of many chance interruptions of ideal sequences, the probability that any theoretical model will produce the expected results can be defined precisely.[15]

The geographer's universe, then, is infinitely complex. Significant regularities in arrangement or in the recurrence of events can be discovered in a variety of ways. Some of these ways are subjective and personal, and are artistic rather than scientific. Some of the methods of seeking significance require the rigorous application of a clearly defined methodology. In any case the geographer must select certain criteria by which he defines areas of homogeneity, or by which he constructs theoretical models of processes. In so doing he disregards other features as irrelevant to his purpose. Becoming expert in the tools and methods of his profession requires experience, training, critical assistance from colleagues, and above all an abiding devotion to the study of geography.

### EXAMPLES OF AVOIDABLE ERROR

The kind of error that we recognize as avoidable usually results from a failure to make expert use of tools and methods. Among the many kinds of examples that might be offered, we shall illustrate the meaning of avoidable error by looking at four possible causes: (1) the inexact use of words; (2) the uncritical use of statistical data; (3) the failure to indicate the reliability of data; and (4) the failure to distinguish among different kinds of spatial distributions.

### *The Inexact Use of Words*

A careful comparison of the latest edition of Webster's International Dictionary with earlier editions brings to light numerous examples of how word meanings change, for better or for worse, as a result of popular misuse. The adjective *nice,* for example, no longer suggests that a person is foolish, simple, or stupid; nor is it widely accepted as referring to a fine discrimination, as in a nice distinction. It used to refer to these things, but people who did not understand the language made use of the word in other senses. Clearly, the popular vocabulary changes through misuse, and language grows "like a language should." But in communications among scholars such errors would seem to be inexcusable. To be sure some words are used in new senses because the writers wish to express disagreement with the ideas connoted by former word usages. But more often the misuse of words results from lack of attention. Probably every writer on this subject would draw up a different list of examples. Here are some usages that bother this writer.

*Geography and Topography*

There is certainly a need to rescue the word *geography,* and its adjective *geographic,* from referring exclusively to man's natural surroundings or perhaps only to the surface of the earth. The adjective *geographic* should refer to anything that is located on the face of the earth, and that is a factor in a problem because of its location. As the title of a lecture there is nothing wrong with "Geographic Factors in National Power," except that a reference to the syllabus shows that the lecturer is supposed to discuss the effect of surface features, climate, resources, and other elements of the physical and biotic earth. Among geographic factors in national power should be included the distribution and density of population, and the arrangement of the facilities for research and development. Then there are government publications which use such headings as "Geography and Climate." This misuse of the word *geography* could be explained if it were only misused by nongeographers, but when geographers use the word in this sense, the result cannot be other than confusing.

The word *topography* once referred to the features of a small area, or the description of a locality. This writer uses the adjective *topographic* to refer to features of the face of the earth that are directly observable from one place at one time. The "topographic symbols" used by the U.S. Geological Survey are those that can be used on large-scale topographic maps. They include not only relief features, but also water bodies, man-made features, and sometimes vegetation. Yet the common misuse of this word to refer only to surface features has made the recapture of the original meaning difficult. There are numerous alternative words that can refer to surface features (*relief, landforms, terrain,* and others), but there is great need for a word to refer to a close look at a part of the surface of the earth, where the degree of generalization is small, and where large-scale maps can be used to portray the details of the landscape.

*Up and Down*

The widespread use of *up* and *down* to mean *north* and *south* is not only irritating, but it is also symptomatic of a deep-seated form of geographic illiteracy. We cannot expect to change the habits of speaking of the general public, including radio and television announcers; yet when we are told that a storm is moving up the St. Lawrence, we may legitimately be puzzled about who should prepare for bad weather. When a geographer gets mixed up regarding the location of the upper Nile, or writes about going down the Rhine to Switzerland, things are in a bad way. The term Sub-Saharan Africa can refer to nothing in the world but the supplies of water and minerals that lie beneath the surface of the Sahara.

It would be interesting to investigate the origin of this error. Did the users of *T* and *O* maps in the medieval period talk about going up to the East, or were these maps never hung on walls? Goldstein quotes the Genoese geographer of the fifteenth century, Toscanelli, writing in 1474, as follows: "you must not be surprised if I call the parts (of the earth) where the spices are, west, when they usually call them east, because to those sailing west, those parts are found by navigation on the under side of the earth. But if by land and on the upper side, they will always be found to the east." [16] Goldstein interpreted this reference to the "under side of the earth" as meaning that Toscanelli was aware of the position of the Spice Islands south of the equator. This interpretation, however, may be doubtful. Toscanelli was thinking of the known world (Europe, northern Africa, southwest Asia) as *up*. In fact he says you can also go to the place where the spices are by going east over the upper part of the earth. The idea that *south* means *down* had probably not been developed in Toscanelli's time. It probably originated when maps were hung on walls with north at the top, or when globes were set upright on stands with the south pole "down under."

Whatever the origin of the misuse of language, geographers should not continue to accept it.

## The Region

The word *region* also causes much trouble because of the many different meanings attached to it. In the popular vocabulary the word *region* has several meanings. It is a major, indefinite division of the inanimate world; or it is a large tract of land with some elements of homogeneity; or it is an administrative area. Among geographers the word also has different meanings. For those who take great delight in speaking sneeringly of "regional geographers" the region is a more or less arbitrary area used as a receptacle for otherwise miscellaneous information, often offered to the bewildered and bored student as geography. Regional courses of this kind are quite correctly subject to criticism. But in the preparation of the manuscript for *American Geography; Inventory and Prospect,* the committee on regional geography, headed by Whittlesey, made a fresh inquiry into the nature of regions. As a result of this inquiry

> the committee came to see the region as a device for selecting and studying areal groupings of the complex phenomena found on the earth. Any segment or portion of the earth surface is a region if it is homogeneous in terms of such an areal grouping. Its homogeneity is determined by criteria formulated for the purpose of sorting from the whole range of earth phenomena the items required to express or illuminate a particular grouping, areally cohesive. So defined a region is not an object, either self-determined or nature-given. It is an intellectual concept, an entity for the purpose of thought, created by the selection of certain features that are relevant to an areal interest or problem and by the disregard of all features that are considered to be irrelevant.[17]

Much of the misunderstanding among geographers concerning the meaning of the "regional concept" is a result of this confusion in word usage.[18] Perhaps it was a mistake for the committee to have attempted a redefinition of the word. Perhaps it is too much to expect that Whittlesey's chapter would be read by many geographers, except by graduate students to whom it was assigned reading. The result is a failure to communicate among people who use the word in different senses.

### The Uncritical Use of Statistical Data

Avoidable error is also introduced into geographical study by those who make uncritical use of statistical data. In fact, some of the scholars who make expert use of the more sophisticated mathematical procedures diminish the geographic importance of their studies by using statistical data gathered by nongeographers, and summed up in enumeration areas that are irrelevant or in time periods unrelated to the processes under investigation.

An example of error of this kind is found in the mapping of population. Zelinksy pointed out that not only are census data lacking for many parts of the world, but even where data are available they are presented in enumeration areas that have little relevance to geographic reality. Very different pictures of the patterns of people can be produced with enumeration areas of different sizes and shapes, especially when population is plotted as if it were evenly distributed over the whole enumeration area.[19] Zelinsky pointed out that "the limitations of anachronistic or arbitrary boundaries for census districts can be reduced by judicious exploitation of large-scale maps and aerial photography where they are available."[20] It would seem, then, that the proper procedure for mapping population would require not only the use of reliable census data, but also the use of information regarding the pattern of settlement derived from nonstatistical sources. Klimm's procedure for identifying areas with no population at once removes these parts of enumeration areas from consideration.[21] Within those parts of enumeration areas where the people are actually located, the relative concentrations of people can be identified by the use of maps of roads and houses. One of the more exciting recent developments is the possibility of constructing maps of population density without any statistical data from traditional sources through the scanning of the earth's surface by orbiting sensors. Geographers should be among the first of the students of population to recognize and take steps to reduce the error resulting from the uncritical use of census data.

The result of using irrelevant enumeration areas is clearly demonstrated in the study of cities, and in the application of rank-size theory. Not only do many nongeographers fail to distinguish the data for political cities from those of whole conurbations, but also there are some geographers who have been guilty of this elementary error. The problem is well illustrated by the difference between political Boston and the whole urban unit that focuses on Boston. Political Boston in 1960 had a population of 697,000 people; but the whole metropolitan area organized functionally around the Boston core had a population of 2,400,000. Writers who list Tokyo as the world's largest city are making comparisons between data for the whole Tokyo conurbation, and data for the political city of New York. Comparing whole conurbations, functionally related to cores, New York in 1960 had 14,114,927 inhabitants while Tokyo had 13,787,766.

On the other hand the concept of megalopolis, as developed by Gottman, makes use of the Census Standard Metropolitan Areas. These include the whole of any county in which there is a city of 50,000 inhabitants.[22] Megalopolis, therefore, includes within its outlines large areas that are strictly not urban at all. When, for the 1960 census, the Standard Metropolitan Areas were redefined as Standard Metropolitan Statistical Areas, this resulted in a decrease of the percent of urban population in New Jersey from 89.9 to 78.9. In other words when enumeration areas, defined for nongeographic purposes, are used uncritically, the result is an erroneous picture of urban growth and spread.

Nor can the rank-size theory of urban hierarchy be tested against observed city sizes unless the data are enumerated for whole conurbations, that is, including all the people functionally related to the nodal, urban region. If such a region cannot be defined without field study, because of the lack of adequate population data, then without field study the rank-size theory cannot effectively be tested.

In any study involving the use of statistical data it is essential to examine carefully the suitability of the enumeration areas.[23] When such areas are too large, the resulting screen may be too coarse to illuminate the geographic patterns, as when megalopolis is defined in terms of whole counties only small parts of which may be urbanized. The size and shape of enumeration areas that can be considered suitable depends on the problem being investigated and on the scale, or degree of generalization of the study. It is possible to apply corrections to the data to minimize the effect of poor sizes or shapes.[24] But there can be no doubt that geographic studies would be improved by identifying meaningful regions in the field and then using these regions as enumeration areas.

Another quite different example of the uncritical use of statistical data has to do with the use of irrelevant periods rather than irrelevant areas. It has long been recognized that weather data averaged by days or months may be much less illuminating than data averaged in terms of weather types on synoptic charts. As early as 1874 Köppen urged the averaging of weather data in terms of weather types rather than irrelevant periods determined by the calendar.[25] But as long as meteorologists held the concept of cyclones as radially symmetrical, the synoptic meteorology with its weather types and air masses was forgotten.[26]

### The Relative Reliability Problem

Much error in geography could be avoided if more attention were paid to the relative reliability of the data. This historians have developed special methods for judging the reliability of sources by comparing them with other sources the reliability of which has been established. Sometimes historical geographers, who are primarily concerned with the geography of past periods rather than with the history, are criticized by historians for making use of secondary sources, or of failing to make adequate tests of reliability.[27] But historians are notorious for accepting maps of dubious quality. So perhaps the score is even.

Error would be avoided if both writers and map makers would specify more precisely the reliability of their sources. Writers of articles can easily provide a commentary in footnotes. But the real problem has to do with the map makers. As Wright pointed out, the map maker must locate a town in one place, even though his sources show the town in several different locations.[28] The geographer in evaluating a map by an unknown author is apt to place more reliance on maps showing much detail than on maps that are broadly generalized. Yet there are examples of spurious detail, and there are examples of maps that are prepared for the purpose of providing support for a theory. Relative reliability diagrams would seem important for any maps covering large areas.

### Kinds of Spatial Distributions

Another source of avoidable error is the confusion of the different kinds of spatial distributions that geographers define on the face of the earth. It is recognized that there are three different kinds of distributions. There are continuous distributions which extend continuously over the earth, but differ only in degree or intensity from place to place. There are discrete distributions where things occupy individually distinct areas, and differ in kind from bordering areas. And there are contingent distributions, where discrete distributions are treated as if they were continuous. For example individual people, each person occupying a discrete area, are summed up in an enumeration area. The result is a figure of density per square mile. The figure is contingent on the size of the enumeration area.[29]

Each of these three kinds of spatial distribution is described by a different method. To bring out the pattern of difference within a continuous distribution lines are drawn to connect points of equal value. These are called isarithms. For example, isotherms, isobars, and isohypses are all specifically located by measurable values. Isarithms are in no sense boundaries between different kinds of regions, but they do show the direction of greatest difference, which is always at right angles to the line.

The discrete distributions, on the other hand, are bounded by lines that separate one category of phenomenon or one association of phenomena from other categories. The areas bounded by these lines are homogeneous in terms of specified criteria, and are, therefore, technically, regions. The lines that separate discrete distributions are boundaries, and they do not necessarily show the direction of greatest difference.

Contingent distributions are dependent on the size and shape of the areas within which the count of individuals is summed up. Lines can be drawn through these distributions to show the direction of greatest difference, for example, lines showing equal population density. But these lines are not isarithms, for they do not connect points of equal value. Rather they are drawn through areas and, therefore, cannot be precisely located.[30] Such lines are called isopleths, or lines of equal ratio. Like isarithms they should not be interpreted as boundaries between unlike areas.

Errors occur when these different kinds of lines are incorrectly used. One very common error results from treating an isarithm as if it were a boundary separating discrete things. Not only in elementary-school classrooms, but also in college classes, and even in graduate schools and among mature scholars, it is not uncommon to find that the ordinary maps colored to show altitude (hypsometric maps) are misread and misused. The lines that separate the different colors are contour lines, not boundaries between different kinds of terrain. Yet many people who should know better think of the low-altitude areas that are colored green as plains, and high altitude places that are brown as mountains. Try identifying the position of the front of the Rocky Mountains in Colorado on a simple hypsometric map where the brown color begins at 5,000 feet above sea level. The error consists in trying to identify a discrete distribution (mountains and plains) on a map designed only to show a continuous distribution (altitude). This kind of error would be something to correct at the level of the High School Geography Project were it not so very common for mature scholars to use hypsometric maps for the purpose of comparing such discrete distributions as land use with underlying surface features.[31]

The point is that expert use of geographic method would require comparing continuous distributions with other continuous distributions, and discrete distributions with other discrete distributions. Categories of surface features can be defined that are relevant to problems of land use, or other kinds of problems in which geographers are interested.[32] Because it is easy to use a hypsometric map that someone else has made does not excuse the widespread and uncritical use of such a map for purposes of identifying areal associations.

## THE IMPORTANCE OF ERROR

Thomas Jefferson, famed as a statesman, was also among the earliest American geographers.[33] In his *Notes on the State of Virginia* he was concerned to find an explanation of the existence of fossil shells in the mountains high above the sea. But his first hypothesis was severely criticized by those who insisted on the scientific accuracy of the Bible. Therefore, in later editions of the *Notes* he suggested two other hypotheses, and to quiet the storm of controversy he added: "the three hypotheses are equally unsatisfactory; and we must be content to acknowledge that this great phenomenon is as yet unresolved. Ignorance is preferable to error; and he is less remote from the truth who believes nothing, than he who believes what is wrong." [34]

Thomas Jefferson was not correct about this. A review of the history of human thought shows quite clearly how understanding progresses from error to error. If no hypotheses were set forth, there could be no reactions to them, no search for evidence to support or to oppose them. Progress in understanding results from the formulation of general concepts and then of the critical consideration of these concepts. But seldom are the conceptual structures of one generation useful to illuminate the problems of the next. In other words the hypotheses confidently set forth by one generation are proved by later scholars to be at least partly in error. Yet the importance of making such errors is evident. There is always the challenge faced by geographers to experiment with ways of gaining a coherent concept of the significance of the arrangement of things and events on the face of the earth, and a more complete grasp of the complex processes of change constantly modifying these arrangements. When a coherent concept is suggested, or a hypothesis formulated, other geographers will not be slow to point out the errors and inadequacies, but geographic learning gains in the process.

Many teachers understand this principle. There is nothing new in the assertion that memorizing facts is futile, and that facts become meaningful only when they are related to a framework of theory.[35] But what is perhaps not so widely appreciated is that the process of learning is greatly stimulated at any age level when general concepts are challenged and subjected to critical evaluation by the students.

The same situation exists in the adult world of scholarship, and especially in the field of geography. A very considerable part of the exploration of the world was motivated by challenging notions that were proved to be wrong. The importance of experimenting with the development of general concepts and hypotheses cannot be overemphasized.

### The Importance of Mythology in Exploration

The kind of error that is called mythology played a major part in stimulating the exploration of the world.[36] Penrose described many such myths, some of which can be traced back to the writings of Homer.[37] There was the idea of the uninhabitable Torrid Zone, and the idea of the *Terra Incognita* with which Ptolemy inclosed the Indian Ocean on the south. Out of the medieval period came the stories of Sir John Mandeville; the legend of Gog and Magog, those giants that ruled inner Asia; the stories of the Land of Ophir and the location of Paradise somewhere to the east of the known world; there were the legends of El Dorado in South America. Plato's story of the fabled land of Atlantis appears even today as a goal of exploring parties. St. Brandan's Island, located somewhere about five degrees west of the Canaries, was not removed from the Admiralty Charts until 1873.

One of the greatest of the myths was the legend of Prester John. According to Penrose, Prester John first appeared as a literary hoax in letters sent by an unknown writer to several of Europe's kings in 1170. The letters tell of a king of vast wealth and power, a Christian who was engaged in fighting the Muslims, and whose realm was placed somewhere beyond the geographic horizons of the Europeans. The search for Prester John was a major stimulant to exploration.[38] After he had been eliminated from Asia as a result of the travels of Marco Polo, by 1340 he was confidently located in the highlands of Ethiopia. In 1520 Rodrigo de

Lima was appointed by the Portuguese king as ambassador to the court of Prester John. The result was the exploration of Ethiopia. The story of Prester John was a geographical error, if not a hoax, but it was a stimulating error, without which the progress of geographic knowledge would have come more slowly.

The myth of the open polar sea was another notion that for centuries stimulated exploration.[39] It was probably started by an English merchant, Robert Thorne, who in 1527 suggested that the shortest way to the Spice Islands would be by way of the North Pole. The search for a Northwest Passage or a Northeast Passage was the purpose of many exploring expeditions to the Arctic from the time of Willem Barents in the late sixteenth century, until beyond the middle of the nineteenth century. The legend was strongly supported in the seventeenth century, when reports of Dutch voyages that almost reached the pole were published. A Dutch geographer, Petrus Plancius, writing in the early seventeenth century, developed a hypothesis to explain the absence of ice in the far north. It was well-known, he said, that the idea of a very hot equatorial region had been disproved. Instead the heat is most intense along the tropics. By analogy, the cold would be most intense at about latitude 70° N., and milder weather could be expected beyond the barrier rim of ice. Many explorers, including Elisha Kent Kane, reported actually seeing the open water toward the pole. Without the argument for and against the existence of an open polar sea the early meetings of the American Geographical Society might have proved quite dull and prosaic. When the president of the society, Charles P. Daly, attacked many of the Arctic experts of his day, the stage was set for the rapid progress of geographic knowledge. The men he attacked included such prominent figures as Elisha Kent Kane, Matthew Fontaine Maury, and the German geographer August Petermann, the founder of *Petermann's Mitteilungen.* The open polar sea was not finally dropped as a subject for debate until after the voyage of the *Fram,* commanded by Fridtjof Nansen. Nansen permitted the *Fram* to become frozen in the ice off the New Siberian Islands in 1893. It drifted across the polar ocean only a few degrees from the pole, and finally emerged in 1896 near Franz Josef Land. If there had been an open polar sea, Nansen would have seen it.

### The Importance of the Challenging Hypothesis

The mythology that stimulated the progress of exploration offers examples of the importance of error in the progress of geography. If a theory is developed on the basis of analogy, as Plancius did, this is little better than the development of theory almost entirely in the absence of observed data. After all, Pythagoras did conceive of the earth as a ball long before there were observations to support such a notion. Even outrageous hypotheses have the effect of stimulating critical thinking.[40]

Let us look at three examples of the important role played by the formulation of challenging hypotheses as essential steps in the progress of knowledge about the surface of the earth and of man's place on it.

### Climate and Landscape

Ever since Alexander von Humboldt had reported a correspondence between vegetation and certain average temperatures in tropical mountains, geographers had been seeking to give the idea wider application. Could a temperature value be found to correspond, for example, with the border between forest and tundra? In 1874 de Candolle had presented a classification of major types of vegetation useful for geographic study.[41] In 1879 Supan suggested that the isotherm most closely corresponding to the southern border of the tundra in northern Europe was that of 10° C. (50° F.) average for the warmest month.[42] In 1900 Köppen offered a classification of climates based in large part on de Candolle's vegetation types.[43] In 1910 Penck presented the hypothesis that climate (not just temperature) so impresses the landscape that classification of climates is possible to apply even in the absence of reliable climatic data.[44] Here is a hypothesis that clearly contains the elements of error, yet it is one that had the effect of stimulating other geographers either to extend and illustrate Penck's idea, or to disprove it.[45] In 1918 Köppen revised his classification of climates to include not only temperature, but also effective moisture and seasonal change.[46] He devised an empirical formula to define the borders of his arid and semiarid regions. A careful comparison of the boundary of Köppen's BW (arid) climate with the boundary between regions where the plants fail to form a complete cover over the ground and regions where the plants fail to form a complete cover over the ground and regions where the plants do form a complete cover (desert and steppe) shows a close correspondence in northern Africa. In other parts of the world there are marked departures between the two lines, especially in the Gobi of inner Asia.[47]

These efforts to apply Penck's ideas on a global scale stimulated a critical review of the whole hypothesis. Not only are some vegetation specialists taking a new look at the traditional categories of vegetation,[48] but also the climatologists have found that available moisture is more significant than temperature in accounting for vegetation differences.[49] In 1948 Thornthwaite outlined a new approach to a classification of climates in which he made use of an empirical formula for measuring evapotranspiration and so arriving at an estimate of the balance between too much and too little water.[50] In recent years Thornthwaite's ideas have been applied in many studies of the relation of available moisture to the growth of plants.[51]

*Hypotheses and Theoretical Models
in the Study of Landforms*

The challenging, and challenged, hypothesis has been of the greatest importance in stimulating progress in the study of landforms. For many centuries there had been almost no new hypotheses presented. Ever since the days of the ancient Greek geographers, it had been customary to explain landforms as resulting from convulsions of nature, or violent cataclysms. To be sure Avicenna, the Arab geographer who lived from A.D. 979 to 1037, had presented a theory of landform development based on the erosive action of running water. But few Europeans knew of his work until the historians of geography pointed it out many centuries later, when the rest of the world had caught up. During the Christian era geographers followed literally the ideas presented in the Bible. The world was perfect before the fall of man, but thereafter it had been all messed up by the actions of an angry deity.

The century following Hutton's book on the *Theory of the Earth,* published in 1788,[52] was one of great excitement as hypotheses and models were formulated, debated, then abandoned or revised.[53] Hutton was immediately attacked by the persuasive German teacher, Werner.[54] But the assistance of Playfair at last turned the tide toward Hutton's idea that landforms could be explained on the basis of processes observable today.[55] Lyell proposed the idea that much of the erosion that had gone on must have been done by submarine currents.[56] Agassiz advanced the ideas of glaciation, which were further elaborated by Guyot.[57] Each of these hypotheses met with challenge, and the challenge led to new field observation and to revised hypotheses. By 1870 there was a large volume of new data available on stream flow, on the capacity of streams to carry load, and on the movement of glaciers. By this time it was recognized that rivers could, in fact, do the work required to explain the landforms of Europe, and there was no need to suppose the existence of marine currents as Lyell had done.

Great advances in the understanding of the processes at work on the earth were made in the United States between 1867 and 1879.[58] This is the period of the great surveys by John Wesley Powell, Clarence King, Ferdinand V. Hayden, and George M. Wheeler. Powell and others first saw and described antecedent and superimposed rivers. Powell developed the concept of base level. Grove Karl Gilbert developed the idea of grade, and also the action of bodies of water in forming shorelines.[59]

The story of the development of the concept of the cycle of erosion (the geographic cycle) by William Morris Davis, and of its subsequent changes, offers a clear example of the importance of the challenging hypothesis, and also of the retardation of the rate of progress in a field that takes place when any one conceptual structure becomes dominant and beyond the range of effective challenge. Davis brought together the ideas of students of landforms not only from the United States, but also from Europe. He described a theoretical model to illustrate what would happen when a plain is uplifted and cut by rivers. His cycle of erosion passed through the stages of youth, maturity, and old age, when the landforms were again reduced to a plain, which he called a peneplain, or almost a plain. He recognized other processes that might be at work, and he also appreciated the variety of forms that would result from differences of underlying structure. All landforms, he insisted, could be interpreted through the use of the formula: structure, process, and stage.[60]

Here is what Davis himself had to say about the utility of his model:

> In the scheme of the cycle of erosion . . . a mental counterpart for every landform is developed in terms of its understructure, of the erosional process that has acted upon it, and of the stage reached by such action stated in terms of the whole sequence of stages from the initiation of a cycle of erosion by upheaval or other deformation of an area of the earth's crust, to its close when the work of erosion has been completed: and the observed landform is then described not in terms of its directly visible features, but in terms of its inferred mental counterpart. The essence of the scheme is simple and easily understood; yet it is so elastic and so easily expanded and elaborated, that it can provide counterparts for landforms of the most complicated structure and the most involved history.[61]

There are many people who insist that Davis retarded the study of landforms by many decades. By his own vigorous and persuasive writing and lecturing, his model of landform development was almost universally accepted, not only in the United States but also among the scholars of Europe. After his demonstration of the method of applying his scheme to the physical history of an area,[62] many such studies were undertaken. From all over the world came reports of the identification of peneplains, now uplifted and redissected. In fact one of the puzzling questions raised by his own students was the scarcity of peneplains that had not been uplifted and dissected. There can be no doubt that the presentation of the Davis model greatly increased the volume of geographic writings. His model was also used as a basis for the teaching of physical geography in the secondary schools. How, then, can it be said that Davis retarded the study of landforms?

The answer is clear, and significant. There was a long delay in the development of critical response in sufficient volume to set up a dialog. To be sure the younger Penck did present a basic challenge to the Davis model,[63] and Passarge insisted on the utility of an empirical approach to the study of landforms rather than a genetic one.[64] Both were promptly attacked by Davis or his disciples.[65] In fact, Davis himself was so effective in his defense of the cycle theory that critical challenges were few. In other words, the theoretical model became the standard of landform study, and Davis was the almost unquestioned authority.

Chorley pointed to some of the dangers inherent in any model.[66] Models are caricatures of reality, from which many distracting elements are discarded as irrelevant. So long as models illuminate a subject, they—like regions—may be judged to be good; when they obscure a subject they are bad. Since the Davis cycle specifically excludes the effect of climatic change or of the continuous movement of base level, it follows that the cycle is a special case and not universally applicable. Where the removal of a foot of rock material from an area of the earth's surface results in the isostatic rise of the rock column beneath that surface by some nine to eleven feet, it follows that eroding mountain ranges must be continuously uplifted, which suggests why peneplains are found to be dissected, and also why the whole peneplain concept needs to be reexamined.

The ideas of Penck have been expanded and clarified in the numerous writings of the South African scholar, King.[67] The question is: do slopes actually flatten during a period of erosion, as Davis suggests, or do slopes retreat parallel to their initial position, resulting in the formation of a pediplain rather than a peneplain? [68] This provides the kind of effective challenge to a theoretical model that we recognize is a promoter of rapid progress in a field of study. And the challenge has been taken up by Budel, who suggests that where a given amount of rainfall produces a large runoff, the Davis cycle becomes operative, but where the same amount of rainfall produces a relatively small runoff (as in the Brazilian Highlands) the King cycle becomes operative.[69]

*Hypotheses and Theoretical Models in Human Geography*

The formulation of challenging hypotheses has also been of the greatest importance in those aspects of geography that focus attention on man. But the development of geographic concepts regarding man and his activities came much later than in the physical aspects of geography. Whereas students of landforms were shaken loose from the hypotheses regarding convulsions of nature during the latter part of the eighteenth century, students of human geography were not similarly awakened until after the middle of the nineteenth century. As in the physical fields, progress results from setting up hypotheses and then challenging them either to raise the hypotheses to the prestige of validated theory, or to demonstrate the existence of error. Haggett suggests that "the sound of progress is perhaps the sound of plummeting hypotheses." [70]

The world of scholarship was startled in 1858 by a paper presented to the Linnean Society of London jointly by Charles Darwin and Alfred Russell Wallace. This was the first statement of the theory of organic evolution and of the survival of the fittest. Since physical geography at this time was already a well-established field of scientific study, it was natural that concepts regarding the relationships of man to his natural surroundings should be closely attached to the physical concepts. The ideas of the close dependence of human societies on the physical earth, and of the survival of those societies capable of adjusting to the conditions of the physical environment gained wide acceptance. This was social Darwinism, and it led to the concept of man as a product of the earth, seeking to adjust his ways of living to fit within the physical limitations imposed by his natural surroundings. [71]

The reaction against these hypotheses appeared first in Germany and France. Ratzel himself, whose first volume of *Anthropogeographie* in 1882 presented the ideas of environmental determinism most plausibly, changed his approach to a modified environmentalism in the second volume published in 1891. [72] Alfred Hettner in Germany and Paul Vidal de la Blache in France led geographic thinking away from strict social Darwinism. [73] The

French geographers, following Vidal, developed the concept of human society as closely interacting with the natural surroundings of which it becomes an essential part. In Germany Weber proposed a body of theory to account for the concentration of manufacturing industry in certain locations.[74] All these efforts at theory-building were based on the recognition of the error inherent in strict social Darwinism.

In the English-speaking world, on the other hand, social Darwinism continued to dominate the conceptual structure of geography. This dominance resulted in part from the authority and prestige of Davis, and in part from the persuasive teaching and writing of Semple and Huntington.[75] The theory of man's response to environment guided geographic research and determined the kinds of field observations that gave support to these theories.

The beginning of an effective revolt against social Darwinism in America came in 1925 when Sauer published an important paper. "Geography under the banner of environmentalism," wrote Sauer, "represents a dogma, the assertion of a faith that brings rest to a spirit vexed by the riddle of the universe." [76] Instead Sauer suggested that geographers should investigate the form and structure of landscape, and the interconnections among the features of the face of the earth that form spatial systems. Through his writings the landscape school of geography was introduced to America.

It is a mistake to hold that geography in that period returned to the empirical regional description of unique situations. The landscape school of geographers abandoned the concept of environmental control. They substituted the assertion that the significance to man of the physical and biotic environment was a function of the attitudes, objectives, and technical skills of man himself. Studies of sequent occupance illustrated the changing significance of natural surroundings with changes in the human culture.[77] Furthermore, theoretical models were set up for the purpose of accounting for observed processes of change and of extending the changes into the future.[78] The models were described in words rather than mathematical formulae, but they were nevertheless theoretical models.

The search for regularities among the patterns of things and events spread in complex association and interaction among the spatial systems of the earth (which is surely what geography is all about) occupied the attention of some geographers, even during the supposedly sterile period of social Darwinism. Jefferson, for example, was examining the distribution of population and cities over the world. In 1908 he presented the idea that urban areas could be defined as having a population density of more than 10,000 people per square mile.[79] Between 1909 and 1941 he published thirty-one papers in the *Bulletin of the American Geographical Society* and its successor, the *Geographical Review*.[80] A study of these papers will reveal the extent to which hypotheses and theories, rather than mere description, constituted the chief concern of this geographer. His studies of city sizes, and of the relation of cities to the areas they serve spanned more than a decade before 1940.[81]

The rank-size theory of cities within any one national state was suggested by Zipf in 1941.[82] His idea was that in each national state there was a primate city (as Jefferson had pointed out), that the second city had about half the population of the first city, and that the population of the other cities followed a descending order by rank. This theory caused a stronger reaction, in America at least, than the earlier studies by Auerbach and Lotka, neither of whose writings were cited by Zipf (which supports the hypothesis that geographers seldom read what other geographers write).[83] The rank-size theory, however, fails to stand up, and now seems to have plummeted.[84]

City sizes and the interchange among cities of different sizes was studied by Stewart, who presented a challenging hypothesis on this matter in 1947. According to Stewart, "The evident tendency of people to congregate in larger and larger cities represents an attraction of people for people that turns out to have a mathematical as well as a merely verbal resemblance to Newton's law of gravitation." [85] The population potential measures the extent of interaction among different populations, based on the concept of population number divided by distance. Stewart's ideas have been applied by Warntz in a study of the geography of price.[86] They could be further applied to an identification of the pole of maximum potential accessibility,[87] which would bring new meaning to the concept of the land hemisphere.

Many years ago the German geographer, Christaller, published a study of the spacing and functions of central places in southern

Germany.[88] This highly original contribution to challenging hypotheses has now stimulated a large number of studies regarding the patterns of central places, and of the services they offer. Central-place theory, as now formulated, tells us that the functions performed in any market center are related to the size of the center and to its position in the hierarchy of central places. Central-place theory also suggests how the service areas of central places will be arranged: the service area of each center tends to take on a hexagonal shape because this is the most efficient subdivision of space.

Central-place theory has become one of the major foci of interest among geographers, where mathematical methods are providing not only a more precise way to formulate hypotheses and theoretical models, but also a more reliable method of testing them.[89]

### The Persistence of Error

The formulation of challenging hypotheses, then, stimulates progress in any field of scholarship, in spite of the inevitable errors they contain. This is the kind of error that Thomas Jefferson did not like, but which we can clearly see is an essential element in the learning process. The kind of error that retards progress is the kind that persists. There was nothing in Davis's concept of the cycle of erosion that held back the study of landforms; rather the delay in the progress of this field can be charged to the ironic situation in which Davis, because of his exceptional mastery of the methods of logical thought and of communication, so far dominated his professional colleagues that his authority was seldom effectively challenged.

What kinds of error do in fact persist, and can we identify conditions that permit such persistence?

### Some Examples of Persistent Error

The history of geographic thought is filled with examples of the persistence of concepts long after their usefulness in illuminating geographic conditions and problems has been lost. Even today we find a widespread use of the idea of the division of the globe into temperate, torrid, and frigid zones, with connotations regarding the habitability of each. The torrid zone is still thought to be excessively hot, in spite of evidence to the contrary presented in writing since the time of Posidonius (who insisted that the highest temperatures are found not near the equator but along the tropics), and in spite of modern evidence in the form of climatic data and maps. The supposed heat of the torrid zone is supposed, also, to reduce human energy to the point where effective economic development is impossible. These ideas are still taught and widely believed.[90] They appear not only in the writings of nongeographers, but also are not entirely absent from the work of those who should know better.[91]

Another persistent practice, inherited from the ancient Greeks, is the use of the continents as units of study. Actually, the three continents—Europe, Asia, and Libya (Africa)—were very useful regional divisions of the known world at the time of Strabo. In each there was a distinctive association of climate, surface features, and cultures. And the concept of the continents gave rise to valuable discussions regarding the placing of the boundaries.[92] Herodotus was especially critical of those who would divide Asia from Libya along the Nile River, and recommend that the dividing line be established at the western border of Egypt, leaving the Egyptians where they belonged, in Asia. Strabo suggested that either one should follow Herodotus or draw no boundary at all. But when these original regional divisions of the Greek world are expanded to continents, the result is geographic nonsense. To be sure Ritter tried to show that each of the continents had been fashioned by an all-wise deity for the particular use of man at successive stages of his development.[93] In modern times, however, the continued use of continents as either units of study or as enumeration areas for summarizing population or economic data can result only in obscuring the significant ideas of world geography.[94]

### The Persistent Use of Wind Zones

The concept of the general circulation of the atmosphere that was developed by Maury in 1850 was, at the time of its publication, the first comprehensive view of atmospheric movement over the earth.[95] Maury had brought together wind data from the logs of many thousands of ships. He had before him a view of atmospheric movements such as no student had ever had before. With this information Maury provided revised sailing directions for ship's captains that greatly reduced the sailing time on established routes. His knowledge of the prevailing winds was as much a factor in the records of the clipper ships as was the new design and rigging.[96] For example, he cut some ten days off the voyage from New York to Rio de Janeiro by instructing the captains to stay close to the Brazilian coast south of Cape São Roque.

Maury as a scholar, although a self-made one, could not view the great collection of empirical data without taking the next step to formulate a theoretical model. His model was presented in the 1850 paper.[97] He showed the belts of calms, the trade wind zones, and the zones of the westerlies. The winds of each zone were shown by straight arrows, in the manner that has become standard since that time. He also showed around the edge of the globe a vertical section of the atmosphere with surface winds and winds aloft. This also became common practice among the writers of texts.[98]

Maury's ideas have had an amazing persistence. Most authors have now eliminated the vertical section of the atmosphere, realizing that the whole height of the atmosphere, drawn to scale, would be less than the width of the black line representing the earth's surface. But the wind zones, with winds shown by straight lines are still with us. As Maury did, the arid west coast of South America is still interpreted as a lee coast in the southeast trade wind zone, in spite of the well-known fact that the winds along the coast are from the southwest. And Maury himself showed the east coast of Brazil south of Cape São Roque as lying in this zone of southeast trades. He was so blinded by the completeness of his theoretical model that the existence of northeast winds along this part of the Brazilian coast was treated as an exceptional condition. Maury was realist enough to make use of these northeast winds in his sailing directions, but not on his world maps.[99] The modern knowledge concerning the atmosphere, in part derived from the experiences of World War II (when the jet streams were discovered), and in part from the data gathered during the International Geophysical Year, render the theoretical models devised more than a century ago by Maury no longer useful.[100] Now there is need for proposals regarding new hypothetical models of atmospheric circulation.[101]

### The Dichotomies

Wright, in his remarkable book on the role of man in geography, discussed the reasons for the long lag between the first presentation of new and better methods or new conceptual structures and their acceptance by the profession. He identified not only the "principle of the persistence of error," but also the "principle of the resistence to novelty." [102] We are concerned about these matters in the history of geographic thought, but Wright freed the geographers from any special opprobrium, because these principles can be identified in all aspects of human affairs and in all fields of learning. This places geographers in the mainstream of humanity, but it does not diminish the need to try to do something about it.

In other words, it is quite natural that when a theoretical model has been developed which is highly successful in simplifying and clarifying the complexities of the geographer's universe the geographers become more and more reluctant to abandon it. But among the persistent oversimplifications, we should provide a special place for the persistence of dichotomies. By their simplicity and apparent clarity they have the effect of ending critical thought: they provide the tired mind with clear-cut categories with which to become associated; perhaps nothing we have discussed above is so pervasive and so ambiguous in promoting the persistence of error.

A dichotomy is the logical division of a class into two subclasses that are mutually contradictory. Between two subclasses so distinguished there can be no overlapping. To assert the existence of a dichotomy is to assert the irreducibility of the difference. Examples of dichotomies include such absolute dualisms as good and evil, body and mind, reason and faith. From the Chinese philosophers comes the dichotomy of *yin* and *yang*: *yin* represents the feminine, passive, and negative aspects of the universe; *yang* represents the masculine, active and creative aspects.

To identify a false dichotomy is not always easy. Theoretically a dichotomy does not exist if one of the two subclasses is derived from the other, or is subordinate to the other. Furthermore, a dichotomy may exist for some people and not for others, depending on the basic—and often unrecognized—premises inherent in a culture.

### Man and Nature

A dichotomy which is embedded in our culture is the dualism of man and nature, which has been accepted in geographic thought for a long time. The teleologists were quite clear about the distinction between man and nature. From Judeo-Christian teaching comes the directive that man should establish his conquest over nature. For the teleologists the natural world was built by an all-wise deity especially to be subdued by man. The dichotomy was the cornerstone of the conceptual structure developed by the social Darwinists.

For the great majority of the world's population no such dichotomy exists. Among the Buddhists and the Hindus, for example, man is not separate from nature, but rather is a part of nature, and the individual hopes eventually to be absorbed in the natural world after he has overcome his ignorance, his lusts, and his angry reactions to frustration. In the Judeo-Christian tradition, on the other hand, the earth is only a stopping place for man on his way to eternity.

### Physical Geography and Human Geography

The man-nature dichotomy might not be so damaging to geographic thought if it had not given rise to a related dichotomy, physical geography and human geography. In the period of the social Darwinists, the physical aspects of geography constituted a well-developed science. When Varenius spoke of general geography, he was referring to the general concepts in the fields of physical and biotic phenomena. The development of laws regarding human action seemed beyond reach, and certainly the study of man and his activities required the use of procedures quite different from those developed for the investigation of physical geography. In recent times the stochastic approach to the formulation of theory dealing with man's activities has opened new vistas of scholarly and scientific accomplishment. But it is easy to assume that in physical geography one can identify laws for which there are no exceptions, whereas in human geography one must fall back on the theory of probability.

The difference, of course, is in the number of individual units being studied. In physical geography laws are based on the behavior of vast aggregates of elements. The physicists who deal with the smallest components of matter find that they, too, must fall back on the theory of probability. The human geographers, like the atomic physicists, deal with a relatively small number of individual elements. Actually, then, the two subclasses—physical and human —are not irreducible.

The distinction in geography between physical and human subclasses becomes a serious source of error when it results in separating these two aspects of geographic study. There are some universities wherein physical geography is offered in a different faculty from the one in which human geography is offered. And the usual division of the academic world between physical and social sciences seems to give additional support to the dichotomy. A major obstacle to geographic study develops when applications for financial aid for research undertakings in physical geography must be submitted to entirely different agencies than those to which applications for the support of studies in human geography are sent. There would seem to be no solution to this problem until a foundation is endowed for the specific purpose of supporting studies in geography.

In other words the common distinction between physical and human geography, which may be useful and convenient, and even necessary for dealing with the academic world, becomes a source of persistent error when it is permitted to become a dichotomy. When this happens these two subclasses are regarded as mutually exclusive, sometimes to the extent that workers in one subclass neglect to communicate, or become unable to communicate, with workers in the other subclass. Much physical geography, in past decades has, in fact, failed to provide what the students of human geography needed, and there are many workers in human geography today who shy away from giving proper consideration to the physical world, either because of the fear that this belongs in another discipline, or because in their earlier years they were scared by the bogeyman of environmental determinism.[103] If it is a useful concept to insist that the significance to man of the physical and biotic features of his habitat is a function of man's culture, then clearly the separation of physical geography from human geography becomes a crippling error. The distinction between physical and human geography is not a valid dichotomy, and every effort should be made to eliminate it.

*Topical and Regional*

Another false dichotomy that causes persistent error in geography is the supposed contradiction between topical (or systematic) and regional geography. The distinction is commonly credited to Varenius [104] who used the term "general geography" to refer to the explanation of the nature and properties of the earth, and the term "special geography" to refer to the application of the general concepts to particular parts of the earth. Varenius never thought of these two parts of geography as forming a dichotomy, for the special geography was derived from the ideas developed in general geography. Although Varenius died too early to complete the studies he planned to do in special geography, he did complete regional studies of Japan and Siam.[105] His major work, which had a lasting influence on geographic thinking, had to do with general geography.[106] It remained the standard text for geography in universities for more than a century. In spite of the clear fact that Varenius himself never saw general and special geography as mutually exclusive, and did think of special geography as derived from general geography, the apparent dualism became commonly accepted as a dichotomy, and geographers began to identify themselves as chiefly concerned with one or the other.

Some geographers who accept topical and regional geography as representing a real dichotomy point to von Humboldt and Ritter as demonstrating its validity. Humboldt is thus described as a topical geographer, and Ritter is named as the great master of regional geography. Nevertheless a careful study of the writings of these two scholars does not support the idea that they followed two exclusively different methods. Humboldt did not establish general principles without reference to particular parts of the earth. When he measured ocean temperatures it was in the water off the coast of Peru; when he established a correspondence between temperature and vegetation zones, he was referring to the Andes of northern South America; when he noted the changing levels of inland bodies of water he was examining the Lake of Valencia or the Caspian Sea. And Ritter made it very clear that he could not have written his comparative studies of special regions without the insights of general geography provided by Humboldt.

Yet it is curious to trace the continued acceptance of this supposed dichotomy between the topical and regional approach. Hartshorne made a careful analysis of the origin and persistence of this idea.[107] He showed not only that topical and regional geography are mutually interdependent, but also that individual geographers, whatever their professions of faith, have in fact worked these two approaches together. All general concepts must be identified from the study of particular places, and all studies of particular places are only made significant (rather than merely descriptive) through the application of general principles. In other words, all topical studies must be done regionally, making use of the regional method, and all regional studies must be done topically.[108] The idea that a dichotomy exists between topical and regional studies is a persistent error, and insofar as the idea leads geographers to enlist in one or the other division and scorn the findings of the other this error also can be crippling.


## The Empirical-Inductive and the Theoretical-Deductive Methods

The distinctions between an empirical and a theoretical approach to learning, and between an inductive and deductive approach have been recognized for a very long time in human thought. The distinction between the deductive and inductive methods was presented in words by Plato and Aristotle. It was Plato, the champion of the deductive method, who described some prisoners chained in a cave with their backs to the cave opening. People passing back and forth in the sunlight cast shadows on the cave wall. The prisoners, seeing only the shadows, came to think of these as reality. But, said Plato, the things people see are only the blurred shadows of reality, which can only be approached through the study of theoretical concepts. Aristotle, on the other hand, insisted on the necessity of looking at things before developing theories. He did not suggest that theories should be avoided; rather, he said, in testing a theory go out and look at things to see whether what you see supports the theory. He was the champion of the inductive method, and the father of geography as a field study.

The deductive method is supposed to start with theory. But it would be difficult to demonstrate that pure theory can be formulated without some kind of preceding observation. Perhaps Pythagoras did theorize that the world was a ball, but this was based on his preconception that symmetry is the essence of beauty, and the most symmetrical form is a ball. We may assume that he also worked from the premise that the earth must be beautiful because it was created as the home of man. Having established the theory of a round earth, he and his followers proceeded to deduce the results of this form, as when Parmenides divided the round surface into slopes, or *klima*. Certainly from Pythagoras to Bunge there are examples of scholars who thought they were starting with pure theory, and who were then more concerned with what should be than with what is.[109] As Wellington Jones once remarked: "A theoretical model shows how a process would work if it did not work the way it does." [110]

The inductive method is supposed to start with observations of things and events. But we have pointed out that observations are likely to reflect the mental images already in the mind of the observer. The inductive method then proceeds to the formulation of hypotheses to account for the things observed. Long ago scholars recommended the formulation of multiple hypotheses in order to minimize the blinding power of one's own preconceptions. The hypotheses are tested against new observations, and if they stand these tests the hypotheses are then elevated to the status of theory. If the hypotheses fail to stand these tests they must be abandoned or modified.

In 1886 Gilbert pointed out his reasons for preferring the inductive method. He wrote: "In the testing of hypotheses lies the prime difference between the investigator and the theorist. The one seeks diligently for the facts which may overthrow his tentative theory, the other closes his eyes to these and searches only for those that will sustain it." [111] This is a good description of what the social Darwinists tried to do.

The geographers who formed the *ad hoc* committee to prepare the monograph on *The Science of Geography* took a big step toward the creation of a dichotomy when they linked empirical with inductive, and theoretical with deductive. They quoted James B. Conant in describing the progress of science as "a dialogue between the empirical-inductive and the theoretical-deductive methods of thought and investigation." [112] If a dialog really exists, then the two approaches are mutually interdependent and no dichotomy exists. But if, instead of a dialog, one finds scholars enlisting in one or the other armies and thereafter waging incessant warfare on all those of the opposite forces, then a dichotomy does exist. The report of the *ad hoc* committee insisted that geography must advance beyond the preliminary stage of empirical-inductive work and become more theoretical. In other words the dialog idea is to be abandoned in favor of a dichotomy.

Linking the word *empirical* with the word *inductive* is more a declaration of faith than an example of careful thinking. In the first place what is an empirical observation? *Empirical* means wholly dependent on experience and observation without any reference to theory. But the discussion of the relationship between percept and concept suggests that anyone who claims to approach the observation of things and events with a blank mind is either fooling himself, or is a candidate for an insane asylum. Truly empirical study, we should be able to assume, does not exist. Nevertheless the follower of the inductive method does try to let his hypotheses develop on the basis of observations. But does anyone wish to insist that the inductive method does not lead to the formulation of hypotheses, the testing of hypotheses, and the elevation of successful hypotheses to the level of theory? How does one arrange for Haggett's plummeting hypotheses without following the inductive method?

There is, of course, a real difference between those scholars who prefer to develop theory first and those who let observation lead to theory. The former have sometimes demonstrated keen intuitive judgment in visualizing theory in advance of conscious observation. But so also have the inductive workers, whose hypotheses are also, on occasion, brilliantly formulated on the basis of subjective judgment.

Both clarity of thinking, and also the avoidance of a dichotomy, might have been promoted by omitting the word *empirical* altogether. This is really a straw-man who can be so spectacularly demolished for the benefit of frustrated egos. But to think more clearly, why do we not distinguish between an inductive-theoretical approach and a theoretical-deductive approach? This would provide us with an important distinction, but would avoid the dichotomy and let a real and much needed dialog develop.

## CONCLUSION

This review of the origin and persistence of error suggests some conclusions. Although there are certain kinds of errors that can be avoided with proper attention to the pitfalls in the geographer's universe, we must recognize that the continuous formulation of hypotheses and hypothetical models, even though they contain errors, is nevertheless an essential accompaniment of progress.[113] The sound of plummeting hypotheses may bring pain to the authors of these hypotheses, but to the profession as a whole the sound is encouraging. The purpose of any hypothesis or model is to bring together things and events that previously seemed to be unrelated, and to place them in some kind of conceptual framework that can be easily comprehended and easily tested against new observations. It is, rather, the persistence of error, the persistent use of familiar theory and well-known models long after they are known to be misleading and obscuring, that is to be deplored.

It is true that there has always been a tendency to accept clear and simple answers to complex problems. These neat conceptual structures are then carefully protected by their proponents from the impact of deviant facts, as when a mathematical geographer removes the deviants from his scatter diagram to make the results look more convincing.

The dichotomies, themselves, are a form of oversimplification of complex matters. Because geographers are human, many find satisfaction in taking extreme positions with respect to a dichotomy, whether or not it is a false one. It is easy and immensely satisfying for a geographer of the right persuasion to proclaim "I am not a regional geographer" or "I am a scientist and I approach the study of geography systematically through the formulation of theory of wide application." The often demonstrated proposition that all topical studies must be done regionally, and that the regional method is fundamental to the proper use of mathematical procedures, does not diminish the sense of superiority this false dichotomy can offer. And although the history of human thought shows clearly that inductive reasoning leads to the formulation of theory, the devoted theorists can enjoy a status of intellectual superiority by cutting off all communication with those who are concerned about the observation of things and events in the field. If the theoretical-deductive workers are not conscious of the sources of their data, so much the worse for the persistence of error.

Now, in the last two decades, the study of geography has been greatly invigorated through the application of mathematical procedures. These procedures are not applied exclusively to the theoretical-deductive approach; far from it, their chief application has been to the inductive-theoretical approach. Mathematical procedures now make it possible to formulate hypotheses and hypothetical models with greater precision than ever before. The use of orbiting sensors and computers makes possible both the collection of more reliable data and also the analysis of the interconnections among things and events of diverse origin. Even the concept of the compage, as developed by Whittlesey, might emerge from the status of an emotional feeling, to the certainty of complex mathematical formulae through judicious use of the computer.

With all these exciting new opportunities it seems essential that all those scholars who are challenged by the complexity of the earth's spatial systems should learn to communicate freely with each other. Whether geography is pursued inductively or deductively, or even whether it is pursued as an art or as a science, is perhaps less important than that it be pursued by honest scholarship, and that the results of this pursuit be communicated. It is important, also, that we learn to avoid the major sources of error. As Wrigley wrote: "the most complete prisoners of the past are those who are unconscious of it." [114] A proper attention to the history of geographic thought makes both the success and failures of those who preceded us a part of our common heritage.

### NOTES

1. Address given by the Honorary President of the Association of American Geographers at its sixty-second Annual Meeting, Toronto, Ontario, Canada, August 31, 1966.

2. J. Leighly, "Error in Geography," in J. Jastrow, ed., *The Story of Human Error* (New York: Appleton-Century, 1936).

3. R. Hartshorne, *Perspective on the Nature of Geography* (Chicago: Rand McNally, 1959), Monograph No. 1, Association of American Geographers.

4. G. de Jong, *Chorological Differentiation as the Fundamental Principle of Geography* (Groningen: J. B. Walters, 1962); E. A. Ackerman, *Geography as a Fundamental Research Discipline* (Chicago: Department of Geography, University of Chicago, 1958).

5. E. Adickes, *Kant als Naturforscher* (Berlin: W. deGruyter, 1925), reference in II, 394.

6. R. Hartshorne, *The Nature of Geography, A Critical Survey of Current Thought in the Light of the Past;* reprinted by the Association of American Geographers from the *Annals,* 29 (1939), 173–658, reference on pp. 140–42.

7. R. Hartshorne, "The Concept of Geography as a Science of Space, from Kant and Humboldt to Hettner," *Annals* of the Association of American Geographers, 48 (1958), 97–108.

8. R. Carnap, *Introduction to Symbolic Logic and its Applications* (New York: Dover Publications, 1958); trans. by William H. Meyer and John Wilkinson, from *Emführung in die symbolische Logik,* reference on pp. 158 ff.

9. N. Ginsburg, "Area," in the *International Encyclopedia of the Social Sciences* (New York: Crowell, Collier, and Macmillan, 1966).

10. R. Hartshorne, *Perspective on Geography,* footnote 3, pp. 22–25.

11. P. E. James, "Toward a Further Understanding of the Regional Concept," *Annals* of the Association of American Geographers, 42 (1952), 195–222.

12. W. Zelinsky, "Of Time and the Geographer," *Landscape,* 15, 2 (1965–66), 21–22.

13. D. Lowenthal, "Geography, Experience, and Imagination: Toward a Geographical Epistemology," *Annals,* Association of American Geographers, 51 (1961), 241–60.

14. J. K. Wright, *Human Nature in Geography* (Cambridge: Harvard University Press, 1966).

15. P. Haggett, *Locational Analysis in Human Geography* (New York: St. Martin's Press, 1966), pp. 23–27.

16. T. Goldstein, "Geography in Fifteenth-Century Florence," in John Parker, ed., *Merchants and Scholars* (Minneapolis: University of Minnesota Press, 1965), pp. 11–32, reference on pp. 14–15.

17. D. Whittlesey, "The Regional Concept and the Regional Method," in P. E. James and C. F. Jones, eds., *American Geography, Inventory and Prospect* (Syracuse: Syracuse University Press, 1954), pp. 19–68, reference on p. 30.

18. V. V. Pokshishevskiy, "Economic Regionalization of the U.S.S.R.," in *Geografiya S.S.S.R.,* No. 2, Academy of Sciences, U.S.S.R., Moscow, 1965; translated in *Soviet Geography,* 7, 5 (1966), 4–32. The Soviet geographers use the word *region* in the administrative sense.

19. O. D. Duncan, R. P. Cuzzort, and B. Duncan, *Statistical Geography: Problems in Analyzing Areal Data* (Glencoe, Ill.: The Free Press, 1961), pp. 57 ff.

20. W. Zelinsky, *A Prologue to Population Geography* (Engelwood Cliffs, N. J.: Prentice-Hall, 1966), pp. 6–9, 17–24, reference on p. 22.

21. L. E. Klimm, "The Empty Areas of the Northeastern United States," *Geographical Review,* 44 (1954), 325–45.

22. J. Gottmann, *Megalopolis, The Urbanized Northeastern Seaboard of the United States* (New York: The Twentieth Century Fund, 1961), pp. 7–9.

23. Haggett, *Locational Analysis,* pp. 185–210.

24. A. H. Robinson, "The Necessity of Weighting Values in Correlation Analysis of Areal Data," *Annals,* Association of American Geographers, 46 (1956), 233–36.

25. J. Leighly, "Climatology since the Year 1880," *Transactions of the American Geophysical Union,* 30 (1949), 658–72.

26. C. W. Thornthwaite, "The Life History of Rainstorms . . . ," *Geographical Review,* 27 (1937), 92–111.

27. C. O. Sauer, "The Road to Cibola," *Ibero-Americana,* 3 (Berkeley: University of California Press, 1932).

28. Wright, *Human Nature,* p. 35.

29. These three kinds of distributions were described as continuities, discontinuities, and discontinuous distributions in James and Jones, *American Geography,* pp. 10–11; see also J. K. Wright, "Some Measures of Distributions," *Annals* of the Association of American Geographers, 27 (1937), 177–211. The terms used here are from Edwin N. Thomas.

30. J. R. Mackay, "Some Problems and Techniques in Isopleth Mapping," *Economic Geography,* 27 (1951) 1–9.

31. P. E. James, "On the Treatment of Surface Features in Regional Studies," *Annals* of the Association of American Geographers, 27 (1937), 213–28.

32. E. H. Hammond, "Analysis of Properties in Land Form Geography: An Application to Broad-Scale Land Form Mapping," *Annals* of the Association of American Geographers, 54 (1964), 11–19.

33. R. H. Brown, "Jefferson's Notes on Virginia," *Geographical Review,* 33 (1943), 467–73; the first edition of the *Notes on the State of Virginia* was published in Paris in 1785.

34. Wright, *Human Nature*, p. 263.

35. A. Guyot, Preface to *Physical Geography* (New York: American Book Co. 1873).

36. J. K. Wright, *The Geographical Lore of the Time of the Crusades* (New York: American Geographical Society, research series 15, 1925).

37. B. Penrose, *Travel and Discovery in the Renaissance, 1420–1620* (Cambridge, Mass.: Harvard University Press, 1952).

38. F. M. Rogers, *The Quest for the Eastern Christians: Travels and Rumor in the Age of Discovery* (Minneapolis, Minn.: University of Minnesota Press, 1962).

39. J. K. Wright, "The Open Polar Sea," *Geographical Review*, 43 (1953), 338–65, also printed in Wright, *Human Nature*.

40. W. M. Davis, "The Value of the Outrageous Geological Hypothesis," *Science*, 63 (1926) 463–68.

41. A. de Candolle, "Constitution dans le règne végétal des groupes physiologiques applicables à la géographie ancienne et moderne," *Archives des sciences physiques et naturelles* (Geneva: May 1874).

42. A. Supan, "Die Temperaturzonen der Erde," *Petermann's Mitteilungen*, 25 (1879), 349–58.

43. W. Köppen, "Versuch einer Klassifikation der Klimate, vorzugsweise nach ihren Beziehungen zur Pflanzenwelt," *Geographische Zeitschrift*, 6 (1900), 593–611.

44. A. Penck, "Versuch einer Klimaklassifikation auf physiogeographischer Grundlagen," *Sitzungs-Berichte der Akademie der Wissenschaften*, 1 (1910), 236–46.

45. S. Passarge, *Die Landschaftsgürtel der Erde, Natur und Kultur* (Breslau: Ferdinant Hirt, 1923).

46. W. Köppen, "Klassifikation der Klimate Nach Temperatur, Niederschlag, und Jahreslauf," *Petermann's Mitteilungen*, 64 (1918), 193–203 and 243–48, reported by P. E. James, "Köppen's Classification of Climates: A Review," *Monthly Weather Review*, 50 (1922), 69–72.

47. P. E. James, *An Outline of Geography* (Boston: Ginn & Company, 1935), p. 18.

48. D. J. deLaubenfels doubts whether the tundra is, in fact, a single vegetation type, comparable to a woodland or a seasonal forest.

49. C. W. Thornthwaite, "Problems in the Classification of Climates," *Geographical Review*, 33 (1943) 233–55.

50. C. W. Thornthwaite, "An Approach Toward a Rational Classification of Climate," *ibid.*, 38 (1948), 55–94.

51. W. D. Sellers, *Physical Climatology* (Chicago: University of Chicago Press, 1965).

52. J. Hutton, "Theory of the Earth; or an Investigation of the Laws Observable in the Composition, Dissolution, and restoration of Land upon the Globe," *Transactions of the Royal Society of Edinburgh*, 1 (1788), 209–304; and *idem, Theory of the Earth, with Proofs and Illustrations* (Edinburgh, 1795).

53. R. J. Chorley, A. J. Dunn, and R. P. Beckinsale, *The History of the Study of Landforms, or the Development of Geomorphology* (London: Methuen & Co., 1964), I, 69.

54. A. G. Werner, *Kurze Klassifikation und Beschreibung der Verschiedenen Gebirgsarten* (Dresden, 1787); and *idem, Neue Theorie von der Enstehung der Gange* (Freiburg, 1802).

55. J. Playfair, *Illustrations of the Huttonian Theory of the Earth* (Edinburgh, 1802; New York: Dover Publications, 1964).

56. C. Lyell, *Principles of Geology* (London: Murray, 11th ed. 1872).

57. Chorley, Dunn, and Beckinsale, *History of Study of Landforms*, 191–234.

58. R. A. Bartlett, *Great Surveys of the American West* (Norman: University of Oklahoma Press, 1962).

59. G. K. Gilbert, *Geology of the Henry Mountains* (Washington, D.C.: U.S. Geological Survey, 1877); *idem, Lake Bonneville* (Washington, D.C.: U.S. Geological Survey, 1890).

60. W. M. Davis, "The Geographic Cycle," *Geographical Journal*, 14 (1899), 481–504.

61. W. M. Davis, "The Progress of Geography in the United States," *Annals of the Association of American Geographers*, 14 (1924), 159–215, ref. p. 189.

62. W. M. Davis, "The Colorado Front Range, A Study in Physiographic Presentation," *ibid.*, 1, 1911, 21–84; *idem*, "The Principles of Geographic Description," *ibid.*, 5 (1915), 61–105.

63. W. Penck, *Die morphologische Analyse* (Stuttgart: Geographische Abhandlungen, 1924).

64. S. Passarge, *Die Grundlagen der Landschaftskunde* (Hamburg: L. Friederichsen & Co., 1919).

65. W. M. Davis, "Passarge's Principles of Landscape Description," *Geographical Review*, 8 (1919), 266–73; Isaiah Bowman, "The Analysis of Land Forms," *ibid.*, 16 (1926), 122–32.

66. R. J. Chorley, "A Re-evaluation of the Geomorphic System of W. M. Davis," in R. J. Chorley and P. Haggett, eds., *Frontiers in Geographical Teaching* (London: Methuen & Co., 1965), pp. 21–38.

67. L. C. King, "Canons of Landscape Evolution," *Bulletin of the Geological Society of America*, 64 (1953), 721–53; *idem, The Morphology of the Earth* (New York: Hafner Publishing Co., 1962).

68. P. E. James, "The Geomorphology of Eastern Brazil as Interpreted by Lester C. King," *Geographical Review*, 49 (1959), 240–46.

69. J. Budel, "Klimagenetische Geomorphologie," *Geographische Rundschau*, 15 (1963), 269–85.

70. Haggett, *Locational Analysis*, p. 277.

71. J. Herbst, "Social Darwinism and the History of American Geography," *Proceedings of the American Philosophical Society*, 105 (1961), 538–44; F. Ratzel *Anthropogeographie* (Stuttgart: J. Engelhorn, I, 1882; II, 1891), I, 26–31; E. C. Semple, *Influences of Geographic Environment, on the Basis of Ratzel's System of Anthropo-Geography* (New York: Henry Holt, 1911).

72. Hartshorne, *Nature of Geography*, pp. 120–26.

73. A. Hettner, *Die Geographie, ihre Geschichte, ihr Wesen, und ihre Methoden* (Breslau: Ferdinand Hirt, 1927), pp. 90–109; P. Vidal de la Blache, *Principes de géographie humaine* (Paris: Armand Colin, 1922).

74. A. Weber, *Über den Standort der Industrien: reine Theorie des Standortes* (Tübingen, 1909).

75. E. Huntington, *Civilization and Climate* (New Haven: Yale University Press, 1915).

76. C. O. Sauer, "The Morphology of Landscape," *University of California Publications in Geography*, 2 (1925), 19–53.

77. J. W. Goldthwait, "A Town that Has Gone Downhill," *Geographical Re-*

*view*, 17 (1927), 527–52; P. E. James, "The Blackstone Valley: A Study in Chorography in Southern New England," *Annals* of the Association of American Geographers, 19 (1929), 67–109.

78. P. E. James, "A Geographic Reconnaissance of Trinidad," *Economic Geography*, 3 (1927), 87–109; ref. pp. 108–09; *idem, An Outline of Geography* (Boston: Ginn & Company, 1935), pp. 126–27.

79. M. Jefferson, "Anthropography of Some Great Cities," *Bulletin of the American Geographical Society*, 41 (1909), 537–66.

80. J. K. Wright, *Geography in the Making* (New York: American Geographical Society, 1952), pp. 294–95.

81. M. Jefferson, "Distribution of the World's City Folk," *Geographical Review*, 21 (1931), 446–65; *idem*, "The Law of the Primate City," *ibid.*, 29 (1939), 226–32.

82. G. K. Zipf, *National Unity and Disunity* (Bloomington, Indiana: Principia Press, 1941).

83. F. Auerbach, "Das Gesetz der Bevölkerungskonzentration," *Petermann's Mitteilungen*, 59 (1913), 76; A. J. Lotka, "Frequency Distribution of Productivity," *Journal of the Washington Academy of Sciences*, 16 (1926), 323; *idem*, "The Law of Urban Concentration," *Science*, 94 (1941), 164.

84. K. E. Rosing, "A Rejection of the Zipf Model (Rank Size Rule) in Relation to City Size," *The Professional Geographer*, 18 (1966), 75–82.

85. J. Q. Stewart, "Empirical Mathematical Rules Concerning the Distribution and Equilibrium of Population," *Geographical Review*, 37 (1947), 461–85.

86. W. Warntz, *Toward a Geography of Price* (Philadelphia: University of Pennsylvania Press, 1959).

87. P. E. James, *One World Divided* (Boston: Blaisdell Publishing Co., 1964), pp. 421–22.

88. W. Christaller, *Die zentralen Orte in Süddeutschland* (Jena: G. Fischer, 1933).

89. P. W. Lewis, "Three Related Problems in the Formulation of Laws in Geography," *The Professional Geographer*, 17 (1965), 24–27.

90. D. H. K. Lee, "Physiological Climatology," in James and Jones, *American Geography*, pp. 471–83; ref. pp. 472–73.

91. B. Ward, *The Rich Nations and the Poor Nations* (New York: W. W. Norton & Co., 1962), pp. 39–40; W. G. East and A. E. Moodie, eds., *The Changing World* (London: G. C. Harrap & Co., 1956), p. 1.

92. *The Geography of Strabo*, trans. by H. L. Jones, I, 243; and Hugo Berger, *Geschichte der Wissenschaftlichen Erdkunde der Griechen* (Leipzig: Von Veit & Co., 1903), pp. 86–87.

93. C. Ritter, *Die Erdkunde* (Berlin, 1822–59), I, 1–88.

94. Compare the treatment of southwest Asia where the culture unity of the region, including Egypt, is recognized by G. B. Cressey, in *Crossroads, Land and Life in Southwest Asia* (New York: Lippincott, 1960), with the treatment of Asia and Africa separately by L. D. Stamp, in Africa, *A Study in Tropical Development* (New York: John Wiley & Son, 1953, 1964).

95. M. F. Maury, "On the General Circulation of the Atmosphere," *Proceedings, American Association for the Advancement of Science*, 3 (1850), 126–47.

96. F. L. Williams, *Matthew Fontaine Maury, Scientist of the Sea* (New Brunswick, N.J.: Rutgers University Press, 1963).

97. Maury, "On the General Circulation of the Atmosphere," p. 137.

98. C. E. Koeppe and G. C. de Long, *Weather and Climate* (New York: McGraw-Hill Book Company, 1958), p. 92.

99. M. F. Maury, *Physical Geography of the Sea* (New York: Harper & Bros., 1855).

100. H. Riehl, *Introduction to the Atmosphere* (New York: McGraw-Hill, 1965): see especially pp. 206–44.

101. P. E. James, "A New Concept of Atmospheric Circulation," *Journal of Geography,* 63 (1964), 245–50.

102. Wright, *Human Nature;* see especially p. 232.

103. These observations were suggested by Edwin H. Hammond.

104. J. N. L. Baker, "The Geography of Bernhard Varenius," *Transactions and Papers, Institute of British Geographers,* 21 (1955); reprinted in Baker's *The History of Geography* (New York: Barnes & Noble, 1963), pp. 105–18. Baker noted that the terms "general" and "special" geography had been used forty years earlier by Bartholomew Keckermann in a book published in Danzig in 1603. Kecherman said the idea came originally from Ptolemy in his distinction between *geography* (Varenius' general geography) and *chorography* (Varenius' special geography).

105. Bernhard Varenius, *Descriptio Regni Japoniae et Siam* (Amsterdam, 1649).

106. B. Varenius, *Geographia Generalis, in qua affectiones generalis Telluris explicantur* (Amsterdam, 1650). Later editions were printed in Latin in 1664, 1671, and 1672. Isaac Newton edited two Latin editions, published in Cambridge, England, in 1672 and 1681. English translations were published in 1693 and in 1712.

107. Hartshorne, *Perspective on Geography,* pp. 100–45.

108. Haggett, *Locational Analysis,* pp. 254–76.

109. W. Bunge, *Theoretical Geography* (Lund, Sweden: University of Lund, 1962).

110. Verbal comment at some meeting made by Wellington Jones, formerly of the Department of Geography, University of Chicago.

111. G. K. Gilbert, "The Inculcation of the Scientific Method by Example," *American Journal of Science,* 3rd ser., 31 (1886), 284–99.

112. *Ad Hoc* Committee on Geography, E. A. Ackerman, Chairman, *The Science of Geography* (Washington, D.C.: National Academy of Sciences–National Research Council, Publication 1277, 1965), p. 12.

113. T. S. Kuhn, *The Structure of Scientific Revolutions* (Chicago: University of Chicago Press, 1962).

114. E. A. Wrigley, "Changes in the Philosophy of Geography," in Chorley and Haggett, *Frontiers in Geographical Teaching,* pp. 3–19.

# 3

## TOWARD A FURTHER UNDERSTANDING
## OF THE REGIONAL CONCEPT

The regional concept constitutes the core of geography. This concept holds that the face of the earth can be marked off into areas of distinctive character, and that the complex patterns and associations of phenomena in particular places possess a legible meaning as an ensemble which, added to the meanings derived from a study of all the parts and processes separately, provides additional perspective and additional depth of understanding. This focus of attention on particular places for the purpose of seeking a more complete understanding of the face of the earth has been the continuous, unbroken theme of geographic study through the ages.

These assertions, however, will not stand unchallenged. Geographers, as well as scholars in other disciplines, do not agree on the content of the regional concept; attaching a variety of meanings to these words, they reach various conclusions. For the sake of clarity we need to distinguish differences of vocabulary from differences of a more fundamental nature.

The purpose of this paper is to seek a further understanding of the regional concept. In a sense this is an essay in geographical semantics, for it discusses the meaning of the symbols geographers use to refer to the objects and concepts with which they deal. Logic, as defined by Aristotle, holds that the definition of a word should (1) place the thing referred to by the word in a class; and (2) tell how it is distinguished from other things in the same class. In accordance with Aristotelian logic a region may be defined as

Reprinted from *Annals* of the Association of American Geographers, 42, 3 (September 1952), 195–222.[1]

"an area on the earth's surface homogeneous with respect to announced criteria." Modern semantics, however, suggests that further clarity can be had only by defining a symbol, like the word *region,* in terms of operations; that is, in terms of what must be done to identify and describe it, or having described it, to make use of it or to show its significance.[2]

This approach is not new. Geographers have been formulating operational definitions for many years, long before Korzybski developed his ideas on semantics. Many of the forty-one volumes of the *Annals* that precede the current one contain essays on operational definitions.[3] The often repeated remark that "geography is what geographers do" points clearly toward an operation as opposed to a logical definition. It is important, however, that most of the geographers who have tried to define a region in terms of what they did about it were experienced field men.

The present writer is well aware that most of what he would like to say about the regional concept has already been said, not once, but many times. He is also aware that many writers from Bucher to Kimble [4] have attacked something which they described by the words *regional concept.* Yet because this concept, as the writer understands it, provides the frame of reference around which all geographic study is organized, he accepts the responsibility, inherent in the presidency of the association, of formulating his own understanding of the matter and of attempting a more exact definition of the referents for which his symbols stand.

The best place for geographers to communicate to each other the meaning of their word and map symbols is out-of-doors in the presence of the things they are discussing. Many professional differences would be resolved and many controversies avoided if we could always talk geography in the field where we could observe directly the things and relationships that we are all trying to understand more clearly. When geographers talk or write about geography indoors they are restricted wholly to symbols; when geography is taught in the classroom it must be presented entirely by devices which impress the eye or the ear and which stand for the objective reality that lies outside. There ought to be much more discussion of what these symbols mean, and the meanings attached to the symbols by one generation should be carefully scrutinized by the next

—not indoors, but always in the field where direct observation is possible.

At the moment, however, we cannot go into the field together. We are forced to attempt to communicate our ideas through the careful definition of our symbols both by the methods of logic and by the description of operations. The writer will attempt to state in logical terms what he means by the regional concept; then he will proceed to a discussion of what he would do to identify a region, and what he would do with it after it has been defined.

## The Logic of the Regional Concept

We can all agree that geography deals with the face of the earth. We assume this to refer to a zone which has not only length and breadth, but also height and depth. There need be no attempt to establish the limits of what we mean by the face of the earth, for each geographer would certainly extend his observations as far down into the earth or as far up into the atmosphere or beyond as the nature of his problems or the degree of his competence made proper.

The things geographers deal with on the face of the earth are not uniformly distributed over it. As Hartshorne points out, geographers have long selected for study those things which are not uniformly distributed and have rejected as lacking geographical interest those things which are uniformly distributed.[5] There are things which are present in some places, absent from others, or which vary in intensity or motion from place to place. They may be referred to as phenomena which result from the operation of processes. A process, as we understand the term, refers to a sequence of changes systematically related as in a chain of cause and effect. A phenomenon is an observable fact or event which represents the embodiment at any one time of the intellectually conceived sequence we describe as a process. A geographical phenomenon is any fact or event not uniformly distributed over the face of the earth.

The phenomena which are irregularly distributed over the earth are also irregularly associated with other phenomena in particular parts of the earth. Those phenomena which are systematically related because they are produced by one kind of process are associated on the face of the earth with other phenomena produced by quite different processes. This is what William Morris Davis means when he writes of "natural but unsystematic groupings." [6] The phenomena associated in a particular place are unsystematically related because they are produced by different processes.

But the geographer cannot wholly isolate one process from other processes operating in the same area. Each kind of process can be made the object of specialized study, and such specialists develop their own kinds of methods and their own instruments in order to measure and describe more precisely the sequence of changes in which they are interested. Some kinds of processes can be isolated in the laboratory, where controlled experiments are devised to eliminate all irregularities or modifications of the sequence introduced by outside influences. Other kinds of processes, notably those related to human behavior, cannot so easily be isolated in a laboratory; these are isolated symbolically by the use of such a phrase as "other things being equal." To a geographer, however, other things never are equal, for his particular mission is to study each process as it operates in particular places, and as it is actually modified in its action by the presence of other unsystematically related phenomena grouped naturally together on the face of the earth. This does not imply that an individual geographer may not be a topical specialist, that is one who achieves special competence in the study of phenomena systematically related to a process or to a closely related group of processes. But the topical specialist in geography can be distinguished from scholars in neighboring disciplines because of the focus of his interest on the differences developed from place to place on the earth by a process rather than on the process itself. This is, of course, a hair-breadth distinction and one of small importance to an individual who is pursuing the factors of a problem back and forth from study of process to study of the differentiated face of the earth. It should never be used to set up a barrier. But it should be kept as a signpost, for the methods of studying a process as it works in an isolated system and the methods of studying a process as a part of the total association in a particular place are quite different.

Geography is not logically defined by the phenomena with which it deals. It deals with any phenomenon, material or immaterial, natural or human, that is not uniformly distributed over the earth. The distinguishing characteristic of geography is its attention to particular places. A geographer seeks to understand the causes and consequences of likenesses and differences between places on the face of the earth. He recognizes that particular places are given distinctive character by the unsystematically associated phenomena that exist in them; he seeks to define likenesses and differences between places, and to see more clearly the meaning of the relative location of one thing with reference to another. Scholars who are identified professionally as geographers are not the only ones who make use of geographic concepts or apply geographic methods. Anthropologists, economists, sociologists, and many others also study processes where other things are not equal, where the process operates as a part of the total association of processes and phenomena in a particular place. Workers in the several social science disciplines do not hesitate to make historical studies or to apply historical methods; they should be encouraged to make similar use of geographic methods, and to do so with a similar degree of expertise. When a social scientist is faced with a problem involving area differentiation he should be expected to make use of accepted geographic techniques, and if he fails to do this, it becomes the responsibility of professional geographers to point out the deficiency.

Obviously no one person could embrace the whole field of geography, any more than one person could embrace the whole of the field of history. A geographer must become especially competent in some restricted part of the field: in the study of a selected group of related processes as they operate in a few specific parts of the world. As Ackerman recognizes, the geographer must specialize both topically and regionally, or topically within regions.[7] He cannot possibly develop a real competence in the study of all possible processes that are at work in even a restricted part of the earth; nor can he possibly understand all the modifications imposed, in all parts of the world, on those processes in the study of which he is competent. Topical and regional specialization are not separable. It does seem true, however, that knowledge of process is more important than knowledge of place for persons working at the extreme physical end of geography, especially in climatology, whereas knowledge of place is more important than knowledge of process at the opposite end where human behavior is involved.

## Likenesses and Differences on the Earth

It is important to understand that no two spots on the face of the earth are identical. Yet one does not have to receive professional training in geography to perceive that there are areas on the earth throughout which a more or less homogeneous association of characteristics exists. The sense of regional uniformities is what we call regionality; regionality is a part of the lay vocabulary and is reflected in many aspects of life, even where a sophisticated definition of boundaries cannot be achieved.[8]

There are, then, areas on the earth which are homogeneous with respect to this or that phenomenon or combination of phenomena. But even the smallest of these homogeneous areas could be subdivided. There is no such thing as a "unit area," an indivisible entity completely uniform in character. Nevertheless, if we are to bring the complexity of the face of the earth into manageable units for the purpose of examining the causes and consequences of area differentiations, it is obviously not possible to examine each minute point separately. The anthropologist defines general classes into which the diverse individuals of a society are grouped; the historian defines certain spans of years as periods each with certain distinctive characteristics; the geologist defines categories of rock in each of which a certain range of characteristics is permitted: this is the method of all science—to define categories in terms of selected criteria.

## The Region as a Geographic Generalization

The region is a geographic generalization. A generalization of the characteristics of area is accomplished by defining categories of area difference in terms of selected criteria. The criteria which are selected must be in terms of a stated objective or problem. For the purposes of a specific problem, it is possible to define and identify areas which are homogeneous in terms of relevant criteria, disregarding, as all generalizations do, conditions which are not homogeneous but which are considered to be irrelevant. A homogeneous area, so defined by announced criteria, must be evaluated, as all generalizations are evaluated, in terms of the purpose for which they are made. A system of regional differences is justified if it illuminates the factors or elements of a problem: it is not justified if it obscures the factors of a problem. Such a generalization of area is based on a selection of parts of a whole for the purpose of clarifying our understanding of a situation which otherwise would remain less clearly understood. Whether, or to what degree, it accomplishes this purpose must be the basis of judgment or critical appraisal. There can be no such thing as a correct system of regions, or a system of "true regions"; no one system of regions is right and all others, wrong: there are as many regional systems as there are problems worth studying.

When a geographer proposes a system of regional divisions to be used in the study of a problem, he is in fact proposing a hypothesis. The regional generalization in geography is the counterpart of a general description of a process, as it is conceived to operate in an isolated system, by workers who are specializing in the study of this process. A process is first given a generalized description as a working hypothesis, and thereafter this generalized description, being confronted with evidence, is either proved valuable in understanding the process or is discarded as inadequate for this purpose. In geographical study, the preliminary system of regional divisions is hypothetical, but after being confronted with evidence, after a successful demonstration of the validity of the system of area divisions, the regional system is advanced from the status of a hypothesis to that of a theory or concept. A system of demonstrated regional divisions provides the theoretical basis, or the conceptual framework, for geographic study.

THE FACE OF THE EARTH

The face of the earth is made up of many overlapping parts. Sten de Geer recognized this when he wrote of the superimposed spheres: the atmosphere, the lithosphere, the hydrosphere, the bio-sphere, and the anthroposphere.[9] The complexity of the problem becomes more apparent when we realize that these various spheres are each produced by a special group of processes, that each kind of process is measured by methods different from those used in the measurement of other processes, that each kind of a sequence of change is proceeding at a different rate from that of all the others, and that each group of processes results in a different kind of area differentiation.

### Static and Kinetic

Areas can be differentiated on the basis of two kinds of conditions. There are the static conditions, the patterns and associations of phenomena which at any one moment of time are fixed and immo-bile. Static conditions have most commonly been used in the defini-tion of regional systems. It is also possible to define area differences on the basis of the pattern of movement at any one period of time, and these might be designated as kinetic regions. Kinetic regions might be based on such phenomena as traffic flow, commuter movement, or tourist travel.

### Lines, Points, Areas, and Volumes

The phenomena which produce likenesses and differences between places on the face of the earth, whether static or kinetic, form four different kinds of patterns. There are patterns of lines, patterns of points, patterns of areas, and patterns of volumes. Because of the importance of the map as a device for the analysis and presentation of geographic phenomena, these different kinds of patterns are commonly shown as areas, with lines forming the underlying base data. Nevertheless on the face of the earth the patterns are distinc-tive, and there are many cases when it is important to distinguish between them. Lines are illustrated among the natural features by drainage lines; many of the phenomena produced by man himself are arranged in linear patterns such as roads, fences, and political boundaries or property lines. The movements characteristic of kinetic regions are usually linear. The nodal region, defined by Whittlesey as being organized around a focus,[10] usually, but not necessarily always, consists of a pattern of lines. We must realize that a line, such as a road, can be transformed into an elongated area by enlarging the scale; on the other hand some lines, such as boundaries, which have the property common to all geometric lines of possessing length but no breadth, remain lines regardless of change of scale. Many settlement forms are arranged in patterns of points, as are also mines, manufacturing establishments, and other human phenomena. Like lines, many kinds of points become discrete areas upon enlargement, but the points used in geodesy remain points at all scales.

Some phenomena form patterns of areas or patterns of volumes. For example, soil types cover areas, as do also many of the forms of land use and forest cover, or the national territories of politically organized units. Air masses and climates are actually volumes, although mapping techniques usually require that they appear as areas.

### Continuities and Discontinuities

Differentiation on the face of the earth, where it is based on patterns of areas or patterns of volumes, involves still another important distinction. There are differences of degree and differences of kind. Where the phenomenon being studied is arranged in a continuous cover over the earth, varying in intensity from place to place, we have what may be described as a continuity, in which differences from place to place are differences of degree, not kind. Examples of continuities are rainfall, air temperature, or degree of slope. Where we are dealing with continuities on a map some kind of iso-line is used, connecting points of equal value or ratio, such as isohyets, isotherms, or contours. These lines do not mark boundaries between different kinds of things, even though they are sometimes so interpreted: they do indicate the direction of greatest variation in intensity, which is always at right angles to the line.

On the other hand, where the phenomenon being studied is arranged in discrete units, each differing in kind from other units about it, we have what might be described as a discontinuity. The core of each discrete unit differs in terms of the criteria by which it is defined from other units; although the cores may be separated by transition zones, the lines which separate one area from another are boundaries and do not necessarily reveal the direction of greatest variation. Area units defined by announced criteria in a continuity do not have cores, for there is a continuous transition from one limit to the other, as from a twenty-foot contour line to a forty-foot contour line. Area units defined by announced criteria in a discontinuity must be interpreted quite differently. Examples of the latter are air masses, soil types, vegetation associations, and forms of land use.

For purposes of analysis with iso-lines, it is possible to transform discontinuities into continuities. For example, the land-use map can be constructed on the basis of such a ratio as that of crop area to total area and thus the actual pattern of discontinuities is changed into a map pattern of continuities. The uses of this technique have been presented by Wellington Jones.[11] Density of population, on the other hand, probably should be related to discrete work areas which form discontinuities, rather than to an arbitrary total territory. The dasymetric map which distinguishes discrete areas of this or that density may have advantages over an isopleth map of population, where the variations of density are treated as a continuity.[12]

## Processes

All these patterns of lines, points, areas, and volumes, whether static or kinetic, and whether arranged as a continuity or a variegated design of discontinuities, are a reflection of processes. And many fundamentally different kinds of processes are at work on the face of the earth. These processes differ in the nature of the sequences of change, the methods of measuring and describing them, and in the tempo of rate of change.

At least three major groups of processes can be distinguished. There are physical and chemical processes which proceed in accordance with the precisely formulated laws of physics and chemistry, and which are studied and described by the fields known collectively as geophysics. Geography is closely related to geophysics because certain kinds of area differences on the earth result directly from this group of processes. There are biological processes which are described by the somewhat less precise laws of the biological sciences. The biological processes, however, are modified in important ways by the physical and chemical processes associated with them unsystematically in particular places, and the study of such relationships is known collectively as ecology. Geography is closely related to ecology because of the many area differences on the earth which are the result of the interaction of the biological processes with those of physics and chemistry. And there are also the cultural processes, which may be subdivided into the traditional economic, social, and political; these processes are still somewhat inadequately described by the principles of human behavior, formulated by the several social sciences. Such cultural processes are modified by their interaction with the processes of biology, physics, and chemistry associated with them unsystematically in particular places. Geography is closely related to studies of human culture— to economics, sociology, political science, social psychology, and social anthropology, because human culture too results in the development of major area differences from place to place in the earth.

The methods of studying these different kinds of processes are notably contrasted. Among the natural sciences, whether they deal with physics, chemistry, or biology, the observer is outside the process he is observing. To be sure the act of observing may so change the thing observed that it is not always possible to look directly at the process itself. But the investigator is still an outsider. In the social sciences, on the other hand, the observer is a part of the process he is observing, and is himself a product of a culture. In the formulation of laws in natural science a rigorously controlled method must be used, but once formulated and tested, any college freshman can apply the laws and can be judged right or wrong on the application. In the formulation of general principles in the social sciences, on the other hand, intuitive judgment plays a major part. In order to evaluate the results of investigations in the social sciences it is essential to be informed concerning the personality of the investigator. The personality of Einstein must be known in order properly to evaluate his pronouncements in the fields of economics or politics, but it is of no consequence at all with respect to his theoretical concepts in physics. It is true that modern social science is formulating forecasts of human behavior based on actuarial methods, but even here the selection of categories of phenomena to count and the interpretation of the results obtained requires a large measure of intuitive judgment.

## Structure, Process, and Stage

Area differences on the earth are a reflection of the operation of all these different kinds of processes as they are associated in specific places. It is true that the processes of physics and chemistry, especially those giving rise to atmospheric differences from place to place, are only to a minor degree affected by the processes with which they are unsystematically associated. Therefore, it is possible for a geographer to specialize topically in some aspect of physical geography, especially in climatology, and find that specialized knowledge of places is of minor importance except, perhaps, for studies of microclimates. But biological processes, as described from laboratory experiment, are modified in important ways by the physical environment in particular places. Knowledge of place in plant or animal ecology is certainly equal in importance to knowledge of process. Cultural processes, it would seem, are more profoundly modified by the conditions of the total environment in which they operate than are other kinds of processes, so that general concepts seem to have less importance than the variations imposed by the unsystematically associated factors. In cultural geography, it appears, knowledge of place is even more important than knowledge of topic.

In any case, area differences can be described in terms of the simple formula proposed many years ago for the description of landforms by William Morris Davis.[13] Structure, process, and stage are the three elements to be considered. Structure, in the case of geomorphology, refers to the geologic structure and earth material on which the processes work. In the case of other processes, structure refers to the total environment, including relict features from the past, on which a process works. The sequence of changes characteristic of a process can be described in terms of stages. Insofar as the sequence of change for a given process is well-known, and insofar as it is not subject to a large degree of modification by the other things in the same area, there is a strong possibility of forecast.[14]

## Two Conclusions

This rapid survey of the kinds of processes and phenomena which exist together on the face of the earth, and, in association, give character to places, suggests two conclusions with respect to the actual operations involved in the definition of the regional concept. The first conclusion stems from our understanding of the contrasts in the kinds of processes at work on the earth. Considering the different methods necessary to measure and describe these processes, and the very different tempos with which they go on, ranging from the relatively slow changes of geologic time to the very rapid tempo of cultural change, we conclude that an attempt to define regions based on phenomena produced by a variety of different processes is dangerous and could lead to serious errors of interpretation. We may find ourselves trying to add things like cabbages and kings. We would be on safer ground if we should define several parallel systems of regions, each based on the operation of one process or a group of closely related processes. We should be very critical of regional systems based on the totality of the content of area, unless and until they have been validated by a comparison of component regional systems.

The second conclusion is that geography cannot be strictly contemporary. If we are to seek the meaning of area differences in terms of causes and consequences, this inevitably involves the time perspective, for processes must operate over time. Historical geography, which deals with the geography of the past and with the changes in geographical patterns through time, would seem to be inseparable from regional geography. We cannot even accept such a restriction as that which would select historical data solely because of their direct causal relation to contemporary conditions. The full perspective of the time sequence insofar as it is related to geographic patterns and processes is essential if we are to read the story of contemporary differences correctly. The regional concept, as it is presented in this essay, embraces not only the idea that patterns and associations of phenomena in particular places give distinctive character to those places, but also that the meaning of likenesses and differences between places is to be understood in terms of complex, continuous change, growing out of the past, and going on into the future.

There are certain dangers involved in the application of this second conclusion. It requires, for example, that we go beyond the things that can be seen by direct observation in the field. The sequences of change which we call processes are intellectual concepts, tested, to be sure, by the direct observation of what we think of as the resulting phenomena of area differentiation. But once a sequence of change has been clearly stated, it is easy to think we have found evidence to support it, and it requires considerable imagination and independence of mind to find conflicting evidence. We need only recall the years during which innumerable peneplains were identified and described—an example, it would seem, of the intellectually numbing effect of a clearly stated, but over-simple theory. Yet in spite of the ever-present and essentially human temptation to find what we are looking for, we cannot well go to the extreme of refusing to look for anything. The deeper understanding of the patterns and associations of phenomena which produce area differentiation involves a search for meanings in terms of causes and consequences; and this search inevitably takes us away from the strictly contemporary.

## The Degree of Generalization

When we attempt to go beyond the logical definition of the regional concept and to indicate what must be done, operationally, to identify meaningful regional patterns, we come at once to the problem of scale, or degree of generalization. Some degree of generalization is required if we are to define a homogeneous area no matter how small, for we must keep in mind that no two points on the face of the earth are identical. There is no such thing as a "unit area" which is truly and completely uniform in all its components. Sometimes we are inclined to think of such a feature as a single field of corn as constituting a unit which is not further divisible. The fact is, however, that in many corn fields less than half of the area of the field has corn on it. The field of corn is a generalization, defined by the presence of corn (which is relevant to a problem involving agricultural land use) and disregarding those parts of the area not used for corn (which are considered irrelevant to the problem). Even the smallest area, examined more closely would obviously be further divisible into more minute parts.

When we view the earth more broadly, the degree of generalization necessary for the identification of homogeneous areas becomes greater, and the scale of the maps we use becomes smaller. What factors determine the degree of generalization most appropriate for a particular kind of problem? What is it that determined the smallest degree of generalization that we consider worth making?

### A Consideration of Scales

Theoretically the range of choice between large and small scales is very wide. In practice, however, we find that most geographic studies in which area differences are identified and plotted on maps fall into two widely separated scale ranges. First, we find many studies in which the original plotting of data on maps is done at scales between $1/10,000$ and $1/62,500$. There are a few examples of area differences plotted beyond these limits: certain Soil Conservation Service maps of individual fields done at $1/8,000$, certain urban studies, and even one attempt to map the rooms inside a house; there are some examples of work done at smaller scales, such as the early land-classification studies of the western United States under the direction of John Wesley Powell, done at $1/125,000$. But the great bulk of what may be called detailed studies are within the scale range described. Such maps include the soil studies of the Soil Survey, the geological maps of the Geological Survey, the various land and land-use maps prepared for planning purposes, and the numerous studies of small areas by individual geographers which have been described as examples of microgeography. In contrast, we find many studies which show regional divisions of various kinds of maps of 1/3,000,000 or smaller. These are the maps of climatic regions, great soil groups, agricultural regions, regions of natural vegetation, and many others. These are examples of macro-geography.

It is interesting that there are few examples of studies involving the original plotting of regions on maps of intermediate scales. There is a wide gap between scales on which one inch represents a mile or less than a mile, and scales on which one inch represents fifty miles or more. Why have geographers not worked at these inter-mediate scales; and why have they not considered it worth while to make area divisions at scales on which one inch represents less than eight hundred feet?

When we examine the studies done in these two scale ranges we find that each is characterized by a fundamentally different method. The studies on large-scale maps with relatively small de-gree of generalization are based on direct observation of area dif-ferences in the field. The studies on the small-scale maps with a rel-atively large degree of generalization are perhaps generalized from large-scale studies, or are based on observations recorded in notes or on census data and other statistics. Since statistics are not usually available for small area units, studies based on such data must make use of scales appropriate to the detail of the informa-tion. But what about the very large-scale studies based on direct field observation: why, for example, is it customary to define a soil type or a phase of a soil type so that it embraces just a certain de-gree of variation and so that we must disregard the still more mi-nute variations that plague the beginner in his first attempts to iden-tify soils in the field?

Linton, in his paper on "The Delimitation of Morphological Regions," [15] makes the statement that "nature offers us two ines-capable morphological unities and only two; at one extreme the in-divisible flat or slope, at the other, the undivided continent." Why does he consider a flat or a slope to be indivisible? Surely, if we could stand out-of-doors together to look at these things directly, we could not find a natural slope so uniform that a close examination of it would not bring to light many minute differences; surely in nature we could not find a flat so utterly flat that minute variations of slope could not be identified and mapped, if it were worth our while. Is it really nature—that is, the phenomena existing outside the human mind—that tells us a flat or slope is not further to be divided?

This writer believes that the answer to the questions concerning the minimum-size units which we consider to be relevant for geographic study must be found in the fact of the physical dimensions of man himself, not in the objective reality of nature. When we identify and record area differences by direct observation, man himself is the instrument of observation. What he thinks of as the smallest indivisible unity is determined not by the facts of area differentiation, but by man's average height and the average distance between his eyes. The observer views the earth from the vantage point of a position between five and six feet above the ground and with a perspective given by the three inches or so between his eyes. What he sees is a result of his preconceptions and the physical dimensions of his body.

To appreciate this more clearly, let us imagine two different situations. First, if men were no taller than ants and were carrying on an ant-size investigation of the area differences on the face of the earth, can it be supposed that what we see as an indivisible flat would appear similarly indivisible to them? Or, if human observers were of such giant stature that the United States, in proportion, would fit within a forty-acre field, can it be supposed that this new kind of geographer would be concerned with what we call soil types? It seems more probable that he would identify as indivisible the area differences we describe as the major physiographic regions, and that in mapping out these areas he would be called a microgeographer. To be sure, the people who are making use of the earth as these contrasted sizes would mark out fields and properties in proportion to their stature: the ant-size men would make ant-size fields, and the giant would think of all North America as his private homestead.

These considerations are not to be dismissed as pure fantasy. If we are to gain a deeper understanding of the differences from place to place on the earth, we must be able to distinguish between nature-given objective realities and those phenomena we see because of our own physical and psychological constitution. Faced with such uncertainties we do not need to abandon the regional concept as a delusion; for it is easily demonstrable that area differences do matter, that meaningful categories of regions can be defined, and that being applied they bring results of value. Much depends, however, on so defining categories of area that they are clearly relevant to an objective, and this requires that the purpose of any geographic study must be clearly and simply stated at the very beginning.

## Objectives

A regional system, we must recall, is to be justified in terms of the purpose for which it is defined. It is justified if it illuminates the factors in a problem; it is not justified if it obscures the factors and relationships we are trying to analyze. Area divisions, when first presented, are of the nature of geographic hypotheses; when they are demonstrated as valid by some acceptable systematic method, they furnish the basic conceptual framework on which geographic scholarship rests.

There is a wide range of problems which are illuminated by studies of the causes and consequences of likenesses and differences from place to place on the earth. Certain kinds of studies are properly considered "basic research" in that they contribute to a more effective formulation of the concepts of our field, to the definition of more illuminating regional systems. This writer suggests that basic research in the field of geography may be aimed at one of the following four objectives: (1) to gain a further understanding of the kinds of area differences observable on the earth, and of the processes which have produced them, and of the foreseeable consequences of the continued operation of these processes; (2) to define more precisely the sequence of changes associated with a specific process as it operates in specific places; (3) to formulate or evaluate broadly applicable concepts or theories regarding the significance of area likenesses and differences on the earth; or (4) to test methods or techniques. Geographic studies may also be applied to economic, social, political, or military problems where the chief contribution to be anticipated from the application of geographic methods is an increased perspective regarding the parts played by the various factors in the problem. Geography, among the social sciences, analyzes the importance of the modifications of specific processes by the other processes with which they are unsystematically associated. Geographic studies contribute to a clarification of the issues involved in decisions of public or business policy by defining the predictable consequences of proposed courses of action when carried out in the total environments of particular places.

### Objectives Served by Small-Scale Studies

On map scales of 1/3,000,000 or smaller it is not possible to record direct observations of area differentiation. Where one inch represents fifty miles, area differences visible to a man are too small to appear on the map. The boundary lines must be highly generalized. To be sure it is possible to establish the position of regional boundaries at certain places and to interpolate between these places, as Shantz and Marbut did in their maps of vegetation and soils in Africa.[16] It is also possible to prepare a generalized map on the basis of detailed studies, as when land use maps are transformed into "Types of Farming Maps," or when maps of soil types are combined into "Soil Associations."

Most regional systems defined for use on small-scale maps are based on statistical data. In some cases the boundaries do not follow specific values, as in many of the agricultural regions which appeared in *Economic Geography*.[17] In many cases, however, regional systems have been defined in quantitative terms; the climatic regions of Köppen or Thornthwaite, or the agricultural regions of Hartshorne and Dicken, for example.

The various kinds of maps prepared at scales of 1/3,000,000 or less do not usually permit close analysis of the area relations of the patterns they reveal. With area divisions based on such highly generalized criteria, in the definition of which so many underlying differences must be neglected in order to identify a kind of homogeneity, comparison of one regional system with another for the purpose of establishing area relations or for the purpose of demonstrating causes and consequences is most difficult. Apparent area relations which seem to exist at these high degrees of generalizations have a habit of disappearing when they are sought on larger-scale maps. Even the generally discredited concept of environmental determinism finds its last refuge in macrogeographic studies.[18] The validity of a concept which can be seen only when viewed very broadly, and which cannot be demonstrated upon close scrutiny would seem to be open to legitimate doubt.

The chief utility of regional systems drawn with a high degree of generalization on small-scale maps would seem to be for teaching purposes. By teaching, this writer refers not only to classroom instruction, but also to the broader aspects of teaching which involve presenting geographic concepts to the general public, to statesmen, or military leaders. For this purpose the desirable qualities to be sought in a system of area differentiation are simplicity and significance to a topic. Over-complicated regional patterns defeat their objective; where the two principles are in conflict, simplicity outweighs significance. But to attempt to measure carefully the relation of one such system of regions to another is obviously futile; the attempt to demonstrate the meaning of such small-scale regions by direct observation in the field leads only to frustration and confusion.

### Objectives Served by Large-Scale Studies

One reason for the rapid development of microgeography during the past thirty years has been the dissatisfaction felt among many geographers with the vague, undemonstrable results of the more highly generalized macrogeography. Detailed studies were brought to sufficiently sharp focus on small areas so that the knowledge that was brought together was of direct use in planning for the better use of land by individual farmers. The Michigan Land Economic Survey, dealing with the cut-over and abandoned lands of the northern part of the state, mapped differences of land quality as small as five acres in extent. More recently the survey of Puerto Rico, carried out under the direction of Clarence F. Jones, found that in such a mountainous terrain where field units were so small, it was necessary to map area differences as small as an acre. Studies of cities require mapping the use of each building, occupying a fraction of an acre.

We may suggest the tentative conclusion that studies which involve the use of land or land resources by individual persons require large-scale treatment with a relatively small degree of generalization. This is true whether the objective is to contribute to basic research or to make application of the results to practical problems. The reason is, again, related to the stature of man. The size of the fields he lays out or of the buildings he constructs is of an order which cannot be reproduced on small-scale maps: the impress on the physical earth produced by the process of human settlement is visible only on large-scale maps. On maps of too large a scale, the human impress goes out of focus, as when we examine the details of a plot of ground four feet square; on maps of too small a scale the specific impress of human occupance is blurred by generalization. Where analysis of area relations is wanted, where it is desired to advise the individual farmer about his use of land, where objective causal connections between phenomena are to be demonstrated, the degree of generalization must be just enough to show the specific impress of man himself—not too large a scale and not too small.

But there are purposes, other than pedagogical ones, which suggest the use of scales smaller than those demanded for the specific analysis of man-land relations. Valuable as the detailed studies have proved to be, the criticism can still be made of them that they do not yield broad concepts of wide application, that their results apply to unique small areas of little general importance. Whether this criticism is entirely justified need not be argued here. Among the geographers are many who feel that the only certain results are to be obtained by mapping and analyzing detail, and there are others who feel the need for broader generalization. Both are in part right.

The fact is that detailed, large-scale studies cannot be completed fast enough to meet the need for them. Geographic analyses of many kinds of problems are urgently needed: there are problems involving business developments; there are problems concerning the results of public-works programs; there are problems of technical assistance; and there are military problems involving the study of extreme and unfamiliar environments. To undertake detailed, large-scale studies of all these problems, as well as of the problems in basic research which interest the geographic profession would be impossible. There simply are not enough trained field geographers to do this work fast enough, even with modern aids such as air photography. The survey of Puerto Rico, covering an area of 3,421 square miles, required the services of eighteen field men under the guidance of an experienced research director over a period of two and a half years. If all the geographical manpower of the Western Hemisphere were made available, it would scarcely be possible to complete more than four or five such surveys in the next five years. Long before the need for the geographical analysis could be satisfied, the problem would have been met with an action program. So it is that action programs are undertaken blindly, lacking the basic knowledge of the relevant phenomena or understanding of the processes combined in the area.

### Objectives Served by Studies at Intermediate Scales

A possible answer to this dilemma is offered by exploration of the intermediate scales. There is a wide range between scales on which one inch represents one mile, and those on which one inch represents fifty miles. What could be done, we may ask, at a scale of 1/1,000,000, where one inch represents sixteen miles. This writer has made some investigation of the possibilities of working at this scale in studies of northeast Brazil.[19] It seems possible that, with some modification of the technique and with the aid of air photography, the mapping of area differences by direct observation at this scale might be possible. The use of intermediate scales, where the degree of generalization is still not far removed from that required for recording the specific impress of human occupance, might make possible the more rapid coverage of larger areas without serious loss of meaning. Before we can discuss the operations involved in working at such scales, however, we must consider some of the problems and methods of recording field observations on maps.

## Mapping at Different Scales

We should recall that the patterns of arrangement developed on the face of the earth and which can be observed at any degree of generalization are made up of lines, points, areas, and volumes. For purposes of this essay we may omit discussion of the problem of mapping volumes, and consider volumes and areas together. In field mapping, the use of lines and points on the one hand, and areas on the other, is important to discuss.

Before any area on the earth can be analyzed and its area relations to other phenomena studied, it is necessary to plot it on a base map. The base data in relation to which the area is plotted are lines and points. Long ago geographers devised a system of lines of latitude and longitude to form a grid over the surface of the earth. Areas were plotted on this grid. Latitude and longitude are significant lines in terms of solar relations, and phenomena plotted on them can be located with reference to the sun and to each other.

But there are many other kinds of relationships that, in certain problems, may be more important than relationships to the sun. It might be desirable, for example, to show such highly generalized features as agricultural regions or density of population with reference to the pattern of climates. For this purpose, the lines of such a quantitative system as that of Köppen might be considered as similar to latitude and longitude lines. Position could be plotted over the framework of climatic lines, and location with reference to the climatic pattern could be read directly from the map—without arguing for or against causal relationship. On large-scale maps the lines in relation to which areas are plotted are usually the roads, railroads, property lines, political boundaries, or other similar features.

In any case, the base map is made up of items selected from the available patterns of lines and points. We suggest that it is desirable to consider carefully the selection of relevant base data rather than uncritically to make use of traditional latitude and longitude. Having selected relevant base data, the area differences are then plotted by direct field observation.

The scale of the field map bears a direct relationship to the size of the smallest area difference that can be recorded. Items too small to show on the map can, of course, be shown by out-of-scale symbols, but those features which are shown to scale must occupy a certain minimum extent of territory to be visible on the map. Field men are in general agreement that where a fractional code symbol is used to express a group of associated phenomena a space on the map something like a quarter of an inch on a side is required.[20] If the categories of area require only a single letter or digit to represent them, the space on the map may be only an eighth of an inch on a side. If, then, the nature of a problem requires the mapping of area differences as small as a single acre, this would require the use of maps with a scale of $1/10,000$ for fractional codes, or $1/20,000$ for single digits. If the smallest area unit necessary to map occupies forty acres, the map scales would then have to be $1/62,500$ or $1/125,000$ respectively. On maps of $1/1,000,000$, the smallest area unit that can be recorded in scale, even with a single-digit symbol, must cover at least four square miles on the ground.

These estimates of map space are, of course, somewhat flexible. Nevertheless there is a direct relationship between the areas occupied by the categories of regional divisions and the scale of the maps on which they can be plotted. The estimates refer to the original plotting of data on field maps, not to the scale of the published maps on which they are presented. The latter, with use of color or solid black, can be considerably reduced.

### Topographic, Chorographic, Global

So important is the consideration of the degree of generalization and the scale of field maps in our operational definition of the regional concept that this writer feels the urgent need for finding acceptable word-symbols to refer to them. The tendency to overlook the significance of the degree of generalization in thinking about regions may be in part due to the loss, through misuse, of the words originally devised for this purpose. In a previous paper this writer suggested attempting to recapture the original meanings of the words *topographic, chorographic,* and *geographic.*[21] *Geographic,* in this sequence, refers to studies of the world as a whole or its larger parts; *chorographic* refers to studies of intermediate areas; and *topographic* refers to studies of small areas. Since the word *geographic* stands for studies of area differentiation at any scale, its use to refer to only the more general kinds of studies would not be accepted; for this reason we suggest the use of *global studies* to refer to this category.

The chief difficulty in this proposal has to do with the use of the word *topography.* At first chiefly by geologists and engineers, but now by many other people including many geographers, the word has been misused until it has lost its original meaning and now refers to surface features or landforms. Yet the term "topographic map" refers to a map of relatively large scale, and the topographic symbols include not only those which stand for relief features, but also those which show hydrography, culture, and in some cases the cover of vegetation and land use. These are all topographic features, when presented on large-scale maps. There is no compelling need for the word *topography* in the sense of landforms, for the words *landforms, surface configuration,* or *relief* are available and clear. But for the smallest degree of generalization there is no word: we must attempt to regain the original meaning of *topography* or invent a new word. This writer, therefore, uses the word *topography* only to refer to degree of generalization.

Whatever terms the profession eventually agrees to use for these scale concepts, it is possible to suggest some sharpening of the definitions. A *topographic study,* as we propose to use the words, is one which makes use in the field of maps of sufficiently large scale to permit the plotting of the smallest relevant area units: such units as soil types; individual fields on a farm; individual clearings in a forest; or in urban studies, the components of the commercial core. When the scale of the maps on which data are originally plotted is too small to permit mapping these details, when the specific detail must be generalized into broader categories which do not show the specific impress of unit processes, we propose to use the word *chorographic.* Chorographic studies, however, are not so highly generalized that effective analysis of the area relations between different systems of regions cannot be carried out. For the highly generalized studies on maps of relatively small scale, where the analysis of area relations cannot be done effectively, we proposed the word *global*.

## Chorographic Methods

The methods of topographic study are well-known and need not be discussed here. Some preliminary experience in chorographic studies suggests certain observations concerning the methods to be used at the intermediate scales. In detailed mapping the observer can frequently see the whole of the area units he is plotting, and, from one spot, he can record the boundaries between categories in specific detail. But at the chorographic scale this is never possible. Even from an airplane it is not possible to see the whole of an area unit in sufficient detail to permit the plotting of all the specific details of its boundaries. We must remember that the smallest area unit that can be shown with its written symbol at 1/1,000,000 is four square miles. At such a scale the observer must synthesize his observations as he moves from place to place, combining the area units he observes directly into more general aggregations that are too big to be seen directly. He plots the outline of these areas in part from memory, and the boundaries he draws are necessarily smoother than those of any of the component details. By making use of the airplane, the air photograph, and other devices, as well as by training his memory, chorographic mapping can be done in the field when large areas, not previously covered by detailed studies, require investigation.

The problem is how to generalize sufficiently to permit more rapid coverage but at the same time not to blur the specific details of man-land relations which are directly tied to specific processes. Man's occupance of the land produces patterns which must be seen in topographic detail. When our purpose is to seek the meaning of area differences in terms of causes and consequences we make use of topographic-scale studies. When our purpose is to present the general results of such studies as in a classroom, we make use of global scales where simplicity is the quality most desired. The rise of the chorographic scale is justified by the attempt to cover larger areas more quickly, but without losing the specific meanings derived from study of details. How is this to be done?

The first suggestion is that the categories of area for use at the chorographic scale be defined as associations of component details. Less satisfactory results are obtained from using the principle of the predominant type, that is, of identifying the feature which occupies the largest area and outlining the whole area in which this type is predominant. The older state soil maps were made in this way, and are very difficult to use in the field for this reason.[22] The newer soil maps where large areas are covered on smaller scales are based on associations of soil types, that is of categories defined in terms of component types which are commonly and repeatedly found grouped together in characteristic patterns of arrangement.[23]

As an example, consider the problem of mapping at the chorographic scale in the Corn Belt. At the topographic scale we could distinguish the use made of each field, and we could distinguish the woodlots from cleared land. But at such a scale as 1 / 1,000,000, where the smallest area division must occupy at least four square miles to be plotted with its written symbol on the map, it is not possible to distinguish the use of individual fields or even whole farms. The screen through which we view the area differences on the earth is so coarse that we cannot distinguish the use of the land by the individual farmers.[24] But for the purposes we have in mind —rapid coverage—we can define an association of uses that we find to be recurrent. The association might include all the land in the prevailing system of rotation and the commonly associated woodlots. This is essentially the makeup of the categories developed by the Department of Agriculture for its "Types of Farming" map. The resulting map is so generalized that one cannot read from it the meaning of area differences as they affect the individual farmer, yet one is not so far from the specific details of occupance as when the whole Corn Belt (defined as producing three thousand bushels of corn per square mile) is described as a homogeneous area on a global scale.

Where associations of component details are defined and mapped, it seems essential to develop some acceptable method of tieing them back to the details of which they are composed. This requires a sampling technique. A considerable amount of experiment is needed to define the size of samples to be studied in topographic detail for the purpose of showing the components of an association. Presumably the larger the number of components included in an association the larger the area that must be covered to provide a true sample, but the arrangement of the components and the average size of the areas they cover must also be considered.[25] Then there is the question of whether samples should be selected by the application of some geometric pattern, or whether the trained judgment of the experienced field man still brings better results.

In any case, the development of chorographic-scale mapping techniques may offer at least a partial answer to the problem of increasing the significance of geographic research. Perhaps this offers the best opportunity to bridge the gap between microgeography and macrogeography, and to demonstrate more fully the essential unity of the whole field of geography.

## THE ANALYSIS OF AREA RELATIONS

It is possible, then, to visualize the regional concept in terms of action. Area differences can be defined in terms relevant to a problem, and can be plotted on field maps with a degree of precision fully as great as that achieved by other non-laboratory sciences. By the development of a sampling technique, a greater degree of generalization can be used to permit wider coverage while at the same time specific details applicable to individual people in their use of earth resources are not lost. Geography seeks geometric precision; that is, it is concerned more than bordering fields of study with the exact measurement of areas and patterns, and from these more exact studies of area differences, it brings to light additional understanding of the role of relative location. Geography cannot find all the answers to economic, social, political, or military problems of a practical nature, but it can contribute to an understanding of the problems by applying its own individual kind of analysis.

Geographers are concerned with a wide range of professional questions. How to define categories of area difference more strictly relevant to objectives; how to observe and map the significant features of a region more exactly yet with fewer man-hours of work; how to present the results of a geographic study, especially so that non-geographers can appreciate the kind of contribution to be expected from such study. One of the facets of professional work has to do with the study of relationships between the phenomena that are mapped.

It is necessary to distinguish between two kinds of relationships in which geographers are interested. There are area relations and there are causal relations. Area relations have to do with the relative positions of things, the spread and patterns of phenomena; area relations are found by observing the space dimension at any specific time. Causal relations, on the other hand, have to do with the changes systematically related to a process; they have to do with origins and developments, and with extensions into the future; causal relations are only to be observed through study of the time dimension. Let us consider briefly some of the ways in which geographers work with the regional concept for the purpose of bringing out more clearly the area relations of phenomena, and for discerning their significance. Of course, the fundamental tool for such research is the map.

### The Map as an Analytic Device

The map serves many functions. In the field it provides the most precise way of recording observations. It reduces the patterns of area differences on the earth to a size permitting close analysis—patterns which otherwise would disappear from view in the merging lines of perspective on the curved surface of the globe. The map is an eloquent form of presentation for those trained to read its symbols—a form much more precise than the word-symbols more commonly used. And between the work in the field and the final presentation of results, the map is used in the office as an analytic device.

Cartographic analysis brings to light different kinds and degrees of area relationship between phenomena. Of course everything on the face of the earth has some relation to everything else, but many relationships are discordant, and many, also, are accordant. Accordant relations are either coincident or correspondent. A coincidence occurs when two phenomena occupy exactly the same area on the earth; in such a case the boundaries outlining the areas occupied by the two phenomena are said to coincide. A correspondence occurs when there is a discernible similarity between the areas of occurrence of two phenomena. Perhaps the boundaries of the two areas are very close together, perhaps coinciding in most places, but departing from each other in a few localities; or perhaps they coincide nowhere, but are so close together that the similarity of the two outlines is apparent. Where two phenomena occupy approximately the same areas this may be called an *in situ* correspondence, but where they occupy wholly different areas, although with similar outlines, this may be called an *ex situ* correspondence. Discordant relationships exist when the patterns of two phenomena are wholly incongruous. These various kinds of area relations are shown by the accompanying diagrams (Figure 1).

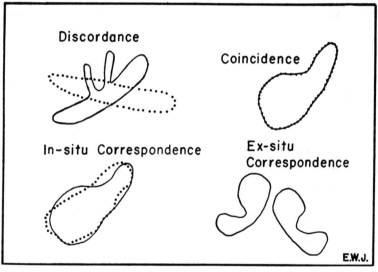

Fig 1. Kinds of area relations.

The identification of an accordant relationship is no proof of a causal relationship, although it may offer a strong indication of the existence of a causal relationship. Coincidence of two phenomena in area does not demonstrate that one is the cause of the other. A third cause may operate to produce the two phenomena mapped, or a coincidence of pattern may be only a temporary condition existing at a moment of time and of little fundamental significance. Although accordant area relationship suggests strongly the existence of some causal connection, perhaps through the operation of a process still not mapped, the demonstration of causal significance must rest on the identification of the responsible process as it operates through time.

This writer cannot accept without reservation the formula suggested by Hettner [26] and reported by Hartshorne,[27] to the effect that phenomena which lack causal connection are to be rejected as data for geographical study. It would seem entirely suitable to map phenomena for the purpose of discovering causal connections, even where the patterns seem at first sight to be entirely incongruous. Our failure to see the congruity of the patterns may be a reflection of the state of our knowledge. Furthermore, if the results of a study of this sort are purely negative—that is, the relationships are found to have no causal connection, and any accordance of pattern is purely a matter of chance—even under these circumstances the work is justified and the conclusions may be of importance.

The dangers of arriving at conclusions regarding causal relationships without study of process in time perspective are amply demonstrated by the history of our professional writings. The concept of environmental determinism [28] was given apparent support by much field evidence during the period when this principle dominated geographical thinking. The evidence, however, was faulty because of the technique used. Again and again in the literature of that period we find coincident area relations between natural and cultural phenomena asserted but not demonstrated. And again and again when we actually measure these area relations we find examples of correspondence but not coincidence. If the places where the two phenomena fail to coincide are examined in detail, we find processes at work which invalidate the theory of determinism as applied to the occupance of land.

### An Example

To illustrate this point more clearly, this writer will describe an imaginary area, greatly simplified by the omission of many elements of the real situation. Let us suppose our purpose is to understand the meaning (causes, in this instance) of the area relationships between the physical quality of the land and a pattern of rural settlement. We shall assume that an individual community of farmers has occupied an intermont basin. The land used for hay fields and for the pasture of cattle was cleared from an initial cover of forest which once extended over the mountain slopes and basin floor alike. The basin itself is made up of gentle slopes on deep volcanic ash of essentially uniform character. It is bordered on all sides by relatively steep rocky slopes with thin soil. This situation is pictured in Figure 2, and mapped in Figure 3.[29]

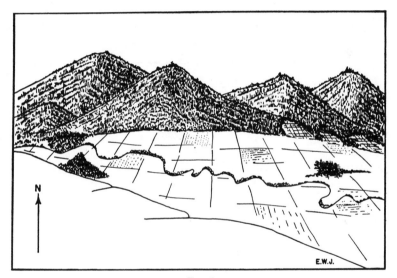

Fig. 2.

Geographers have often been confronted with this kind of situation and there are many reports describing fundamentally similar relationships. There are two ways of proceeding, so far as the mapping and the cartographic analysis are concerned. One is to observe the essentially coincident relations between basin and land cleared for farming, and to record the observation in descriptive notes and on a field map. Two categories of area are defined: steep, rocky slopes still covered with forest; basin floor cleared and used for hay

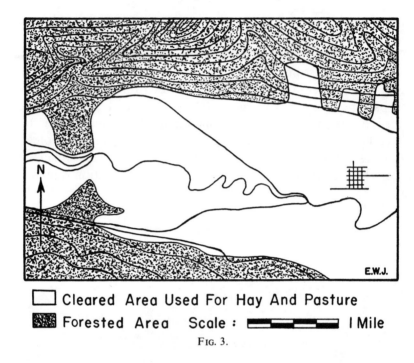

☐ Cleared Area Used For Hay And Pasture
▓ Forested Area    Scale :  ▬▬▬▬  I Mile

F IG. 3.

and pasture. One might be led to assert that the settlers were engaged in adjusting themselves to the determining quality of the
land, or, in the terminology of determinism, that here was a response to environmental influence.

But the close observer, trained to be critical of his preconceptions, would note that at the eastern side of the basin there was a
small but not inconsiderable area where the steeper mountain
slopes had been cleared and were used for hay and pasture, and
that in the western part of the basin floor there were patches of uncleared forest. If the two categories of area are to be distinguished
by a single line, where is that line to be drawn? [30] Is the bit of
cleared mountain slope to be included with the mountain or with
the cleared land? Are the patches of forest on the basin floor to be
included with the forest on the slopes, or the basin which is mostly
cleared? Of course, the problem makes no sense and therefore cannot be answered. It arises from the attempt to define categories of
area which include the association of too many unsystematically related phenomena; whatever decision is made, the result is to ob-

scure the meaning of the area relationships, the factors in the problem.

The other methods of proceeding does perhaps require more careful observation of details in the field, and certainly involves more precise mapping. The component parts of the area are separated, and each is mapped as an individual item. Whether this mapping is done on separate bases or with a fractional code symbol on one base is a matter of convenience. The important thing is that the associated phenomena be examined as separate, overlapping patterns. Examination of the resulting maps in the office reveals an *in situ* correspondence between basin and cleared farm land. The search for causal connections, however, leads one to concentrate attention not on the places where the two phenomena are coincident, but rather on those places where they do not coincide.

As soon as the analysis of area relations reveals the existence of a problem, attention is focused on the process of clearing and settlement, viewed as a sequence of changes extending from the past, through the merely contemporary, on into the future. Suppose that we find that the movement of the settlers into the basin was from the east, and that a series of maps showing the spread of the cleared land at various stages could be prepared. We might then find that the relict patches of forest on the western part of the basin floor had not yet been cleared because the movement of new clearing had only just reached them; we might also find that when the basin floor which was more accessible and desirable had been occupied, settlement was in fact spreading onto the bordering mountain slopes. We would recognize, then, that the contemporary picture of a near coincidence between cleared land and basin was only a momentary stage in a process, which in the course of time would result in the complete disappearance of the coincident relationships. We would, then, be led to examine the slopes for evidence of erosion, and we would seek in the culture of the inhabitants for previous experience with these different qualities of land.

### The Significance of the Land

A major concept of modern geography holds that the significance to man of the physical quality of the land is not something which remains the same for all men at all times; rather it is determined by the attitudes, objectives, and technical abilities of the settlers, and with each change in these elements of the culture, the physical land, or resource base, must be reevaluated. Modern geography does not deny the importance of the physical quality of the land: it differs from the deterministic concept by asserting that only when the land itself changes does it exert a positive force on what people do with it; as long as the land remains relatively unchanging, man himself determines how the land affects his use of it. This concept is supported by field evidence in which process is investigated through time, and it can be validated not with respect to broad, highly generalized areas, but for the most intimate details that are revealed by topographic study.[31]

## The Degree of Generalization in Area Relations

One further warning regarding the methods of examining area relationships needs to be offered. When two phenomena are to be analyzed cartographically for the purpose of discovering accordant or discordant relations, it is essential that they be mapped originally on the same scale with similar degrees of generalization. To seek for area relationships, let us say, between the highly generalized lines of the Köppen climatic system, drawn on a global scale, with the much more detailed boundaries of "Types of Farming Areas" [32] drawn on a chorographic scale would be methodologically unsound. Nor should the boundaries of a system of climates plotted on a global scale be compared with patterns of vegetation plotted in chorographic or topographic detail. When comparisons of this sort are undertaken, the phenomena being analyzed should each be developed as a system of regions separately, but with the same degree of generalization.

### CONCLUSIONS

The regional concept involves the idea that there are associations of phenomena to be observed on the earth; that these associations, and the patterns of their individual elements, are significant of the interacting processes at work on the earth; and that these associations give character to particular places. For some purposes the synthetic approach to the definition of area associations may be justified: especially for pedagogical purposes the simplicity of a synthetic region, like the basin floor cleared for farming, and the steep, rocky, uncleared slopes, may offer a compelling reason supporting this kind of approach. Some geographers, however, will prefer to develop their more highly generalized regional systems on the basis of the cartographic analysis of component parts, building up by analysis rather than asserting by an initial synthesis.

By these various methods, however, geographers are seeking accordant relationships, and having discovered them to demonstrate the causal connections through the study of the processes involved. Simply to define and map a system of regions without investigation of underlying processes operating through time, and without showing clearly the relevance of the regional system to the underlying purpose, comes perilously close to what Kimble calls "doodling." The regional concept, as presented here, involves the time perspective as an integral part.

Geographcial study based on the regional concept recognizes the need for focusing attention on place rather than on isolated process. It accepts from other fields the illumination cast by knowledge of process as it operates in an isolated system, and clearly recognizes the extraordinarily fruitful methodology of process study. But the geographical field also can make distinct contributions. It contributes to an understanding of the meaning of area differentiation, and of the operation of processes in particular places. It focuses attention on the modifications in the operation of processes by the other things that are not equal, by noting the actual operation of processes in particular places modified by the presence of the other things unsystematically associated there.

Individual scholars do not attempt to cover this whole broad, complex field. Rather they specialize in small parts of it, topically in certain groups of related processes, and regionally in certain limited areas where conditions are similar. Competence in geography is not easily gained, and even for a limited sector requires a lifetime of devotion. Geographers, whatever their specialties, are united by the concept which underlies all their investigations, and by the cartographic field methods and methods of analysis which lead to a deeper understanding of the meaning of area difference. The concept to which we have attempted to give both a logical and an operational definition is the concept of area differentiation based on patterns and associations of phenomena and meaningful in terms of continuing processes of change. This, the common denominator of geographical study, is what we know as the regional concept.

## NOTES

1. Presidential address delivered at the forty-eighth annual meeting of the Association of American Geographers, Washington, D.C., August 7, 1952. I am indebted for many suggestions and criticisms to Derwent Whittlesey, Lester E. Klimm, Clarence F. Jones, and Clyde Kohn, and to my colleagues at Syracuse University.

2. Anatol Rapoport, "What Is Semantics?" *American Scientist,* 40 (1952), 123–35.

3. See especially the many writings of William Morris Davis in which he discussed the methods of doing and writing geography. For example: "An Inductive Study of the Content of Geography" (presidential address at the second meeting of the AAG, 1905), published in the Bulletin of the *American Geographical Society,* 38 (1906), 67–84, "The Colorado Front Range, A Study in Physiographic Presentation," *Annals* of the Association of American Geographers, 1 (1911), 21–83; and "The Principles of Geographic Description," *Annals* of the Association of American Geographers, 5 (1915), 61–105.

4. August L. Bucher, *Von den Hindernissen welche der Einführung eines besseren Ganges beym Vortrage der Erdkunde auf Schulen im Wege Stehen* (Cöslin, 1827); George H. T. Kimble, "The Inadequacy of the Regional Concept," in L. Dudley Stamp and S. W. Wooldridge, *London Essays in Geography* (Cambridge, Mass.: 1951), pp. 151–74.

5. Richard Hartshorne, "The Nature of Geography, A Critical Survey of Current Thought in the Light of the Past," *Annals* of the Association of American Geographers, 29 (1939); 173–658; ref. Chap. 8.

6. William Morris Davis, "The Principles of Geographic Description," p. 62.

7. Edward A. Ackerman, "Geographic Training, Wartime Research, and Immediate Professional Objectives," *Annals* of the Association of American Geographers, 35 (1945), 121–43.

8. Merrill Jensen, ed., *Regionalism in America,* (Madison, Wisc., 1951).

9. Sten de Geer, "On the Definition, Method, and Classification of Geography," *Geografiska Annaler* (1923), 1–37.

10. See the chapter on "Regional Geography" prepared by a committee of which Derwent Whittlesey was chairman, in Preston E. James and Clarence F. Jones, eds., *American Geography, Inventory and Prospect* (Syracuse, N.Y.: Syracuse University Press, 1954).

11. Wellington D. Jones, "Ratios and Isopleth Maps in Regional Investigation of Agricultural Land Occupance," *Annals* of the Association of American Geographers, 20 (1930), 177–95.

12. John K. Wright, "A Method of Mapping Densities of Population, with Cape Cod as an Example," *Geographical Review*, 26 (1936), 103–10; see also *idem*, "Some Measures of Distributions," *Annals* of the Association of American Geographers, 27 (1937), 177–211.

13. William Morris Davis, "The Geographical Cycle," *Geographical Journal*, 14 (1899), 481–504.

14. Among the many discussions regarding the identification and description of regions see especially: Vernor C. Finch, *Montfort: A Study in Landscape Types in Southwestern Wisconsin*, Bulletin No. 9 (Chicago: Geographical Society of Chicago, 1933); Preston E. James, Wellington D. Jones and Vernor C. Finch, "Conventionalizing Geographic Investigation and Presentation," *Annals* of the Association of American Geographers, 24 (1934), 77–122; Ralph H. Brown and others, "A Conference on Regions," *Annals* of the Association of American Geographers, 25 (1935), 121–74; Vernor C. Finch, "Geographical Science and Social Philosophy," *Annals* of the Association of American Geographers, 29 (1939), 1–28.

15. D. L. Linton, "The Delimitation of Morphological Regions," in L. Dudley Stamp and S. W. Wooldridge, eds., *London Essays in Geography* (Cambridge, Mass., 1951), pp. 199–217; ref. p. 215.

16. H. L. Shantz and C. F. Marbut, *The Vegetation and Soils of Africa*, Research Series No. 13 (New York: American Geographical Society, 1923).

17. Series of papers on agricultural regions of the continents, indexed in the *Ekblaw Memorial Index* to volumes 1–25, Worcester, 1950.

18. Griffith Taylor, ed., *Geography in the Twentieth Century* (New York and London, 1951), ref. Chap. 1.

19. Preston E. James, "Observations on the Physical Geography of Northeast Brazil," *Annals* of the Association of American Geographers, 42 (1952), 153–76.

20. Vernor C. Finch, *Montfort*.

21. Preston E. James, "The Terminology of Regional Description," *Annals* of the Association of American Geographers, 24 (1934), 78–92.

22. W. J. Latimer and others, *Soil Survey (Reconnaissance) of Vermont*, Bureau of Chemistry and Soils, No. 43 (Washington, D.C.: U.S. Dept. of Agriculture, 1930).

23. Yearbook 1938 *Soils and Men*, (Washington, D.C.: U.S. Department of Agriculture, 1938), ref. pp. 979–89, and attached map; Charles E. Kellogg and others, "Soil Classification," *Soil Science*, 67 (1949), 77–191.

24. G. D. Hudson, "The Unit Area Method of Land Classification," *Annals* of the Association of American Geographers, 26 (1936), 99–112.

25. Preston E. James, "The Blackstone Valley, A Study in Chorography in Southern New England," *Annals* of the Association of American Geographers, 19 (1929), 67–109; M. J. Proudfoot, "Sampling with Transverse Traverse Lines," *Journal of the American Statistical Association*, 37 (1942), 265–70.

26. Alfred Hettner, *Die Geographie, ihre Geschichte, ihr Wesen, und ihre Methoden* (Breslau, 1927), ref. pp. 110–32.

27. Richard Hartshorne, "The Nature of Geography," p. 240.

28. Griffith Taylor, *Geography in the Twentieth Century*, p. 16.

29. See, for example, Roderick Peattie, "The Conflent: A Study in Mountain Geography," *Geographical Review,* 20 (1930), 245–57; Preston E. James, "Regional Planning in the Jackson Hole Country," *Geographical Review,* 26 (1936), 439–53.

30. This same problem with somewhat different elements is exhaustively analyzed in Siegfried Passarge, "Wesen, Aufgaben, und Grenzen der Landschaftskunde," in *Hermann Wagner's Gedächtnisschrift, Petermanns Mitteilungen,* Ergänzungsheft 209 (1930), pp. 29–44.

31. Preston E. James, *A Geography of Man* (Boston: Ginn and Co., 1951), pp. 40–45, 234–54.

32. Map by the U.S. Department of Agriculture.

# PART II

# On Research and Writing

# COMMENTARY

James's formulations of the special character of geography were firmly grounded in experience, in having worked as a geographer at every scale from the topographic to the global. Certainly much of the clarity of his thinking about those "associations of phenomena that give character to particular places" is derived from detailed field study of a number of particular places. Some thirty different products of such research appear in his bibliography, representing field seasons in Latin America, the British West Indies, and the United States. World War II was a major interruption, and thereafter he became increasingly heavily involved in various tasks of leadership, such as his work with numerous national committees assessing the status of geography, reforming the teaching of geography in the schools, and promoting research support for others. Despite the decrease in his own time devoted to it, he has never wavered in his insistence that intensive field work in local areas should be part of the basic training of all geographers. Several examples of such work are included in this section, selected not only because they seem representative but because each has from time to time been cited by James himself as illustrative of a certain type of geographic work (for example, notes 77 and 78 in article 2, notes 25 and 29 in article 3). All of these examples are preceded by another paper typical of the man, wherein he attempts to bring order to a broad subject by clarifying objectives, defining categories, and discussing methods.

"The Blackstone Valley" is an oft-cited paper in American geography for it was one of the first to reflect the impact of Carl Sauer's famous programmatic call in "The Morphology of Landscape" in 1925. Although James, like Sauer, would later move away from that rather narrow concept of "landscape interpretation," it remains an interesting example of what he defined in article 4 as an "exploratory study," a controlled description at topographic scale, based firmly upon detailed field observation, mapping, and measuring. James has referred to it as a study of "sequent occupance," but it is not basically organized as such

118

(though the short section on Millbury is). A sequence of Indian, early European, and several industrial phases is noted, but the main description is a cross-section as of 1927 in which the landscape elements produced by these several phases are studied as they were then areally associated. Thus it is not only a good example of a type, but like all such studies it has in time taken on new value as a historical document on the area, a base line against which to study subsequent changes.

In the summer of 1933 James and several colleagues and students from the University of Michigan undertook a field study project in Wyoming. One of the results was article 6, an example of a "remedial" study dealing with the incompatible objectives of competing interests in Jackson Hole. James has insisted that the scientific investigator of controversial public issues should remain as objective as possible, limiting his purpose to "the clarification of the issues involved," and leaving policy decisions to the vote of citizens or their elected officials. That this study served to do just that is suggested by the fact that it was reprinted by the state government for the information of Wyoming legislators.

Preston James has long been the leading geographer-interpreter of modern Latin America to the English-speaking world and has had much influence upon Latin Americans as well. It is a regional interest which has spanned his entire professional career, beginning in 1921 with his field work for his doctoral dissertation and continuing yet today. The modest paragraph in article 7 hardly does justice to his contributions, but that brief survey does serve to set his research in historical perspective. It is rather surprising to find that this man, who is still so active today, was in fact one of the very first geographers to specialize in the study of Latin America.

The two brief papers on Trinidad form a somewhat unusual set in the literature on geography. The first contains a brief description of the geography of the three leading crops on the island as determined from his field reconnaissance of 1924. In the conclusions he sets forth what he would later refer to as a "theoretical model," a three-stage sequence in the adjustment of land use to physical and locational conditions, on the basis of which he made some predictions about future crop patterns. As he notes in the opening paragraph of article 9, a return trip to Trinidad in 1955 allowed him to check his predictions and to suggest the reasons for the main discrepancies. It is typical of his style and broader interests that the article is actually not tightly focused upon testing the degree of correspondence between the patterns of the two dates. Each article is but a small part of a more general reconnaissance study of Trinidad.

From 1930 on James took a special interest in Brazil. Articles from his several research trips and extensive commentaries on the studies of other scholars of that country are sprinkled through his list of publications. Article 10 is one of several studies of cities by James and is a very good, if brief, example of the morphological emphasis of the time. The next item is related in topic but different in type and scale. It is in fact of special historical significance for it is a careful assessment completed just before the decision was made to proceed with the building of Brasília (note the Postscript). It is another excellent example, at a different scale than the Jackson Hole study, of a geographer's attempt at "clarification of the issues" in a controversial matter of public policy. Dr. Speridião Faissol, the co-author of the article, is one of James's former students, having received his Ph.D. from Syracuse University in 1955. Long prominent in Brazilian geographical and planning circles, he is currently in charge of the preparation of a Brazilian national atlas.

The first appearance of *Latin America,* in 1942, established James as an outstanding authority. As a geography text it set a new standard in style and theme, and it was immediately admired, widely adopted, and at times quite explicitly emulated (as, for example, by O. H. K. Spate, who acknowledged in the Preface to his own monumental *India and Pakistan,* "the inspiration I have received from . . . Preston James's *Latin America, . . .* the best regional geography in English known to me"). As a geographical interpretation it offered a perspective on a major part of the earth and its people which was essential to any depth of understanding and quite unobtainable from any other field; thus it has had many readers far beyond the college classroom. An obvious measure of its success are the successive editions and the publication of condensed versions; more diffuse but significant evidence is the fact that it is so widely regarded as an essential work by scholars in other fields. It is an "exploratory study" at a very different scale than the previous examples, but like them it is soundly based upon field research. The latest edition is the culmination of nearly fifty years of study which have included half a dozen research seasons, a dozen shorter sojourns, and wide-ranging reconnaissances which have taken him into every major region of this huge area. A brief excerpt from the opening chapter of that edition is included in article 12 to suggest something of the broad range of fundamental matters which the author seeks to illuminate; the book as a whole still stands as an uncommonly good exhibit of one of the grand traditions of the field: the geographer as regional interpreter.

# 4

## FORMULATING OBJECTIVES OF
## GEOGRAPHIC RESEARCH

At the beginning of any serious research study it is essential that the objectives be clearly and unambiguously stated. Although few geographers would disagree about the need for this, we have developed the habit of taking this preliminary step in a research project for granted—certainly not giving it the careful thought it requires. A perusal of the published results of research in recent professional periodicals indicates that in many instances the reader gains nothing from the opening paragraph that he did not gain from the title. When either the research worker, or the reader of published research, cannot clearly identify the objectives of a study there is no way to distinguish the relevant from the irrelevant, or a completed work from one that is incomplete. We need to give more thought to the formulation of objectives.

### A COMMON DENOMINATOR

Consideration of the objectives of geographic research raises at once the question whether or not there is a common denominator which makes it possible to add one piece of geographic research to another. There are some geographers—and some our most productive ones—who have gone so far with a systematic or regional specialization that they find their ties to other geographers less meaningful than those which connect them with non-geographers. Some of these specialists have expressed doubt whether a geographic

Reprinted from *Annals* of the Association of American Geographers, 38, 4 (December 1948), 271–76.

common denominator is worth seeking. This paper takes the stand that such a denominator does exist, and that it is worthwhile to discuss its nature and the methods of formulating objectives in terms of it.

## *Three Categories of Problems*

It might clarify matters if we suggest the existence—generally in all fields of study—of three categories of problems. First, when systematic, organized knowledge is inadequate or nonexistent, the problem is to find a means of gathering, organizing, classifying, and presenting such knowledge in a way which will be meaningful. Studies built around such a problem can be described as *exploratory*. Second, when some organized knowledge exists, questions are raised regarding the operation of cause and effect processes, and the answers not only reveal new and hitherto unobserved data, but also make forecasting possible. Studies built around problems of this sort may be described as *genetic*. Third, when organized knowledge illuminated by understanding of cause and effect processes exists, questions are raised concerning the desirable direction of changes in the conditions man finds and the most effective means of making such changes. Studies built around problems of this sort may be described as *remedial*.

There are, of course, ways to identify studies in all three categories which are geographical in nature. First, such studies have to do with the surface of the earth—with the zone of overlapping spheres where the lithosphere, the hydrosphere, the biosphere, and the atmosphere are intermingled, and where mankind develops out of the materials of the other spheres, those myriad forms and patterns which we describe as the anthroposphere. But this zone of interest is not exclusively geographic, since it is also occupied by geophysics, biology, and the social sciences. Geographic studies have to do with the nature and causes of area differentiation on the surface of the earth—with differences from place to place. But also geophysics, biology, and the social sciences deal with differences from place to place. The relation of geographical studies to studies in these other fields can only be defined in terms of objectives: if the basic objective is to gain an understanding of area differentiation, then the study is geographic; if the basic objective is to gain an understanding of physical, biological, or social processes then the study can be properly described as lying beyond the normal scope of geography, although geographers may make important contributions to the knowledge of process.

We should understand at once that the only purpose of making such a distinction between geographic and non-geographic is to provide a frame of reference for the establishment of a common denominator. Some of the most significant work in recent years in geophysics, biology, and social science as well as in geography has been carried out by scholars who are disdainful of arbitrary categories or academic distinctions, and who pass freely back and forth, both ways, from preoccupation with process to preoccupation with resulting area difference. A definition of the scope of the broad field of geography will be misused if it in any way restricts the free approach of scholarship to whatever ends trained curiosity may lead.

With this reservation concerning its use, the following one-sentence description of the scope and purpose of geographical study can be offered: it is the study of the significance of differences from place to place on the earth. The word *significance* in this brief description of the field implies an inquiry into both the causes of area differences and also into the consequences. This preoccupation with the significance of area differences on the earth constitutes the common denominator of geographic research.

## Exploratory Studies

In no one of the three categories of problems is the precise formulation of objectives more important—and sometimes more difficult—than in those which have been described as exploratory.

Exploratory studies are essentially descriptive, and might be so named were it not for the faint aroma of discredit attached to what is termed by some of our professional colleagues "mere description." We need not elaborate on the point that description without clearly defined objectives, without a conceptual framework which is being filled out with new information, is indeed not scholarship. To this kind of descriptive writing the word *mere* might well be applied. But description for a stated and limited objective is quite another matter.

Professional geographers will, of course, agree that complete description of any part of the earth, even one farm, is impossible. The complex face of the earth cannot be reproduced at any scale less than one to one: at any smaller scale it becomes necessary to select some data as relevant, and to reject others as irrelevant. Relevant and irrelevant to what?

Geographers are always dealing with categories of things. No two points on the face of the earth are alike; yet differences, similarities, and relationships are identified and analyzed in terms of categories in which similar things, but not identical things, are grouped together. Since the selection of categories can determine the kinds of relationships identified, it is highly important that they be selected in such a way that they can be evaluated by one's professional colleagues. This requires a statement of the objectives, for only in terms of objectives can categories be evaluated.

This is a point we frequently overlook. One cannot simply go into an unfamiliar area to answer the question "what is the area like?" The answer, as so many geographic papers demonstrate, depends on the concepts, conscious or unconscious, which the geographer carries with him. Since it is obviously impossible to go into an area with a blank mind, it is essential to identify one's own preconceptions and to formulate clearly the nature of the conceptual framework which the exploratory study is designed to supply with relevant data. Description controlled in this manner is not *mere*.

What is a geographical concept? It is a generalization regarding the meaning of differences, similarities, or relationships on the earth. A concept which has to do with causal relationships is, of course, a hypothesis, or, if it has stood the test of time and is widely held to be true, it is a theory. But there are also area relationships which are not necessarily causal. In fact, the total environments with which a geographer must deal involve many elements which are areally but not causally related to each other. A geographic concept is a generalization regarding the significance of area differentiation on the earth. The conceptual framework around which an exploratory study may be organized consists of the general geographical ideas that the worker holds to be true. Since such geographical ideas are in most cases based on intuitive judgment rather than objective proof, the clear formulation of them is all the more important.

## Sequent Occupance

For example, "sequent occupance" is a geographic concept. This term refers to the successive patterns of settlement impressed upon a given physical and biological environment by a succession of people with differing economic techniques. It rests upon the generalization that the significance to man of the physical and biological features of the land is determined by the culture, or way of living, of the people. It is entirely possible to set up exploratory studies the purpose of which is to provide additional data to enrich or fill out this concept. Categories developed with this concept in mind can be evaluated—they have a meaning which is broader or more general than can be applied to the local settlement patterns of any one area at any one time. Exploratory studies in sequent occupance add up to something.

## The Regional Concept

The regional concept can also provide a frame of reference for an exploratory study. I am not referring to the concept of the region as an organic unit, which was so effectively demolished by Hartshorne in *The Nature of Geography*. The regional concept identifies a region as possessing an over-all aspect of unity, superimposed on strong internal diversity, and with many of the regional elements extending beyond the area into neighboring regions. New England, for example, is a group of states which most people agree possess regional unity. Yet within New England there are strongly contrasted parts, and the contrasts are physical, biological, economic, social, and political. An exploratory study of New England would attempt to define the complex area relationships between these different categories of things. It would throw new light on how the internal differences contribute to or detract from the unity of the region as a whole; it would investigate the causes and the consequences of unity. It would serve to enrich the regional concept as a geographical generalization.

Each systematic and regional field of geography has a number of concepts around which exploratory studies might effectively be organized. To identify and formulate these concepts is one of the purposes of the Centennial Studies Program.

## GENETIC STUDIES

The formulation of the statement of objectives in the case of genetic studies is, in many ways, simpler than it is in the case of exploratory studies. It is not always easy to make clear, unambiguous statements about concepts, many of which are held unconsciously. But the objectives of genetic studies are presented simply in the form of questions concerning cause and effect relations. The difficulty with genetic studies will be in the rigorous method which must be followed in finding and demonstrating the correctness of the answer.

Geographers are not always clear about the difference between cause and effect relations and simple area relations. Any two phenomena located on the earth's surface have an area relationship to each other. In a previous paper on this subject,[1] the terms "coincidence," "correspondence," and "discordance of pattern" were suggested. A coincidence of pattern occurs when two phenomena occupy precisely the same geographic area—this is the kind of fact which might be established by an exploratory study, and as one of the results of the study the existence of a cause and effect problem would be discovered. But even such a close area relationship does not establish the existence of a causal relationship, plausible as such a relationship might be made to seem. To demonstrate a cause and effect relation it is necessary to show the existence of a process connecting a previous cause to a presently observable effect.

Consider, for example, the study of urban morphology. A purely exploratory problem is raised by the question whether or not the position of residence districts has an area relationship to wind direction. One is faced with the formulation of the conceptual framework which lies back of the identification of categories of residence districts, or categories of duration and intensity of wind. One studies as many cities as possible, in as many different parts of the world. A variety of possible area relationships between residence patterns and wind direction might be discovered and described. The greater the degree of correspondence brought to light the more plausible it becomes to believe that there is a causal relationship. But the nature of the relationship, and even its existence remains uncertain.

A genetic study might start with a causal hypothesis: that the wind direction is a factor in the location of residence districts in cities. The question is whether and to what degree the hypothesis is supported by observation. The resulting study would be quite different in its procedure from the study based on an exploratory objective. It would be necessary to prove that the persons responsible for the arrangement of residences did in fact give consideration either directly or indirectly, consciously or unconsciously, to the wind factor.

These two kinds of studies, the exploratory and the genetic, need to be clearly distinguished. Items relevant to one type might or might not be relevant to the other. Results can only be evaluated when the geographer is clear regarding the kind of objective he is seeking. Yet obviously, the two are closely related and might even constitute two distinct phases of one research project. The understanding gained by the genetic study might well establish the conceptual framework on which new and more meaningful exploratory studies could be set up. But whether there are two phases to one project, or whether there are two quite different projects carried out by different people with different intellectual interests, the clear distinction of the two kinds of objectives must be made if the two parts are ever to be added together.

## REMEDIAL STUDIES

Another kind of problem is presented when any physical, biological, or cultural condition exists on the earth which is thought to be undesirable. The constructive application of geographical understandings contributes to the creation of conditions more satisfactory to man.

The statement of objectives for such remedial studies commonly defines the condition to be remedied and the desirable direction of change. In some cases the condition to be remedied is simply the absence of something, and the direction of change is essentially the plan for development—as when new colonies are planned in a previously unsettled country, or when retail stores are located where none existed before. In other cases the condition to be remedied requires a decision of policy either on the part of responsible public officials or through the votes of citizens. In the latter case there is considerable argument in favor of limiting the objectives of the geographical study to the clarification of the issues involved in the policy decision.

Whatever may be the nature of the remedial study, the formulation of objectives requires a careful statement of the conceptual framework. In many instances the concepts involved are taken for granted—and this may be justified where the studies involve immediate practical application. But where the studies are directed toward the increase of broader understanding rather than specific application, then the statement of the conceptual framework cannot be taken for granted. The kinds of economic, political, or social conditions which are thought to be undesirable, and the changes which are recommended are all determined by the normative concepts which the worker brings with him to his task. The statement of objectives for a remedial study should leave no room for doubt regarding the kinds of conditions which are postulated as good.

Remedial studies are not necessarily applied studies. Actually the distinction between academic or pure geography and applied geography has little meaning. In the fields of physical science if studies are undertaken for the purpose of using the results outside of the field they are immediately identified as applied. But among the social sciences which deal with man no results can be so academic that they are not of immediate practical use—unless, of course, *academic* is a synonym for *poor, trivial,* or *meaningless.* Pure geography is geography studied with the objective of increasing professional understandings; applied geography is geography studied for objectives outside of its own domain. In social science this becomes almost a distinction without a difference.

It is important that we, as geographers, give more thought to the careful formulation of our objectives. But we should avoid permitting any formula to become so standard in its application that it controls the direction of geographic thinking. Any categories which are set up, including those presented in this paper, have a limited and specific utility in relation to a stated objective. Each new research undertaking in a field such as ours requires the fresh approach, as unrestricted as possible by traditional forms and procedures. But no fresh approach starts in by being vague: there is always the basic requirement that objectives be clearly and unambiguously stated whatever may be their form.

### NOTE

1. P. E. James, W. D. Jones, and V. C. Finch, "Conventionalizing Geographic Investigation and Presentation," *Annals* of the Association of American Geographers, 24 (1934), 77–122.

# 5

## THE BLACKSTONE VALLEY, A STUDY
## IN CHOROGRAPHY
## IN SOUTHERN NEW ENGLAND

### INTRODUCTION

To the geographer, southern New England offers a fascinating and challenging problem in landscape interpretation. Occupied successively by the Indians, by European agriculturists, and by manufacturers, the several cultures have left their own peculiar impressions in the landscape. Thus a confusing array of earlier and later forms, of impression set on impression is presented to the eye. Southern New England, with its long history and its several periods of development, possesses a landscape composed of a complex of relict forms, intricately involved with the more recent forms. The investigation set forth herein was limited to a strip about forty miles long and four miles wide, extending along the valley of the Blackstone River from the southern outskirts of Worcester to the northern margin of Pawtucket and Providence. Within the 178 square miles included in this purely arbitrary unit are found represented the chief types of landscape of southern New England. Valley manufacturing towns, upland farms, wooded, rocky slopes, and many other types of less areal significance appear. It is the character and mutual relationships of these landscapes which we set ourselves to describe and interpret, not as a finished picture, but as a living, changing, developing expression of the earth's exterior.

Reprinted from *Annals* of the Association of American Geographers, 19, 2 (June 1929), 67–109. For the drafting of the maps and charts and for assistance in the field the author is indebted to Charles Crittenden.

## PHYSICAL CHARACTERISTICS

The main events in the evolution of the present landforms in southern New England are already familiar to most geographers.[1] During the Cretaceous the surface of the area was reduced to a lowlying peneplain, possibly even smoothed by an invasion of the sea, so that rocks differing greatly in resistance to the forces of erosion were worn down to a nearly uniform baselevel.[2] On the surface of this peneplain were spread detrital sands worn from the still upstanding highlands to the north and west. With the uplift and southward tilting of the land, consequent streams began to establish their courses, flowing, in the area with which we are dealing, in a southerly direction. However, the uniform mantle of detritus which masked the varied rock structure beneath was soon cut through, and the streams were superposed on a series of rock formations, largely pre-Cambrian crystalline rocks, which varied to a marked degree in resistance. In the belts of weaker rock, broad open valleys were quickly excavated, but in the bands of more resistant strata, the valley forms remained youthful. A conspicuous amount of readjustment through shift of channel and through piracy followed, so that the present irregular drainage lines vary to a large degree from the courses of the earlier consequents, and the surface forms are characterized by valleys of irregular width, by water gaps, and by abandoned drainage lines. The original peneplain surface appears in the strikingly level skyline of New England; it is found in the area we are studying in the many irregular patches of graded upland which have not yet been dissected by the tributary streams, and which lie between four hundred and six hundred feet above sea level (Figure 1).

### The Blackstone Valley

The present course of the Blackstone River results from two notable captures.[3] The first took place between Woonsocket and Millville. (See Figure 3 for places mentioned in the text.) A small tributary of the Pawtucket River was finding relatively easy cutting along the strike of a weak phyllite member of the Westboro quartz-ite, with its outlet in the lowlying carboniferous depression of the Narragansett Bay.[4] Aided by these advantages, this river succeeded in cutting headward across the resistant Milford granite and the Bellingham conglomerate, and in capturing the ancestor of the present Blackstone a little west of Millville. The original channel of this river led southward through Ironstone toward the sea.

The second capture, aided no doubt by the first one, took place near Worcester, as a tributary stream cut across the resistant outcrops of schist at Millbury, and the ridge of quartzite south and east of Worcester to divert the headwaters of the present French River. The whole Worcester depression, excavated in a belt of weaker rock, was transferred to Blackstone drainage, the divide being shifted to a point between Auburn and Oxford.

In this way the present Blackstone Valley, in the northwest corner of the map (Figure 1), is a broad lowland excavated in weak rock. At Quinsigamond Village there is a narrow water gap. Weaker rocks immediately southeast result in a wider stretch, but at Mill-bury resistant layers force the river to pass over a succession of rapids where water power is abundant. Below Farnumsville the valley gradually broadens to its widest point near Uxbridge. Then a sharp bend to the southeast at Melville leads to the narrow irregularly winding trench incised in the resistant formations around Woonsocket, where again water power is available through falls and rapids. Below Woonsocket in Rhode Island, the deep gorge of the lower Blackstone results from the excavation of a weaker rock between stronger material on either side, which continues to retard the process of valley widening. In the southeastern corner of the map the Blackstone Valley loses its identity in the broad Narragansett Lowland.

### Glacial Forms

The major features of drainage and ridge lines were established before the Glacial period, but the ice modified in an important way the forms of the surface. The more prominent hills were scraped

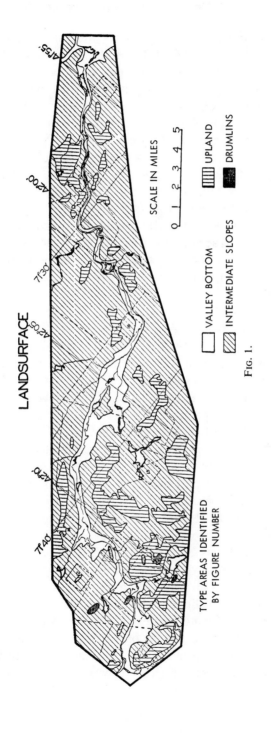

LANDSURFACE

SCALE IN MILES

0 1 2 3 4 5

VALLEY BOTTOM

INTERMEDIATE SLOPES

UPLAND

DRUMLINS

TYPE AREAS IDENTIFIED
BY FIGURE NUMBER

FIG. 1.

bare of soil, and their southern sides were steepened. The valleys were broadened and polished. But still more important in this area, a thin veneer of glacial drift and outwash was strewn over the surface. Low hills of gravel, marshy hollows filled with a confusion of round boulders, lakes, the bottoms and shores of which are paved with rocks, soil in which the plow encounters in every furrow stones too big to move, a thin covering of coarse sand or gravel barely concealing the ribs of crystalline bedrock below—such is the heritage of the ice age. A few conspicuous drumlins in the neighborhood of Millbury and Sutton dominate the landscape. In the valley, the torrential waters from the melting ice left an aggraded floor of sand and gravel roughly stratified, and now remaining as a broad terrace on either side of the river channel. The present channel is slightly degraded in harmony with the gradual erosion of the resistant rock sills lower in the course of the river.[5]

### Climate

·The climate of this area is as unfriendly as its surface. Providence, close to the sea, enjoys relatively mild winters, but inland the severity of the cold waves and the depth of the snow increases. The average January temperature[6] at Providence is 27.2° F and at Worcester 24.8°. July in Providence averages 73.4° and in Worcester 71.4°. The growing season is approximately 160 days.[7] The rainfall is very nearly the same throughout the area, the stations recording for the most part averages between 40 and 45 inches, and with a conspicuously uniform distribution throughout the year.[8] During the years 1841–1920, during which time Worcester has received on the average 43.7 inches of rainfall a year, the lowest amount received was 30.9 in 1914, and the highest 61.8 in 1852 (61.7 in 1888).[9] Applying the symbols of Köppen's classification,[10] Providence is on the poleward margin of the Cfa climate, and Worcester has a Dfb climate. Most of the area of this study probably falls within the climate expressed by the symbol Dfa. Cyclonic storms crossing New England, or passing near it at short intervals especially in winter, provide the rapid non-periodic variations of weather for which this part of the world is justly famous.

## Forest

The whole area was originally covered with a dense virgin forest of the oak-hickory association.[11] In certain of the glacial lake beds of New England and along the valley bottoms of the larger rivers, the first settlers found grassy meadlowlands without brush cover and shaded only by scattered, graceful elms—a landscape of great beauty to which was given the name *intervale*.[12] It is possible that a small intervale of this type may have existed in the broad part of the Blackstone Valley near Uxbridge, but elsewhere in the narrower portions and on the slopes of the upland, and probably even on the drumlins, a dense forest sheltered the wild game on which the first inhabitants depended for their existence.

## THE DEVELOPMENT OF THE LANDSCAPES

Into this not too hospitable land came man, and with man came those modifications of the original terrain which it is our special task to analyze. Three distinct periods in the modification of the original terrain can be discerned. First the native Indians with their primitive methods of land occupation created landscape forms characteristic of their culture. Then came the European settlers, first interested in farming, and these people developed out of the earlier landscape, largely obliterating it, a new set of forms reflecting a more advanced agricultural economy. Finally, industrial cities with an entirely new set of cultural forms were imposed upon the rural landscape, not by any means obliterating it, but rather forming patches scattered especially in the valley, and forming vivid contrasts with the earlier landscapes in which they are embedded.

## Landscape Modifications
### Resulting from the Indian Culture

The Nipmuck Indians, inhabiting the area of the Blackstone Valley, were hunters and primitive cultivators.[13] As was common throughout New England, the permanent, stockaded villages were located either on a knoll of higher ground in the midst of a swamp, or on the flattish tops of the hills whence could be had a commanding view in all directions.[14] Pakachoag Hill, just south of Worcester, is said to have been the site of one of these villages, and another was situated at Grafton. Occupying an area of only three or four acres, the wigwams were arranged around the edge of a clearing, the center of which was left open for games and ceremonies. The wigwams themselves were constructed of poles bent together, and fastened at the top and covered with mats or bark.[15] Villages were crowded into a small space and became very dirty in course of time so that the natives suffered severely from various diseases.

Although agriculture was carried on in clearings usually on the upland remnants where the soil is a little less stony, the occupation of the land was distinctly temporary. Land was cleared, used for a time for the cultivation of such crops as Indian corn, squash, pumpkins, or beans,[16] and then abandoned in favor of a new clearing elsewhere. The villages, too, were shifted frequently in this typical form of migratory agriculture. Thus much of the flatter portions of the uplands and hilltops were cleared and later permitted to grow up in a tangle of brush.

To supplement the products of the soil, the Indians depended on the abundant fish of the rivers and lakes and on the larger game of the forests. Temporary villages were established every summer, particularly during spawning time, at the outlets of the lakes, or at the falls on the rivers.[17] The site at the outlet of Singleterry Pond near Millbury (Figure 7) was a frequent camping place for the Indians, for this place in addition to offering the advantages of fishing in the pond, was also located near an outcrop of steatite or soapstone which the Indians used in the manufacture of utensils of many sorts.[18] The signs of similar temporary villages are to be found at such points throughout the area.

Trails connected the various parts of the country, and travel over these trails was important, although there was probably little exchange of products. Two east-west trails crossed the area we are discussing.[19] The more important one led from the vicinity of Boston to the Connecticut Valley. It passed Grafton, and crossing the Blackstone through the site of Millbury, climbed to the upland to

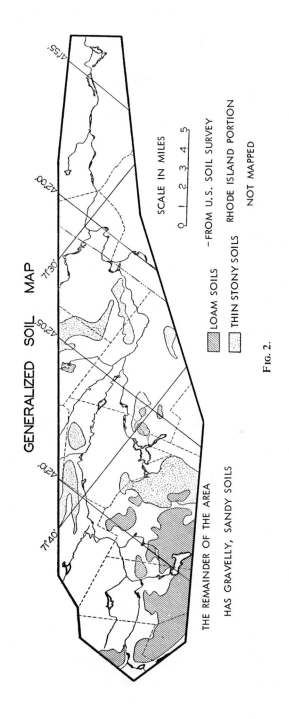

GENERALIZED SOIL MAP

SCALE IN MILES

0 1 2 3 4 5

LOAM SOILS

THIN STONY SOILS

– FROM U.S. SOIL SURVEY

RHODE ISLAND PORTION

NOT MAPPED

THE REMAINDER OF THE AREA

HAS GRAVELLY, SANDY SOILS

42°55'

42°00'

7°30'

42°05'

42°10'

7°40'

FIG. 2.

the west through the valley of Singleterry Brook (Figure 3).[20] A
second one led westward from Mendon, across the valley near Whitinsville, and westward along the southern shores of Whitins Pond.
Following the lines of least resistance across the country, these
trails were the precursors of the later roads, although the railroads,
making use of deep cuts, have found somewhat different routes
westward.


## The  Rural  Landscape  of  the  European  Settlers

Not until after King Philip's War (1675) did the frontier of European settlement reach and cross the Blackstone. As early as 1635 a
band of English colonists had crossed our area en route for the
Connecticut Valley, probably following the Indian trail through
Grafton and Millbury.[21] When the Indian wars broke out, Mendon,
at the time the outpost of the English settlements, was the first town
to be destroyed. Mendon is located just east of our area. As soon as
the country had been cleared of hostile Indians, however, the English began to occupy and cross the Blackstone Valley, settling
Worcester for the first time in 1685.[22]

On the outer fringe of the westward-expanding settlements
were scattered clearings, isolated from the main area of established
farms by as yet uncleared wilderness. Simple cabins of rough-hewn
logs, with chimneys of mud and roofs of thatch, formed the homes
of the pioneers.[23] In many cases the first crops of corn grew among
the tree stumps, on land only partially cleared, or recently burned
over. With the enormous labor of clearing off the virgin forest before
them, and with an overabundance of wood on every side, fire was
frequently resorted to as the cheapest and quickest method of preparing the area for the raising of crops or the pasturing of animals.
The hilly country in the neighborhood of the present Douglas was
repeatedly burned over in the spring by settlers from the eastern
side of the valley in order to keep it covered with grass for their
cattle,[24] for in that climate, a clearing which is abandoned speedily
grows up with brush as a first step in the return to a forest cover.
But difficulties meant little to these people. With remarkable rapidity, the landscape was radically transformed. From a virgin forest

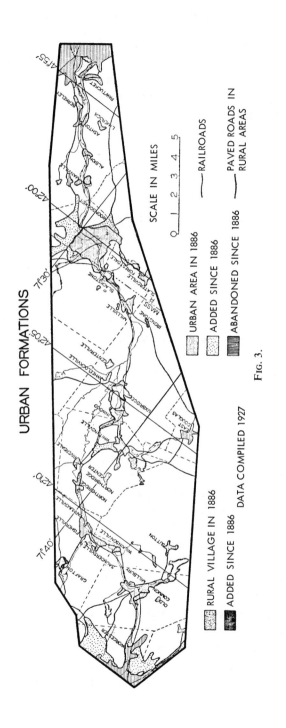

URBAN FORMATIONS

SCALE IN MILES

0 1 2 3 4 5

URBAN AREA IN 1886

ADDED SINCE 1886

ABANDONED SINCE 1886

RURAL VILLAGE IN 1886

ADDED SINCE 1886

DATA COMPILED 1927

——— RAILROADS

——— PAVED ROADS IN
RURAL AREAS

FIG. 3.

with scattered clearings appeared open fields, waving with corn or grain, or dotted with cattle and sheep, interspersed with scattered patches of relict woodland. Even the areas of poorer soils and all but the rougher slopes were thus placed in use. Only twenty or thirty years after the first fringe of settlement had invaded this territory,[25] the isolated clearings with the rude log cabins had become things of the past. In 1715, two-story houses, built of clapboards and with gambrel roofs, had supplanted the cruder house forms, although at this time a few of the log cabins are described standing side by side with the more pretentious homes, reminders of the rapidity of the course of settlement.[26]

### Agriculture

During this period the labor expended in agriculture was enormous. Not only did the forest have to be cleared and the stumps removed, but also the boulders and stones in the soil had to be pulled out. With these were constructed the famous stone walls which form so characteristic a part of New England landscape. The height and width of the walls reflected the amount of stone encountered in the fields, as the care with which the rounded boulders were fitted together reflected the perseverance of the people. Fields were set off in irregular patterns, conforming somewhat to the surface, but showing nothing of the right-angle regularity of the fields in the Middle West. In sections where land was devoted to the raising of hay or grain, fields were set off which could be mowed by one or two workers with scythes in a single day. With the introduction of machinery about 1850 or 1860,[27] the small size of these fields, and the immobility of the stone walls which bounded them became distinct handicaps.

In addition to clearing the land of forest and boulders, the early settlers constructed in some cases local systems of irrigation. Brooks were dammed and small glacial marshes converted into little reservoirs. Canals, in some cases carefully lined with stone flags, carried the water to the fields of hay or grain, where yields were apparently sufficiently increased to stimulate a spread of similar systems. On one old farm which was studied, canals wind like contours around many of the morainic hills, and cross lower areas on small stone-lined aqueducts, all of which must have required many years of patient work for construction. The irrigation system was used until 1880, when the farm was abandoned. At the present time irrigation ditches, excepting the better ones, are only faintly to be discerned.

### Rural Hamlets

In the midst of the better agricultural areas, small rural villages or hamlets appeared. Sutton, Uxbridge, Grafton, and Douglas were among those incorporated early in the eighteenth century. With few exceptions, such as Uxbridge, these towns were on the uplands, and the most prosperous of them were in areas of loam soil (Figure 2). A group of farm homes stringing out along the highways, a store at the four corners, a blacksmith shop, and, most important of all, a white-painted church with its tall steeple: such is the aspect of these "hill towns." The church steeple in its conspicuous position on the upland is a landmark for miles around. Before the development of the manufacturing cities of the valley, these rural communities were of dominant importance. Their function was as much religious and political as it was commercial, for the town meeting to the New England colonist was an affair of the greatest importance, and every Sunday families for miles around gathered in the little meeting house for worship. While Uxbridge and Douglas have changed their form with the advent of manufacturing, Grafton, and especially Sutton, remain virtually unchanged, declining with the decline of the functions for which they existed.

### The Decline of Agriculture

Agriculture in this area was never easy. As the little soil fertility was depleted, and as the more productive plains west of the Appalachians were occupied, the old New England rural economy gradually crumbled. Emigration, first to the new areas of the west, and later to the nearby cities, took from each generation its most ambitious sons. Gradually the fields which had been reclaimed from the wilderness at such a cost in human labor, and in so short a time, were allowed to revert to brush. Old farms—the ancestral homes of the present generations of city dwellers—were abandoned and fell slowly into picturesque ruin. There is probably less cleared land today in the area of this study than in the opening years of the last century.[28] Hidden in the scrubby woods which cover much of the terrain today, crumbling stone walls alone tell of the period when the land was cleared and cultivated.

### The Growth of the Urban Landscape

The combination of superposed rivers in the process of readjustment to underlying structure of varying resistance and the minor damning and shifting of drainage lines resulting from glaciation gave New England a multitude of small waterpower sites. At the same time, a uniform rainfall and a runoff regulated by many lakes and marshes insured for these sites an even flow of water. During the period of agricultural predominance, many small power sites were used for gristmills which were established to take care of the local grain production. In the urban growth which came later at these same sites, the old gristmills of the Blackstone have almost entirely disappeared, although town records and the stories of old-timers still tell of their existence.

The first successful cotton mill in America was established by Samuel Slater in 1790 at Pawtucket.[29] The plans which Slater had memorized in England, united with the capital accumulated by the New England traders in such cities as Providence, was a dynamic combination. By 1800 there were twenty-nine other cotton mills in the neighborhood of Pawtucket. Waterpower sites were at a premium: textile factories were built at Woonsocket, Blackstone, Millville, Uxbridge, Millbury, and soon each little power site was the nucleus of a new and thriving landscape formation. The rumble of the water wheel and the clatter of the shuttle filled the valley with strange new sounds, ominous for the hardworking farmers of the upland. The urban landscape had come to stay, and in it the hard-pressed agriculturists one after another sought a decent living.[30]

Occupying but a relatively small part of the country's area, the manufacturing cities soon collected the greater part of the population, and by far the greater part of the wealth. The hard life of the farm with its characteristic lack of material comforts, and the relatively easy and prosperous life of the city is perhaps nowhere more strikingly set in contrast than in southern New England where the older rural landscape remains to this day on the sheltering upland looking out over the bustling activity of valley manufacturing towns.

## Communications: The Canal

During the agricultural period communication was by means of wagons drawn by horses or oxen over roads, and one of the characteristics of the rural landscape today is the absence in it of railroads and in most cases of paved roads. The development of manufacturing towns, however, created an insistent demand for more efficient means of transportation, especially since most of the raw materials had to be brought in from Providence, and most of the finished products sent out that way. Unfortunately the need for easier communications came just a little before the beginning of railroad development with the result that the first connection with the sea was through a canal.

The Blackstone Canal was started in 1824 and completed in 1828.[31] Starting at Providence, it ran up the Blackstone Valley, on the west of the river below Farnumsville, and on the east above that city as far as Worcester. The canal was forty-five miles long, and in that distance fell 451 feet through a number of locks. The Blackstone was never a large river: at best the supply of water was small, and by this time the mills along the stream were jealously guarding their water rights. In order to fill the canal and its locks, therefore, a number of the ponds in the neighboring uplands were dammed and turned into reservoirs in which the waters from the melting snow of spring could be saved for the low water period of the summer. This had the very desirable result not only of providing enough water for the canal but also of further regulating the flow of water for the mills in guarding against both droughts and floods.

The canal gave a tremendous impetus to the growth of the urban landscape. Along its banks many new mills were located. In the town of Millbury, for example, at least a thousand new inhabitants came to live permanently in 1830. This was a boom period: a dynamic period when growth and change were rapid, continuous, and healthy. Many of the mills of this period produced cotton textiles, but on the other hand the valley was not by any means exclusively a textile valley. From the very start its manufactures included a widely diversified list.[32] In addition to the gristmills and linseed oil presses, there were makers of agricultural tools, iron foundries, and establishments for the manufacture of nails and wire. At an early date there was a rubber mill making use of raw rubber from the tropics which was being landed at Providence.[33] In response to the demand for textile machinery, factories specializing in this type of product were established at Whitinsville. Pawtucket, in 1925, had 228 different mills manufacturing sixty-six different kinds of products.[34] There were and are many baskets for the industrial eggs in each of the larger urban communities.

### Railroads

For several reasons the canal did not prosper. The rapid growth of industry dependent on waterpower was overtaxing the low water resources of the river, and the mill-owners, especially those in Rhode Island where the canal was not so vital a factor in their prosperity, waged bitter warfare against the diversion of water.[35] Then again, in times of very low water, the portions of the canal which made use of the main stream were not navigable, and the whole route was closed four or five months of the year by ice. A railroad project, not by any means the first in the vicinity, was surveyed, and in 1847 the Providence and Worcester railroad began operation. The canal survived this competition only one year, and ceased business in 1848. It can be seen in a few places today, its tow path overgrown with bushes, its channel clogged with vegetation. Railroads now provide ample connection not only down-valley to Providence, but also eastward and westward, through Worcester or Woonsocket, with the larger markets and sources of raw material. The predominant position of Worcester as a commercial and manufacturing center is due among other things to its position on the main line of east-west transportation, and with its right-angle connection to Providence through the Blackstone.

### The Changing Character of Manufactures

As long as the power for the use of the factories was derived directly from the flow of the stream, there was a tendency for small isolated manufacturing communities to spring up wherever the combination of power site and outside connection was favorable. About 1840, however, steam began gradually to supplant water power. Since coal arrived in those days chiefly by water, the cities near the coast had a distinct advantage over those farther inland.[36] However an urban community is not easily shifted. The early start of the up-valley industries, aided by the construction of railroads to the coal supply and to the coast was able to maintain and continue the development of the interior cities. It is interesting to speculate on what might have happened if before the development of manufacturing had begun, the use of steam had been perfected. At any rate, at the present time, the water of the river is utilized largely for the boilers of the steam plants. Recently electric power sent over transmission lines from the Connecticut Valley has reached the Blackstone and is becoming of increasing importance in the power resources of our area. The tall steel towers of the power lines, set in clearings through the brush and woodland, or marching imperiously across open fields, are among the arresting features of the modern landscape which tell of the dominance of industrial life, and of the many intricate connections of that life with the outside world.

Not all the manufacturing enterprises were successful in the Blackstone area. Many of the factories built for the spinning of cotton turned later to a variety of other products. Many factory buildings were later abandoned and allowed to fall into ruin alongside the more prosperous successful mills. In the days when factories were built of wood, or of brick walls with wooden interiors, and when fire-fighting was a social event, the records of destruction by fire are very numerous. In Millbury one plant which burned during the winter season was completely destroyed before the arrival of the fire engine, drawn by oxen. Another company lost three mills on the same site in twelve years.[37] There are records of periods of prosperity and periods of depression, of successes and failures. Time and again industries were saved by clever inventions or by the business sagacity of the owners.

For a number of reasons which have been extensively treated elsewhere,[38] the Civil War brought about a tendency in New England for the shift from cotton textiles to the manufacturing of worsteds. This tendency was especially marked in the smaller towns of the Blackstone Valley, where none of the cotton factories had achieved as outstanding importance as those elsewhere. The lesser mills, none too prosperous in cotton, turned eagerly to the new worsted industry.

### The Present Condition of the Landscapes

The landscapes assumed approximately their present condition many years ago. We have already shown that the amount of land cleared and under cultivation or pastured probably began to decline about the middle of the last century in the particular area we are studying. Figures for Massachusetts as a whole show an increase of forested area beginning about 1850 or 1860.[39] Since then much of the formerly cleared land has been allowed to grow up in brush, pine, or hardwoods. Over much of the territory, the second growth of pine has been cleared away as a result of the increasing demand for lumber for packing cases and for firewood.

The map (Figure 3) shows the changes in urban area since 1886, when the U.S. Geological Survey Topographic Map of this area was made. Of the cities, Worcester, Whitinsville, and Woonsocket are the only ones to show any marked increase of area; but Pawtucket, although it shows no change of outline in the area of our study, has grown in other directions. Millbury, Northbridge, Uxbridge, Blackstone, and some of the towns along the lower Blackstone in Rhode Island show insignificant gains. The rest of the urban areas remain the same except for Ironstone, which no longer exists as a town. Of the rural villages, only Grafton shows a slight increase of area. In other words, in the course of some forty years, the landscape has remained in an apparently static condition excepting around the margins of the larger cities, where at the present time limited suburban residential subdivisions held by real estate companies are in evidence. But static landscapes of long duration, especially in the new world, and probably in most of the old one, must be rare. "Change is the essence of nature," is a commonplace saying. Even while the areal relations of the landscapes of the Blackstone have remained largely unchanged for forty years, the small changes are of great significance as presaging greater ones to follow, and certain modifications of the character of the landscape show that the apparently static condition is actually only a temporary phase of development.

## Changes in the Urban Landscape

There is a distinct tendency, similar to developments in other regions, for the smaller communities to decline while the larger communities continue to grow. At Ironstone an abandoned factory—a great hollow brick frame with broken windows, surrounded by a group of workingmen's cottages—forms a picturesque ruin, a symbol of the change which is less noticeable but just as real elsewhere. In the summer of 1927, Manchaug, lying a little west of the western margin of the area, offered its mill and mill properties at auction. Wilkinsonville, shortly after the hectic war days when it manufactured khaki cloth, closed its factory, and its inhabitants now seek work in neighboring towns, some even in Worcester. There are closed factories in many of the other towns, especially textile mills, for textiles, whether cotton or woolen, are on the decline in this area. Evidences of this decline are visible on every side in the smaller towns. Meanwhile in the larger cities, where opportunities for employment are more varied, where the modern necessary luxuries are to be had at less cost, where labor is more plentiful, and where for many other reasons, mankind in the industrial areas of the world is tending to concentrate, a steady and solid growth is taking place.

## Changes in the Rural Landscape

The development of the urban landscape in the bosom of the earlier one has had certain important reflections in the surrounding country. The growing network of transmission lines is one of these changes. Another significant change is the increase of concrete roads connecting the cities and towns. To be sure these roads (Figure 3) are chiefly in the valley, and the upland roads are prevailingly of gravel, narrow, and winding. But a few concrete roads cross the upland, as for example from Whitinsville to East Douglas, or eastward from Uxbridge, or from Millbury to Sutton. There is an increasing use of motor trucks in moving the raw material and the finished product from the more isolated mills to the markets, or to such commercial centers as Worchester, Providence, and even Boston. For such short hauls, the railroads can scarcely compete with motor trucks. The concrete roads are obviously related to the city landscape.

A more essentially rural change is the use of farming land for vegetable and fruit raising. Although vegetables and apples are raised in small quantities on almost all of the farms to supplement the income from dairy cattle, only a few large-scale vegetable and fruit farms are to be found in the area. There is a distinct tendency throughout this section of New England, which has gained momentum in recent years, to plant apple orchards, especially on the hill slopes where air drainage is good. The ready market for fruit and vegetables in the nearby cities should stimulate this development. In the analysis of the landscapes which follows, representative farms of this sort will be described at greater length.

## THE ANALYSIS OF THE LANDSCAPES

The foregoing sections lay the basis for the description and interpretation of the "areal scene," which is the objective of chorographic investigation.[40] This involves the synthesis of the distribution of the landscape forms, that is the recognition of the

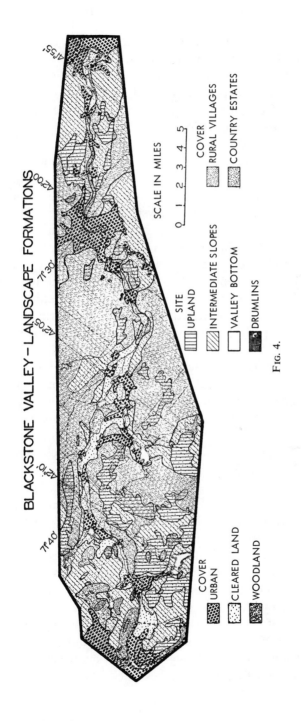

BLACKSTONE VALLEY – LANDSCAPE FORMATIONS

SCALE IN MILES

0  1  2  3  4  5

SITE
▦ UPLAND
▨ INTERMEDIATE SLOPES
☐ VALLEY BOTTOM
■ DRUMLINS

COVER
▦ URBAN
▦ CLEARED LAND
▦ WOODLAND

COVER
▦ RURAL VILLAGES
▦ COUNTRY ESTATES

FIG. 4.

characteristic associations of these forms which create the varying expressions of the face of the earth. For such a combination of forms, we suggest the term landscape *formation*. A formation, thus defined, is a landscape composed dominantly of a definite set of cover forms (vegetation, crops, buildings, etc.), coinciding in area with a definite combination of the elements of site (landforms, soils, etc.).

Synthesis, however, unsupported by analysis is weak. A geographer trained in field investigation can usually recognize and describe the outstanding formations of a region by reconnaissance. More detailed mapping and analysis, at least in representative sections, is necessary in order that the formations may be defined in quantitative terms. In the present stage of geographic field technique it is no longer necessary that such a concept as the landscape formation should remain a matter of individual impression. Its identity can be objectively established: it can be defined in terms of percentage of a site occupied by the different forms of the cover. Several such analyses will be attempted in the paragraphs which follow.

In the area of the Blackstone Valley several landscape formations were recognized and mapped (Figure 4). Analyzing these formations, we see that they are composed of four characteristic sites, associated in various ways with five different combinations of the forms of cover. The sites are: (1) the valley bottom, composed of flood plain and terrace lands, with sandy or gravelly soils and with extensive marshy areas; (2) the intermediate slopes, the surfaces above the valley bottoms which have been eroded below the peneplain level, characterized by steep slopes with thin stony soils and many outcrops of grayish bedrock, and with numerous short brooks which disappear now in boulder-strewn marshes and now reappear to race noisily down the steeper inclines or to pour over the rock ledges; (3) the upland, mostly remnants of the peneplain smoothed by the ice sheets and covered in many places, but not throughout, by the loam soils, relatively free from stones, which make some of the best farmland soils in New England; [41] and (4) the drumlins, few in number but conspicuously different in land form and soil, the latter being, in almost every case, a dark greenish-yellow loam five or six inches thick, known technically as the

Paxton Loam, which is outstanding in its capacity to hold moisture during periods of drought.[42] To complete the concept of these sites, the position of the area across the narrow east coast extension of the Dfa climate must be kept in mind.

The combinations of cover are: (1) urban; (2) rural hamlets or villages; (3) cleared farmland, including small patches of woodland but being chiefly utilized for hay and pasture or fruit and truck farming; (4) woodland, including small clearings of farmland; and (5) a few large estates with extensive lawns and gardens, neat, well-kept buildings, and herds of superior cattle. Of the possible twenty combinations with the sites, sixteen actually occur. The most significant of these landscape formations are: (1) urban areas in the valley bottom and the neighboring intermediate slopes; (2) the cleared farmland on the upland and the gentler intermediate slopes; (3) woodland on the steeper intermediate slopes, especially along the steep sides of the main valley of the Blackstone; (4) rural hamlets on the upland. Tables 1, 2, and 3 show the areas occupied by each of the formations, and present a statistical analysis of the relationships between site and culture.

These tables show quantitatively the existence of certain expect-

TABLE 1

AREAS OCCUPIED BY THE SEVERAL LANDSCAPE FORMATIONS

(In square miles)

| | Valley | Slopes | Upland | Drumlin | Cover Totals |
|---|---|---|---|---|---|
| Urban | 9.1 | 13.5 | .5 | .1 | 23.2 (13%) |
| Cleared Farmland | 7.4 | 49.1 | 18.4 | .8 | 75.7 (42.3%) |
| Woodland | 2.1 | 70.5 | 6.3 | .2 | 79.06 (44.1%) |
| Rural Villages | — | .1 | .5 | | .62 (.3%) |
| Estates | — | .1 | .1 | | .11 (.2%) |
| SITE TOTALS | 18.6 (10.4%) | 133.3 (74.7%) | 25.8 (14.4%) | 1.1 (.5%) | 178.8 |

TABLE 2

PERCENTAGES OF THE SITES OCCUPIED BY THE DIFFERENT COVERS

|  | Urban | Cleared Farmland | Woodland | Rural Villages | Estates |
|---|---|---|---|---|---|
| Valley | 49.2 | 39.7 | 11.1 | 0 | 0 |
| Slopes | 10.1 | 37.0 | 52.8 | .1 | 0 |
| Upland | 1.8 | 71.8 | 24.6 | 1.8 | 0 |
| Drumlins | 5.0 | 76.0 | 19.0 | 0 | 0 |

TABLE 3

PERCENTAGES OF COVERS IN THE DIFFERENT SITES

|  | Valley | Slopes | Upland | Drumlins |
|---|---|---|---|---|
| Urban | 39.4 | 58.2 | 2.1 | .2 |
| Cleared Farmland | 9.7 | 65.0 | 24.4 | 1.0 |
| Woodland | 2.8 | 89.0 | 7.9 | 2 |
| Rural Villages | 0 | 24.2 | 75.8 | 0 |
| Estates | 0 | 54.5 | 45.5 | 0 |

able areal relationships. The valley bottom, for example, has about 50 percent of its area in cities. The greater part of the intermediate slopes with their thin, stoney soils are in woodland, while 71 percent of the upland is cleared farmland. Analyzing from the point of view of the covers, only about 40 percent of the urban areas are in the valley. This being too narrow to contain the expanding cities, 58 percent of the urban area has spread onto the adjoining intermediate slopes, but only 2 percent is on the upland, separated as it is from the lines of communication essential for urban existence. It is important to note that only about a quarter of the cleared farmlands is on the upland, a large percentage lying on the poorer slopes, and that of the wooded areas, almost 90 percent occupy the slopes. The actual distribution of these landscapes is shown in Figure 4.

The mapping of such landscape formations in an area can be accomplished by a reconnaissance, but before such a generalization becomes of scientific value some closer inspection of the character of the units is necessary. In this study, ten representative areas were chosen for detailed study and were surveyed on a scale of 1:10560.

These topographic [43] studies are intended to illustrate the character of the landscapes in detail, and are themselves subject to statistical analysis so that the description can be made quantitative. Only in this way can landscapes be described accurately so that later on, after more detailed information has been gathered, the beginnings of scientific landscape classification can be made. The first of the following topographic studies deals with the town of Millbury; the other nine studies each cover a square mile of area so placed as either to exhibit a typical expression of a formation, or to illustrate the character of a boundary between different formations.

### Millbury, An Urban Study

Millbury (see Figure 7), like many of the other towns along the Blackstone, occupies a narrow section of the valley. Within or immediately contiguous to the city area the relief of the surface is about four hundred feet. The Blackstone itself, at this town, descends rapidly over the resistant outcrops of Brimfield schist, and at its conspicuous eastward bend within the city, it is joined by Singletary Brook draining from the upland. Singletary Brook is remarkable as a power resource in that its flow is maintained by the lake which it drains—now dammed to furnish additional uniformity of flow—and in that it falls 212 feet in a distance of about 1.25 miles. The immediate valley sides, both of the valley and its tributary, are steep and rocky and thus poorly adapted to agricultural or pastoral use.

In a country where waterpower is utilized, such a site inevitably came into prominence. The first industry to be established here was a gristmill, located on Singletary Stream within fifty feet of the outlet of Singletary Pond.[44] At this advantageous location the upland agricultural area around Sutton was served without the necessity of descending and ascending the steep slopes to and from the main stream. Shortly after the gristmill was built, the demand for construction timber in the growing community called for a lumber mill, and in order to provide water for this, Singletary Pond was dammed. Both these mills were built and running in 1720. During the eighteenth century a number of other mills were built along

Singletary Brook, and a few along the main stream. The variety of industries operating in 1792 has already been mentioned, these including iron foundries, rolling mills, tool manufacturing plants, powder mills, and others. The first textile establishment was started in 1828 in an old building refitted for the manufacture of cotton batting.

The detailed record of the building and changing fortunes of the various manufacturing plants of Millbury contained in the Centennial History is striking in three respects.[45] In the first place each building is used in the course of its existence for many different kinds of production. Again and again there are records of renovations or of refittings, in many cases with radically different kinds of manufacturing following each other. One building, for example, was utilized as a linseed oil mill, as a paper plant, as a machine shop, for the manufacturer of fancy cassimeres, and finally for the manufacture of woolens. The second striking feature is the repeated burning of mills, losses due to fire appearing in the records of almost every mill site in the town. In some cases, burned mills were speedily replaced, but in many others the old site was abandoned and the faint trace of a foundation, overgrown with bushes, is all that remains. The third point is that after the opening years of the present century, there has been almost no additional construction. Mills, are shut down or abandoned, but growth is conspicuously lacking. The maps (Figures 5, 6, and 7) show the areal extent of Millbury in 1851,[46] the additions between that date and 1886, and those added since that date. The town had reached essentially its present development in 1851, lacking chiefly the narrow connection of residences between the Singletary Brook section and the main urban center in the valley of the Blackstone. Additions since 1886, chiefly residential, are minor. Millbury is a city of past achievements, a cradle of inventions which have influenced other mills and other cities wherever manufacturing is carried on, but today its period of youth and growth is over. It has no real estate subdivisions on its periphery. It has no group of citizens to tell of its future. The signs along the highway to welcome the passing motorist are broken and rusted. It reeks of that atmosphere which one finds in a small New England manufacturing town, and which tells of a struggle not to move forward but to keep from decline.

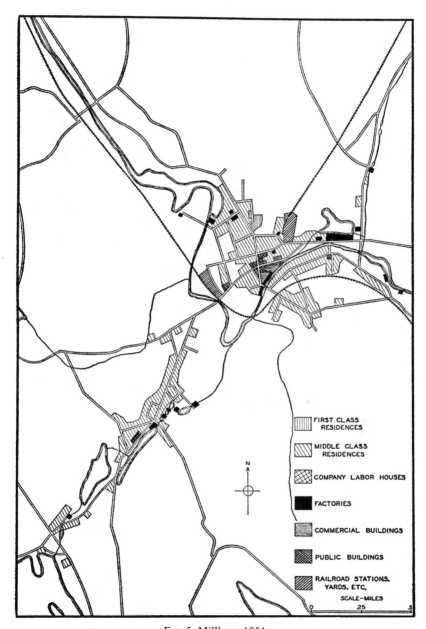

FIRST CLASS
RESIDENCES

MIDDLE CLASS
RESIDENCES

COMPANY LABOR HOUSES

FACTORIES

COMMERCIAL BUILDINGS

PUBLIC BUILDINGS

RAILROAD STATIONS,
YARDS, ETC,

SCALE-MILES

0 .25 .5

FIG. 5. Millbury 1851.

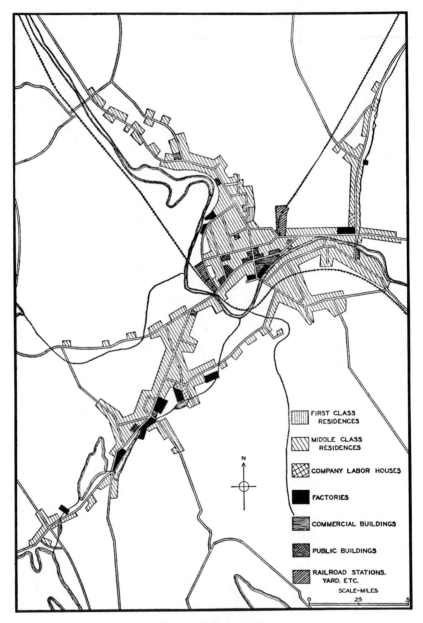

FIG. 6. Millbury 1886.

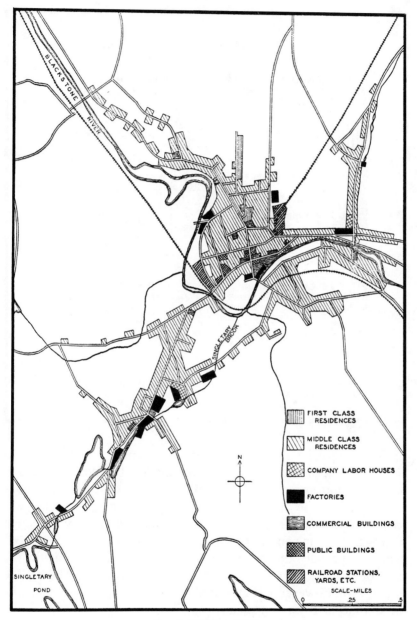

F<small>IG</small>. 7. Millbury 1927.

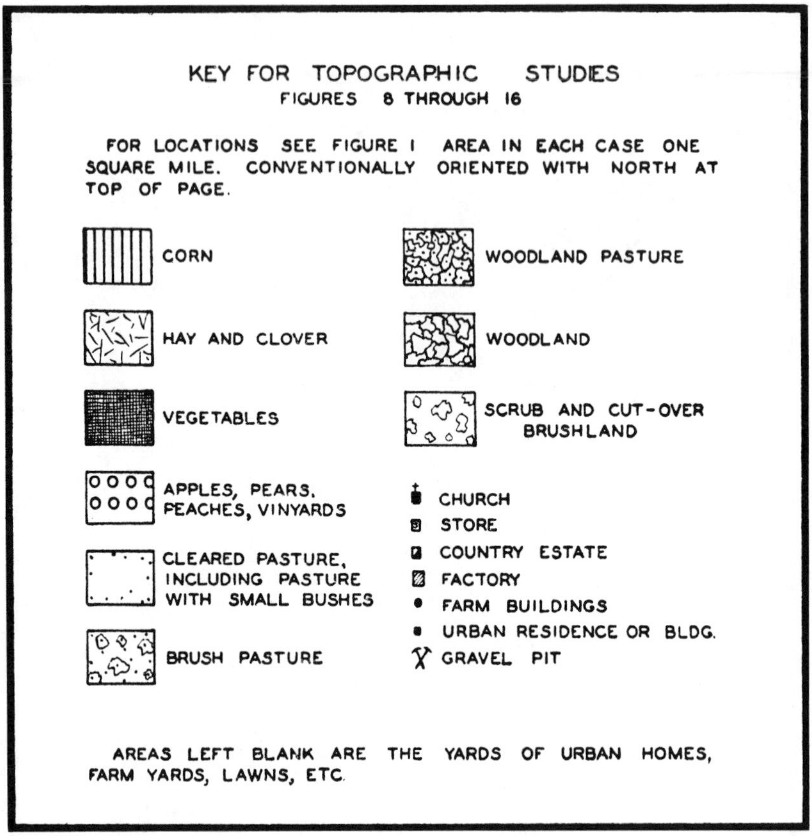

KEY FOR TOPOGRAPHIC    STUDIES
FIGURES   8 THROUGH 16

FOR LOCATIONS SEE FIGURE I   AREA IN EACH CASE ONE
SQUARE MILE. CONVENTIONALLY ORIENTED WITH NORTH AT
TOP OF PAGE.

 CORN

 WOODLAND PASTURE

 HAY AND CLOVER

 WOODLAND

 VEGETABLES

 SCRUB AND CUT-OVER
BRUSHLAND

 APPLES, PEARS,
PEACHES, VINYARDS

 CHURCH
 STORE

 CLEARED PASTURE,
INCLUDING PASTURE
WITH SMALL BUSHES

 COUNTRY ESTATE
FACTORY
FARM BUILDINGS
URBAN RESIDENCE OR BLDG.

 BRUSH PASTURE

GRAVEL PIT

AREAS LEFT BLANK ARE THE YARDS OF URBAN HOMES,
FARM YARDS, LAWNS, ETC.

The internal structure of Millbury is similar to other towns along the Blackstone (Figure 7). Its commercial center is located in the valley bottom near the junction of the side valleys where roads join or cross. The mills are found along the streams near the water-power sites which gave them birth, and are scattered through the town from one end to the other like beads on a string. The residences, especially the better-class ones, prefer a location on the sides of the valley where these sides are not too steep. The outline of the town, however, strings out along the valley, altogether unlike the outline of towns on plains.

### Wilkinsonville

The little community of Wilkinsonville, just below Millbury along the main valley (Figure 8), may be taken as an example of the several one-factory towns.[47] The group of mill buildings is along the river, while the residence area is on one of the terraces of the valley bottom, never having reached sufficient size to climb far onto the steeper slopes. The rudimentary commercial center is found at the cross-roads along the main highway. At the present time, after a period of feverish activity during the war, the mills in this town are

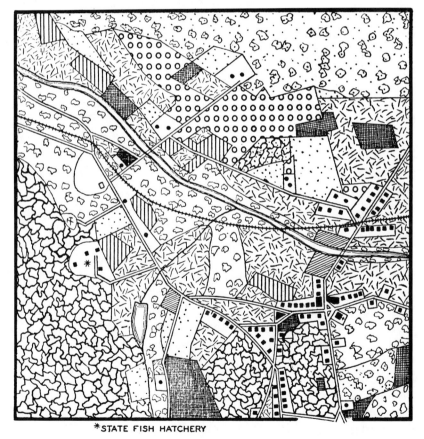

*STATE FISH HATCHERY

Fig. 8. Wilkinsonville and Vicinity.

closed and the few families still living in its residential area seek work elsewhere.

### The Urban Margins:
### Worcester South of Pakachoag Hill

The definition of the urban as opposed to the rural landscapes cannot, as yet, be stated in quantitative terms, although further study will no doubt make such a statement possible. The boundaries in this study are drawn on the basis of the qualitative combination of a number of criteria. House architecture is the most conspicuous feature; but since expanding city margins often include many converted farm houses, this form alone cannot be used without other checks. The occupation of the families using the houses is a criterion of importance; although in the Blackstone area this led to some confusion as many of the persons living in the country on farms sought work at certain seasons of the year in the towns, and usually, when this was the case, derived a large part if not the larger part of the family income in so doing. Another criterion may be found in the arrangement of the houses. Closely set homes, with small lots utilized for vegetable gardens or for hen yards, are obviously urban, while isolated farmhouses, with barns, sheds, and other outbuildings, and surrounded by extensive fields, are typically rural. Other criteria include the road pattern, the presence of street lights, and public utilities such as gas, water, sewers, etc. Then, too, the intent in ownership is in some cases critical, since it seems desirable to include platted real estate subdivisions where roads and other improvements have been already made, in the urban formation. It should be noted that only rarely is the political boundary of a city of any value as a geographic criterion.

In the Blackstone area the boundary between urban and rural landscapes is in most places fairly sharp and easily identified. Isolated urban houses are, it is true, found outside of the main body of the city, and in some cases farms are still found within the geographical city limits. A static city, such as most of the smaller ones in the Blackstone, generally has sharply defined limits, whereas an expanding city merges with the surrounding rural areas through a broad transition zone of relict farms within the city, and isolated suburban homes or platted subdivisions scattered through the country. Worcester has expanded in recent years into the cleared farmland on the upland south of Pakachoag Hill (Figure 9). In this section modern suburban homes of flimsy construction, closely packed together, rub elbows with a few scattered farmhouses now converted to urban uses, or maintained as farms in spite of the encroachment of the city. Of the latter there are few, for the value of such land in a growing residence section makes profitable farming impossible. Since the soil is a mellow loam in this area, much of

ON THE UPLAND SOUTH OF PAKACHOAG HILL

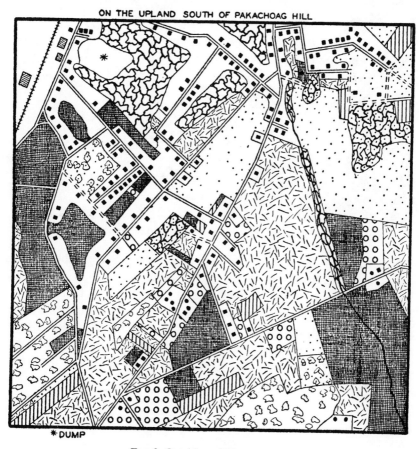

*DUMP

FIG. 9. Outskirts of Worcester.

FIG. 10. Manville and the southern margin of Woonsocket.

the peripheral farmlands are used for growing vegetables, with years of rotation in which they are planted to hay or clover. A large greenhouse and a creamery along the main road face growing ranks of urban homes. Farther back in the area occupied by the city, former pastures or farms not yet built up appear as idle brush land. However, small vegetable patches and orchards in the back yards of the urban homes tell of the attraction of the rural activities when they can be enjoyed on a modest scale.

## Woonsocket and Manville, Rhode Island

Woonsocket, too, is expanding, but, at least in a southerly direction, its expansion is not as vigorous as that of Worchester. Manville, located just below Woonsocket, has struggled up the sides of the narrow valley (Figure 10) both to the northeast and the southwest, but chiefly in the former direction. The suburbs of Woonsocket have already reached out and, on paper, have joined the northeastern edge of Manville. However, although the slope of the valley has been marked off into roads and house lots, little construction has yet taken place. The few homes which mark the outposts of the city are still reached by rudimentary streets with pretentious names, but have not yet been connected with sewers and gas. In the idle land beyond, irregular patches of vegetables are found, perhaps cultivated by squatters. The soil of this section is stoney and infertile, so that truck farming on a large scale is lacking. The farmland is in hay or pasture, while the steeper slopes and the marshy area along the small brook are left in scrubby timber.

## The Cleared Farmlands: Sutton

The expression of the cleared farmland varies with different conditions of site. On the upland, and especially in areas of loam soil, the cleared farmland appears somewhat as illustrated by the country north of Sutton (Figure 11). In order to present the description of this landscape quantitatively the following statistical analysis is used (Table 4). In the interpretation of these figures it is necessary to keep in mind that they do not represent simply the land use in an area of varied natural conditions. They measure, rather, the relative areal importance of the cover of an essentially uniform site. Because of the uniformity of the basic physical conditions, this analysis may be taken as the quantitative definition of a landscape formation.

The analysis shows that, in the square mile which was studied, fields of hay and cleared pastures make up almost half of the area, while about a quarter is covered with woods and brush.

CLEARED FARMLAND ON THE UPLAND

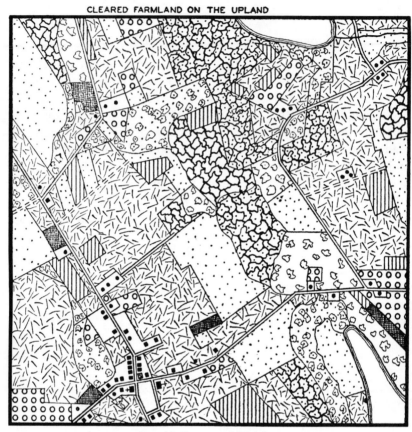

FIG. 11. Sutton and Vicinity.

New England farmland shows a close adjustment to surface and soil, not only in general, but also in detail.[48] The 27 percent of wood and brushland in the Sutton area is found almost exclusively in the small valley where the side slopes are steeper and stonier, and where the bottom is marshy. The hay fields and pastures are marked off as previously described into small units by the inherited stone walls, and along these walls there is such a thick growth of bushes and trees that one gains the impression of a larger amount of wooded land than actually exists. Small patches of corn, truck crops, and fruit orchards are scattered throughout the area. The village of Sutton itself is located at the intersection of two high-

TABLE 4

UPLAND NEAR SUTTON

(Cleared farmland and rural hamlet, on upland and drumlin. Soil: chiefly loam.)

| | |
|---|---|
| Hay | 35.1% |
| Cleared Pasture | 10.8 |
| Brush Pasture | 7.0 |
| Woodland Pasture | 10.4 |
| Scrub and Brushland | 6.0 |
| Woodland | 4.0 |
| Corn | 4.4 |
| Truck Crops | 1.0 |
| Orchards | 3.2 |
| Farmsteads–Village Land | 8.0 |
| Water | 3.0 |
| | 100.9 |
| All Pasture | 28.2% |
| All Woodland and Brushland | 27.4% |

ways. The road leading in from the northwest was formerly one of the chief traveled highways of this part of the country, following approximately the line of the old Indian trail, and not until railroads found an easier westward path by making deep cuts through intervening ridges did this road definitely lose its importance. At the present time, unlike the other roads on the upland, this road is paved, thus giving the village of Sutton, and the dairy and other farm products which originate in the neighborhood, an excellent connection with the valley markets through Millbury.

## Brigham Hill

The cleared farm landscape reaches the expression found in the neighborhood of Sutton only in areas of the better loam soils. Elsewhere, on the gentler intermediate slopes, in areas of sandy, gravelly, or stoney soils, the amount of land devoted to pasture increases at the expense of hay. Brigham Hill may serve as one example of this formation (Figure 12), a statistical analysis being presented in Table 5.

In this square mile, pasture—cleared, brush, and woodland—make up about 60 percent of the area. A little less than half is cov-

CLEARED FARMLAND ON INTERMEDIATE SLOPES

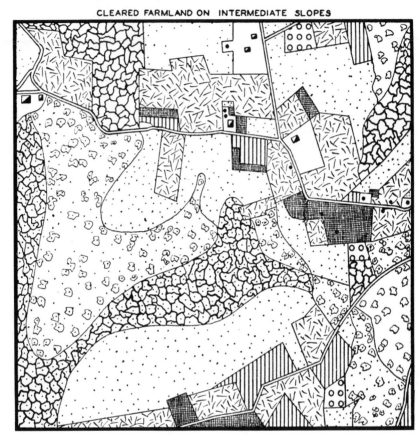

Fɪɢ. 12. Brigham Hill.

ered by woods or brush, most of the woodland being also pastured. The cultivated fields show a marked tendency to border the roads, leaving the area farther back in pasture, although this land may be physically as well suited to cultivation as the more accessible fields. A number of large estates appear in this study—beautiful houses surrounded by well-kept lawns, and utilizing the surrounding pasture lands for high-breed dairy cattle or horses.

Brigham Hill Farm itself, the second estate on the road entering Figure 12 in the northwest corner, has had an interesting and somewhat typical history. The oldest part of the present building was started in 1728, and took five years to complete. Timber from the farm itself was used, and the rocks which were dug out of the

TABLE 5

Hᴏʟʟʏ Cᴏᴜɴᴛʀʏ Aʀᴏᴜɴᴅ Bʀɪɢʜᴀᴍ Hɪʟʟ
(Cleared farmland with country estates, on intermediate slopes.
Soil: stoney fine sandy loams, chiefly Gloucester.)

| | |
|---|---|
| Hay | 16.3% |
| Cleared Pasture | 26.6 |
| Brush Pasture | 19.8 |
| Woodland Pasture | 12.7 |
| Scrub and Brushland | 3.8 |
| Woodland | 6.6 |
| Corn | 4.3 |
| Truck Crops | 3.6 |
| Orchards | 0.8 |
| Estate Grounds and Buildings | 2.5 |
| | 97.0 |
| | |
| All Pasture | 59.1% |
| All Woodland and Brushland | 42.9% |

fields were used for the foundations and for the large stone walls. For approximately a century the farm was profitable, but about 1825 its rocky soils began keenly to feel the competition of better areas in the immediate neighborhood. The farm was handed down in the Brigham family, being gradually divided into smaller and smaller units. The present owner, having retired from business, now lives on the original farm which does no more than pay for its up-keep. On the three hundred acres which remain, the owner, using hired labor, raises about eighty tons of hay a year, sells small amounts of cabbage and sweet corn in the Worcester markets, where he also sends the milk from his herd of dairy cattle. While the buildings still perform in a certain way a farm function, they are more properly classified as belonging to a country estate, since without the support of money earned elsewhere they would no longer be kept in repair or perhaps even in use. In almost every case, large, prosperous looking farms in rural New England are found to be maintained in this way.

### The Farmland North of Pawtucket

The remnants of the New England peneplain become fewer and of less extent as one goes southward into Rhode Island. Similarly, the

CLEARED FARMLAND ON THE INTERMEDIATE SLOPE

*LIME QUARRY

FIG. 13. Intermediate slope north of Pawtucket.

loam soils of the upland are encountered less frequently. Although no soil survey is available for the Rhode Island section, observation leads us to the belief that the soils are distinctly stonier and less fertile than the soils farther north. The cleared farmland of this part of our area should, then, exhibit the expression typical of these smoother intermediate slopes with stoney soils, such as was illustrated by the Brigham Hill study. In the square mile surveyed a little north of the outskirts of Pawtucket (Figure 13), the statistical analysis (Table 6) shows the expected resemblance.

Pasture, by a significant coincidence, occupies the same percentage of the area, and the amount of land left in woods or brush

TABLE 6

HILLY COUNTRY NORTH OF PAWTUCKET

(Cleared farmland, on intermediate slopes. Soil: stoney and gravelly, sandy loams.)

| | |
|---|---|
| Hay | 21.6% |
| Cleared Pasture | 29.9 |
| Brush Pasture | 10.4 |
| Woodland Pasture | 19.4 |
| Scrub and Brushland | 0.9 |
| Woodland | 5.7 |
| Corn | 2.3 |
| Truck Crops | 1.6 |
| Orchards | 2.4 |
| Farmsteads | 3.1 |
| Water | 1.9 |
| | 98.8 |
| All Pasture | 59.7% |
| All Woodland and Brushland | 36.4% |

is comparable. The small amount of agriculture, in spite of the proximity of a large city, reflects the poverty of the soil, and forms an interesting contrast with the loam soil upland south of Pakachoag Hill, where soils are relatively fertile. The cultivated fields, as common to this landscape formation, show a marked tendency to border the roads.

If we may apply these topographic studies to the formations shown on Figure 4, we may say that about 65 percent of the cleared farmland occurs on the intermediate slopes, and therefore has an aspect similar to that described for Brigham Hill and the outskirts of Pawtucket (see Table 3), whereas only about a quarter is of the type illustrated by the Sutton study. However, the cleared farmland has a third expression which is of growing importance, and which reflects the influence of the urban landscape most vividly. This is the large-scale fruit and truck farming, located for the most part on the upland.

### The Fruit and Truck Farming Expression: Fisk Farms

Along the hill top south of Grafton a large-scale fruit and truck farm enterprise has been started (Figure 14). The exposure and air

**✳FARM HOUSES ABANDONED**

FIG. 14. Upland and slopes south of Grafton.

drainage as well as the loam soil are favorable for the growth of
apples, pears, and peaches. The Fisk Brothers, owners of the farms,
are fruit and vegetable wholesalers in Providence, to which city the
products of these farms are sent by motor truck. On the five
hundred acres near Grafton, a part of which appears in our topographic study, most of the land is devoted to apples, with smaller
amounts planted with pears and peaches, and with still smaller
fields of cabbages, sweet corn, tomatoes, celery, beans, and other
truck crops. At the present time new land is being cleared of woods
and brush and planted with apples. At its easternmost extent, the
orchard area has reached the end of the upland and of the area of
loam (Figures 1 and 2), and further expansion in that direction will

be stopped by the steep slopes and thin, stoney soils below. Expansion southward along the ridge top, however, will be relatively easy. The Fisk Farm employs a regular force of seventeen men, and during harvest time drafts the services of between seventy and ninety. Judging from the upkeep of the buildings and the lands alone the business is a profitable one, and of a type which is rapidly spreading in rural New England. The same company operates another similar fruit farm on the upland a little east of Sutton. In every case where large-scale orcharding is proving successful, the trees are set out on hill tops or upper slopes, as, for example, the orchards on the drumlin northwest of Wilkinsonville (Figure 8). Apparently a marketing organization—in the case of the Fisk Brothers, concentrated in the hands of one company in a large city—is all that is needed to make at least a small part of the New England farmlands again productive. However, judging from other areas, some prediction can be made regarding the development of this truck farming and orcharding expression. At the present time, it occupies almost exclusively those areas best suited to orchard culture, under which conditions it may be considered as in a first stage of adjustment. As the possibilities of deriving profits from such an industry become apparent, more and more land will be devoted to orchards and truck farms, but in this expansion land not so well suited to such uses will be occupied. This may be considered as a second stage. Later, the lands which are unsuitable because of poor soil, liability to early and late frosts, difficult accessibility, or other reasons will be abandoned, and this expression will become more permanently adjusted to the better areas, but with more intensive methods of cultivation than are practiced at present. This may be thought of as a third stage.[49] The individual disaster and suffering which is brought about by a too rapid or too wide expansion is one of the unfortunate aspects of this progress from the second to the third stage.

### The Woodland Landscapes:
### A Study of West Whitinsville

Areally speaking, the two most important types of cover—cleared farmland and woodland—are about equally divided (Table 1). As we have already pointed out, much of the present woodland was once cleared and cultivated. The woods at the present time are found to a marked extent occupying the steeper and stonier lands, nearly 90 percent being located on the rougher intermediate slopes (Table 3).

The woodland landscape on these stoney slopes may be illustrated by a square mile lying on the intermediate slopes west of Whitinsville, an area of thin, gravelly soil alternating with marshy stretches along the narrow brook bottoms (Figure 15). The statistics for this landscape stand in interesting contrast to those of the

WOODLAND ON THE INTERMEDIATE SLOPE

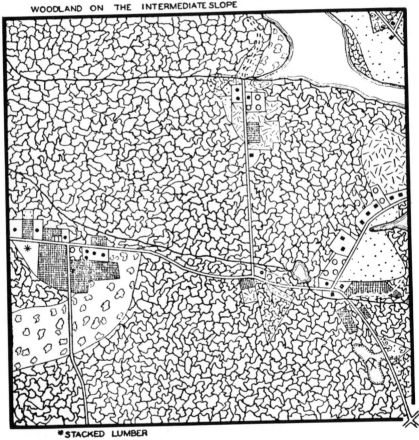

*STACKED LUMBER

FIG. 15. Intermediate slope west of Whitinsville.

cleared farmlands (Table 7). In the first place 78 percent is un-grazed woodland, and only about 12 percent is cleared. Crops and pasture, therefore, form only small percentages of the whole. The trees are mostly hardwoods, generally too small in this area for use as timber. However, much of the woodlands has been thinned for firewood, and piles of logs are found at many places along the roads.

TABLE 7

HILLY COUNTRY WEST OF WHITINSVILLE
(Woodland, on intermediate slopes.
Soil: stoney, sandy, and gravelly loams, with narrow belts of meadow.)

| Hay | 2.5% |
|---|---|
| Cleared Pasture | 4.0 |
| Brush Pasture | 0.4 |
| Woodland Pasture | 1.5 |
| Scrub and Brushland | 5.2 |
| Woodland | 78.1 |
| Corn | — |
| Truck Crops | 2.4 |
| Orchards | 0.7 |
| Farmsteads | 2.0 |
| Water | 3.0 |
| | 99.8 |
| Cleared Land | 11.6% |

Small areas are found where the whole forest has been recently removed, leaving only a waste brush land, not even suitable for grazing, as in the semicircular belt near the southwest corner of Figure 15. The old sawdust piles in such areas of brush, even after the cords of firewood have been removed, reveal the earlier pres-ence of at least a scrub forest. Apparently it takes only a few years, about twenty or twenty-five at the most, for brushlands or aban-doned farmlands to grow up with dense stands of poor timber.

The clearings which are found within the woodland landscape are miniatures of the larger body of cleared farmland outside. So common is this inclusion of small detached pieces of a larger land-scape formation within the body of a neighboring formation that the term "ectochore" is proposed for them. In the area of this study, the ectochore lying just west of Burt's Pond (the body of

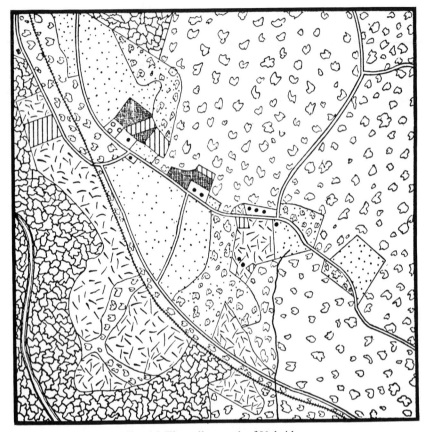

FIG. 16. The valley south of Uxbridge.

water near the northeastern corner) has had an interesting and typical history. The farm in this clearing was built in 1786, requiring several years for its construction from local timber. It was on this land that the irrigation system described earlier was built to increase the yields of grain. A large herd of dairy cattle was kept on the extensive cleared pastures, and the farm was reputed to be among the most prosperous in the neighborhood. With the gradual decline in agricultural prosperity, however, the farm was gradually abandoned, and finally stopped production in 1880. The present owner points out areas now densely forested which in those days were used for pasture. After living for a time in the city, he returned to the farm in 1919, clearing off some of the growth of brush by using sheep. At the present time, the owner works in the shops at Whitinsville nearby, raising on his small farm about ten tons of hay, and keeping two cows, a horse, and some poultry. Here again, it is found that the major part of the family's income is derived from work in the city—a condition which is probably widespread in this part of rural New England.

The boundary between the cleared farmland and the woodland formations is, in most cases, sharply defined and easily recognized. This is illustrated by a study along the valley, a little south of Uxbridge (Figure 16). Here the cleared farmland, chiefly hay and pasture, is clearly set off from the brushland. At one time there was an ectochore of farmland along the road which extends toward the northeast corner of the map but, this having been abandoned and the house having burned down, is today scarcely distinguishable. Recently the woods were cut, so that the bulk of the area is waste brushland, covering a thin, stoney soil.

## CONCLUSION

Thus the landscapes of the Blackstone area are made up of a complex of cultural impressions set one upon the other. The three chief cultures, the native Indian, the rural European, and the urban manufacturing, have each modified the natural setting in a unique and characteristic way. Forms developed by the Indian culture are visible even today in the shell mounds, the deposits of chipped stones and broken utensils, or the scarcely discernible trails. The forms of the rural European culture are visible on every side, some of them continuing without change of function to the present, others significantly modified in their use, and others remaining as weather-beaten ruins or brush-entangled fields to tell of a period which exists no more. In the course of time, however, the cleared farmland landscape has developed different expressions in different situations. Only the graded uplands with their loam soils exhibit the characteristics of the area around Sutton. On the stonier intermediate slopes, many of the cleared fields are no longer planted to crops, but are used instead for pasture, and in many cases are growing up with brush. Where the surface is very rough and the soil thin, the complete abandonment of the land for either crops or grazing is common, and a scrubby woodland, thinned for firewood, now dominates the landscape. In a few places, an entirely new expression of the cleared farmlands is appearing under the influence of the city markets, namely, the large-scale orchard or truck farm. Finally, the urban landscape, in spite of its relatively small area, has come to occupy the position of commanding importance around which the economy of the region is oriented. Yet change still continues. The urban landscape, too, reached a zenith of growth and prosperity, and is now gradually shrinking in the smaller, less effectively located units, and concentrating in the better and larger units, where production is maintained by a more intense and efficient activity.

It seems probable that the present tendency to concentrate in the larger cities will continue for some time, leading perhaps eventually to the complete loss of urban function by the smaller single-mill towns. With the concentration of the people in cities, especially as those cities are located in the midst of a hilly land with poor soils, the railroad connections with other parts of the country and with the sea ports, and the paved highways must continue to grow in importance, for over these must pass not only the exported manufactured products, but also the imported raw materials and food-stuffs. The large-scale orcharding which is now beginning is due for a rapid over-development, followed later by a decline of the poorly located farms, and a concentration of such activity in the better areas. The cleared farmland expression found near Sutton will be modified no doubt by an increase of area in fruit and truck. In another half-century, abandoned orchards will be listed with abandoned crop and pasture land on the poorer areas as a relict form. Eventually the definite use of such lands for timber production and recreation may come to be widespread.

NOTES

1. W. M. Davis, "The Physical Geography of Southern New England," *Nat. Geogr. Soc. Monograph* (New York, 1896).

2. W. C. Alden, *The Physical Features of Central Massachusetts* (U.S. Geological Survey: Bulletin 760-B, 1924), pp. 155 ff.

3. *Ibid.,* p. 20.

4. B. K. Emerson, *Geology of Massachusetts and Rhode Island* (U.S. Geological Survey: Bulletin 597, 1917), p. 26.

5. W. C. Alden, *Central Massachusetts,* p. 56.

6. From *Summary of Climatological Data by Sections,* Sec. 105, U.S. Weather Bureau.

7. Atlas of American Agriculture, Part II, Climate, Sec. 1, *Frost and Growing Season* (Washington, D.C., 1920).

8. X. H. Goodnough, "Rainfall in New England," *Journal of New England Water Works Association,* 40, 178–247.

9. *Summary of Climatological Data.*

10. W. Köppen, *Die Klimate der Erde* (Leipzig, 1923).

11. W. Lincoln and C. C. Baldwin, "History of the County of Worcester," *The Worcester Magazine and Historical Journal,* 1 and 2 (Worcester, 1826), 86.

12. *Ibid.,* p. 129.

13. J. C. Crane, "The Nipmucks and Their Country," *Worcester Society of Antiquities,* 1897.

14. G. W. Ellis and J. E. Morris, *King Philip's War* (New York, 1906), p. 12.

15. L. B. Chase, "Early Indian Trails Through Tantiusque," *Quinabaug Historical Society Leaflets,* 1, 78.

16. G. K. Dresser, *The Indians of This Locality,* pp. 108–109.

17. *Ibid.,* p. 111. Also L. B. Chase, "Early Indian Trails," p. 73.

18. *Centennial History of the Town of Millbury, Massachusetts* (Millbury, 1915), p. 27.

19. Chase, "Early Indian Trails," pp. 69–84. Also, L. B. Chase, "Interpretation of Woodward's and Saffery's Map of 1642, or the Earliest Bay Path," *Quinabaug Historical Society Leaflets,* 1, 85–98, with map.

20. L. B. Chase, *The Bay Path and Along the Way* (Boston, 1919), pp. 185, 191.

21. Chase, "Early Indian Trails," p. 81. Also, Lincoln and Baldwin, *History of Worcester,* p. 113.

22. Lincoln and Baldwin, History of Worcester, pp. 164, 193.

23. Ellis and Morris, *King Philip's War,* p. 6.

24. W. A. Emerson, *History of the Town of Douglas, Massachusetts* (Boston, 1879), pp. 17–18.

25. Lincoln and Baldwin, *History of Worcester,* p. 139 ff.

26. W. B. Weeden, *Economic and Social History of New England* (Boston, 1891), p. 283.

27. *Yearbook,* U.S. Dept. of Agriculture, 1924, article on hay, p. 298.

28. R. M. Harper, "Changes in the Forest Area of New England in Three Centuries," *Journal of Forestry,* 16 (1918), 442–62. Also, note in the *Geographical Review,* 7 (1919), 50.

29. M. Keir, *Manufacturing Industries in America* (New York, 1920), p. 145.

30. J. T. Adams, *New England in the Republic, 1776–1850* (Boston, 1926), pp. 110–18.

31. *Centennial History of Millbury,* pp. 110–18.

32. P. Whitney, in his *History of Worcester County* (Worcester, 1793), enu-

merates the following industries in Millbury: a paper mill, a linseed oil mill, ten grist-mills, six sawmills, three fulling mills, seven triphammers, five scythe- and axe-makers, one hoe-maker, several nail factories, and six potash factories. Quoted in *Centennial History of Millbury*, p. 82.

33. Keir, *Manufacturing Industries*, p. 63.

34. Pawtucket Chamber of Commerce figures.

35. *Centennial History of Millbury*, pp. 117–18.

36. M. Keir, "Some Influences of the Sea Upon the Industries of New England," *Geographical Review*, 5 (1918), 403.

37. *Centennial History of Millbury*, p. 131.

38. "The New England Economic Situation," *Harvard Undergraduate Economic Studies* (New York, 1927). Also, Keir, *Manufacturing Industries*.

39. Note in the *Geographical Review*, 7 (1919), 50.

40. For an elaboration of this viewpoint, see C. O. Sauer, "The Morphology of Landscape," *University of California Publications in Geography*, 2, 2 (October, 1925).

41. W. J. Latimer, R. F. R. Martin, and M. O. Lanphear, *Soil Survey of Worcester County, Massachusetts* (U.S. Dept. of Agriculture, 1927), p. 1572.

42. *Ibid.*, p. 1566.

43. *Topography* is used in this paper in the original sense used by the U.S. Geological Survey and given in the dictionary: the detailed description of a particular place, not only as regards its surface forms, but also the other forms of its landscape. Topography, then, is in a series with chorography, the description of a larger area or region, and geography, the description of the earth or a major part of it.

44. *Centennial History of Millbury*, p. 240.

45. *Ibid.*, pp. 240–89.

46. From a Map of Millbury and Vicinity in 1851, by Walling and Harkness.

47. Figures 7–16 were surveyed in the field during the summer of 1927. The location of these representative areas is shown on Figure 1.

48. I. G. Davis, and C. I. Hendrickson, *Soil Type as a Factor in Farm Economy, The Town of Lebanon*. Bulletin 139, Agricultural Experiment Station (Storrs, Connecticut, 1926).

49. P. E. James, "A Geographic Reconnaissance of Trinidad," *Economical Geography*, 3 (1927), 108.

# 6

## REGIONAL PLANNING IN THE JACKSON HOLE COUNTRY

Too many regional plans and too many regional planners have succeeded only in stalling the process of settlement in the Jackson Hole country of western Wyoming. This situation is the result of the impact of two opposed projects: one that looks toward the progress of settlement and the shift from cattle ranching to more intensive forms of economy; and another that calls for the removal of the settlement already established, the return of the area to its natural state, and the maintenance in it of herds of wild game. Thus there has been created an economic and political situation for which a compromise is difficult to discover.

### THE LAND

The territory involved in these matters is an intermontane basin, some forty miles long by eight miles wide, lying at an elevation of six thousand to seven thousand feet in the midst of the Rocky Mountains of western Wyoming, just to the south of Yellowstone National Park. On its west side Jackson Hole is overshadowed by the abrupt and imposing front of the Teton Range, a block of ancient crystalline rocks tipped toward the west. The sharp pinnacles of crumbling rock, excavated on the upstanding edge of this block by the valley glaciers of the Pleistocene, reach elevations of more than thirteen thousand feet. Towering seven thousand feet above the floor of the basin, they provide some of the finest alpine scenery

Reprinted from *Geographical Review*, 26, 3 (July 1936), 439–53. Six photographs in the original publication are not reproduced here.

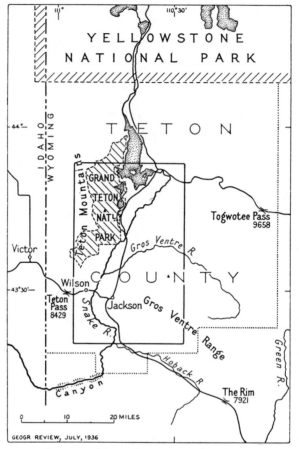

Fig. 1. Location map of the Jackson Hole region. Scale 1:2,000,000.

of the western United States. Some small glaciers still exist on the east side of the range.[1] The east side of Jackson Hole, on the other hand, is bordered by the Gros Ventre Mountains, which rise more gradually through a wide zone of foothills to summits between ten thousand and twelve thousand feet above sea level, but placed well to the east and south. These and other, smaller ranges, together with the high Yellowstone Plateau to the north, combine effectively to isolate the Jackson Hole country. Even the Snake River, which drains the basin, departs southward through a narrow, winding canyon.

This asymmetry of the east and west borders of Jackson Hole is a fundamental feature of the area. Within the basin itself are corresponding contrasts between the eastern and western parts. On the west side the glaciers from the Teton Range extended beyond the mouths of the mountain valleys and left a number of marginal lakes behind morainic festoons along the mountain front (Figure 2).[2] Glaciation was active in the Gros Ventre Range also, but because the cirques on this side lie so far to the east, the glaciers failed to emerge from the mountain valleys. From both sides came floods of coarse outwash gravels which covered the floor of the Hole to a great depth, but those from the Gros Ventre side, being farther from the ends of the glaciers, contain a slightly larger proportion of fine material mixed with the cobble. Whatever may have been the original character of the basin floor, it was leveled off by this accumulation of gravel; only three steep-sided buttes stand conspicuously above the outwash. Then, during the late stages of the Glacial period, a thin covering of loess fell, chiefly on the east side, and from some of the Gros Ventre valleys postglacial alluvial fans are extending over the outwash. Thus the regolith on the east side is not quite so coarse as that on the west, and no rough morainic surfaces border the mountain front.[3]

The drainage, too, is asymmetrically developed. The Snake River, from the outlet of Jackson Lake to the south end of the basin where this river enters its canyon, forms somewhat of a median line, lying, however, a little to the west of the exact center. On its west side the river receives only short, turbulent tributaries descending almost directly from the relict glaciers high on the cirque walls; on its east side, on the contrary, the Snake is joined by several large tributaries with extensive drainage basins, the largest of which is the Gros Ventre River.

## THE COURSE OF SETTLEMENT

The occupance of this country by the cattle ranchers developed a pattern that also reflects this basic asymmetry. The first people to establish themselves permanently on the land came, in 1883, from the Mormon settlements of Utah and Idaho. Forming a back eddy

# JACKSON HOLE

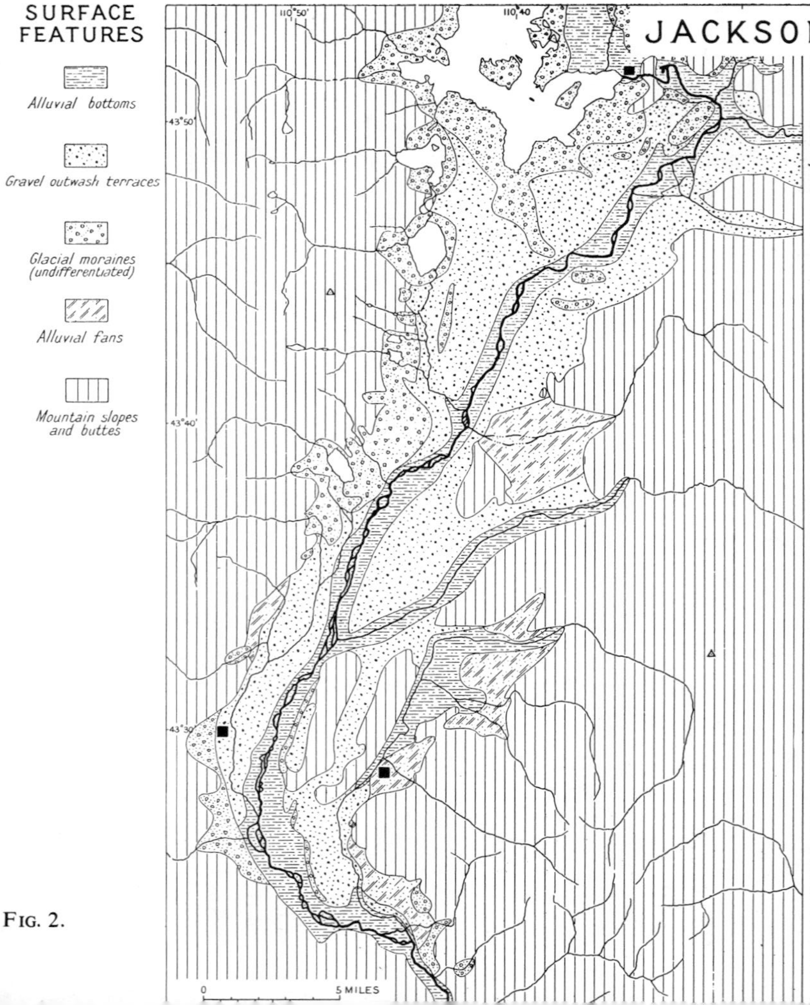
SURFACE FEATURES
Alluvial bottoms
Gravel outwash terraces
Glacial moraines (undifferentiated)
Alluvial fans
Mountain slopes and buttes
110°50'
110°40
43°50'
43°40'
43°30'
0
5 MILES

FIG. 2.

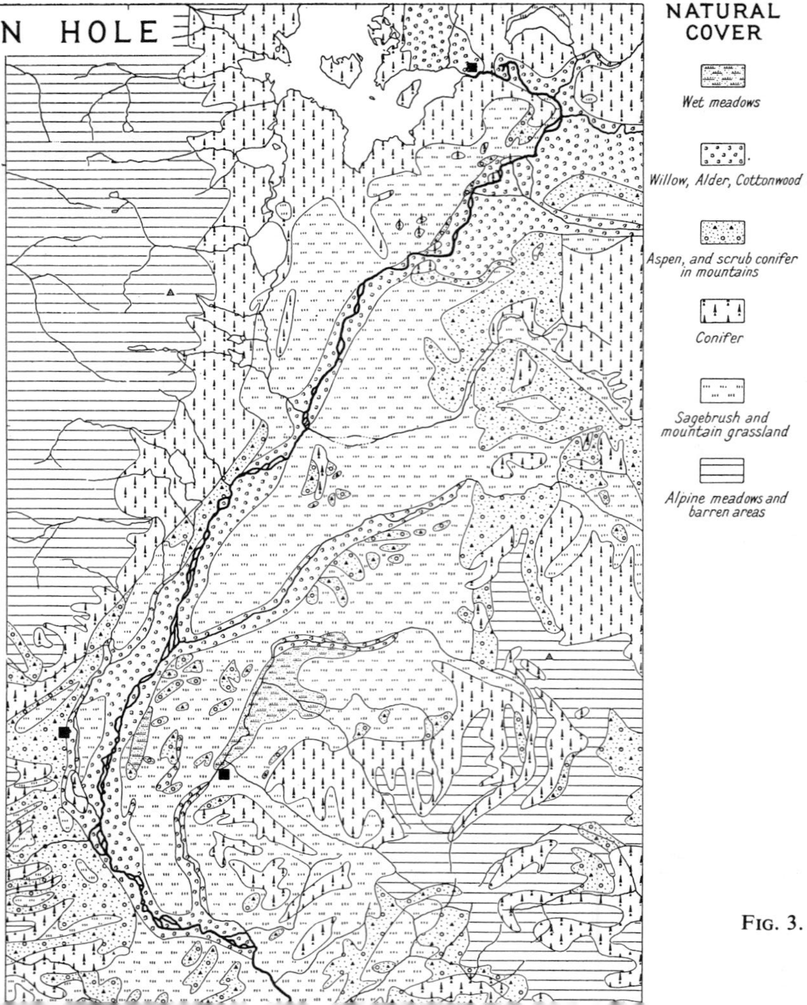
NATURAL COVER
Wet meadows
Willow, Alder, Cottonwood
Aspen, and scrub conifer in mountains
Conifer
Sagebrush and mountain grassland
Alpine meadows and barren areas

FIG. 3.

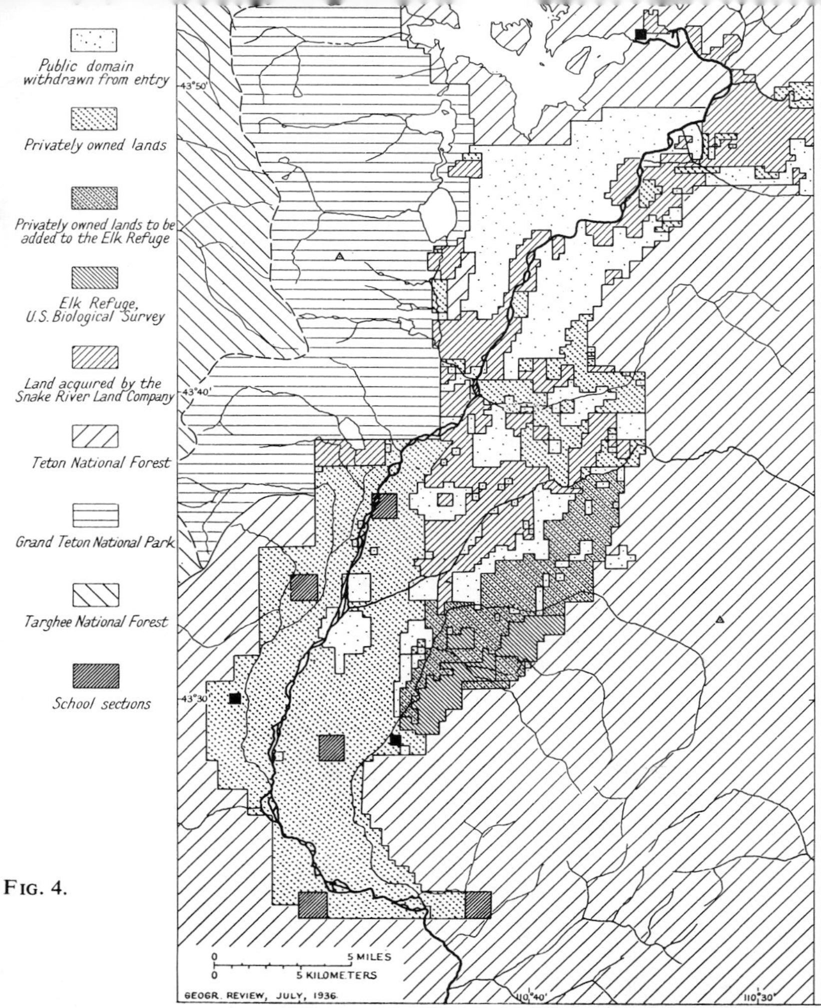

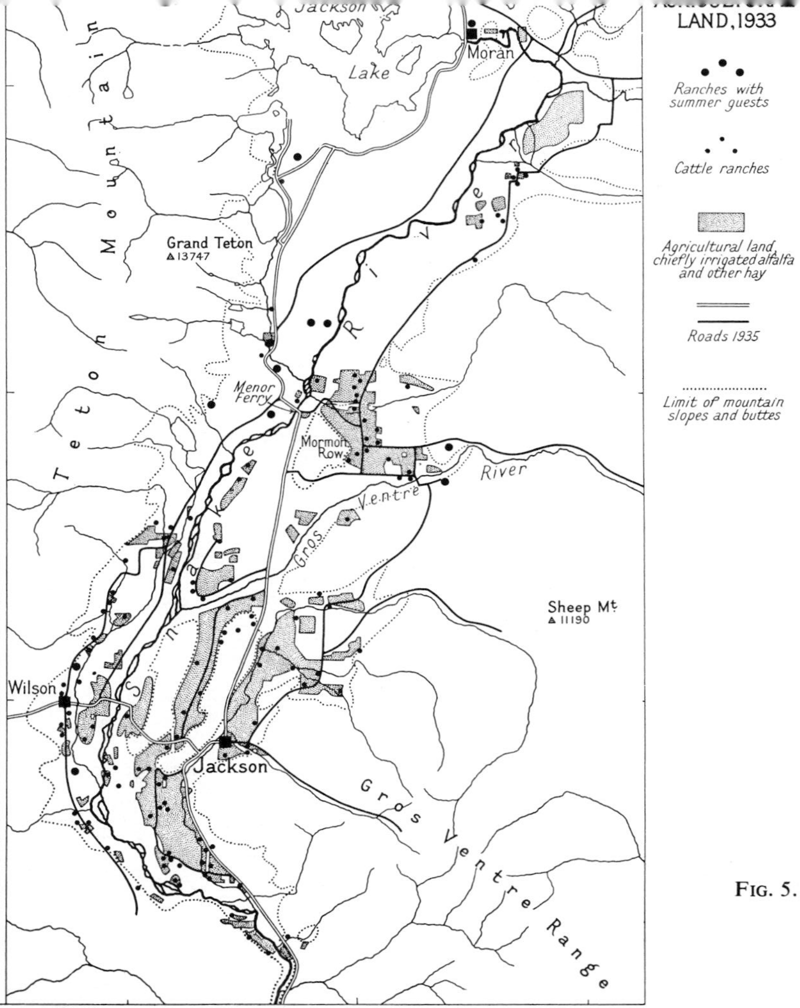

LAND, 1933

● ● ●  Ranches with
      summer guests

∴ ∴ ∴  Cattle ranches

▦  Agricultural land,
   chiefly irrigated alfalfa
   and other hay

═══  Roads 1935

⋯⋯  Limit of mountain
    slopes and buttes

FIG. 5.

Jackson
Lake

Moran

Snake River

Grand Teton
▲ 13747

Menor Ferry

Mormon Row

Gros Ventre River

Gros Ventre

Sheep Mt.
▲ 11190

Gros Ventre Range

Teton Mountain

Jackson

Wilson

Public domain
withdrawn from entry

Privately owned lands

Privately owned lands to be
added to the Elk Refuge

Elk Refuge,
U.S. Biological Survey

Land acquired by the
Snake River Land Company

Teton National Forest

Grand Teton National Park

Targhee National Forest

School sections

110°30'

43°50'

43°40'

43°30'

0        5 MILES

0    5 KILOMETERS

GEOGR. REVIEW, JULY, 1936

FIG. 4.

in the prevailing westward course of migration, two families with a hundred head of cattle crossed the Teton Pass and entered what had been up to that time wild territory—a haven for hunters, trappers, and fugitives from the law. These first homesteaders crossed to the east side of the Hole and chose a place near the present site of the town of Jackson because there the heavy winter snows are not quite so deep as in the western and northern parts of the area and because of the presence of a natural meadow of wild hay (Figure 3). The cattle herd passed the winter in the open on this meadow.

The following years saw a rapidly increasing stream of new settlers pouring into Jackson Hole. They came not only from the Mormon group in Utah and Idaho but also from various parts of the eastern United States. The chief period of increasing population was from 1889 to 1909: by 1909 it was estimated that there were some fifteen hundred people in the basin. Nearly all of them were cattle ranchers, feeding their animals during the summer in the Gros Ventre Mountains and maintaining them through the winter on wild or cultivated hay.

For a number of reasons this ranching occupance followed the example of the firstcomers and concentrated in the eastern part of the basin (Figure 5). Unfortunately, snow measurements are not available for the various parts of the area, but local testimony confirms unanimously the statement that the snowfall is much deeper along the west side than on the east and somewhat deeper in the north than in the south. Then, too, the east side, where the supply of water is more abundant, can be irrigated in general more successfully. The Snake in its course through Jackson Hole is so deeply incised below the lowest terrace of the series cut by the river since the Glacial period that use of its water for irrigation is difficult here, and most of the local water supply must come from the tributaries. These, as has been pointed out, are largest and most dependable on the east side. Furthermore, the somewhat finer regolith on the east side of the basin retains moisture better.

In fact, the porosity of the regolith constitutes one of the chief problems of the agricultural use of the land. The climatic data available in the area, chiefly from Jackson and Moran (Figure 5), indicate no deficiency of moisture. The average annual rainfall at

Jackson for the period 1924–33 was 15.3 inches (ranging from 11.7 in 1933 to 21.2 in 1930). At the relatively low temperatures of the area this amount is enough to class the station among the humid climates (Dfb for Jackson, Dfc for Moran).[4] The natural vegetation on the outwash gravel is sagebrush, which in this case is edaphic rather than climatic in its requirement. Good stands of lodgepole pine mark the more compact glacial moraines (Figure 3). This porosity of the outwash gravels requires the irrigation of cultivated hay in most parts of the area. Also, where irrigation has raised the water table almost to the surface it has created new meadows of wild hay, similar to those that existed previously where natural conditions had created a high water table, as near Jackson (Figure 3). In a climate really deficient in moisture such spots would have been ruined by the accumulation of alkali.

## PROBLEMS AND PATTERNS OF CIRCULATION

The rectangular plan of the General Land Office has controlled the pattern of settlement in this country. To be sure, the first routes of travel were developed unsystematically across the sagebrush flats, shifting from time to time with changing currents of circulation. The topographic map, surveyed in 1899,[5] is of little use today as far as roads are concerned, so great has been the shifting. The fencing of the ranch lands increasingly forced the roads into the standard rectangular arrangement. The two main north-south roads, however, still preserve their irregular courses (Figure 5).

Roads were built, and later improved, over the Teton Pass (8,-429 feet), the Rim (7,921 feet), Togwotee Pass (9,658 feet), and northward into Yellowstone Park (Figure 1), but every winter they are blocked for five or six months by deep snows. For many months the only contact with the outside world is by airplane. To reach a market in the fall the cattle are driven some thirty miles over the Teton Pass to the railroad at Victor, Idaho. The paving of some of these roads in recent years has been stimulated by the increasing number of automobile tourists entering Yellowstone from the south. In the winter of 1935–36 funds to keep the Hoback and Teton Pass roads open the year round were made available for the first time.

The isolation of the area was the reason for the creation of Teton County with a county seat at Jackson. Although the population and taxable values were still well below the minimum required for the establishment of a county in Wyoming, in 1922 a special act of the state legislature gave the people of Jackson Hole a government center that they could reach throughout the year.


WILD GAME

Meanwhile an important shift was taking place in the distribution of the wild game. The elk, originally a plains animal, were slowly being driven farther and farther into the mountains by the advance of settlement. Before the arrival of the ranchers in Jackson Hole a large herd of these animals was accustomed to spend the summer on the wild-hay meadows of the basin and on the north-facing slopes of the buttes and lower Gros Ventre foothills, where there are patches of aspen or pine shading a grassy floor. During the winter the animals migrated southward into the Green River country. By the last decade of the nineteenth century, however, the Green River basin had been occupied to such an extent that the elk were forced to seek even more isolated pastures. At the present time their migrations are fairly well fixed. During the summer they are found only in the higher pastures of the Gros Ventre Mountains or farther north, in the Yellowstone, but during the winter they seek refuge on the hay meadows of Jackson Hole, especially in places where they are fed, and on the south-facing slopes of the buttes and foothills. As a result many of the slopes have been grazed bare of their scanty vegetation cover, and all are marked by the familiar terracelike trails. There is even more contrast now than formerly between the generally wooded shady slopes, which one sees in a view toward the south, and the very dry-looking sunny slopes, which one observes toward the north.

The presence of this large herd of elk together with a great variety of other game animals and an abundance of fish gave the mountains and basins of western Wyoming a considerable reputation for hunting and fishing. Attracted by the wildlife and also by the spectacular natural scenery, an increasing number of people came to the area for recreation rather than permanent settlement. In fact, many of the later settlers first came as hunters. "Dude ranching" and hunting became important sources of revenue, in some cases independent of the cattle business, but more often as a profitable sideline. One or two of the dude ranches achieved a national reputation and attracted each year a number of eastern visitors of wealth and position. Climbers were increasingly drawn to the Tetons. "This superb range is at last coming into its own among mountaineers." [6] The beauties of Jackson Hole and its magnificent Teton Range were widely heralded.

### Projects for the Preservation
### of the Natural Scenery

The various projects for preserving the natural scenery can be attributed largely to the eastern visitors. Unlike those of the Yellowstone country, these projects were conceived in the Jackson Hole region after ranching settlement had already become established— too late, therefore, for the acquisition of uninterrupted territory for recreational purposes. The supporters of the projects were, and are, obviously led by a variety of motives. Some are sincere idealists, filled with an almost religious zeal for the preservation of the natural scene—witness the little log chapel at Menor Ferry, with its plate-glass window behind the altar through which the majestic Tetons can be seen by the worshipers. Some motives, however, are more mundane. And the plans set forth are as varied as the motives. Some favor park extension; others are opposed to park extension but favor some other form of administration for lands devoted exclusively to recreation. The original plan, it seems, contemplated the creation of a "national recreation area," to include the entire basin and its bordering mountains.[7] The plans actually put into operation, however, represent a compromise between this larger concept and the interests of those settlers who have resisted the movement to "buy them out."

These various recreational developments within the basin have had their most successful expansion on the west side. Some time before park extension was seriously discussed cheaper forms of recreation service had made their appearance, especially on the margins of the lakes at the base of the Tetons: a dance hall, a number of second-rate tourist cabins, a rodeo field, a succession of hot-dog stands along the highway, and the familiar advertisements. These things were not exactly in harmony with the background of forest, lake, and mountain. To many they constituted nothing less than a sacrilege, and much of the support for park extension sprang from a desire to eliminate them. In 1929 the Grand Teton National Park was created, with boundaries drawn to include the mountain peaks and the fringe of marginal lakes and moraines within Jackson Hole proper (Figure 4).

The presence of these various recreational developments has had its effect on the pattern of circulation. Had Jackson Hole remained a purely ranching country, the main highway in all probability would have followed the east side of the basin. As it is now, the main surfaced road through the area follows the eastern route for part of the distance and the western route for the remainder. In the south the concentration of political and commercial interests serves to bring the main roads to a focus on the east side at Jackson. But proceeding northward the main road crosses to the west side at the Menor Ferry Bridge, leads to the borders of the national park, and thence returns eastward to follow the eastern shores of Jackson Lake.

Meanwhile a considerable movement was a foot to provide increased protection and more winter feed for the now growing elk herd. As early as 1918 parts of the public domain not yet taken up by homesteaders were beginning to be removed from entry. Several subsequent withdrawals eventually closed to settlement most of the territory on the east side of the basin north of the town of Jackson. A bill in the United States Congress provided for the addition of a considerable area to the holdings of the Biological Survey, under whose care the elk herd was placed. The Survey, which deprecates the feeding practice as degrading, suggests the addition of more land for maintenance of the herd under natural conditions at about twenty thousand head.[8]

These various plans and projects might have accomplished relatively little, however, had it not been for a gift of some two million dollars from Mr. John D. Rockefeller, Jr., for the aid of park extension. With the money the Snake River Land Company was incorporated, and through its agents it began the evaluation and purchase of ranching properties throughout the northern part of the basin, chiefly north of the Gros Ventre River. A large part of the settlement has now been removed from this territory—removed so completely that only when viewed from the air or from the summit of one of the buttes can the faint traces of the occupance patterns be discerned. A conspicuous though interrupted "island" of settlers has been left in so-called Mormon Row, on land that has been described as the most fertile of the whole basin.

Thus the normal course of settlement has been retarded. The cattlemen have found their summer pastures in the mountains restricted in favor of the elk; new settlers seeking either ranch lands or summer homes have found the public domain closed to entry: yet the groups interested in park extension have found a strong opposition on the part of those, especially, who realize that the withdrawal of so much land from the taxpaying category will render impossible the continuation of county government in Teton County. During the two decades from 1910 to 1930 the population of Jackson Hole increased only 480, to 1,980, still below the three thousand required for the support of a county government. If a reservoir should be built flooding most of the land south of Jackson and Wilson, as is projected, and if most of the land north of these places should be cleared by the purchase and removal of settlement, the people left in between would be faced with considerable loss in valuations even if they were permitted to remain on the land. Whether the town of Jackson could survive solely on income from the summer tourists and fall hunters is a question.

## Is Jackson Hole "Submarginal"?

Some of the proponents of park extension maintain that cattle ranching or other forms of farming activity cannot be carried on with financial success in Jackson Hole. The theory of the marginal producer, like most economic theories, is easy to set forth in general terms but difficult to apply in reality, largely because there are so many "other things which are not equal." One approach to the problem, however, is to examine the existing situation and discover how it came about, the prediction of the future being left to others more courageous.

The difficulty with Jackson Hole, in addition to its isolation, lies in the length and severity of its winters. The snow does not leave the basin floor in the average year until early in May. The growing season is between the middle of May and the middle of September, but killing frosts may be feared, especially in the lower places along the rivers, during all months of the year. The first snows appear in the mountains in late September, and by the middle of November the basin floor is covered and the mountain roads have become impassable. At Jackson barely four months average above 50°F., and in most parts of the area there are only three months above 50°. During the winter the temperatures not infrequently drop below −30°.

The shortness of the growing season places Jackson Hole near the limits of agriculture. Yet parts of the basin have regularly and successfully matured vegetables and potatoes and such grains as wheat, barley, and oats. The most successful of such areas is the so-called Mormon Row. Located on the gentle slopes of an alluvial fan and on one of the higher gravel terraces, this area is especially free from early and late frosts. If spring rather than winter wheat is grown, it is not so much because of climatic necessity as the result of the depredations of the hungry elk.

Most of the agricultural land, however, is devoted to hay, and most of it is irrigated. Alfalfa is widely grown, but there is a considerable acreage of wild hay where the water table lies at or close to the surface. The irregularly spaced and oriented haystacks, each protected from the elk by sturdy log fences, form prominent features of the landscape.

Aside from the hay purchased for the winter feeding of the elk, most of the crop is fed to the cattle. Feeding is necessary for four or five months—from December to April (Fig. 6).[9] The cattle are driven to the spring range on the lower slopes of the Gros Ventre Mountains between the middle of May and the first of June. By the first of July they are on the summer pastures, where they remain until September or early October. The annual drive to the nearest railroad, at Victor, or to Opal, Wyoming, one hundred sixty miles

# THE MARCH OF THE SEASONS

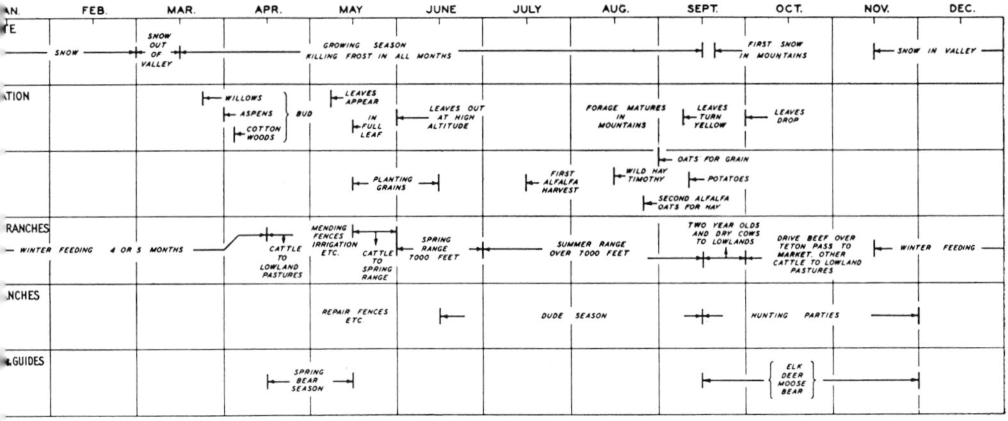

SNOW — SNOW OUT OF VALLEY — GROWING SEASON / KILLING FROST IN ALL MONTHS — FIRST SNOW IN MOUNTAINS — SNOW IN VALLEY

VEGETATION: WILLOWS, ASPENS, COTTONWOODS — BUD — LEAVES APPEAR — FULL LEAF — LEAVES OUT AT HIGH ALTITUDE — FORAGE MATURES IN MOUNTAINS — LEAVES TURN YELLOW — LEAVES DROP

PLANTING GRAINS — FIRST ALFALFA HARVEST — WILD HAY TIMOTHY — OATS FOR GRAIN — POTATOES — SECOND ALFALFA — OATS FOR HAY

RANCHES: WINTER FEEDING 4 OR 5 MONTHS — CATTLE TO LOWLAND PASTURES — MENDING FENCES IRRIGATION ETC. — CATTLE TO SPRING RANGE — SPRING RANGE 7000 FEET — SUMMER RANGE OVER 7000 FEET — TWO YEAR OLDS AND DRY COWS TO LOWLANDS — DRIVE BEEF OVER TETON PASS TO MARKET. OTHER CATTLE TO LOWLAND PASTURES — WINTER FEEDING

RANCHES: REPAIR FENCES ETC. — DUDE SEASON — HUNTING PARTIES

GUIDES: SPRING BEAR SEASON — ELK DEER MOOSE BEAR

Fig. 6.

south in the Green River basin, takes place during October and early November.

Winter feed is the critical item in the cost of producing cattle in this area. On the average a ton of hay will carry a steer through an ordinary winter, though on fourteen selected successful ranches for which statistical information is available (Table 1) about a ton and a half were consumed a head. The average yield of hay to an acre is about a ton, so that for the area as a whole about an acre or perhaps a little more than an acre of irrigated hay land to a head of cattle is necessary. Again the figures for the fourteen selected ranches are a little higher than this.

According to a report of the supervisor of the Teton National Forest,[10] using 1932 figures, there were 7,827 head of cattle from Teton County, which means practically Jackson Hole, summering in the national forest. There were also six thousand head from outside areas. Even this, however, represented only 80 percent of the capacity of the forest for summer grazing. The forest supervisor suggested increasing the Jackson Hole cattle herd by some three thousand head and, in addition, in order to utilize the total possible amount of hay land, increasing the number of dairy cattle summering as well as wintering in the Hole by some two thousand head. This plan, however, would require the use of all the irrigable land, a large part of which has been removed from production by the activities of the Snake River Land Company.

TABLE 1

DATA ON SELECTED CATTLE RANCHES *

(In Jackson Hole and neighboring mountain valleys)

| | Number of Cattle | | Acres of Hay Land | | Hay Production (Tons) | | Acres of Pasture in Lowlands |
|---|---|---|---|---|---|---|---|
| | 1925 | 1932 | 1925 | 1932 | 1925 | 1932 | 1932 |
| 1 | 250 | 350 | 215 | 220 | 500 | 375 | 20 |
| 2 | 350 | 582 | 250 | 500 | 350 | 1000 | 720 |
| 3 | 170 | 150 | 200 | 100 | 275 | 212 | 40 |
| 4 | 200 | 275 | 270 | 300 | 300 | 420 | 100 |
| 5 | 54 | 100 | 100 | 100 | 140 | 170 | 60 |
| 6 | 600 | 1050 | 740 | 1100 | 900 | 1228 | 1200 |
| 7 | 90 | 130 | 100 | 150 | 100 | 150 | 290 |
| 8 | 200 | 350 | 350 | 380 | 600 | 800 | 260 |
| 9 | 220 | 355 | 480 | 480 | 500 | 490 | 80 |
| 10 | 160 | 150 | 150 | 160 | 250 | 112 | 120 |
| 11 | 74 | 55 | 135 | 120 | 90 | 75 | 200 |
| 12 | 90 | 90 | 100 | 150 | 204 | 315 | 290 |
| 13 | 75 | 100 | 300 | 200 | 150 | 300 | 300 |
| 14 | 80 | 80 | 250 | 300 | 200 | 225 | 360 |

*Summary:* Average acreage per head, 1.12; hay consumption per head, 1.54; hay production per acre, 1.38 tons; grazing land per head, 1.05 acres.

* Data are from U.S. Forest Service.

Whether or not the ranchers can make a profit depends not only on the physical possibilities of the region but also on the energy and ability of the operators and on the price in the outside markets. Although a number of the ranches were financially embarrassed and so were glad to sell to the Snake River Land Company, most of them were making a clear profit, according to the testimony of the Jackson banker.[11] Interviews with several of the successful ranchers yielded the estimate that cattle from Jackson Hole could be placed on the market without losing money as long as a price of six cents a pound could be obtained.

This evidence seems to indicate that Jackson Hole can scarcely be considered submarginal from the point of view of the cattle producer. It is not listed as a problem area by the Department of Agriculture. But what other, more intensive forms of land use could be developed? Here again we are forced to fall back on estimates supported by the evidence of what has actually been accomplished. The area seems to possess all the necessary climatic requirements for producing first-class butter and cheese. In 1934 a cooperative creamery was opened in Jackson, and Jackson butter now finds a steady and increasing market in towns outside the basin. However, there is agreement that the dairy business in order to prosper must enlist the services of men trained in dairy work. Beef-cattle producers make notoriously poor dairymen. There is reason to believe that, if conditions of settlement were more favorable, experienced dairymen would be attracted to the region.

Dude ranching and the development of summer homes are also forms of land use that would have a considerable growth in the Hole if the territory were still open to settlement. A large number of applications for the construction of summer homes, especially along the shores of Jackson Lake, have been filed away by the Forest Service. It is stated that if these applications had been granted the taxable values in the county would have been increased enormously.

## CONCLUSION

So it is that for more than a decade now the process of settlement in the Jackson Hole country has been stalled. Neither of the two opposed plans for the area has been able to gain a clear decision and the chance to proceed without interruption. Any decision one might make is likely to be colored by the preconceptions one brings to the problem. To the outsider the concept of a wide extent of territory returned as nearly as possible to its natural state has a strong appeal, especially when one views by comparison the devastated landscapes of the lumbering and mining areas of our western states. But there are real difficulties involved in the creation of such a territory after settlers have already become attached to the land.

## NOTES

1. Fritiof Fryxell, "Glaciers of the Grand Teton National Park of Wyoming," *Journal of Geol.*, 43 (1935), 381–97.

2. The field survey on which the maps are based was carried out during the summer of 1933. The author was assisted by A. J. Gray, O. E. Guthe, Eric Faigle, and L. J. Zuber.

3. For an explanatory description of these landforms see Fritiof M. Freyxell, "Glacial Features of Jackson Hole, Wyoming," *Augustana Library Publications, No. 13* (Rock Island, Ill., 1930).

4. Both stations are D' in Thornthwaite's classification—humid, but deficient in temperature efficiency.

5. Since this was written a revision of the Jackson Quadrangle has been issued, 1935. The U.S. Geological Survey also has in preparation a map of the Grand Teton National Park (scale 1:62, 500). Use has been made of these maps in the drawing of the base for Figures 2–5. Incidentally, the difficulties of representation of a braided stream, such as the Snake River, may be pointed out.

6. Fritiof Fryxell, *The Teton Peaks and Their Ascents* (1932), p. 3.

7. For an informative exposition of the plans see "Investigation of Proposed Enlargement of the Yellowstone and Grand Teton National Parks: Hearings before a Subcommittee of the Committee on Public Lands and Surveys," United States Senate, Seventy-Third Congress, Second Session, Pursuant to S. Res. 226, 72d Congress, (Washington, 1934).

8. H. P. Sheldon, O. J. Murie, and W. E. Crouch, "The Present Plight of the Jackson Hole Elk," *U. S. Dept. of Agriculture Bureau of Biological Survey, Wildlife Research and Management* Leaflet BS-12, 1935.

9. For aid in the preparation of Figure 6 and for advice and assistance in the collection of other information, the author is indebted to the District Forest Ranger, Mr. F. Buchenroth.

10. A. C. McCain, "Economic Survey of Jackson's Hole and Plan of Development" (Jackson, 1933). In manuscript.

11. "Investigation of Proposed Enlargement of the Yellowstone and Grand Teton National Parks," p. 65.

# 7

## STUDIES OF LATIN AMERICA
## BY GEOGRAPHERS
## IN THE UNITED STATES

The National Conference of Latin Americanist Geographers brings together most of those geographers who are currently contributing to Latin American studies. The committee which planned the conference identified four major objectives: (1) to review the record of geographical study in Latin America, and to offer a critical appraisal of what has been accomplished; (2) to evaluate current research in relation to the professionally accepted paradigm defining the conceptual structure, the scope, and the methods of geographical study; (3) to identify neglected fields in which major problems exist which need to be examined by geographical methods in the years ahead; (4) to discuss the contribution of geography to interdisciplinary programs.

The purpose of this introductory paper is to place the current studies of Latin America in the perspective of what has been done before. This previous experience with the study of Latin American problems is a part of our heritage which should be understood in part to reduce the persistence of old error, and in part to pay tribute to those who have created the discipline within which we work. The pioneer studies of Latin America should not be judged in terms of the needs and understandings of today, but rather in the context of their time and in relation to what had been done before. The scholar who formulates a hypothesis which later proves untenable should not be belittled for his lack of acumen: rather he should be honored for having taken one of those essential steps on

Address delivered at the National Conference of Latin Americanist Geographers, Ball State University, Muncie, Indiana, April 30, 1970.

which any field of learning must be based. For any hypothesis clearly and vigorously stated results in new observation, new processes of analysis, and eventually in the formulation of new and more illuminating concepts. To quote Peter Haggett's remark, "the sound of progress is perhaps the sound of plummeting hypotheses" (Haggett 1966:277).

The study of Latin America by geographers from the United States can be said to have started during the first decade of the twentieth century. To be sure Louis Agassiz was in the Amazon region in 1865; William Morris Davis was observing the weather at Córdoba (Argentina) from 1870 to 1873; and Mark Jefferson held a similar position from 1883 to 1887, after which he spent two more years in Argentina as assistant manager and treasurer of a sugar cane plantation near Tucumán. From 1905 to 1907 George M. McBride was living in Santiago, Chile, where he was the director of the English Language Institute; and from 1907 to 1915 he lived in La Paz, Bolivia, as director of the American Institute. During this time he was not carrying out actual field studies, but he was storing up observations about the land and people which he used later in his studies of Chile and Bolivia.

### Isaiah Bowman
### and the American Geographical Society

Specific geographical studies began when Isaiah Bowman directed the Yale South American Expedition of 1907. This was the first of three field seasons in which Bowman worked on the Andes of Peru and the borderlands of Bolivia, Argentina, and Chile. In 1911 he was the geographer and geologist on the Yale Peruvian Expedition which was headed by Hiram Bingham—on which expedition Bingham rediscovered the lost Inca ruins at Machu Picchu. In 1913 Bowman received a grant from the American Geographical Society for a third expedition to Peru. The results were published in the book *The Andes of Southern Peru* (Bowman 1916).

> The geographic work of the Yale Peruvian Expedition of 1911 was essentially a reconnaissance of the Peruvian Andes along the 73rd meridian. The route led from the tropical plains of the lower

Urubamba southward over lofty snow-covered passes to the desert coast at Camaná. The strong climatic and topographic contrasts and the varied human life which the region contains are of geographic interest chiefly because they present so many and such clear cases of environmental control within short distances. . . .

My division of the Expedition undertook to make a contour map of the two-hundred-mile stretch of mountain country between Abancay and the Pacific Coast. [Bowman 1916: vii]

We do not need to throw out Bowman's work because of his reference to "environmental controls." This was a part of the geographic paradigm in 1916. But what else was he trying to do? It is clear that out of the mass of specific detailed observations made he was trying to arrive at some kind of useful generalization that would communicate to others the characteristic associations of people and land in the Peruvian Andes. Bowman's imaginative innovation in this study was his use of the "regional diagram." He recognized in the high Andes six kinds of what he called "topographic types":

1. An extensive system of high-level, well-graded, mature slopes (around 15,000 feet in altitude), below which are:

2. Deep canyons with steep, in places, cliffed sides and narrow floors, and above which are:

3. Lofty residual mountains composed of resistant, highly-defored rock, now sculptured into a maze of serrate ridges and sharp commanding peaks.

4. Among the forms of high importance, yet causally unrelated to the other closely associated types, are the volcanic cones and plateaus of the western Cordillera.

5. At the valley heads are a full complement of glacial features, such as cirques, hanging valleys, reversed slopes, terminal moraines, and valley trains.

6. Finally there is in all the valley bottoms a deep alluvial fill formed during the glacial period and now in process of dissection. [Bowman 1916:185–86]

The actual topographic maps show all these features in their complex arrangement and with the many variations that make each view unique. The regional diagram, on the other hand, shows these various types in their characteristic arrangement, simplified and compressed within small rectangles. "This compression, though great, respects all essential relations. For example, every location on these diagrams has a concrete illustration but the accidental relations of the field have been omitted; the essential relations are preserved. Each diagram is, therefore, a kind of generalized type map" (Bowman 1916:51).*

After Bowman became the director of the American Geographical Society in 1916, several events contributed to the further development of Latin American studies. During World War I Bowman worked on The Inquiry, a group of scholars from a variety of disciples who worked together on boundary problems in Europe. Bowman was at the Peace Conference as advisor to President Wilson. At about this same time Guatemala and Honduras were quarreling over their common boundary. When they asked the United States Secretary of State to arbitrate the dispute, Robert Lansing turned to the man with whom he had dealt on such questions in Paris. He asked Bowman to study the Guatemala-Honduras boundary area and suggest a solution. The American Geographical Society organized a survey team under the direction of Major Percy H. Ashmead to prepare a detailed map showing not only the terrain, but also the distribution of people and their ways of using the land. The survey was made in 1919 and submitted to Lansing. The negotiations took fourteen years, but the settlement accepted in 1933 was based on the maps and suggestions of the American Geographical Society.

Bowman's work in Peru, Bolivia, and Chile, as well as his experience in the Guatemala-Honduras dispute, made it clear to him that there was a very real need for the preparation of a reliable map of Latin America. With the methods of surveying then in use it would have taken many decades to carry out the surveys in the field. But Bowman realized that there were numerous original surveys in manuscript form that had been done by private companies

---

* The regional diagrams were also used in the English translation of Jean Brunhes' *Human Geography* (Chicago: Rand McNally, 1920). See also P. H. Stevenson, "Notes on the Human Geography of the Chinese-Tibetan Borderland," *Geographical Review*, 22 (1932), 599–616; regional diagram on p. 605.

for a variety of purposes. He proposed to the Council of the American Geographical Society that the Society should undertake a major research program leading to the compilation of a map of Hispanic America on a scale of 1:1,000,000 conforming to the standards of the International Map of the World (Wright 1952: 300–19; R. R. Platt 1927). Raye R. Platt reviewed the completion of the Million Map Project in 1946 and quoted the annual report of the council for 1920 as follows:

> The first step in the development of this program aims at the review and classification of all available scientific data of a geographical nature that pertains to Hispanic America. . . . The work will involve the compilation of maps—topographic and distributional—on various scales; but always including sheets on the scale of 1:1,000,000 which will conform to the scheme of the International Map. . . . The undertaking is an ambitious one, but the Society is happy to say that assurances of cooperation have been given by the whole group of Hispanic American countries in a cordial spirit that augurs well not only for immediate scientific results but also for the fostering of mutual understanding and sympathetic relations towards which the field of geography offers a peculiarly fortunate approach. [R. R. Platt 1946:2] *

As part of the Map of Hispanic America project, the society supported the publication of a series of research studies. Some were based on actual field study, such as the reports of European colonization in Chile, Argentina, and Brazil by Mark Jefferson (1921a, 1921b, 1926a, 1926b), or the studies of land-settlement problems in Chile, Bolivia, and Mexico by George M. McBride (1921, 1923, and 1936), or the studies of Peruvian Highways by McBride and his son (1944). Other research studies were compiled in New York from the drawings of the Millionth Map supplemented by Bowman's copious notes and other documentary materials in the society's library (Wrigley 1916; Ogilvie 1922).

* Geographers who took major parts in the mapping program, including the field survey of areas not otherwise covered, included O. M. Miller, Robert Shippee, and Charles B. Hitchcock (Miller 1929; Shippee 1932; Hitchcock 1947, 1954).

BAILEY WILLIS AND WELLINGTON D. JONES

In 1902, when Argentina's claim to Patagonia was confirmed by arbitration with Chile, carried out by Thomas Holdich for the king of England, the Argentine government started construction of several railroads running inland from the Atlantic coast. One of these started at the port of San Antonio and was to extend up the valley of the Río Negro to Neuquen and eventually to Lake Nahuel Huapí. The Argentines were well aware of the experience of the United States when surveys had preceded the construction of the transcontinental railroads. They appealed, therefore, to the United States Geological Survey for help in carrying out a study of the water resources and other potentialities of the northern part of Patagonia. The Geological Survey assigned the Stanford geologist Bailey Willis to the task of organizing and operating such a survey, which became known as the *Comisión de Estudios Hidrológicos*. The *Comisión* was set up in January 1911, and the final report was completed in 1914.

It happened that Bailey Willis had served as a visiting professor with T. C. Chamberlin and Rollin D. Salisbury at Chicago, which, at this time, had the only separate department of geography for graduate study in the United States. Naturally Willis turned to Salisbury to recommend a young man trained in economic geography to work on the survey. The young man selected by Salisbury was Wellington D. Jones, then a graduate student. During the 1912 field season the expedition surveyed a strip of territory along the Andes for some ninety miles north and south of Lake Nahuel Huapí. Jones surveyed the area north of the lake (Willis 1914:290–91).

The surveys were carried out at a scale of 1:200,000, and included six categories of existing and potential use: (1) potential and actual agricultural land; (2) forest land (virgin forest); (3) brushy growth which either marks old burns or occupies the transition zone along the lower mountain slopes; (4) recent burns (which were extensive south of Lake Nahuel Huapí); (5) grass-covered foothills and adjacent plateaus to the east, suitable only for the grazing of cattle or sheep; and (6) alpine pastures and barren mountain slopes over 1,500 meters in altitude.

The conclusion was reached that the chief use of the land would be for raising high-grade beef or dairy cattle, and that crops could not occupy any large areas. In certain of the lower valleys descending from the Andes fruit could be raised without irrigation, but in most places irrigation would be necessary. Large areas of forest would have to be preserved on the watersheds to maintain the supply of water for irrigation and for hydroelectric power.

It was this experience in Patagonia that inspired Wellington Jones, together with his fellow graduate student at Chicago, Carl Sauer, to suggest the importance of detailed field mapping of agricultural areas. For the first time it was suggested that maps of land use should be prepared at the same scale and degree of detail as the maps of land types or soils (Jones and Sauer 1915).

### STUDIES BY INDIVIDUAL GEOGRAPHERS

After World War I there were a few geographers in the United States who began to focus their attention on Latin American problems. In addition to Bowman, McBride, and Jefferson—who were associated with the American Geographical Society Map of Hispanic America program—four individuals returned repeatedly to Latin America starting in the early 1920s. These four were Carl O. Sauer, Robert S. Platt, Clarence F. Jones, and the writer of this paper.* It may be appropriate here to characterize the contributions of these early area specialists.

Carl Sauer made Latin America the focus of his field studies after he became a member of the faculty at Berkeley in 1923. With his graduate students he worked chiefly in the northwestern part of

* C. O. Sauer, after his appointment at Berkeley in 1923, turned his attention to Mexico. During the late 1920s and the 1930s he led field parties into Mexico almost every year for periods ranging from a few weeks to several months. Most of his graduate students wrote dissertations on Mexican problems. Robert S. Platt was in the field in Latin America for periods ranging from several months to a year on the following dates: 1922, 1923, 1928, 1930, 1933, 1935–36, 1947, and 1948. Clarence F. Jones worked in the field on the following dates: 1925, 1928, 1931, 1933, 1941, 1948, 1949–55, 1956, and 1959. This writer's field work in Latin America was done in 1921, 1924, 1930, 1938, 1949–50, 1956, 1959, 1960, 1965, and 1969.

Mexico. His first publication in this field was with Peveril Meigs in 1927. Sauer's approach to geographical studies in Mexico was quite different from his earlier attention to the practical problems of land classification in Michigan. Influenced by his California colleagues in history and anthropology he focused on the evidence in the cultural landscape of the course of human settlement. He was interested in how man changed the face of the earth, whether intentionally or unintentionally. For him culture history made a sequential impact on the physical earth and its cover of plants, and the task of deciphering this sequence captured his imagination (Sauer 1941). One of his early works along these lines reconstructed the course of the road connecting Central Mexico with the Pacific Northwest and California (Sauer 1932). To be sure the historians took him to task in this study for making use of secondary sources, but his contribution went beyond anything the historians could have done with primary sources, when he reconstructed the position of the road on the basis of field observation. He and his students did much with prehistoric Indian settlements, which led him later to generalize about early man in America, and about the origins and dispersal of agriculture.*

Robert S. Platt started his higher education as a major in philosophy and history at Yale. After graduating in 1914 he accepted a teaching post in China, and one of the subjects he was asked to teach was geography. In China he discovered an abiding interest in people and places, but not until his return to the United States in 1915 did he discover that the field in which he had found an interest was called geography. At the age of twenty-five he started graduate work at Chicago and completed his Ph.D. in 1920. Here is what he had to say about what it was that attracted him to the study of geography:

> In comparison with my philosophy major, geography offered the advantage of dealing with tangible and visible things forming a solid basis on which to build ideas, instead of beginning and ending with abstractions. In comparison with my history minor, geography had the advantage of going more into the field for direct ob-

* A bibliography of Sauer's writings is included in the selections from his writings edited by John Leighly, *Land and Life* (Berkeley: University of California Press, 1963).

servation instead of going to the library to read about things no longer visible. In comparison with geology, geography had the appeal of dealing with the world of people instead of only rocks and fossils. [Hartshorne 1964:631]

In his first field study in the Antilles in 1922 he realized the inadequacy of the theme of environmental controls, and thereafter he became one of the most effective spokesmen for those who abandoned the concept of environmental determinism. In a study of a small Wisconsin community in 1928 he was the first American geographer to discuss the functional organization of earth space. Each of his papers after 1928 made use of a small unit of human occupance to illustrate the application of a method (Platt 1931, 1932, 1933, 1934, 1935, 1936, 1938a, 1938b, 1939, and 1949). Those who did not follow his writings, and especially his papers presented to the annual meetings of the association, sometimes failed to see the broader patterns of ideas that his details were intended to build. When he was accused of describing only unique things and having nothing to do with the construction of general concepts, this revealed a common difficulty among scholars: a failure to read or listen carefully. His 1942 book placed a selection of his many detailed studies into the perspective of larger themes. The ideas with which he came to grips were actually too complex to be thoroughly analyzed before the age of the computer. If Platt were alive today he would be a leader in the use of spatial systems theory—for this is what he had been writing about for forty years.

One example of his penetrating attacks on the concept of environmental controls can be used to illustrate this aspect of his work. In 1930 he began to experiment with the observation of settlement patterns from the air. On an air traverse of Central America he prepared a strip map distinguishing five categories: (1) urban settlement; (2) rural settlement that completely covers the ground; (3) dense, but not complete, rural settlement; (4) sparse rural settlement; and (5) empty areas (Platt 1934:31). Before that time it was common to find geographers explaining the division of this part of Latin America into six small states as the result of the difficulties of travel through rugged, mountainous terrain. But Platt demonstrated that the political boundaries between countries were not drawn along mountain ranges, and that the boundaries did pass through areas of sparse settlement or entirely empty areas separating the densely settled cores. The sparsely settled areas were not related to especially rugged terrain. Amazingly, not many geographers took notice of this important revision of the deductions from the concept of environmental control.

Clarence F. Jones began his studies of Latin America in 1925, and continued to work in the field at intervals until his retirement in 1961. Among his many important contributions to the understanding of Latin American problems perhaps the outstanding one had to do with the survey of Puerto Rico carried out between 1949 and 1952. This was one of the conspicuous examples of the application of geographic methods to an inventory of land resources and land uses as a basis for planning economic development.

In 1949 Rafael Picó (who holds a Ph.D. from Clark University in geography), then chairman of the Puerto Rico Planning Board, invited the Department of Geography of Northwestern University to undertake the job of making a land-use map of Puerto Rico on a scale of 1:10,000. G. Donald Hudson, chairman of the department, and Clarence F. Jones went to Puerto Rico to work out details of the contract with Picó. The pilot survey—a strip across the island on which to experiment with the categories to be identified—was carried out in the summer of 1949 under Jones's direction. The survey of the island was done by teams, each consisting of an advanced graduate student in geography from the United States and a Puerto Rican student. The whole island was mapped between July 1949 and August 1951. Using a fractional code system of notation on vertical air photographs, the teams identified eight categories of land use (in the numerator) and the characteristics of the physical land (in the denominator) including soil types, degree of slope, conditions of drainage, rate of erosion, amount of stoniness, and rock exposure.

The maps of the Puerto Rico Rural Land Classification Program proved to be of inestimable value. On the basis of the information about the physical character of the land and the existing land use, plans were drawn up for the improvement of agriculture, for the establishment of a number of small manufacturing plants, and for the routes to be followed by new highways. The cost of the survey was more than covered by the money saved in the process of economic development programs (Jones and Berrios 1956).

This writer's studies in Latin America cover a wide range of topical fields. Mostly, but not exclusively, concentrated in Brazil, I have written on geomorphology, climatology, population and settlement, economic development, urban problems, and problems of political geography. The observed conditions in Latin America are illuminated by placing them in historical perspective—by tracing their changes through time. These papers illustrate both the advantages and the limitations of this approach (James 1932, 1933, and 1953). Nevertheless this writer has not entirely neglected the formulation of hypotheses and models.*

INTERDISCIPLINARY PROGRAMS

Geographers have participated in a number of interdisciplinary programs of Latin American study. One of the earliest was an informal collaboration among members of the faculty at the University of California at Berkeley. Here Carl Sauer found congenial supporters—H. E. Bolton, historian, and A. L. Kroeber, anthropologist. Three outstanding scholars with different backgrounds and approaches came together on the study of Latin America. The combination proved to be enormously stimulating to the participants, and also to the many graduate students who worked with them. In 1932 a new collection of monographic studies known as *Ibero-Americana* was started. It was planned to include substantial contributions to the understanding of Latin American cultures— native and transplanted, pre-European, colonial, and modern.

* In the study of Trinidad in 1924 I correlated the size of coconuts with the rainfall of the year before (coefficient of .733, probable error of ± .072—James 1926:117). I hypothesized that each new form of land use would be located first in the place most accessible to the chief port, that it would then spread all over the island, and finally would retreat to the area most favorable in terms of physical conditions (1927:108–109). Some twenty-five years later I tested the validity of the hypothesis by looking again at Trinidad, and found that some of the forecasts came true while others did not (1957). My book interprets observed contemporary conditions and problems in Latin America as the result of the spread of innovation from source regions along lines of maximum accessibility (1942 and 1969).

Studies of physical and racial backgrounds were to be included, but it was anticipated that most of the monographs would be contributions to culture history. The first of the monographs was written by Sauer and Donald Brand (1932), dealing with a prehistoric Mexican frontier on the Pacific coast.*

In the 1930s several efforts were made to bring scholars from different disciplines together for the study of Latin America. One of the most successful of these efforts was started by Professor Max S. Handman, a sociologist at the University of Michigan. Handman was able to get funds from the Social Science Research Council to hold a preliminary meeting of Latin Americanists in the Middle West. The meeting, incidentally was held in a cottage on the Indiana Dunes owned by Robert S. Platt. The meeting included geographers (James and Platt), economists, anthropologists, sociologists, and students of Latin American literature. A conference of some thirty scholars in a wide variety of fields met at the Social Science Research Council offices in New York in 1934. From this meeting came the annual *Handbook of Latin American Studies,* edited at first by the historian Lewis Hanke, and published by Harvard University Press.† It includes a selection of the most important publications in all fields dealing with Latin America. The social programs and exhibits were organized to increase the understanding of Latin American problems. The first such institute was held at the University of Michigan in the summer of 1939, and included musical programs and art exhibits as well as panel discussions of economic, social, and political problems. A second institute was held in the summer of 1940 at the University of Texas. Thereafter the institute program became a war casualty.

Interdisciplinary programs contributed to the war effort. In many ways the agencies that were organized to consider and advise on policy questions during the war brought home to scholars in many fields that the best, if not the only, way to attack such questions was by teams made up of representatives of different disci-

---

* James J. Parson's monograph on *Antioqueño Colonization in Western Columbia* was number 32 in the series (1949). In 1968 the fiftieth monograph was published.

† The *Handbook,* now in its thirty-fourth year, is edited by Howard Cline at the Hispanic Foundation of the Library of Congress, and published by the University of Florida Press.

plines. In the rush of demobilization after the war the experience gained was largely forgotten, at least for a time, and only more than a decade later did it become common to attack major problems with interdisciplinary teams.

In this new era of the electronic computer and remote sensing the problems are much too big to be effectively handled by single disciplines. As Kenneth Hare points out there is need for a new kind of discipline which approaches policy question through synthesis rather than analysis. He writes: "I suggest that the past century was the era in which we achieved great things by dissecting reality so that we could look at its fine texture; and that is how most of our existing disciplines got going. The next century will be that in which we learn to cope intellectually with complexes of things, and especially with those that make up the environment of man" (Hare 1970:353).

But is that not precisely what geographers have been trying to do for generations—the study of man in his environmental setting? For the first time this becomes possible through the use of electronics and other aids to the collection, storage, and manipulation of data, and through the formulation of procedures for handling systems of interconnected elements. There is a brilliant sunrise ahead for those who can bear to look at it.

## NOTES

Bowman, I. 1909. "The Distribution of Population in Bolivia," *Bulletin of the Geographical Society of Philadelphia,* 7:74–93.

———. 1916. *The Andes of Southern Peru* (New York: Henry Holt for the American Geographical Society).

Hare, F. K. 1970. "How Should We Treat Environment?" *Science,* 167:352–55.

Hartshorne, R. 1964. "Robert S. Platt, 1891–1964," *Annals* of the Association of American Geographers, 54:630–37.

Hitchcock, C. B. 1947. "The Orinoco-Ventuari Region, Venezuela," *Geographical Review,* 37:525–66.

———. 1954. "The Sierra de Perijá, Venezuela," *Geographical Review,* 44:1–28.

James, P. E. 1926. "Geographic Factors in the Trinidad Coconut Industry," *Economic Geography,* 2:102–25.

———. 1927. "A Geographic Reconnaissance of Trinidad," *ibid.,* 3:87–109.

———. 1932. "The Coffee Lands of Southeastern Brazil," *Geographical Review,* 22:225–44.

———. 1933. "Rio de Janeiro and São Paulo," *ibid.,* 23:271–98.

———. 1953. "Trends in Brazilian Agricultural Development," *ibid.,* 43:301–18.

———. 1957. "Changes in the Geography of Trinidad," *Scottish Geographical Magazine,* 73:158–66.

———. 1969. *Latin America,* 4th ed. (New York: Odyssey Press).

Jefferson, M. 1921a. *Recent Colonization in Chile,* (New York: American Geographical Society Research Series No. 6).

———. 1921b. *The Rainfall of Chile* (New York: American Geographical Society Research Series, No. 7).

———. 1926a. *Peopling the Argentine Pampa* (New York: American Geographical Society Research Series, No. 16).

———. 1926b. "Pictures from Southern Brazil," *Geographical Review,* 16:521–47.

———. 1928. "An American Colony in Brazil," *ibid.,* 18:226–31.

Jones, C. F., and Berrios, H. 1956. "Report on the Rural Land Classification Program of Puerto Rico, 1949–1952," *Revista Geografica,* 18 (44), 23–40.

Jones, W. D., and Sauer, C. O. 1915. "Outline for Field Work in Geography," *Bulletin of the American Geographical Society,* 47:520–25.

McBride, G. M. 1921. *The Agrarian Indian Communities of Highland Bolivia* (New York: American Geographical Society Research Series, No. 5).

———. 1923. *The Land Systems of Mexico* (New York: American Geographical Society Research Series, No. 12).

———. 1936. *Chile: Land and Society* (New York: American Geographical Society Research Series, No. 19).

McBride, G. M., and McBride, M. A. 1944. "Peruvian Avenues of Penetration into Amazonia," *Geographical Review,* 34:1–35.

Miller, O. M. 1929. "The 1927–1928 Peruvian Expedition of the American Geographical Society," *ibid.,* 19:1–37.

Ogilvie, A. G. 1922. *Geography of the Central Andes* (New York: American Geographical Society, Map of Hispanic America Publication, No. 1).

Platt, R. R. 1927. "The Millionth Map of Hispanic America," *Geographical Review,* 17:301–308.

Platt, R. S. 1928. "A Detail of Regional Geography: Ellison Bay Community as an Industrial Organism," *Annals* of the Association of American Geographers, 18:81–126.

———. 1931. "Pirovano: Items in the Argentine Pattern of Terrene Occupancy," *ibid.,* 21:215–37.

———. 1932. "Six Farms in the Central Andes," *Geographical Review,* 22:245–59.

———. 1933. "Magdalena Atlipac: A Study in Terrene Occupancy in Mexico," *Bulletin of the Geographical Society of Chicago,* 9:45–75.

———. 1934. "An Air Traverse of Central America," *Annals* of the Association of American Geographers, 24:29–39.

———. 1935. "Coffee Plantations in Brazil," *Geographical Review,* 25:231–39.

———. 1936. "A Curaçao Farmstead," *Journal of Geography,* 35:154–56.

———. 1938a. "Conflicting Territorial Claims in the Upper Amazon," in Charles C. Colby, ed., *Geographic Aspects of International Relations,* (Chicago: University of Chicago Press), pp. 241–76.

———. 1938b. "Items in the Regional Geography of Panamá, with some Comments on Contemporary Geographic Method," *Annals* of the Association of American Geographers, 28:13–36.

———. 1939. "Reconnaissance in British Guiana, with Comment on Microgeography," *ibid.*, 29: 105–26.

———. 1942. *Latin America: Countrysides and United Regions* (New York: McGraw Hill).

———. 1949. "Reconnaissance in Dynamic Regional Geography: Tierra del Fuego," *Revista Geografica*, 5–8:3–22.

Sauer, C. O. 1932. *The Road to Cíbola* (Ibero-Americana 3) (Berkeley, Calif.: University of California Press).

———. 1941. "The Personality of Mexico," *Geographical Review*, 31:353–64.

Sauer, C. O., and Brand, D. D. 1931. *Aztalán, Prehistoric Mexican Frontier on the Pacific Coast* (Ibero-American 1) (Berkeley, Calif.: University of California Press).

Sauer, C. O., and Meigs, P. 1927. "Site and Culture at San Fernando de Velicatá," *University of California Publications in Geography*, 2 (9), 271–302.

Shippee, R. 1932. "Lost Valleys of Peru, Results of the Shippee-Johnson Peruvian Expedition," *Geographical Review*, 22:562–81.

Willis, B. 1914. *Northern Patagonia, Character and Resources* (Buenos Aires: Ministry of Public Works).

Wright, J. K. 1952. *Geography in the Making, The American Geographical Society 1851–1951* (New York: American Geographical Society).

Wrigley, G. M. 1916. "Salta, An Early Commercial Center in Argentina," *Geographical Review*, 2: 116–33.

———. 1919. "Fairs of the Central Andes," *ibid.*, 7:65–80.

# 8

## SOME GEOGRAPHIC RELATIONS
## IN TRINIDAD

The British colony of Trinidad provides some remarkably interesting geographic material. With a mountain range along its northern
shore, and plains and hilly belts to the south of this (Figure 1); with
a rainfall of over one hundred and twenty inches in the northeast,
and less than sixty inches in its sheltered western parts (Figure 2);
and with a cultural landscape varying from open, sunlit fields of
sugarcane to densely shaded forests of cacao, Trinidad exhibits a
great variety of geographical conditions. Although justly famous
for its asphalt and oil, these resources are rather indirectly important to the average citizen of the colony, since the chief interest lies
in the major crops—cacao, sugarcane, and coconuts. The present
notes deal with the adjustment of these three industries to the natural setting in Trinidad.[1]

### Distribution of the Chief Crops

The chief crop industries of the island are, at the present time, distributed in fairly definite areas. Sugarcane is localized on the sunnier western side of the island in an area which we may term the
"sugar district." Very little sugar is now produced outside this area.
Cacao, on the other hand, is widespread over the island, but occupies in general the rainier parts, especially the humid valleys of the
mountainous and hilly belts. Coconuts are found in many parts of
Trinidad, but thriving plantations are largely confined to three co-

Reprinted from *The Scottish Geographical Magazine*, 42, March 1926, 84–93.
Five photographs in the original publication are not reproduced.

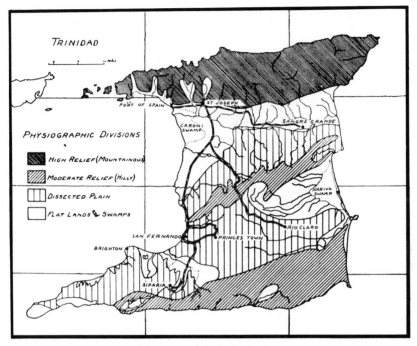

FIG. 1. The relief of Trinidad.

conut districts, one of the southwestern peninsula, the Cedros district; one along the eastern coast, the Nariva-Mayaro district; and one along the northern coast, the North Coast district.

By far the greatest densities of population, outside of Port of Spain and its suburbs, are found in the sugar district, where the East Indians, especially, are concentrated in response to the many labor requirements of a cane industry (Figure 3). The cacao district is marked by a distinctly sparser population, and the coconut districts contain even fewer people.

### THE SUGAR DISTRICT

The sugar district is located along the western or gulf coast of Trinidad from Port of Spain in the north to the Oropuche Swamp, a little south of the town of San Fernando (Figure 1). In the northern

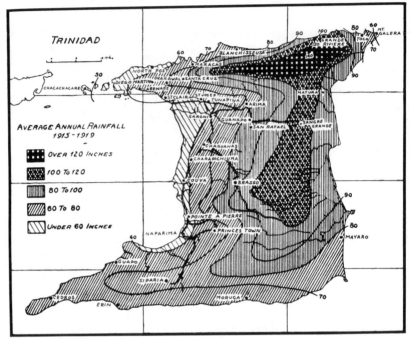

FIG. 2. The rainfall of Trinidad.

part it occupies the flat Caroni Plain, an area filled with alluvium, formerly swampy, and now possessing a rich black soil, but demanding, in consequence of its low relief, considerable attention to drainage. The area around San Fernando is probably the richest sugar land on the island. Here a dissected plain with a relief of about one hundred feet provides good natural drainage. The sugar district as a whole receives between fifty and seventy-five inches of rainfall. The average rainfall, therefore, being sufficient for the best cane growth, the critical climatic element is sunshine, which increases the sugar content of the cane. Penetration eastward into rainier areas may increase the yield of cane, but it also increases the likelihood of cane diseases and decreases the sugar content. The sugar district, therefore, represents the area best suited by natural conditions for the growth of sugarcane in Trinidad.

The sugar industry first achieved an important position in the economic life of the colony in the vicinity of San Fernando, where a number of small estates were established, using primitive methods of cultivation and extraction. The prosperity of the sugar market, however, resulted in the spread of sugarcane to almost all parts of the island. In 1836, although the largest acreage is reported for the area around San Fernando, sugar is also reported from the southwestern peninsula of Cedros, and even from distant Toco on the rainy northeast coast, as well as from many other places.[2] Probably at this time, however, the extent of the sugar industry was diminishing, due to the increasing scarcity of labor. The slaves were emancipated in 1834, and since that time the sugar industry has been faced with an almost chronic labor shortage. The East Indians brought in under contract during the period 1845 to 1916 have only partly remedied this condition. Sugar was grown in Cedros on the southwestern peninsula up to 1890, at which time coconuts were introduced, and, owing to the lighter labor requirements, this new crop proved better adapted to those points distant from Port of

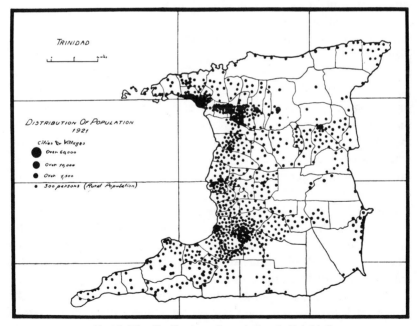

Fig. 3. The distribution of population in Trinidad.

Spain and from the railroads which give access to the shipping port.

At the present time scarcely any sugar is grown outside of the sugar district. Production from this area, however, is increased by more efficient methods. The large sugar companies are carrying on soil surveys and are experimenting with various types of cane in the attempt to reach a closer adjustment to the natural conditions. Production is becoming more and more intensive, although much yet remains to be done.

## THE CACAO DISTRICT

Cacao has been the chief crop of Trinidad since early colonial times. About 17 percent of the island is devoted to that crop at present. The cacao district includes areas of very different natural equipment. In the northern part of Trinidad, cacao is grown in the flat-floored, bottle-shaped valleys of the Northern Range (Figure 1), which are shut in by steep mountain slopes covered by a dense tangle of vegetation. The heavy rains on the mountainsides run off into the valleys in many torrential streams. So rapid is the decomposition in these latitudes, and so dense is the covering of vegetation, that torrential streams carry sediments which are for the most part finer than would be carried in middle latitudes by streams of similar velocity. This material is spread out on the valley floors, so that the soil there is constantly replenished, and never reaches the extremity of leaching and eluviation which is found on flatlands where wash from neighboring highlands is not received. Thus in these mountain valleys, and in the valleys of Montserrat a little farther south in one of the hilly belts, the best natural conditions for cacao on the island are to be found. The cacao district, however, includes also the flat country just south of the Northern Range and in the rainy eastern part of the island. Here the soil has been leached of its soluble minerals until a highly infertile yellow clay, entirely lacking in humus, is left.

The earliest cacao plantations were set out in the valleys of the Northern Range which open out on the Caroni Plain near Port of Spain, and were in consequence easily accessible from the early white settlements. Other plantations were located in Montserrat. The popularity of chocolate in Europe stimulated the production of cacao in the tropics, especially in Trinidad, where, as a result of much attention to the process of fermentation, a very high quality was attained. Under the influence of high prices and cheap land, cacao soon spread beyond the more favorable parts of Trinidad. A large income could be derived even from infertile soils. Land was so abundant that it was more profitable for an estate owner to plant two hundred acres of trees and do little more than collect the pods when they ripened than to plant one hundred acres and increase production by attention to fertilization of the soil, care and selection of the trees, and the other activities associated with a more intensive agriculture. On the neighboring island of Grenada, where arable lands are more limited, very much more attention is given to cultivation.

During the war, cacao prices rose to new high levels. In 1919–20 the planters received $23.90 per bag of 112 pounds. Then came the worldwide economic crisis, and in the following year the planters received only $10.00 per bag.[3] On many of the estates this price could not even cover the expense of picking the crop and maintaining the plantations. Especially in the poorer areas, many estates have stopped picking their cacao, and have even cut down some of their trees and used the area thus cleared to plant coconuts. On the edge of the sugar district some of the land has been cleared and replanted with cane. Unfortunately in most cases these changes in land use have taken place on low-grade cacao sites, which are also poor sugar sites, and very poor coconut sites. Sugar, as mentioned above, cannot thrive where the rainfall is very heavy. Coconuts are very much affected by the drainage of ground water through the soil, so that thriving plantations are only found where the soil is sandy. Clay soils, such as exist throughout most of the cacao district, are ill-suited to coconut palms. Therefore these shifts in land use are temporary expedients rather than permanent solutions of the problem, and represent a change from one maladjustment to another. In all probability, the poor cacao lands, being unsuited to the permanent production of any crops, excepting perhaps rubber, should be utilized for the production of timber. Such advice as this is obviously not particularly encouraging or even acceptable to the small landowners in these areas, for they lack the capital necessary to start a timber or a rubber plantation, and are forced, therefore, to produce the best-paying crop within their means which is, at the present time, coconuts.

## THE COCONUT DISTRICTS

Ideal conditions for coconut palms are dependent primarily on soil and drainage. Apparently soil texture is of greater importance than soil fertility, for coconuts are found growing on many kinds of soil, but only thrive where the soil is sandy. The palms must have a ready supply of ground water seeping constantly among their roots, but never remaining stagnant even for short periods. Clay soils through which the ground waters move slowly and with difficulty are unsuited to this crop. Plantations on clay are characterized by small trees with low yields of nuts and, in many cases, are ravaged by such tree diseases as Bud Rot and Red Ring. Coconut palms can stand salt water, but do not require it. Most commonly the best sites are found close to the sea, where the ground-water drainage from the higher land behind passes through a sandy shore. Ideal conditions may occur inland, but are not so common.

There are three areas in Trinidad with an ideal natural equipment for coconuts. One is the famous Nariva Beach along the eastern shore. Here a long sand bar, almost sixteen kilometers in length, has been built by the waves across the sea face of the Nariva Swamp (Figure 1). The waters of the swamp, derived from a large drainage area with a heavy rainfall, seep constantly and easily through the sand of the bar. These waters contain much organic material in solution, and this is left in the soil, imparting to it a rich black color. A more ideal coconut setting would be difficult to find.

The other two areas are almost as well endowed by nature. The end of the southwestern peninsula of Cedros is composed of a series of sandy spits enclosing marshy lagoons. Owing to a smaller drainage area, this district is more prone to suffer from the effects of protracted drought than Nariva Beach. The third area occupies a marine terrace, cut on the slopes of the Northern Range where the mountains rise abruptly from the Caribbean Sea. Water from the northern ridges drains through a sandy soil on the terrace, providing excellent conditions for coconuts.

Coconuts have achieved a place of importance in the economic life of Trinidad more recently than the other two chief crops. In the data previously quoted for 1836 no mention is made of coconuts. Yet in 1870 Kingsley [4] described the coconut forest of the Cocal along Nariva Beach. Coconuts had lodged here, perhaps drifting from a wrecked ship nearby, and a forest of palms had grown up. Even today the Cocal is operated almost as a reproducing forest, little or no cultivation other than picking the ripe nuts being carried on. Cedros at one time produced sugar, but about 1890, with the withdrawal of sugar from lands less well adapted to its production, coconuts assumed first place in that district. The north coast district has been even more recently developed.

The industry today is definitely localized in these three most favorable areas, and production is, for the most part, extensive. Yet, with the crisis in the cacao industry, much land is being planted with coconuts outside of the three coconut districts, and young plantations are appearing in many parts of the island, often located in areas unsuited by soil or drainage conditions for coconut production. The three coconut products—whole nuts, copra, and coconut oil—are commanding such favorable prices on the markets that this crop, rather than any other, seems most profitable to the estate owners who are unable to find a market for their cacao.

## CONCLUSIONS

The development of the cultural landscape of Trinidad appears to have progressed through three stages of adjustment to the natural conditions. Each of the major crop districts appears to be at a slightly different point in the suggested stages. The first stage is one of extensive agriculture, in which the most accessible high-grade sites are used. Thus, the first sugar estates were located in the highly favorable area near San Fernando; the first cacao plantations were made in the valleys of the Northern Range and in Montserrat; the first coconut plantations were established in the three most favored districts, especially the famous Cocal along Nariva

Beach. But this stage is soon passed through, the development being hastened if the crop in question can command a high price on the world markets.

The second stage is inaugurated when, under the influence of high prices and cheap land, the crop begins to spread to areas less suited to its production. High yields may be expected for a time on virgin soils, even with extensive methods of cultivation, and this spread to poorer lands is usually a period of great prosperity. The sugar industry had spread in this way almost completely over the island, so that in 1836 sugar acreage was reported even for the rainy northern coast. Cacao is today overexpanded, being grown on lands unsuited by soil and other conditions for its permanent and best production. Cacao, however, since the crisis of 1920, is beginning to retreat from these poorer areas and to be concentrated in the better areas again, while coconuts, under the influence of high prices, are spreading to many parts of the island, and are thus fast losing the harmony of the first stage.

The third stage of adjustment is represented only by the sugar industry. Retreating from the less favored areas, sugar at last concentrated on only those areas best suited by natural conditions. Here production was increased by more intensive agriculture, by attention to the maintenance of soil fertility, by the selection of varieties of cane to suit the varying character of the soil, by the selection of better yielding canes, by more efficient estate organization, and by many other changes which aided more efficient production. Theoretically the ultimate goal of this stage will be reached when every piece of land is used as efficiently as possible for the production of the crop best suited to it. Actually, however, such close adjustment may be interrupted by the spread of crop diseases, by war or political disturbances, or by the many natural and human events which change the normal courses of things.

On the basis of this thesis, a prediction may be ventured concerning the cacao and coconut industries of Trinidad. The cacao industry will tend more and more to give up the poorly endowed areas, and to concentrate more and more upon the better sites, with an increasing attention to the preparation of the cacao bean for the markets, to the fertilization of the soil, and other cultivation practices. The coconut industry will unquestionably take advantage of high returns and spread to a far greater extent than now over the island; but the plantations located on the poorer lands should be considered as of the nature of speculations rather than investments, for eventually, when the third stage is reached, production will again concentrate in such highly favorable areas as the Cocal, and there intensive agriculture will be the order. However, these changes must take place for the most part blindly. The method of trial and error in the past has served to locate the best sugar district: it may be allowed to do the same for cacao and coconuts—in its haphazard, inefficient, expensive way. The only substitute is a careful, scientific land classification made by geographers who, through training, are competent to handle such a survey. Trinidad could produce to great advantage many of the tropical products which the northern world is coming more and more to demand as necessities rather than luxuries; but its attainment of permanent agricultural prosperity must await the time when there shall be a closer harmony between its natural and cultural landscapes.

## NOTES

1. The sketch-maps forming Figures 1, 2, and 3 are reproduced here by the kind permission of the editor of *Economic Geography*.

2. *The Trinidad Almanac and Public Register for the Year of Our Lord 1837* (Port of Spain, 1838), p. 80.

3. Prices quoted by the Cocoa Planters' Association of Trinidad.

4. Charles Kingsley, *At Last: A Christmas in the West Indies* (London, 1871), Chap. 13.

# 9

## CHANGES IN THE GEOGRAPHY
## OF TRINIDAD

Most of the predictions that geographers make lie safely buried in libraries. Unlike the laboratory scientists who can bring the processes they study down to observable size and period, the geographers must await the slow operation of real processes, modified by all the unsystematically associated features of particular places. The process in a specific context is the essence of geography. But not always do we have the opportunity to watch the outcome of a forecast and so to provide ourselves with a check on the reliability of our concepts.

The author had such an opportunity recently on the island of Trinidad in the British West Indies. In the summer of 1924 he made a hurried survey of the island, identified its major parts, described its physical character, and indicated how the processes of land use and settlement were bringing about changes. The results were published in a series of articles in *Economic Geography*,[1] in *The Scottish Geographical Magazine*,[2] and elsewhere.

### THE PHYSICAL CHARACTER

Along the northern coast is a range of steepsided mountains, some three thousand feet in elevation. This range, an eastward continuation of the coastal mountains of northeastern Venezuela, rises abruptly from a series of terraces along the Caribbean. On the southern side the dissecting streams have opened several pouch-shaped

Reprinted from *The Scottish Geographical Magazine,* 3 (December 1957), 158–66. Three photographs in the original publication are not reproduced.

valleys. To the south two lower hilly belts cross the island, also more or less east to west. Their rounded summits are only about one thousand feet above sea level. In between are dissected terrace lands and low swampy plains.

The climate is equatorial. Temperatures are never excessively high, and there is never any cold weather. The easterly trades are strong on the east-facing coast and are felt throughout the island except in the lee of protecting heights. Rainfall is heavy, with the greatest amount falling between June and December, but with no season that is really dry. The heaviest rainfall is of more than one hundred fifty inches on the eastern end of the Northern Range; a belt of more than one hundred inches extends southward a little back from the east coast. Each day convectional storms develop in this belt of over one hundred inches and drift westward. Rain comes in the form of heavy showers, separated by periods of brilliant sunshine. The annual rainfall diminishes toward the west, being somewhat less than sixty inches along the shore of the Gulf of Paria. Trinidad lies far enough south to escape hurricanes; only once in the past century did it feel the violence of one of these storms.

These physical characteristics of the island combine to form a checkerboard of habitats. In the east: wet mountains, wet plains, wet hills, wet plains, and wet hills again; in the west a similar succession of mountains, plains, and hills, but with somewhat less rain and more sunshine.

## TRINIDAD UP TO 1797

Trinidad was neglected during the first three centuries of European settlement in the Antilles. Efforts by Spain to colonize the island in 1532 and again in 1577 were not followed up. Sir Robert Dudley and Sir Walter Raleigh both visited the island and ravaged the Spanish settlements. Raleigh used asphalt from the Pitch Lake to caulk his vessels. During the seventeenth and eighteenth centuries, when the Dutch, the French, and the British were starting to plant sugarcane in the Antilles, Trinidad shared but little in this movement. While many of the other islands changed hands several times in this

*On Research and Writing*

turbulent period, the island remained under loose Spanish administration. In 1783, however, many French settlers came to Trinidad
where they were permitted to establish small plantations, and by
the end of the eighteenth century there was a small population of
Spanish, French, and British planters with their Negro slaves. In
1797 British forces captured many of the colonies of other European nations in the Antilles, including Trinidad. While most of the
colonies were returned to their former owners by the Treaty of
Amiens in 1802, Britain retained Trinidad and British Guiana, and
Trinidad has been a British colony since that time.

By direction of the commander of the British forces in 1797
Captain F. Mallet made a new map of Trinidad which was published in London in 1802. The map shows the extent of the Spanish land grants, and distinguishes the properties used to produce sugarcane from those used for other purposes. This map is the basis
for the map of Trinidad in 1797 (Figure 1). Most of the island,
after some three centuries of Spanish administration, was still
clothed in tropical rain forest, interrupted in only a few places by
what Mallet called "natural savannahs," presumably old clearings
made by the Indians. There were four Indian missions around
which the miserable remnants of the native inhabitants were clustered. All except the more remote parts of the island—parts which
Mallet described as "inaccessible and covered with incorruptible
woods"—were marked off in Spanish grants, each grant subdivided on paper into small three hundred and twenty acre areas. But
few of these subdivisions were actually occupied. The map shows
that almost all the settled areas were along the immediate shores,
especially on the shores of the Gulf of Paria on the drier western
side of the island. The chief concentration of people was around
Port of Spain, along the southern base of the Northern Range and
in the valleys of that range north of the port. The mangrove-filled
Caroni Swamp was unoccupied, but south of it was a continuous
belt of settlement to, and somewhat beyond, the Pitch Lake. Isolated clusters of settlers occupied the end of the southwestern peninsula, the Mayaro Bay District in the southeast, and the northeastern extremity of the island. None of these settlements were
connected to Port of Spain overland, for only a few Indian trails
passed through the uncleared virgin forest. Connections with Port

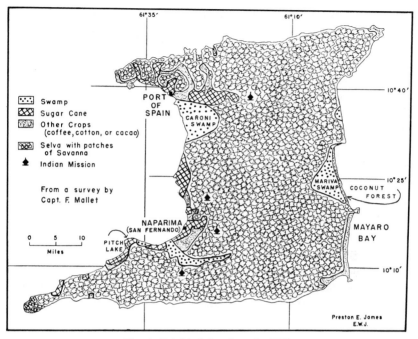

Swamp

Sugar Cane

Other Crops
(coffee, cotton, or cacao)

Selva with patches
of Savanna

Indian Mission

From a survey by
Capt. F. Mallet

0   5   10

Miles

FIG. 1. Trinidad: Land use in 1797.

of Spain were by boat, and for this reason the most accessible places were along the immediate shore.

The areas devoted to various land uses were also indicated on Mallet's map (Figure 1). The sugarcane area was along the sunnier western shore of Trinidad. Each small plantation had its own crude mill for grinding the cane, and its huge castiron pans for evaporating the juice over open fires. The other plantations were mostly used for the island's chief crop, cacao, and also for coffee and cotton but Mallet does not distinguish these. His map also shows a forest of coconut trees along the sand bar that separates the Nariva Swamp from the ocean.

## TRINIDAD UP TO 1924

In the early years of British rule in Trinidad there was no marked change in the pattern of settlement or in the methods of land use.

The acquisition of Trinidad and British Guiana caused a sufficient increase in the British sugar supply to bring a disastrous drop in prices. The earlier prosperity of places like French Sainte Domingue and British Jamaica was never reproduced in Trinidad. At the end of the slave period Trinidad was still a poor colony with a large amount of undeveloped but potentially productive land.

Slaves were freed in the British colonies in 1834, and between 1834 and 1838 there was a brief period in which the Negroes were treated as apprentices and retained on the sugarcane plantations. But in 1838, when restrictions were removed, the Negroes all through the British West Indies left the sugarcane plantations wherever they could do so. So many left the plantations in Jamaica, where there was an abundance of empty land in the interior, that between 1835 and 1838 there was a 50 percent drop in sugar production. In British Guiana matters were even worse, for there was the whole empty backland into which the former slaves could escape. Only in Barbados, where there was no empty land and no escape from the plantations, did sugar production actually increase during this period. In Trinidad, however, the drop in production was only 20 percent because the governor at once levied a tax on those who tried to occupy the crown lands. Still the basic problem for the sugarcane planters was to find a sufficient number of workers. The census of 1844 gives Trinidad a population of about 60,-000, compared with 377,000 in Jamaica, and 122,000 in Barbados.

In Trinidad an effort was made to solve the labor problem by bringing in East Indians, mostly from Calcutta, and mostly Hindu. The East Indians were brought in on a five-year contract, after which many elected to remain in Trinidad and became small freeholders. This immigration started in 1845, and by 1883 there were 48,000 East Indians in a total population of 153,000. Indian contract laborers continued to enter Trinidad until 1916. By 1921 the population had reached 342,523, of which East Indians, whites, and Negroes each made up about a third.

It was the East Indian laborers who made possible the rapid expansion in the production of sugarcane from twenty thousand tons in 1850 to sixty-seven thousand tons in 1879.[3] Sugarcane spread not only around the original plantations along the Gulf shore, but also to other parts of the island. Cane was planted even in the far southwest, on the northeast point, and along Mayaro Bay. The forest was cleared, the cane fields planted, and the small sugar mills set up.

The technological revolution that changed sugar production from a primitive, small-scale, high-cost operation to a large-scale business came to Trinidad during the last quarter of the nineteenth century. It was forced on the West Indian planters by the competition of beet sugar, although for a long time they resisted the change and sought protection by government subsidy. The first modern, large-scale central factory was built in Trinidad in 1871, located a short distance inland from San Fernando—the Usine St. Madeleine, still the largest producer of sugar in Trinidad. Soon the transformation of the sugarcane plantations was in full swing. Whereas each small mill had been supplied with cane from the fields immediately around it and had been operated by the planter himself, the new large central factories needed at least thirty-eight square miles of cane plantations to operate efficiently.[4] Some of the large corporations used wage-workers to plant cane on their own lands, but an increasingly large proportion of the cane is now supplied by independent small planters.

The change from small-scale production to large-scale production brought important changes in the pattern of land use. Sugarcane withdrew from the parts of the island suited to cane and concentrated, to the exclusion of other crops, on the better-suited lands. The map of land use in 1924 (Figure 2) shows that the sugarcane district occupied the western side of the island south of the Caroni Swamp where the average annual rainfall is over fifty inches. Penetration eastward had shown that in the wetter areas, although cane growth was greater, the sugar content of the cane was lower because there was less sunshine. The optimum sugarcane area in Trinidad had been found by trial and error, and was clearly marked by 1924. Here the population was also concentrated, with densities in 1921 of over two hundred people per square mile.

Meanwhile, cacao was still Trinidad's most valuable product. According to George Viers [5] the cacao tree grew as a wild plant along the Amazon and Orinoco Rivers and in Trinidad. In 1797 the chief cacao area was in the pouch-shaped valleys of the North-

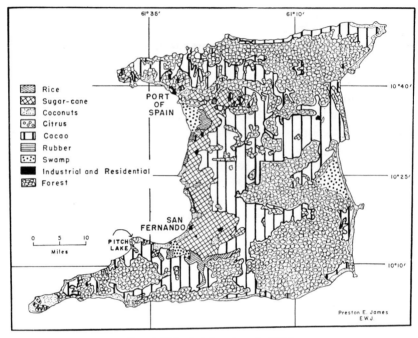

Rice
Sugar-cane
Coconuts
Citrus
Cacao
Rubber
Swamp
Industrial and Residential
Forest

PORT
OF
SPAIN

SAN
FERNANDO

PITCH
LAKE

0    5    10
Miles

61° 35'          61° 10'

10°40'

10°25'

10°10'

Preston E. James
E.W.J.

FIG. 2. Trinidad: Land use in 1924.

ern Range near Port of Spain. But the big increase in cacao planting came at the same time as the big increase in sugarcane—after
1850 when the East Indian immigration was providing Trinidad
with an important new labor force. In 1850, Trinidad produced
some four million pounds of cacao; by 1879 it was producing
twelve million pounds. Whereas the expansion of sugar cane resulted
in the elimination of the forest, the expansion of cacao was carried
on under the shade of taller trees. By 1895 Trinidad was second
only to Ecuador in cacao production.

The map of land use in 1924 (Figure 2) shows how the cacao
plantations had spread over the island. After several centuries,
cacao was still Trinidad's major export, and the prosperity of the
local economy was closely geared to the rise and fall of cacao earnings. High cacao earnings continued in the early part of the present
century until, in 1920, there was a sharp break in the world market, due to overproduction and to the increasing competition of the

Gold Coast and Brazil. The price per bag of cacao in 1919–20 was $23.90; the price in 1920–21 dropped to $10.00.

The spread of cacao under the stimulus of high prices had brought land that was definitely inferior under cultivation. In fact doubt was expressed as a result of the survey in 1924 whether optimum conditions for the planting of cacao existed in Trinidad.[6] The difficulty is that the cacao tree is very susceptible to dryness. Its tender surface roots are injured when the surface layers of the soil dry out, as they would do almost anywhere in the tropics when exposed to direct sunshine. Wind, also, has a drying effect, even in areas of abundant rainfall. Wind dries out the small stems by which the pods are attached to the trunk and branches of the tree. In Trinidad the rainy eastern part of the island is exposed to the full sweep of the trade winds, even where the cacao trees are planted among taller shade trees. But in the western part of the island, where there is more protection from the wind, the rainfall is much less. Even in the sheltered pouch-shaped valleys of the Northern Range near Port of Spain, the rainfall is only about half as great as in the windy eastern part of the range. The drop of prices after 1920 was reflected in the fact that many plantations were left without cultivation and many trees were not harvested.

By 1924 there were several other crops to be seen. The natural coconut forest along Nariva Beach was being harvested, if not cultivated. Coconuts had been planted elsewhere, chiefly along the eastern shores, at the tip of the southwestern peninsula, and around Port of Spain. Conditions for coconuts were described in 1924 as excellent, and coconut plantations were at that time in process of spreading. There were also a few areas devoted to citrus fruits, rice, and rubber.

On the basis of information available in 1924, a forecast was made regarding the development of the land-use pattern.[7] Sugarcane would remain in approximately the same area, with increased production or decreased costs derived from more intensive methods. The cacao area would shrink, first from the more exposed, less suitable areas, eventually concentrating in the better areas. In the absence of a modern soil survey it was difficult to be certain of the location of the better areas, but it was suggested that the pouch-shaped valleys of the Northern Range and the hilly lands northeast of San Fernando probably offered the best conditions for cacao planting in Trinidad. It was suggested, also, that the planting of coconuts would become more widespread, invading areas not so well suited to this crop as the areas in use in 1924.

## Trinidad in 1955

Some twenty-five years later it is possible to look again at the land-use patterns of Trinidad. The map (Figure 3) is based on a survey carried out in 1950 by the Imperial College of Tropical Agriculture. Since 1924, too, a soil survey of Trinidad has been completed and published by the college.

The map shows the extent to which the forecast has been verified. The sugarcane district still occupies approximately the same area as it did in 1924. The cacao area has undergone a marked shrinkage, but not exactly as anticipated. Throughout much of the drier western end of the Northern Range, including the pouch-shaped valleys, there is now only scrub, second-growth woodland and patches of derelict cacao. The excellent cacao lands on the central hilly belt, northeast of San Fernando, have proved to be, in fact, about the best in Trinidad, and are still productive. But the plantations on the windy, eastern side of the island are also still producing. The cacao plantations in the southern hilly belt, mostly operated by East Indians, are also continuing to produce, and have become derelict only in the Mayaro Bay area, and around the Pitch Lake. There has been little or no expansion of coconuts; in fact a considerable area of coconuts near Port of Spain has disappeared.

Meanwhile, a number of unforeseen events have taken place. During World War II, Trinidad became an important strong-point in the defense of the Caribbean. United States military forces occupied parts of the island—the whole northwestern peninsula, and a large air base east of Port of Spain, about midway between the east coast and the west coast. Large amounts of money were spent by military personnel in Port of Spain; many roads were built or improved; a modern airport was built near Port of Spain. Port of Spain itself increased from 70,334 people in 1931 to 105,744 in 1950. The map for 1950 shows a notable expansion of the area classified as "industrial and residential." San Fernando grew from

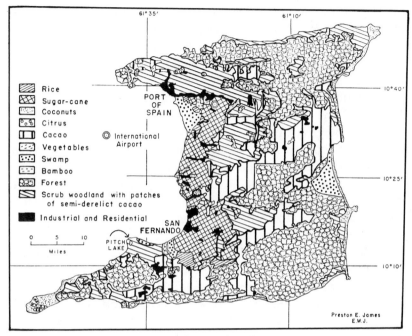

FIG. 3. Trinidad: Land use in 1950.

14,353 in 1931 to 32,867 in 1950, and entirely new industrial areas appeared in the hilly belt southeast of the Pitch Lake. The fact is that Trinidad has become an important oil producer. Not only is asphalt removed in increasing quantities to pave the roads of Britain, but new oilfields were opened up. Oil now makes up about 75 percent by value of the exports of Trinidad. Oil and asphalt production gives employment to some 17,000 workers; whereas sugarcane production employs less than sixteen thousand workers throughout the year, and only a little over twenty-one thousand at the peak of the harvest season. There are ten thousand people employed in manufacturing industries, and an equal number employed in service occupations.[8] The government, observing the success of the program of industrialization in Puerto Rico, has declared a five-year tax holiday for new manufacturing industries locating in Trinidad.

The government has also undertaken to regulate and support the agricultural activities of Trinidad. Sugarcane has been given support. In 1949, 158,890 tons of cane were harvested, which was the largest production on record. This was accomplished by the use of new methods of cultivation and improved technology in the extraction of the juice and the preparation of sugar. Unseasonable rains in 1950 brought a much-reduced harvest, but this was only a temporary setback. Cacao dropped to its lowest point in 1945 with a production of only twelve million pounds—about the same as in 1879. But by 1950 it had climbed back to some sixteen million pounds. The government-sponsored Cocoa Rehabilitation Scheme had distributed over two hundred thousand new cacao seedlings, and had supported the replanting of some five hundred sixty acres. A subsidy was made available for any cacao planter who desired to convert his plantation to some other crop. An expansion of citrus fruit, especially grapefruit, was being supported, and also a program to increase the production of rice. Rice acreage was doubled between 1938 and 1948. Meanwhile the coconuts of Trinidad have ceased to be exported. The whole production of copra is purchased by the government to be made into edible oil, margarine, and soap. During the war the imports of olive oil were cut off, and it was necessary to find a local product to use as a substitute in cooking. The price set for the sale of coconuts and copra provides the planters with adequate compensation, but does not lead to further expansion. . . .

NOTES

1. Preston E. James, "Geographic Factors in the Trinidad Coconut Industry," *Economic Geography*, 2 (1926), 108–25; *idem*, "A Geographic Reconnaissance of Trinidad," *Economic Geography*, 3 (1927), 87–109.

2. Preston E. James, "Some Geographic Relations in Trinidad," *Scottish Geographical Magazine*, 42, 2 (1926), 84–93.

3. J. H. Parry and P. M. Sherlock, *A Short History of the West Indies* (London, 1956), p. 238.

4. Raymond W. Beachey, "The British West Indies Sugar Industry, 1865–1900," Ph.D. dissertation, University of Edinburgh, 1951.

5. Geoges Viers, "Le cacao dans le monde," *Les Cahiers d'outre-mer*, 6 (1953), 297–351.

6. James, "A geographic Reconnaissance of Trinidad," p. 100.

7. James, "Some Geographic Relations in Trinidad," p. 93.

8. Colonial Reports, *Trinidad and Tobago* (1950, published 1952); and Starck, A. R., "Overseas Economic Surveys," *British West Indies, Eastern Caribbean* (1951).

# 10

## BELLO HORIZONTE AND OURO PRETO, A COMPARATIVE STUDY OF TWO BRAZILIAN CITIES

Bello Horizonte and Ouro Preto are representative of two distinct phases of Brazilian settlement. Ouro Preto is old; its buildings, its narrow, irregular cobble-paved streets, its layout, and the less tangible "atmosphere" of the place which these material forms combine to create, are all relics of the eighteenth century. Ouro Preto had its origin as a gold-mining camp, one of the richest of the state of Minas Geraes, at a time when Brazilian wealth was flowing largely from the gold and diamond mines north of Rio de Janeiro. But gold and diamonds have declined in importance in Brazilian economic life, and with this decline the mining communities have crumbled after the manner of mining communities the world over. The difficult accessibility of Ouro Preto, the cramped site it occupied, together with other considerations, led in 1896 to the removal of the political center of Minas Geraes to another location. Bello Horizonte is a new city; unencumbered by history or tradition, since about every man-made feature of this urban center is less than forty years old, this city belongs to the future. It is a response, however misguided, to an ideal.

Both Bello Horizonte and Ouro Preto are located in the economic hinterland of Rio de Janeiro. They are both most easily reached from this port (Figure 1). Both lie close to the center of the great interior state of Minas Geraes, the most populous of all the states in the Brazilian federation. In climatic situation they occupy

Reprinted from *Papers, Michigan Academy of Science, Arts and Letters,* 18 (1932), 239–58. Ten photographs and one diagram in the original publication are not reproduced.

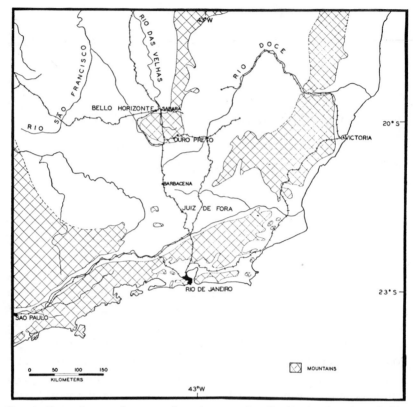

Fig. 1. General map of a part of southeastern Brazil, showing location of cities mentioned in relation to mountains.

a plateau near the margin of the low latitudes at such elevations that the tropical heat is modified, but without the weather variations characteristic of the middle latitudes (Cw).[1]

## OURO PRETO

The earliest settlements in Minas Geraes were mining towns which were established soon after the discovery of gold in 1694.[2] Bands of restless Paulistas, whose efforts resulted in the exploration and settlement of much of the interior of Middle Brazil, soon located colonies in the neighborhood of the richest ores or placer deposits.

One of these Paulistas established the first settlement on the site of Ouro Preto in 1698.[3] All these settlements—notably Villa Rica (Ouro Preto), Sabara, Tejuco (Diamantina), and São João d'el-Rey —are of the same general character. In common with all purely mining towns they show a disregard for those qualities of site and situation which are so important in the location of commercial towns. The mine is the *functional nucleus* of such towns; a focal location with easy accessibility to the surrounding territory, or even a favorable terrain on which to place the streets and buildings, is a matter of minor importance. The most favorable terrain close by the functional nucleus is chosen for the site, and access to the town is gained by the best available route, however difficult it may be.

## *The Terrain*

Ouro Preto lies on the lower mountain slopes of the northern side of the valley of the Ribeirão do Funil. To the north the Serra de Ouro Preto raises an even crest to somewhat over 1,550 meters above sea level; to the south lies another mountain range, culminating in the curiously shaped Pico de Itacolomi. Between these two mountain ranges extends a broad, mature valley, with its graceful curves sweeping down to a bottom elevation of between 1,100 and 1,150 meters. Into the bottom of this mature valley recent rejuvenation has caused the Ribeirão do Funil to sink a narrow, youthful gorge, in places with vertical walls.[4] The tributaries to this stream have fretted the floor of the earlier broad valley. In their lower courses, near their junction with the main stream, they have cut gorges nearly as narrow and steepsided as the gorge through which the Ribeirão do Funil makes its turbulent way; but upstream, toward the base of the mountains, the tributary valleys broaden to an amphitheatral shape. Near the mountain base they have been widened until only narrow ridges, now slightly below the level of the earlier valley floor, separate their drainage basins. The chief remnants of the earlier surface are the flat-topped hills which overlook the main gorge and which mark the less dissected downstream ends of the insequent divides. Ouro Preto is strung out along the mountain base, running across three of the amphitheatral valley heads and festooned over the narrow divides which separate them.

## The Urban Morphology

Irregularity of street pattern is a characteristic feature of the Brazilian colonial culture. In fact, one may look at Lisbon with its irregularly arranged core for the prototype of the Portuguese colonial settlements throughout Brazil. In other words, the apparently haphazard arrangement of Ouro Preto (Figure 2) is not imposed solely by the hilly nature of its site, but the flexibility which permits intimate adjustment to the qualities of the terrain was inherent in the culture of its period of origin.

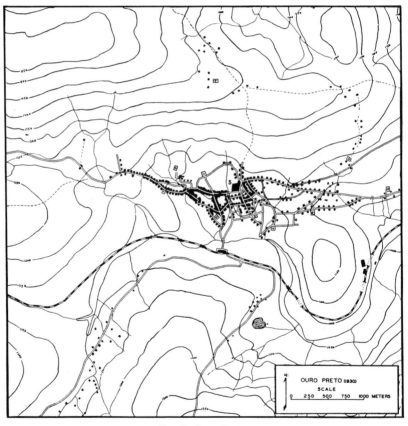

FIG. 2. Ouro Preto.

The essential feature of the origin of a pattern such as came to be developed at Ouro Preto is the lack of any major plan. Each street was established much as paths are worn on vacant lots, following the easiest route from one place to another, turning aside to avoid even minor and temporary obstacles. Once established, houses were built along it, and what had been the result of a more or less unconscious choice on the part of a small group of people became crystallized as a part of the pattern of the urban landscape. In general, the roads of Ouro Preto follow the contour of the surface, in the steeper places forming a series of terraces one above the other, with short ascents or descents from one level to another by the most expedient routes. When, in 1888, the railroad from the west reached Ouro Preto, the line followed the valley bottom, avoiding only the deepest parts of the inner gorge. The station was placed where a road already descended from the city to cross the valley to some scattered mining communities on the southern side. Little extension of the city toward the railroad station has taken place.

The houses of Ouro Preto stand very close together or actually touching. Each street is practically shut in by the houses or walls which rise directly from the narrow sidewalk. One gains the impression of crowding, even near the limits of the town, where the houses string out along a single street after the manner of a typical *Strassendorf,* and where there is no view of the gardens and open fields lying so close at hand. From the air, or from a neighboring elevation, however, one gets quite the opposite impression. Even the insides of the blocks contain trees and gardens, and the urban forms are seen to exist only as an outline or skeleton. The houses themselves are one or two stories in height, mostly of whitewashed adobe plastered on a framework of either wattle, as in the newer ones, or brick, as in the older ones. The red-tile roof is characteristic. The architectural types, especially near the center of the town, show many fine examples of the mode of the colonial period.

Undoubtedly the most striking feature of this urban landscape at the present time is the large number of churches. Scattered throughout the town are about twenty-one imposing structures, some of which contain magnificent carvings and paintings. Almost any view of Ouro Preto is dominated by one or more of these buildings, not only because they stand high above the one- or two-story dwellings in their vicinity, but also because they are commonly located on such commanding eminences of the terrain as the ridges between the amphitheatral valleys. This close juxtaposition of the artistic and the crude is quite characteristic of frontier settlements, but it is all the more striking in Ouro Preto because the usual development of the frontier town was arrested with the decline of the mines and the removal of the political function. Most of the churches stand idle, with their art treasures in serious danger of damage or loss.

There is little differentiation of functional areas in Ouro Preto at the present time. The mines for which the settlement originally was established are now abandoned; their openings, partly caved in, are still visible along the mountainside in the upper part of the town. The old government buildings, now utilized by the School of Mines, occupy a central position (shown by the letter *S* on Figure 2). If there is any commercial center it is located in the area south and west of the School of Mines, but there is actually little to differentiate this section from any other section, except that there are fewer vacant plats and fewer of the buildings are standing unoccupied. It is in this part of the town that the much-reduced present-day population has established itself, leaving the outlying parts to fall into obvious decadence.[5]

### The Relation of Ouro Preto to the Larger Region

The structure of Ouro Preto as regards its functional areas cannot be interpreted, however, without reference to the relation of this urban center to the larger region, the surrounding parts of southeastern Minas Geraes. As we have pointed out, the town owes its location to the presence of gold ores. Being one of the richest of the mining communities, it became the political center of the state early in the nineteenth century,[6] but this additional function was due to the wealth and power already congregated around the mines at Ouro Preto. During the nineteenth century there were as many as thirty-five or forty thousand people in Ouro Preto.[7]

During all this time, however, Ouro Preto remained dominantly a mining community, and the mining economy ruled the politics of the state. It is a characteristic inherent in mining communities to be located at the end of the road, rather than at a focus of roads. Roads perhaps are extended to such mining settlements from several directions, but the greater part of the traffic over the roads originates at the mine and moves away from it. Thus during the eighteenth and nineteenth centuries roads reached Villa Rica from Rio de Janeiro, from São Paulo, from the east coast by way of the Rio Doce, and from distant Bahía by way of the São Francisco Valley.[8] But Ouro Preto was the inner end of these roads rather than the focus of them. It does not occupy a position which is in any way a natural focal point of routes of travel. For this reason it was always handicapped in the performance, for the larger region, of political, commercial, or manufactural functions.

In 1896 the capital of the state of Minas Geraes was transferred officially to the new city of Bello Horizonte. With it went any attempt on the part of Ouro Preto to perform the commercial functions for the larger region. The change was stimulated, then, not only by the cramped nature of the site of Ouro Preto, but also by its unfavorable situation with respect to routes of travel.[9] In 1896 Ouro Preto had approximately thirty thousand inhabitants; at the present day it has about six thousand. It still has its School of Mines; it is a potential center for art; but its other functions have been taken away, and there remains only the empty shell—the relict pattern stamped on the face of the earth by the activities of other days, now rapidly falling into decadence.

## BELLO HORIZONTE

In the most complete contrast to Ouro Preto stands Bello Horizonte. The contrast is not only one of site and functions, but also one of pattern, aspect, and that immaterial quality of atmosphere or personality which is so easy to appreciate but so difficult to portray. Bello Horizonte is the expression of the modern era. Whereas in other cities which have continued their growth into modern times the new features and patterns have been developed as additions to the older parts, or as modifications of preexisting patterns,

Bello Horizonte is completely new, with the exception, as we shall see, of one minor connection with the earlier occupance on this site. Bello Horizonte is facing the vision of its future; Ouro Preto recalls the memories of its past.

## The Terrain

When the *mineiros* decided to establish a new capital they looked for a site which would give plenty of room for growth. But anything approaching level land in Minas Geraes is difficult to find. This part of southeastern Brazil is made up of crystalline plateaus lying eight hundred to a thousand meters above sea level. The plateaus are surmounted by such mountains as those around Ouro Preto (Figure 1), and are dissected by streams which without exception show the usual indications of recent rejuvenation.[10] Level surfaces, then, are to be found only in a very few, isolated bits of valley flat along the deeply incised river valleys, or on the youthful interfluves which the tributary streams have not yet dissected.

The site chosen for the city of Bello Horizonte is of the latter type. It lies just north of the Serra do Curral, a part of the Serra do Espinhaço of central Minas Geraes, and a little west of the deep, youthful valley of the Rio das Velhas where it emerges from the mountains on its way toward the Rio São Francisco. In this region a plateau level at about a thousand meters in elevation is extensively preserved, with broad, open valleys cut below the higher level to another at about eight hundred meters. The main streams, like the Rio das Velhas, flow through narrow, youthful canyons with intrenched meanders incised in the valleys of the eight hundred-meter level, and tributaries of the main streams are extending their V-notch valleys headward into the plateaus. About eight kilometers downstream from Sabara, the Rio das Velhas is joined by a left-bank tributary, the Ribeirão Arrudas, at an elevation just under seven hundred meters. This stream has extended its youthful gorge some fourteen kilometers into the upland west of the Rio das Velhas, but beyond this it flows through a valley only slightly below the general eight hundred-meter level, having the characteristic open V-profile of youthful headwater streams. Just

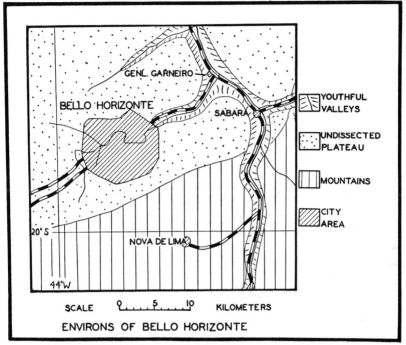

FIG. 3. Environs of Bello Horizonte.

above the gorge of the Ribeirão Arrudas, in a broad, open, basin-like valley which curves down from the thousand-meter remnants on either side to the eight hundred-meter level in the middle, is the site of Bello Horizonte (Figure 3).

## The Urban Morphology

This site was occupied before 1890 by the small rural village of Curral d'el-Rey (Figure 4). Although the village was not a mining settlement, its pattern, like that of Ouro Preto, was characteristic of the colonial culture. Its irregularity was in no way related to a rough terrain. Curral d'el-Rey owed its location to the convergence of three locally significant roads, in this respect differing from the mining type of settlement illustrated by Ouro Preto. One road led down the gorge of the Ribeirão Arrudas and up the valley of the

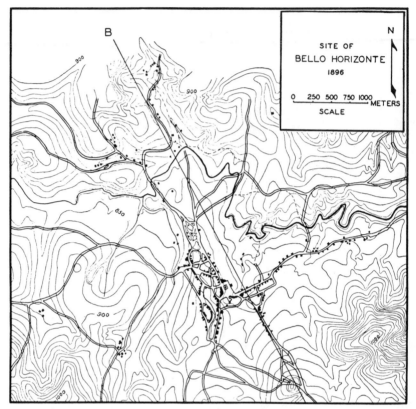

FIG. 4. Curral d'el-Rey, the site of Bello Horizonte in 1896.

Rio das Velhas to Sabara; the second, into the Serra do Curral to the south; and a third into the wilderness, or *sertão,* toward the north. At the junction of these three roads was an open *praça,* or plaza, in the center of which was a church. This was the historical nucleus of the settlement, its "point of attachment" to the earth. Around it the characteristic unplanned street pattern, with the strings of houses, had developed—all the more irregular because of the gentle slopes of the terrain.

The development of a city of a hundred thousand people on this site might have been made with Curral d'el-Rey as a base. This would have been the usual course of events. Even Rio de Janeiro and São Paulo carry in their centers the narrow, irregular street pattern of such an unplanned beginning. But when the new capital was projected, it was determined to wipe out the existing settlement and begin again. The remarkable thing to record is that this apparently was accomplished without the graft and political corruption so frequently exhibited under similar conditions elsewhere.[11] Only one remnant of Curral d'el-Rey was suffered to remain: the church which marked its center. It alone served as the point around which was oriented the otherwise entirely new pattern of Bello Horizonte.

During the closing years of the nineteenth century the acme of perfection in city plans was supposed to be Major L'Enfant's layout of Washington, D.C. Accordingly, a rectangular system was used as a base, then another, but more widely spaced, system of avenues was superimposed on the first and oriented at an angle of 45° to it. Around the periphery of the city a broad boulevard was laid out (Figure 5). With the specter of too narrow roadways before them, the town planners made the basic system of streets twenty meters wide, and the avenues thirty-five meters—widths which have imposed on the city a heavy financial burden in paving costs.[12] This pattern of streets was oriented conveniently on the terrain with the old church of Curral d'el-Rey as a pivot. The location of this church in present-day Bello Horizonte is marked by a black star on Figure 5.

In 1930 the original layout of the city had still not been entirely built up. A considerable section in the southwest was composed only of grassy fields crossed by the traces of the roadways. Beyond the limits of the original city, however, an extensive zone of suburban subdivisions had been platted and partly developed. These subdivisions have somewhat irregularly rectangular plans, variously articulated with the main city.

Before turning to a discussion of the pattern of functional areas, the relation of this city to the larger region must be considered.

*The Relation of Bello Horizonte to the Larger Region*

The urban functions which center on Bello Horizonte are chiefly political and commercial. As state capital this new city became im-

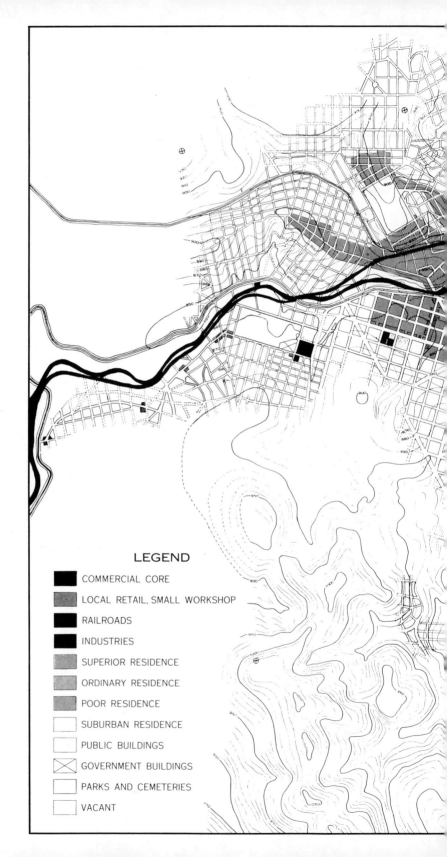

LEGEND

COMMERCIAL CORE

LOCAL RETAIL, SMALL WORKSHOP

RAILROADS

INDUSTRIES

SUPERIOR RESIDENCE

ORDINARY RESIDENCE

POOR RESIDENCE

SUBURBAN RESIDENCE

PUBLIC BUILDINGS

GOVERNMENT BUILDINGS

PARKS AND CEMETERIES

VACANT

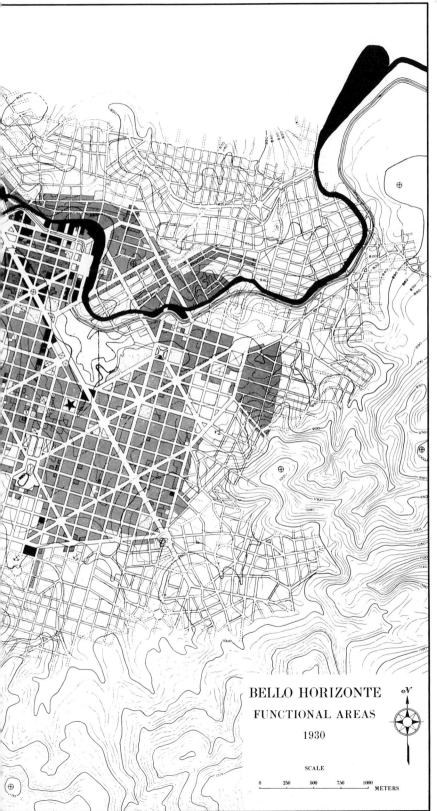

BELLO HORIZONTE

FUNCTIONAL AREAS

1930

SCALE

0    250    500    750    1000
                              METERS

Fig. 5.

mediately an important focus, but for various reasons it has not yet achieved a preeminent position in the commerce of the state. In other words, the territory which it serves in the function of political center is much more extensive than that for which it serves as commercial center or as collecting point for the shipment of local products to the coast. The territory reached by its manufactures is still more narrowly limited.

The reason for this is, in part, the location which was chosen for it. In addition to the selection of a site sufficiently level to accommodate a large city, a point was desired somewhere near the center of the state of Minas Geraes. Bello Horizonte lies very close to the center of this political unit. But Minas Geraes is a very large state, and one which contains within its borders a very great variety of conditions. The population is concentrated in the southern and eastern parts of the state, whereas to the north and west lie the vast expanses of plateau grasslands (with Aw climate), in part utilized for great cattle ranges and with only scattered and isolated pioneer settlements, and in part quite uninhabited except by Indians. Thus Bello Horizonte is not actually in the middle of the settled portion of Minas Geraes, but is located almost on the pioneer fringe. Furthermore, its position on the north and west of the Serra do Espinhaço, which forms a distinct barrier to movement, shuts it out from easy communication with the most populous districts of the state which lie to the south and east of this range (Figure 1).

Railroads, to be sure, now reach Bello Horizonte from various directions. The main line to the south does not follow the more direct route through the Serra do Espinhaço, but bends around its western edge. From Sabara in the valley of the Rio das Velhas, a line extends northward to the isolated outpost of Pirapora on the São Francisco, and another crosses the mountains eastward to Santa Barbara. From Bello Horizonte itself another railroad runs westward into the western part of the state. The capital city has become a railroad focus of a sort, but the focus is a highly artificial one. Bello Horizonte represents no more of a regional focus of natural lines of travel than does Ouro Preto, especially when we recall that the territory to the north is virtually unsettled. Barbacena is much more of a natural focus of routes, since both ridges and valleys radiate from this high point on the plateau and since it is easily accessible to the most populous districts. Juiz de Fora, as the southern outlet of the state, might have become the collecting point for shipments from a wide area of the interior. Instead, however, the lines of travel have radiated from the port of Rio de Janeiro, and no all-embracing focus of routes has developed in southern Minas Geraes. With the opening of the railroad outlet by way of the Rio Doce, another and widely divergent outlet will be provided, still further scattering the commercial orientation of the state.

Bello Horizonte, then, will increase its commercial importance only as the territory to the north is settled. In this respect it is a city of the future, built in response to a vision. But for the present the fulfillment of its vision is incomplete.

TABLE 1

INCREASE OF POPULATION IN BELLO HORIZONTE [13]

| | |
|---|---|
| 1900 | 13,472 |
| 1905 | 17,191 |
| 1910 | 32,300 |
| 1915 | 45,741 |
| 1920 | 52,619 |
| 1925 | 85,224 |
| 1930 | 120,000  (estimated) |

The enormous increase in population, as shown by Table 1, is partly the result of the depopulation of smaller places elsewhere in the state. Although these shifts in population within Brazil have not been adequately studied, their reality is recognized. Bowman describes, for instance, the withdrawal of the frontier of settlement in the north as a result of the construction of railroads farther south.[14] No doubt a part of this decline visible on the frontier accounts for the numbers of people who have moved into the suburban zones of Bello Horizonte and exist there with no very lucrative source of employment.

## Functional Areas

These functional relationships of Bello Horizonte to the larger region are reflected in the present pattern or arrangement of the areas within the city which are devoted to the various urban functions.[15] Unlike Ouro Preto there is a distinct differentiation of Bello Horizonte into such areas (Figure 5).* The political function centers on the governor's palace, located in the midst of a park at the intersection of two of the wider avenues near the southern end of the built-up part of the city. This site was chosen, no doubt, to take advantage of the high ground of a spur somewhat below the thousand-meter level. Several other government buildings are located near the palace, but still others are scattered throughout the city, some even in the suburban fringe.

The commercial function centers in the "commercial core"— the commercial and business area which serves the larger region beyond the immediate urban limits, as opposed to the local retail stores, which are differentiated from the commercial core. In arrangement this core is distinctly attenuated, extending along the sides of one of the broad southeast-northwest avenues, and at right angles to this along another avenue, which leads down to the railroad station. These avenues extend conveniently across the gentle lower slopes of a spur on the inside of a bend of the Ribeirão Arrudas. Much of the remainder of the area inside this bend is taken up with a characteristic Brazilian complex of small retail stores and workshops, and with manufacturing establishments interspersed with poor residences. The railroad lines and the associated warehouses and shops follow the lower part of the valley.

The manufacturing units of Bello Horizonte are various, but mostly of only local significance. On Figure 5 only those industrial establishments which occupy their own buildings, or at least the greater part of a building, are classed as industries. The small workshop and local retail area includes a number of small units occupying restricted quarters and, in many cases, carrying on the retail sale of their products along the street front. The nature of the manufacturing in this city is indicated by Table 2 for 1927,[16] which includes all establishments, whatever may be their size.

A better idea of the relative importance of these industries, however, is gained from Table 3, which shows the percentage of

* It has not been feasible to reproduce this figure in its original colors, and thus to differentiate clearly among the several categories in the legend.

the electric power used for different classes of industry in Bello Horizonte during the first six months of 1930.[17]

This list of industries is a typical one for the cities of the Brazilian plateau. High protective tariffs permit the existence of many small establishments, especially textile, throughout the interior. Even Ouro Preto has its textile mill. However, the local nature of these manufacturing activities is attested not only by the small scale on which they operate, but also by their independence of rail connections. The manufacturing areas of these cities are not tied to

TABLE 2

NUMBER OF MANUFACTURING ESTABLISHMENTS
IN BELLO HORIZONTE

| | |
|---|---|
| Woodworking shops, including furniture | 14 |
| Printing shops | 13 |
| Pharmaceutical supplies | 10 |
| Alcoholic beverages | 10 |
| Marble cutters | 7 |
| Shoes | 7 |
| Coffee mills | 6 |
| Textiles | 5 |
| Confections | 5 |
| Macaroni | 5 |
| Soap | 5 |
| Machine shops | 5 |
| Miscellaneous | 37 |
| TOTAL | 129 |

TABLE 3

PERCENTAGE OF TOTAL ELECTRIC POWER
USED IN INDUSTRIES

| | Percentage |
|---|---|
| Woodworking shops | 19 |
| Textiles | 11 |
| Metal works | 10 |
| Food manufactures | 7 |
| Quarries | 7 |
| Transportation | 5 |
| Miscellaneous | 41 |

the railroads, as in similar cities of North America. Although many of the industries of Bello Horizonte are in the valley of the Ribeirão Arrudas, by no means are all of them so located. And for most of those which are in the valley, cheap land and not proximity to the railroads is the cause.

The residence districts of Bello Horizonte are divided into four classes: poor, ordinary, superior, and suburban. Of these classes, superior and poor are quite distinct and easy to recognize. The houses of the superior residence district are more elaborate and expensive and occupy relatively larger lots, with a street frontage of generally over twenty meters. The poor residence districts, on the other hand, are composed of small houses of cheap construction, on small lots. Only the main thoroughfares of these districts are paved, and the red clay of the underlying soil tinges the sidewalks, the walls of the buildings, and even the inhabitants, both animal and human, with an orange hue. Between these two extremes, the ordinary residence district represents somewhat greater variation of type. Where less than 50 percent of each block has been built up, or otherwise developed, a fourth residence district is recognized. In character the suburban zone most closely resembles the poor residence district. Its streets are with few exceptions unpaved, and such public services as water or light are rare.

The distribution pattern of these residence districts is not unusual. The superior district is concentrated on the higher part of the spur close by the governor's palace and the neighboring group of government buildings. Ordinary residences fill in most of the rest of the original layout not taken up by commerce or industry. The poor residence districts are mostly along the lower sections of the valley and on the northern slopes. Suburban residences form an almost complete ring around the outskirts of the city.

A quantitative analysis of functional areas of this city is of interest, especially when compared with one of a North American city. In Table 4 the percentage of the total area devoted to the various uses we have just described is compared with a similar analysis of Vicksburg, Mississippi.[18] In both studies the total areas in reference to which the percentages are measured are the inner parts, in which at least 50 percent of each block has been built up or otherwise developed for urban use. In order to make such quantitative analyses strictly comparable, this definition of the geographic urban area has been adopted. The reason for the exclusion of the suburban zone, where less than 50 percent of each block is built up (or developed as parks, etc.), is that in many cities the outer limits of this zone are very difficult to establish with precision, whereas the limits of the more continuously built-up or developed area can be precisely recognized. It should be noted that Vicksburg is a much smaller city, having a population in 1930 of about 23,000, as compared with 120,000 for Bello Horizonte. The smaller percentages of area devoted to commercial core and industry in the case of Bello Horizonte reflect the relatively small extent to which this city performs these functions for the larger region.

TABLE 4

QUANTITATIVE ANALYSES OF BELLO HORIZONTE
AND VICKSBURG, MISSISSIPPI

| Bello Horizonte | | Vicksburg | |
|---|---|---|---|
| | Percentage | | Percentage |
| Commercial core | 1 | Commercial core | 3 |
| Small retail and workshop | 7 | Wholesale | 2 |
| Railroad | 3 | | |
| Industries | 2 | Industries | 7 |
| Superior residence | 3 | Superior residence | 7 |
| Ordinary residence | 27 | Ordinary residence | 30 |
| Poor residence | 5 | | |
| Government buildings | 3 | | |
| Parks, etc. | 8 | Parks, etc. | 1 |
| Vacant land within the urban limits | 13 | Vacant land within the urban limits | 9 |

## CONCLUSION

Bello Horizonte and Ouro Preto represent two extremes among Brazilian cities. They also illustrate two common problems which cities in their development have to face. The first problem arises when the growth of an urban center brings to it functions and activities for which no adequate plan had previously been devised. The unplanned irregularity of the colonial cities, even of the major ones, is an indication that their inhabitants were essentially rural minded. Most cities cannot be transplanted, and so must do the best they can to perform the functions of a city within the framework of a rural village. In Minas Geraes, however, a number of factors led to the creation of a new city, unencumbered by an inadequate inheritance. Ouro Preto, as a mining settlement, was located without reference to those qualities of site and situation which are usually called upon to explain urban growth. With rugged terrain, without the advantages of even a local, natural convergence of routes, Ouro Preto could not easily adjust itself to carry on the additional political and commercial functions for the larger region.

A people less imaginative than the Brazilians might have struggled to find a local solution to this difficulty. With the examples of Washington, Canberra, and La Plata before them, the *mineiros* set out to build for themselves an ideal city. Bello Horizonte is an entirely modern city, built by an idealistic and capable people. Yet it, also, is not without its problems. The difficulty of forecasting the future of a city is inherent in all city planning. To plan for one destiny may be to provide inadequately for a lesser one. Bello Horizonte, near the center of the state of Minas Geraes, looks to a future when it may truly become the focus of a widespread population—when the Northwest as well as the Southeast shall have been won from the wilderness. For the present, some other location might have been more satisfactory, such as Barbacena or Juiz de Fora. The spread of population into the North will involve many problems regarding the suitability of these lands for human settlement; and even if they prove hospitable, it is not at all unreasonable to predict that the cooler plateau of the South, with its dependable rainfall, will remain the center of population. Bello Horizonte, however, is placed to serve the northern frontier. Its future is bound up with the advance of settlement into these new lands; it is planning and preparing for a destiny which cannot yet with confidence be predicted.

### NOTES

1. Bello Horizonte is Cwa: its coldest month (July) is 16.8°C (62.2°F); its warmest month (February) is 22.3°C (72.1°F); its total annual rainfall is 1,500

mm. (59 in.), coming chiefly from October to March. Ouro Preto is Cwb: its coldest month (July) is 13.9°C (57.0°F); its warmest month (February) is 19.6°C (67.3°F); its total annual rainfall is 2,136.3 mm. (84 in.), coming chiefly in summer.

Figures from *Boletim de Normaes de Temperatura, Chuva, e Insolacão, correspondentes aos annos de 1914 a 1921* (Estado de Minas Geraes, Commissão Geographica e Geologica, Seccão Central do Serviço Meteorologico, Bello Horizonte, 1923).

2. Delgado de Carvalho, C., *Geographia do Brasil* (Rio de Janeiro, 1929), p. 33.

3. Ouro Preto has been known under several names: São João Baptista de Ouro Preto, from 1698 to 1711; Villa Rica de Albuquerque, from 1711 to 1720; Villa Rica de Ouro Preto, from 1720 to 1823; and Imperial Cidade de Ouro Preto, from 1823 to the present day. Vasconcellos M., *Vias Brasileiras de Communicacão*, 2a. Edicão (Rio de Janeiro, 1928), p. 326.

4. The Portuguese word *Funil* means *funnel*.

5. Saint-Hilaire, Auguste de, *Voyage dans les provinces de Rio de Janeiro et de Minas Geraes* (Paris, 1830), p. 138. The following account was written in 1816: "On compte, à Villa Rica, environ deux mille maisons. Cette ville était florissante, lorsque les terrains qui l'environnent fournissaient de l'or en abondance; mais à mesure que ce metal est devenu plus rare ou plus difficile à extraire, les habitants ont été peu à peu chercher fortune ailleurs, et, dans quelques rues, les maisons sont presque abandonnées."

6. Jacob, R., *Minas Geraes no XX°º Seculo* (Rio de Janeiro, 1911). See especially the table on p. 141.

7. See Dos Santos, L. J., *Historia de Minas Geraes* (São Paulo, 1926).

8. Delgado de Carvalho, *Geographia do Brasil*, p. 334.

9. Haushofer, A., "Ouro Preto und Bello Horizonte: Eine städtegeographische Studie," *Mitt. der Geog. Gesell. in München*, 18 (1925), 293–311.

10. Delgado de Carvalho, C., *Physiographia do Brasil* (Rio de Janeiro, n.d.).

11. Verdussen, J., "Bello Horizonte, nouvelle capitale de l'état de Minas Geraes," *Rev. de l'Am. Latine*, 18 (1929), 434–38.

12. Machado, C. M., *Mensagem apresentada pelo Prefeito . . . ao Conselho Deliberativo de Bello Horizonte, em 10 de Outubro de 1929, e relatorios annexos* (Bello Horizonte, 1929). See especially pp. 71–79.

13. Figures from *Algumas Notas sobre o Estado de Minas Geraes* (Bello Horizonte, 1930). "Estado do Minas Geraes, Serviço de Estatistica Geral," in manuscript.

14. Bowman, I., "The Pioneer Fringe," *"American Geographical Society*, Special Publication, No. 13 (New York, 1931), 301.

15. A workable classification of urban "functions" is given on p. 572 of a paper by M. Aurousseau, "The Distribution of Population, A Constructive Problem," *The Geographical Review*, 11 (1921), 563–92.

16. Table from statistics in *Indicador agro-pecuario, industrial, commercial, e bancario de Minas Geraes*, Anno I, 1927 (Estado de Minas Geraes, Serviço de Estatistica Geral, Bello Horizonte, 1928).

17. Information from the local power company.

18. James, P. E., "Vicksburg, A Study in Urban Geography," *The Geographical Review*, 21 (1931), 234–43. Reference on p. 241.

# 11

## THE PROBLEM OF BRAZIL'S
## CAPITAL CITY

For more than half a century the maps of Brazil have shown a rectangular area near the geographical center of the national territory designated as the "Future Federal District." In recent years the Brazilians have been giving serious consideration to plans for moving the capital from Rio de Janeiro to some place, not yet officially selected, in the backlands. The decisions that must be made involve complex issues. They cannot be based on the advice of engineers and city planners alone, for they require an understanding of Brazil's historical background and of the areal relations of population, economic production, and the underlying characteristics of the land. They also involve a forecast: to what extent are the present patterns of population and the present relationships between settlement and land quality likely to be changed or modified in the future?

### HISTORICAL BACKGROUND

Brazil is a country in which the patterns of population and settlement have been notably fluid. In contrast with most Spanish-American societies, no social class in Brazil has developed a strong sense of attachment to a particular place. The large landowners, with few exceptions, gain little prestige from the mere ownership of land; usually the Brazilian takes a poor view of holding unproductive property. Brazilians of all classes, especially the

Reprinted from *Geographical Review*, 46, 3 (July 1956), 301–17. Speridião Faissol is the co-author of this article.

poorer people whose poverty seems hopeless, are always ready to gamble, to seek new ways to quick wealth. The rich Brazilian not only shifts his capital from one kind of economic activity to another but shows no reluctance to move from one part of the country to another. The result has been a notable lack of permanence in the details of settlement and a great amount of movement within the country by persons of all classes.

This mobility of the Brazilian people, shown statistically for the first time in the census data of 1950, is best revealed by direct observation in the field. One can see the crowding of passengers on Brazilian coasting vessels, or in the third-class railroad cars, or on the decks of river steamers, or in the little automobile stages that provide low-priced transportation even to the most remote parts of the country. One family interviewed in 1950 in a frontier of new settlement in central Goiás had taken five months to walk overland from Maranhão. Many Brazilian novelists have also recorded this mobility and have described the motivation behind it.[1]

Yet the result of more than four hundred years of settlement has not been a uniform peopling of the national territory. On the contrary, the pattern of population remains one of separate clusters, of distinct areas of concentration (Figure 1). Most of these settled areas are set off from one another by thinly peopled country, and most of them form the cores of individual states. Furthermore, these areas have been built up during different periods of Brazil's economic history: those of the Northeast came into existence during the period of the sugar cycle (1532–1700); those of the Southeast, which form the hinterland of Rio de Janeiro, appeared during the gold cycle (1700–1800); those of the São Paulo region were supported by coffee (1850–1930); and other smaller concentrations are similarly related to periods of speculative development. Around the margins of most of these areas waves of new pioneer settlement are advancing away from the central city that forms the nucleus of each cluster. But behind the frontier the older settled land nearer the cities shows a decrease of population as the settlers move either into the urban areas or out onto virgin land where yields and profits are high. The result is the "hollow" frontier.[2]

There is another significant fact about these areas of concentrated settlement. Most of the settled area of Brazil is on land that

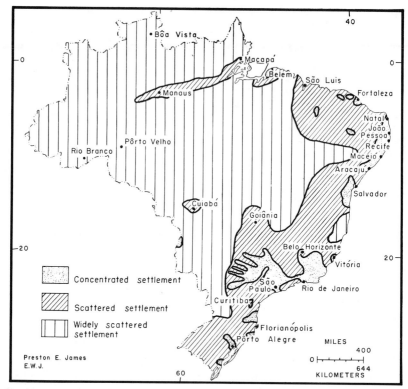

FIG. 1. Settlement areas of Brazil in 1950, based on Map 1 in James, *Latin America* (New York: Odessey Press, 2nd ed., 1950).

was originally covered with tropical forest.[3] This is a kind of forest less dense than the rainforest of the Amazon Basin and parts of the Atlantic coast, but much more dense than the thin scrub forests of the backlands. Today it occupies a relatively small part of the national territory; most of the virgin stands of tropical forest are gone.

During the course of Brazilian economic history, when successive areas have been developed in cycles of speculative profit followed by decline and decadence, the administrative center of Brazil has shifted. In colonial times, when great wealth was being amassed by the sugarcane planters of the Northeast, the capital was at Salvador in the state of Bahia (Figure 1). But by the end of the seventeenth century the sugar cycle was at an end, and early in the eighteenth century there was a rapid new settlement of the country behind Rio de Janeiro from which came gold and diamonds. In 1763, the capital of the colony was transferred to Rio de Janeiro. From 1808 to 1822, Rio was the capital of the Portuguese empire, and in 1822, when Dom Pedro I declared the independence of Brazil, the city was sufficiently powerful to maintain dominance over all the other settled areas of this vast country. But by the end of the empire in 1889, São Paulo was already on the rise, supported by the beginnings of the great coffee cycle. In the constitution adopted in 1891 there is a provision to the effect that the capital of the country shall be removed from Rio de Janeiro and established at a place near the geographical center of the country. Since then, a "Future Federal District" has appeared on all official maps even though its precise position and outline have never been firmly established.

Brazil is exceptional among the countries of the world in that it has no "primate city." [4] The largest city is not twice the size of the second city; in fact, Rio de Janeiro and São Paulo, less than three hundred miles apart, are almost exactly equal in population. Since 1899, much of Brazilian life has reflected the intense rivalry of these two places. Rio, which owed its start to the export of gold and diamonds, was greatly advanced by the arrival of the Portuguese court and achieved its present stature in large part because of its position midpoint between the North and the South, the effective hub of Brazil's domestic commerce, the geographical center of the populated parts of the country. São Paulo, for centuries the primary center from which the *bandeiras,* or exploring expeditions, went out into the backlands, owes its modern growth first to the development of coffee planting in its hinterland, more recently to a development of manufacturing industry which is the largest in all Latin America. São Paulo is more "modern" than Detroit, and the vitality of its economic life is in the strongest contrast with other parts of Brazil. The state of São Paulo alone produces nearly 40 percent of the revenue of the Brazilian treasury. For many years before 1930 Brazilian politics were controlled by São Paulo and Minas Gerais, and these two states can today control the political destiny of the country except when all the other states combine in opposition.

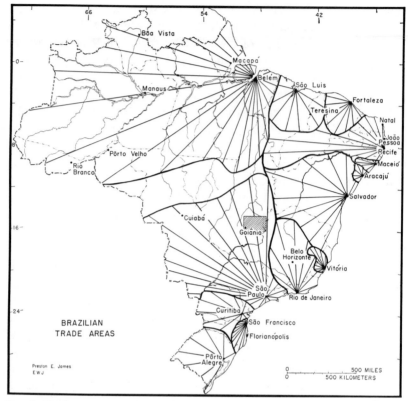

Fig. 2. Trade areas, or hinterlands, of the major Brazilian cities, compiled by James and Faissol.

To a much higher degree than Rio de Janeiro, São Paulo is an "inland" city, since it is in a better position than any other city to serve the interior of the country. Already its hinterland extends farther into the backlands than that of any other Brazilian center except Belém (Figure 2). Anything that promotes the economic development and settlement of the Brazilian backlands south of the Amazon forest, including the removal of the capital to the geographical center of the country, will give additional support to the growth of São Paulo.

In spite of the constitutional provision, there are great numbers of people who do not favor moving the capital away from Rio de Janeiro. But there are also great numbers who favor such a plan.

No Gallup Poll forecasts how a vote on the question might go. Nevertheless, there should be some objective analysis of the ideas that the Brazilians themselves hold on this problem.

## REASONS FOR MOVING THE CAPITAL

In the first place, it is necessary to appreciate the feeling that almost every city-bred Brazilian has for the backlands. He calls these thinly peopled lands the *sertões* (singular, *sertão*). To him they are lands of mystery, lands where the brutal forces of an unfriendly nature are marshaled against the spirit of man, and where only the strongest of men can survive. But they are also lands that contain a hidden wealth of natural resources, lands in which the strong and the brave can find new ways to spectacular riches. Few Brazilians would not give support to almost any plan to populate the interior. For the past two decades a major policy of the government has been the promotion of a *marcha para oeste,* a westward movement. All this gives wide general support to the idea of moving the capital inland.

There are also more specific reasons for supporting the plan, of which four are particularly significant. First, there is the widespread desire to provide an internal, central focus for national life that is a phase of the rising tide of nationalism. Rio de Janeiro lies too exposed to the world outside. To escape from the conflicts and frustrations of the world of great powers and international exchange, there are many who would pull inward, seeking shelter in the interior and a highly centralized, self-sufficient kind of life. To these people the movement of the capital is an essential first step.

Second, there is the feeling that the federal government in Rio is so closely concerned with the problems of this one place that it finds difficulty in viewing the problems of the rest of the country in proper perspective. The press of Rio de Janeiro and São Paulo is thought to have too much influence. Administrators and lawmakers are in danger of losing sight of the country as a whole when they must do their work in the midst of Brazil's great metropolis. Their decisions, some think, would be more clearly in the national interest if they worked in a small capital city (of perhaps some five hundred thousand people) removed from direct contact with any of the major centers of settlement.

Third, there is the concept of a "dream city." Admittedly, life in Rio de Janeiro, pleasant though it may be for tourists and foreign visitors, is trying for permanent residents. With the advent of automobiles, the street pattern of Rio de Janerio became intolerable. Bottlenecks confine the morning and evening flow of commuters to and from the center of the city. The mountainous setting of Rio provides spectacular scenery, but it also presents all but insuperable physical obstacles to growth and development. In contrast, the Brazilian engineers and architects envision a kind of dream city —a city of wide avenues, tall modern buildings, spreading suburbs, and happy people. Already Belo Horizonte and Goiânia have been built where no cities existed before. One can point to the success of Canberra and Washington, both planned capitals—but also to the endless frustration that arises from the off-center position of Washington in the modern period. No one who has been trained as a city planner, or who is capable of contributing to the technical improvement of Brazilian life, can fail to respond to the challenge of building a new capital, a city planned from the start without the encumbrances of inherited street patterns or obsolete buildings.

Finally, we must not forget the possibility of profit. Although the more extreme forms of dishonest profit were avoided in the development of the two new state capitals—Belo Horizonte and Goiânia—and probably could be avoided in the movement of the federal capital, there are nevertheless a great many people who stand to gain honestly from any such undertaking. Engineers and architects, merchants and laborers, would find new job opportunities and new sources of income. And someone is also likely to gain from the "unearned increment" deriving from increased land values.

## REASON FOR OPPOSING THE MOVE

Each of the reasons for favoring the plan appears to other persons as a reason for opposing it. Certainly a realistic appraisal of the possibilities of economic development in the backlands strips away the idea that these lands contain great stores of untapped wealth. No person of understanding would venture to forecast either the possibility or the impossibility of widespread agricultural development without a geographical survey of land quality and an inventory of basic resources. The one forecast that can be made with confidence is that never will Brazilian settlement be spread uniformly over the whole of the national territory. The application of scientific farming methods will have the effect of increasing the density of population in the cities rather than of supporting a new wave of farm settlement beyond the present frontiers. If the backlands are transformed into farmlands, it is likely to be accomplished by the use of machinery on large properties, with relatively few workers. The geographical center of the national territory is not likely also to be the geographical center of the Brazilian population.

Those who subscribe to the idea of international interdependence rather than of national self-sufficiency prefer to maintain the accessibility to the outside world enjoyed by Rio de Janeiro. Furthermore, they assert, Rio's problems are not insuperable. Engineers and architects have already drawn up plans for the construction of subways and for widening the avenues of approach. In the center of the city the Avenida Getúlio Vargas has been carved out of a maze of narrow, winding streets and blocks of antiquated buildings. Some years ago one of the hills in the center of the city was washed down by hydraulic streams and deposited in the bay to make the Santos Dumont airfield. Now a similar undertaking is removing the Morro Santo Antônio to fill in the bay all the way from the Santos Dumont airfield to the Gloria Hotel. The fact is that the people of Rio are making strenuous and effective efforts to solve some of their most pressing problems.

The argument, advanced by some who favor removal, that Rio de Janeiro has an enervating, seductive climate is an interesting survival from the climatic ideas of the Greek geographers. Many people assume that because Rio de Janeiro lies in the tropics its climate must contribute to the weakening of the physical and spiritual fiber of those who inhabit the place. Carefully documented studies on the effect of temperature and humidity on human energy have yet to make much impact on those who still believe in the myth of tropical heat. There is no doubt that Rio is hot in summer, though certainly no hotter than many places in the United States. The average temperature in Rio in February is 78.2°F., the rainfall 4.4 inches; comparable (July) figures for Charleston, South Carolina, are 81.4° and 6.14 inches; for St. Louis, Missouri, 80.2° and 2.87 inches. The fact is that Rio is no more unpleasant in summer than Washington, D.C. In neither city can people be comfortable in dark clothes and neckties.

## THE PLANALTO CENTRAL

The part of Brazil to which the capital would be moved if it were taken away from Rio de Janeiro is the Planalto Central in southeastern Goiás. This is the area described earlier in some detail by Waibel.[5]

The Planalto Central occupies the drainage divide between the headwaters of the Tocantins, the São Francisco, and the Paraná-Plata. It lies in the central part of the Brazilian highlands near the geographical center of the national territory. Between the headwaters of these great river systems the surface, some nine hundred meters above sea level, is an ancient peneplain developed on rocks of varying resistance. Local relief is slight. On this ancient surface, long exposed to the percolation of rain water (more than fifteen hundred millimeters of rain falls each year), the soil is in an advanced stage of lateritic development. The upper horizon is coarse and heavily leached; underneath there is a cemented layer of iron oxide known as *cangá*. A more sterile soil for shallow-rooted crops would be difficult to find. Reflecting both the unproductive nature of the soil and the concentration of rain in one season, with a long and very dry season during the southern hemisphere winter, the vegetation is a mixture of deciduous scrub woodland and coarse savanna grass known as *campo cerrado*. The forest occurs in patches —trees cover a large part of the surface in wet spots or where the water table is relatively high—interspersed with areas where grass predominates and the trees are farther apart. The trees are mainly deciduous, though a few species retain their leaves during the dry season.

The rivers that flow out of this high-level surface are cutting back into it to develop a typical dendritic drainage pattern. At the headwaters the high surface is dented with what Waibel describes as "dales"—broad, shallow depressions with gentle marginal slopes. Farther downstream, however, the stream dissection creates a hilly terrain with steep slopes and narrow V-shaped valleys. For the most part the dales are covered with *campo cerrado,* but the dissected hilly areas support tropical forest, in which some of the tall trees are deciduous, some evergreen.

The largest of the "islands" of forest is developed on the headwaters of the Tocantins, north of Goiânia and northwest of Anápolis (Figure 3). This is the region known as the *Mato Grosso de Goiás,* Brazil's latest and much-publicized pioneer zone, where one of the last remaining areas of virgin tropical forest is in the process of rapid clearing.[6]

Brazilian agricultural settlement has for four centuries been directed to hilly areas covered with tropical forest.[7] Rarely is agriculture found on flat land, even where such land is available. The undissected parts of the Planalto Central are largely left for poor range. Since Brazilian agriculture has the effect of producing pasture in the previously forested areas at the end of each cycle of clearing, burning, and cropping, and since these pastures are better than the undeveloped *campo cerrado* pastures, the latter are used only as open range and never for fattening.

Can the *campo cerrado* be used for agriculture? Most previous attempts have ended in failure, yet in a few places crops have been raised successfully, chiefly in the dales. Where the *cangá* is unbroken, shallow-rooted crops do poorly, and to break the *cangá* requires dynamite and bulldozers. Still, we must recognize that the *campo cerrado* is by no means uniform throughout; it varies, apparently, with the depth of the water table. Here is an area in pressing need of a detailed land-classification survey; without such a survey no useful appraisal of the potential productivity of the vast Brazilian backlands can be made and certainly no pioneer-settlement projects should be attempted. Modern agricultural methods that include the use of machinery, soil conditioners, and fertilizers have created productive farms in places long considered to be low in productivity. Yet these methods, which require a large capital in-

Fɪɢ. 3. Distribution of forest and *campo cerrado* in the Planalto Central, based on field studies by Faissol and the examination of aerial photographs. The rectangle indicates the area within which the site of the Federal District is to be located.

vestment, would probably yield better returns in terms of lowered food prices in the great cities if they were applied to the older agricultural lands nearer the urban centers and within the present areas of concentrated settlement.

## STUDIES OF SITE AND SITUATION

To carry out the provisions of the constitution, the Brazilian government established the "Comissão de Estudos de Localização da Nova Capital do Brasil," originally under the direction of the late General Djalma Polli Coelho. Two expeditions were sent out to study the broad area within which the capital might be located, one under the direction of Professor Francis Ruellan, the other under Professor Fabio de Macedo Soares Guimarães.[8] Much of the field and office work was done by the professional geographers employed in the Conselho Nacional de Geografia.

The principles that guided these studies were clear and simple. The first objective was to find an acceptable site somewhere near the demographic center of the country. It was recognized that the geographical center of the national territory might not necessarily be the best place, and that the demographic center would not itself be acceptable because of the great contrasts in economic development and production around Rio de Janeiro and São Paulo. The center of equilibrium among the various communities must therefore be identified on the basis of both demographic center and economic center. Second, the place selected for the capital must be provided with transportation to make it accessible from all parts of the country with the greatest possible ease. And third, the federal district should lie if possible on the border between two or more states rather than wholly within any one state.

Applying these principles to the central area of Brazil, the geographers employed on the field surveys selected an area in the Paranaíba Valley near the town of Tupaciguara (Figure 3). This town is located in the western extension of the state of Minas Gerais which lies between São Paulo and Goiás and which is known as the *Triângulo Mineiro*. From the geographical point of view, the area enjoys a number of advantages. It is close to the boundaries of three states rather than in the center of any one state. Water could be furnished by gravity flow, and nearby sources of waterpower could be harnessed to provide electricity. Furthermore, the area is within the zone of settlement that focuses on São Paulo, in a place where there are still some forest remnants left. But the commission, composed of men who represented a variety of political opinion, was less inclined than were the professional geographers to give so much weight to the quality of the site. They wanted an area farther north, nearer the geographical center of the country. Actually, two reports were finally issued: the majority report recommended an area in the vicinity of Formosa and Planaltina; the minority report recommended the area in the vincinity of Tupaciguara.

The Chamber of Deputies then set up another commission to make the decision. This body consisted of twenty-two members, one representing each of the states. The inevitable result—approval of the area recommended in the majority report—stemmed from one of the basic facts of Brazilian political geography: the region known as the Northeast comprises nine states, whereas the region known as the Southeast, with Rio de Janeiro and São Paulo as foci, comprises only four states. In short, the voice of the Northeast in national decisions is more powerful than its relative productivity and wealth would suggest.

The area finally selected, within which the government was to look for a specific site, is indicated on Figure 3. It includes Formosa and Planaltina in the North but extends a little farther to the South than was recommended in the report of General Polli Coelho's commission. At the West is the edge of the Mato Grosso de Goiás, and in the southwest corner is the city of Goiânia, the new capital of Goiás. The surface features of this area are sketched on Figure 4. The area selected occupies the drainage divide between the headwaters of the Tocantins, the Paraná, and the São Francisco. It lies well to the south of the demographic center of Brazil, which, in 1940, was located on the eastern side of the São Francisco between Pirapora and Montes Claros. It lies within the most densely populated part of Goiás and definitely within the tributary area of São Paulo (Figure 2). It extends eastward from the Mato Grosso de Goiás a short distance into the state of Minas Gerais.

Somewhere within this general area a site must be found for the new capital. When the site has been selected, a federal district five thousand square kilometers in area will be drawn around the site.

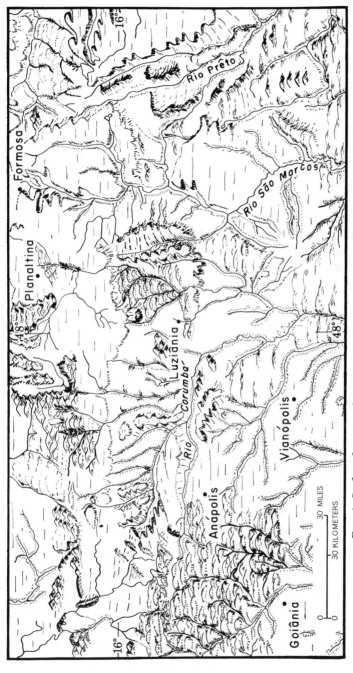

FIG. 4. Surface features of the rectangular area shown on Fig. 3, based on field studies and the examination of aerial photographs by Faissol.

## THE SELECTION OF A SITE

Eight principles, which the Brazilians arrange in the following order of importance, guide the selection of a site: (1) gently sloping terrain—not too steep, not too flat; (2) a comfortable climate with no extremes of temperature or rainfall and no violent winds, and at an elevation high enough to offer freedom from malaria; (3) a water supply adequate for a city of half a million people, preferably available by gravity flow; (4) nearby forested areas where agriculture can become established for the supply of vegetables and milk, and where wood can be procured for fuel; (5) a source of low-cost electric power located within one hundred kilometers; (6) locally available building materials, including lime for cement; (7) a subsoil suitable for building foundations and for the excavation of sewers and subways; (8) an attractive landscape and nearby recreation areas.

It can be said at once that, within the rectangle outlined above, no fully acceptable site is to be found. The major problems are water supply and hydroelectric power. The kind of terrain desired is found in the headwater dales that are indented below the untouched high-level surface. But in no case could an adequate water supply be found. In this headwater position, high enough to be free from malaria (that is, more than nine hundred meters in the north of the rectangle and more than eight hundred meters in the south), water must be pumped up to the dales from the valleys lower down. This in turn places emphasis on the importance of a dependable source of electric power. Unfortunately, however, such sources of power are found mainly on the Rio Paraníba and its tributaries where these streams pass over outcrops of diabase, and they are more than two hundred kilometers distant from the sites that possess other desirable qualities. The rivers that have a sufficient flow for hydroelectric development are also those best suited for use as sources of potable water.

Nor are all the other requisites to be found easily. In this central part of Brazil there are three principal areas of forest: a ribbon of forest along the Paraníba and its tributaries; an island of forest near Patos in the state of Minas Gerais; and the Mato Grosso de Goiás (Figure 3). The Brazilians, however, are inclined to overlook the effects of destructive land use in a forested area, the kind of land use that has created empty areas in the very suburbs of Rio de Janeiro and São Paulo. The clearing of the forest and its frequent reclearing close to a big city soon exhaust and erode the soil, fill the rivers with silt, and greatly reduce the productive capacity of the land. If Brazil's new capital were placed on the edge of the Mato Grosso de Goiás, for how many years could that small area of once-forested land continue to produce vegetables and milk at low cost? Not many, unless Brazilian agriculture undergoes a fundamental change.

Even an enthusiast for the pioneer zone of Goiás cannot say much for the beauty of its landscape. The *campo cerrado* has a kind of mystery—the mystery of vast, level, empty plateaus—and the forested areas are attractive when they are still forested. But nothing is more depressing to a lover of the land than the devastated forest areas of Brazil.

In 1954, the Belcher Associates, a private engineering firm with headquarters in Ithaca, New York, which undertakes city-planning operations throughout the world, was employed to examine several sites tentatively selected by the Brazilians. This company undertook a large-scale survey based on new vertical air photographs and some field study. The result is a thoroughly competent judgment regarding the city-planning and engineering aspects of the problem. In the end, the Belcher people selected five possible sites within the area of the rectangle outlined.

## THE ISSUES

However, the decision that the Brazilians must make involves much more than architectural and engineering problems. Let us suppose that some way can be found to pump water up to a city located on the stream divide, that electricity can be produced at low cost, that the city can be connected by lines of communication with the existing centers of settlement, and that these new overland lines are more efficient and less costly than those at present connecting Rio de Janeiro with the rest of Brazil. The question that remains to be answered, and that is fundamental to the whole problem, is whether Brazil's pattern of population and economic production is likely to change significantly in the years ahead. The Planalto Central is obviously not central at the present time in terms of population and settlement; will it become central in the future as a result of a major movement of people into the thinly peopled backlands?

In the first place, it should be clear that the establishment of the capital in the interior will not, of itself, create a westward movement. Pioneer settlement does not start in a city and move out from it; on the contrary, cities attract people away from rural areas. When Belo Horizonte was established as the new capital of Minas Gerais, replacing Ouro Preto, no movement of new settlement pushed northward into the *sertão*. Belo Horizonte was located on the margin of concentrated settlement. Beyond it to the north was sparsely settled backland. But the establishment of the new capital resulted in a further thinning of the population of the backlands of Minas Gerais, not in a new northward thrust of the frontier. Similarly, the establishment of Goiânia as the new capital of Goiás has not produced a new wave of settlement. Pioneer settlement in the Mato Grosso de Goiás has proceeded from Anápolis, not from the capital. It is a mistake to think that patterns of circulation and settlement can be created by administrative decree; these geographical phenomena develop slowly, and once developed have a tendency to persist.

Can the *campo cerrado* support a substantial increase of settlement, a true *marcha para oeste?* This is perhaps the most important question to be analyzed. And in formulating a forecast it is necessary to keep in mind that the delimitation of the part of the Brazilian backlands is certainly too highly generalized to be useful. There are many significant variations of soil and water, perhaps reflected in the varying nature of the *campo cerrado* itself, that remain to be identified and mapped. However, enough is known about the region to be certain that its soils are not highly productive by nature. As agriculture is at present practiced in Brazil, the *campo cerrado* represents poor land; its grasses are not nourishing for animals, its soils are not naturally rich for shallow-rooted crops. There is nothing here that remotely resembles the black soils of mid-latitude grasslands, of the kind that supported the great move-ment of new pioneer settlement in the United States in the latter half of the nineteenth century. Let no one be misled by the words of ignorant people: the *campo cerrado* is not among the world's naturally productive regions.

But the productivity of any region is determined not only by its natural qualities but also by the technical skills of the people who inhabit it. The black prairie soils and chernozems of the middle lat-itudes were long considered poor for agriculture until a variety of new techniques and skills changed their productivity during the past century. Before the introduction of barbed wire, no one could properly fence a treeless prairie; before the coming of steam rail-roads, surplus food could not be moved cheaply to urban markets, and large urban markets could not themselves exist. Is it not possi-ble that changes in agricultural techniques may radically change the patterns of land use, the pattern of what is considered first-class land? The answer is that such changes are imminent. But they must be superimposed on existing patterns of settlement. In Brazil the centers of population and economic production will not be dis-placed by changes in agricultural technology. The chief markets of Brazil remain Rio de Janeiro, São Paulo, and numerous smaller cities. If large-scale manufacturing industry is to be established suc-cessfully in these cities, some way must be found to supply food at less cost to the workers.

Modern agricultural methods may well change the productive capacity of *campo cerrado* lands. But modern agriculture involves the use of machinery rather than men; it has the effect of reducing the number of people engaged in farming. Even if the *campo cer-rado* is successfully occupied by people raising food crops, this will not change the basic patterns of population and settlement, the po-sition of the major markets for food. Furthermore, modern meth-ods may well be applied to the redevelopment of lands whose productivity was lost as a result of centuries of exploitation and destructive practices, such as the *Baixada Fluminense,* the lowlands behind Rio de Janeiro. The application of modern methods of farming in Brazil may have the effect of bringing the remote back-lands into productive use, but it will also increase the density of population in the already well-populated places.

Even though the present patterns of population and economic production persist, the development of overland communication facilities might make it desirable to place the administrative center of the country in the interior. Even though Rio de Janeiro continues to be the hub of domestic commerce, based on its position with reference to cheap water transportation connecting the major areas of concentrated settlement, government might be carried on more efficiently from an interior position, connected to the densely settled areas by air lines and highways. Yet highways and air lines passing through or over sparsely populated country would be costly, much more costly than in the areas of concentrated settlement. These are some of the issues involved in the decision concerning Brazil's capital city.

*Postscript.* While this article was in press, a newspaper despatch from Rio de Janeiro reported that a request for the final authorization of the site near Anápolis has been sent to the Brazilian congress. Expropriation of four hundred square miles of land has been completed, and surveys for streets and sewer lines have been begun. The despatch further reported that the probable name of the new capital will be Vera Cruz.

## NOTES

1. See, for example, Erico Verissimo, *O Tempo e O Vento* (Pôrto Alegre, 1950), trans. L. L. Barrett and published in this country as *Time and the Wind* (New York, 1951), and Jorge Amado, *Terras do Sem Fim* (Rio de Janeiro, 1943), trans. Samuel Putnam and published in this country as *The Violent Land* (New York, 1945).

2. See P. E. James, "The Changing Patterns of Population in São Paulo State, Brazil," *The Geographical Review,* 28 (1938), 353–62; reference on p. 361.

3. For the distribution of this forest in Brazil, see map of the natural vegetation of Brazil in P. E. James, "Trends in Brazilian Agricultural Development," *ibid.,* 43 (1953), 301–28; map on p. 304.

4. Mark Jefferson, "The Law of the Primate City," *ibid.,* 29 (1939), 226–32.

5. Leo Waibel, "Vegetation and Land Use in the Planalto Central of Brazil," *ibid.,* 38 (1948), 529–54.

6. Speridião Faissol, "O Mato Grosso de Goiás," *Biblioteca Geográfica Brasileira,* Ser. A. No. 9 (Rio de Janeiro, 1952).

7. James, "Trends in Brazilian Agricultural Development," *The Geographical Review,* 43 (1953).

8. For this latter expedition, Leo Waibel served as technical consultant.

# 12

## GENERAL INTRODUCTION TO
## LATIN AMERICA

In no other major part of the earth are the conditions of life being so rapidly and fundamentally transformed as they are in Latin America.[1] Traditional Latin America is to be found today in only a few isolated spots. The graceful and sophisticated society of the aristocratic landowners is rapidly disappearing; disappearing also are the churchmen concerned only with men's souls, and the bemedaled army officers who back their positions of power with force. The tourists will be disappointed who expect to see that picturesque peasant dozing in the shade of a cactus with a large sombrero pulled down over his eyes. There are multitudes of formerly sick, hungry, illiterate, and hopelessly poor people who are now sensing that an improvement in the conditions of life is possible. Ignorance and apathy are no longer terms that describe the people of Latin America. Ignorance is being swept away by a flood of half-understood items of new knowledge, and apathy is being replaced by a rising chorus of vigorous protest.

Changes of so fundamental a nature cannot be neglected. In a world brought closer together than ever before by modern technology, a change in any one element of the system inevitably leads to changes in all the other elements. Yet many people in the United States who must deal with Latin American problems are not informed about the nature of the transformations currently taking place to the south. And many people in Latin America conceive of the United States only in caricature. There is pressing need for

Reprinted from *Latin America* (New York: The Odyssey Press, 4th ed., 1969), pp. 1–4, 51.

more effective communication and more mutual understanding within the American hemisphere.

Mutual understanding is difficult to achieve until the nature of the basic processes of change is made clear. Latin America is not an isolated island of conflict. The industrial revolution and the democratic revolution first appeared as major movements affecting the lives of vast numbers of people during the latter half of the eighteenth century around the shores of the North Sea in Europe —primarily in Great Britain, France, and the Netherlands. Both revolutions have been spreading from the area of origin, setting up conflicts and reactions wherever the new ways of living came into contact with preindustrial and predemocratic societies. Both revolutions have been further developed as they spread, especially in the culture region of Anglo-America. In Anglo-America the results of continued technological innovation have been an unprecedented increase in economic production until more than 40 percent of all the world's goods and services are produced in this one region.

The innovations associated with the industrial and democratic revolutions are sweeping over present-day Latin America. Millions of Latin-Americans are joining in a demand for better conditions of life and for an end to the social inequities of traditional Latin-American society. But these demands are not exactly like those with which we are familiar in Anglo-America. Equality in northern America refers to equality of opportunity and the right of each individual, regardless of economic status, to be treated as an equal. In Latin America the idea of equality means the equal right of every individual to be different and to be treated as a uniquely different person. When businessmen and government officials from the United States attempt to establish what they consider to be a sound process of economic development, they are baffled by the reaction they get even from educated Latin Americans. North Americans discover that for many Latin Americans the increase in the volume or efficiency of production is not the most important goal. Many Latin-Americans demand a change in the traditional system of inequity first.

Another problem is the lack of confidence the average Latin American feels regarding people in power over him. This refers not only to army officers and other politically powerful people, but also to the owners of capital and the managers of businesses. In Latin America those who have gained positions of power have all too frequently misused that power for personal advantage. Dishonesty and corruption are often accepted as normal, and the exploitation of people with less power by those with more power is expected. The system in which those with power exploit those with less power has a name in Latin America—it is called capitalism. When people from the United States talk about capitalism and free enterprise, their Latin American audiences think of unregulated exploitation of those who do not own capital.

Both the people and the natural resources of Latin America have long been exploited. That this is not a new land is a fact that many North Americans find difficulty in understanding. Some of the lands that lie to the south of the United States had been exploited and abandoned by the Indians before the arrival of Columbus. In the centuries that followed Columbus the so-called New World was ransacked by Spaniards, Portuguese, British, French, Dutch, and other peoples of European origin. There are many parts of Latin America for which up-to-date information is lacking, for which there are not even reliable maps, but there are few parts which have not been explored and exploited first by one group and then by another. Actually Latin America is not a virgin land, awaiting the arrival of the pioneer—it is an old land, much trampled, many of its sources of accumulated treasure exploited and abandoned, many of its landscapes profoundly altered by the hand of man. Yet it is a land in which large areas remain comparatively empty of human inhabitants.

International events have made it imperative that we, in Anglo-America, become acquainted with the conditions and problems faced by these other Americans. We must understand why Latin America is in turmoil. We must gain an appreciation of the problems of economic development in very poor countries. We must have some idea what resources are available to support economic growth, and what capital requirements there are if these resources are to be put to use. We must understand why North Americans are not everywhere popular. The common tendency to regard the changes in Latin America as a result of the Communist conspiracy is a dangerous oversimplification. We must know why Castro had such a following in Latin America until he proclaimed himself a Marxist-Leninist. We must know which of the Latin American states are unified and coherent and clearly viable, and which ones are composed of uncoordinated elements. We must appreciate the states which have achieved a high degree of democracy, and know the names and locations of those which are still under autocratic rule. These are the questions we wish to ask about the people who occupy the American hemisphere with us and who have entered into cooperative agreements with us within the frameworks of the United Nations and of the Organization of American States.

People and land are the basic elements of the story. A human society is not understandable unless it is considered in relation to the land it occupies; nor is the significance of the land with respect to human settlement determined without reference to the varying kinds of human societies. In Latin America four principal characteristics may serve to summarize the conditions of the people and the land. These are: (1) a relatively small population that is rapidly increasing; (2) a clustered pattern of settlement; (3) a Latin American population that is composed of a great diversity of racial and cultural elements; and (4) a great variation from place to place in the character of the land. . . .

The struggle to establish order among these diverse elements is a basic theme which endows the present-day arrangement of people in Latin America with meaning. In each independent state, in each separate cluster of people, this struggle takes a somewhat different form and has reached somewhat different stages. As a result, the significance of the elements of the land—the potential value of the natural resources—differs from place to place and from time to time. In extreme cases we find two or more diverse groups mixed but not blended in the same area of concentrated settlement, each group motivated by different attitudes and objectives and consequently each reacting differently to the variegated background of the land. In a few instances we are encouraged by what seems to be a real advance against the forces of disunity. When we examine the map of people in detail in the light of this theme we can no longer see it only as a pattern of apparently uniform dots irregularly clustered—we see each cluster as possessing a distinct individuality, as composed of people who have made a separate and distinctive contribution, even if only a negative one, to the struggle toward the development of a coherent society.


### NOTE

1. The name "Latin America" refers to the southern part of the American hemisphere, but with no suggestion that its inhabitants are all of Latin origin. Similarly we refer to the northern part of the American hemisphere as "Anglo-America," recognizing that the population includes a great variety of people of other than British origin. Latin America, the part of America that lies south and southeast of the United States, is one of the world's major culture regions.

PART III

# On the World and Its Regions

# COMMENTARY

The very nature of geography forces a continual search for generalizations at global scale for the development of concepts which can bring a useful order to the infinite variety on the surface of the earth. Every geographer must perforce carry in his mind some sense of world patterns, of how things are areally arranged. Just what patterns he considers most useful will depend upon his training as well as his special interests, and his training will likely reflect the dominant themes of a particular time. The work of Preston James is of especial relevance to this topic because his textbooks have long had an important influence upon the basic training of American geographers.

A survey of the whole sequence of James's work makes his review of Wladimir Köppen's "Classification of Climates," seem particularly significant. Köppen's famous scheme was one of the first to offer a comprehensive generic system using numerical data for the regionalization of the earth. Because the categories were based upon temperature and rainfall values considered critical to broad patterns of vegetation, this system of world climates came to be used (though often much too naively) as in some degree a surrogate for the delineation of "natural regions" or "habitats." Although Köppen's work had been reviewed by others in America, James, in 1922, was the first to present the full criteria of the categories and also the diagram of the "hypothetical continent." His dependence upon Köppen as a guide to basic world patterns of the physical environment is apparent in all of his textbooks (for example, see article 15), but his review is mentioned here simply as an indicator at the outset of two important features of his career: his emphasis upon a regional approach to world geography, and his interest in the work of important European geographers.

The first exhibit of James's response to the challenge of how to generalize effectively about the entire world was a mimeographed college text of 1929, "Regional Geography, A Chorographical Study of the

World." We can now see it clearly as a work in process, a kind of rough draft of *An Outline of Geography* (1935). This, his first published book, was the first text of its time in America to attempt to treat the world entirely within the framework of a system of regions. Welcomed as "a significant advance in American geography" by George B. Cressey, in *Science,* 84 (October 2, 1936), 311–14, it quickly became one of the most widely used and influential books in the field. Fourteen years later it was metamorphosed into *A Geography of Man* (1949), which in time underwent further extensive revisions, in 1959 and in 1966, to become the book now current under that name.

In the Preface to the 1929 volume, James stated that he had "attempted to develop his subject on the basis of the European geographic philosophy which has been remarkably slow to gain appreciation in this country." His most important sources of that philosophy are specified in the Preface of the 1935 book. *An Outline of Geography* was therefore not just another college textbook but a means of implanting in America a rather different philosophy of the field than the ones then dominant. Thus James had a role in the reformation of American geographic thought during the fifteen years before World War II complementary to those of Carl Sauer and Richard Hartshorne, and *An Outline of Geography* can be seen as a logical and felicitous expression at a world summary scale of some of the more important European philosophical and methodological ideas set forth in *The Morphology of Landscape* (1925) and *The Nature of Geography* (1939).

In 1964 another book, *One World Divided,* written for the same introductory college level but organized on an entirely different set of regions, appeared. Its most obvious antecedent is *The Wide World,* his high school text published in 1959, and his general world-culture area approach would seem to owe much to the innovative American textbook of R. J. Russell and F. B. Kniffen, *Culture Worlds* (1951), which was based, in turn, upon the ideas of Carl Sauer. Nevertheless, on closer look *One World Divided* appears to be an equally characteristic development of James's thought, expressing the same philosophy of geography as his other work, grounded on the same basic principles, and expounding many of the same themes, but all with a quite different emphasis and elaborated within a quite different framework.

The selections in this section offer interesting exhibits of some basic conceptual problems in geography. Spanning more than three decades and written by a man whose interests have always embraced the full breadth of his field, such books certainly could be expected to mirror rather clearly much of the development of American geography as a whole, as indeed they do. A sequential reading of the four Prefaces of the single evolving work is a concise sampling of four phases in recent American developments (article 13). Note, for example, the change in key terms: "landscapes" (1935); "area differentiation" (1949); "processes" and "characteristics of places" (1959); "spatial systems" (1966)—a sequence which carries us from Passarge and Brunhes (by way of Sauer) to Hartshorne to Ackerman and Berry. So, too, the titles of, or in, the Introductions in each book reflect a shift in balance and an elaboration of concepts: "The Face of the Earth" (1935); "Man on the Earth" (1949); "Population," "Culture," "Land" (1959); "The Habitat" and "Culture" (1966) (only the first and excerpts from the last of this sequence are reprinted in this collection). It is an accurate glimpse of the general trend in America toward an increasingly culture-centered geography. The change in title to *A Geography of Man* is of course a bold mark of such a shift, though it belies the magnitude of change, for there is a continuity of theme in James's work despite a shift in emphasis.

In a way, *One World Divided* (1964) with its culture-area organization and the concepts of the Industrial Revolution and the democratic revolution as major themes, appears to be the culmination (despite its date) of this sequence. Its connections with the other works will be readily apparent if the full introductions and conclusions are examined. Even in these excerpts we can now see the brief mention of the "machine civilization" in the Conclusion of *An Outline of Geography* (1935) as an intimation of the "Industrial Society" with each subsequent edition. In *One World Divided* it is magnified and extended in time and space to be seen as a vast cultural process developing out of a Northwest European hearth and spreading unevenly and with varied results over the several broad culture areas of the world.

But of course while *One World Divided* is sequential in the development of such ideas, it is also concurrent, for with the 1966 version of *A Geography of Man,* it is one of a pair of books offering alternative ways of dealing with the human geography of the world. Together they represent an unusual package in American geography—two views of the world by the same mind; two expressions of a single philosophy;

two results of the regional approach, using entirely different but equally valid criteria. Complementary, not contradictory, they are an unusually interesting display of an inherent methodological feature of geography.

These short pieces of these several works are offered here, therefore, not for what they tell us about the world (for that we need the whole of the books), but for what they tell us about how one geographer has looked at the world, and what that in turn tells us about some of the ways the field as a whole has organized its data at that scale.

# 13

## FOUR PREFACES

### An Outline of Geography (1935) *

The face of the earth, especially in its role as the home of man, was made the subject of description and interpretation probably even before the beginning of written history. Homer, that somewhat legendary bard of ancient Greece, was among the first writers about the earth; and from him, through classical antiquity, there descends a long line of contributors to the growing literature of geography. Even in ancient times the description of the phenomena on the face of the earth was developed both as an art and as a science. On the artistic side the word pictures of mountains, deserts, seacoasts, cities, or the manifold occupations of mankind achieved a vigor and clarity of expression difficult to surpass. On the scientific side the systematic collection and classification of data, the interpretation of cause-and-effect relationships, and even quantitative measurements were all carried to a rather remarkable degree of perfection. Anyone who doubts the scientific nature of ancient geography should read the works of Strabo and Ptolemy.

Geography as a science, however, has always suffered from one important handicap. This handicap is in the background of Strabo's eloquent arguments concerning the importance of geographical writings to statesmen and warriors—arguments which have been repeated throughout the course of history down to the present. In the modern world this handicap reveals itself, for instance, in the deplorable attitude of certain schoolmen who believe that the subject can be adequately presented by teachers who lack specific geographic training. Geography is handicapped by the fact that most

* Reprinted from *An Outline of Geography* (Boston: Ginn and Company, 1935), pp. vii–ix.

people are so familiar with the details of their immediate surroundings that it seems as if any attempt to describe, classify, and interpret these familiar phenomena could lead only to an elaboration of the obvious; and, sadly enough, in the hands of the untrained teacher much that passes for geography becomes little more than this. In most sciences the obvious things are the broad, general relationships, and the penetration of greater detail brings forth facts and principles of a more subtle character. In geography the phenomena to be described and understood are much larger than the observer—it is, actually, the details which are obvious—but the broader patterns and relationships can only be studied or described by reducing them to observable size on maps. To a very small creature living, let us say, on the surface of a half-tone photograph, the details of the printed dots would become quite familiar, and any attempt to study or classify these dots would seem to be a needless application of scientific technique to a very obvious matter; yet the larger patterns of those dots, which are combined in the general areas of light and shade to form the lineaments of a picture, would not really be at all obvious. It is this apparent familiarity with the details of geography which constitutes today, as it has in the past, a major handicap to the development of the subject.

The things which exist together on the surface of the earth can be studied from a number of different points of view. Each set of phenomena can be studied systematically: for example, the landforms, the plants, the animals, or the social organization of the human communities all can be made the subject of description, classification, and interpretation. Geography has been called "the mother of the sciences," since many of these systematic groupings, once handled by geographers only, have become fields of specialization in their own right—for example, physiography, botany, zoology, and some of the social sciences.

But the various objects which exist together on the face of the earth can be studied in another way: in their unsystematic but natural groupings. In other words, landforms, plants, animals, or human communities, instead of being made the subject of special studies, can be investigated with regard to their mutual arrangement on the earth. The face of the earth itself is made up of a mosaic of spaces, each space being composed of a complex of elements grouped together in intricate and intimate relationship. In detail these spaces are what we call "landscapes"; in a broader way they are "regions" in which more general combinations of phenomena may be observed. The face of the earth can be made the subject of description, classification, and interpretation. This we maintain to be the general field of geography.

Certain writers have attempted to define geography in a somewhat different way. Some would describe the field as "a study of the influence of environment on man." Others, less extreme, would define it as "a study of the response of man to his environment," or "a study of the adjustment of man to his environment." These definitions of the geographic objective are held to be inadequate, especially insofar as they have led many less critical writers to seek only those interpretations of man's activities which could be considered as responses or adjustments to environment. A truly scientific discipline could not admit of a definition of its field which would permit only a one-sided approach to a problem or which would limit the subject to the study of any one principle. To define biology as the study of evolution would be analogous to defining geography as a study of the adjustment of man to his environment. Not that adjustments are to be denied, any more than one would deny the principle of evolution, but the scientific student must approach his problem without prejudice as to what he is to find. In any given instance the facts must first be described, then classified, and finally interpreted without limitation as to the kind of interpretation which shall be discovered. Geography as the study of responses or adjustments is in the stage of medieval alchemy; geography as the study of the mutual space relationships of phenomena on the face of the earth is a science.

The professional reader will readily discover the debt which the author owes to certain of the great figures in the geographic world. From the stimulating chorologic works of Siegfried Passarge and Alfred Hettner have come the germs of many of the ideas elaborated in these pages. Passarge's *Die Landschaftsgürtel der Erde* gave a definite direction to the classification of the world into "landscape groups." To the master of French geographers, Paul Vidal de la Blache, and his disciples Jean Brunhes and Camille Vallaux, the author owes the crystallization of many principles regarding the relation of man to the earth. More especially in America, the author is very greatly indebted to Carl O. Sauer and Isaiah Bowman for their important contributions to the clarification of geographic thought and technique. . . .

## A Geography of Man (1949) *

Geographers observe and catalog the facts of area differentiation on the earth and analyze the significance of these facts. They attempt to discover what it is that makes one area differ from another, or in what respect differing areas have certain aspects in common. The facts which combine to produce differences from place to place are of many diverse kinds, including those which result from physical processes, operating in obedience to the precisely formulated laws of physics, chemistry, or biology, and those which result from cultural processes, operating under the much less precise principles of the social sciences. Geographers must deal with these varied phenomena insofar as they lead to area differentiation on the earth.

But geographers do much more than observe and catalog. They also analyze the significance of differences which are observed from place to place. To discover the significance, or meaning, of a fact of area differentiation requires inquiry into both causes and consequences. The present nature and arrangement of things on the earth have meaning with respect to the operation of physical or cultural processes in the past. To understand the significance of what is observed on the earth today it is necessary to go back to origins and trace developments. But it is also necessary to forecast the consequences. Only when the present nature and arrangement of things on the earth have been projected both into the past and into the future has the significance of the differences from place to place on the earth been fully analyzed.

One of the basic factors in area differentiation is the distribution and density of population. It is this aspect of geography which forms the core of this book. A geographer is not interested in popu-

* Reprinted from *A Geography of Man* (Boston: Ginn and Company, 1949), pp. v–viii.

lation density as a statistical fact to be analyzed by statistical methods. He must see the pattern of population on the earth in its area relations, that is, in its relative position with respect to other differentiating features of the earth. In this book the facts of population density are shown, . . . [and] the patterns of natural vegetation and surface configuration—two aspects of the physical land which, together, outline the major lineaments of the face of the earth. These patterns are drawn on the same outline maps as those used for the population density, so that by a comparison of the corresponding maps the major area relationships of man on the earth can be identified. These . . . make it possible to see the pattern of mankind in relation to certain physical and cultural elements of the total environment which are assumed to be relevant.

This is the beginning of geographic study. At once the problem is raised: what is the significance of the differences of population density which are observed from place to place on the earth? The answer involves an evaluation of the various processes which have led to the present arrangement of people on the earth, and it also involves a forecast of the consequences of this present arrangement with respect to the economic, social, political, or strategic situations which we face.

The analysis of the significance of human distribution on the earth involves certain concepts of a theoretical nature. These concepts are, in fact, generalizations regarding man's relation to the land. The theoretical concepts which guide a field of study must never be accepted as beyond challenge—they must be subjected again and again to critical examination as they are confronted with new data. Yet as long as they survive such challenge, the concepts themselves must inevitably affect the kind of data that are gathered. There can be no such thing as a complete description of the content of an area. The facts which are selected as relevant are identified in terms of the theoretical concepts. For example, for many years geographers have observed what they called "human responses" to specific physical conditions, guided by the theoretical concept that man's activities were in large measure determined by the relatively unchanging facts of the physical earth. This concept now seems inadequate and inaccurate, since it can be shown quite clearly that the significance of any physical feature of the earth is different for different groups of people; that the meaning of the physical environment so far as man is concerned is determined not by the inherent character of the environment, but by the importance attached to the environment by man.

In this book there are five basic concepts regarding man's relation to the land. These concepts are elaborated and illustrated throughout the book, but may be stated in brief form as follows: (1) that the significance to man of the physical features of the land is determined by the culture, or way of living, of the people; and therefore any change in the attitudes, objectives, or technical abilities of a people inhabiting an area requires a reevaluation of the significance of the land; (2) that an exception to this first generalization occurs when the character of the physical earth itself changes rapidly in the presence of a particular group of inhabitants —as when there are volcanic eruptions, when harbors silt up, when rivers change their courses, or when there are actual changes of climate; and that in such circumstances the land exerts a positive influence on man; (3) that there is one basic necessity in man-land relations—that any human society, if it is to survive, must form a workable connection with the resources of the land; (4) that the simple cultures, in which the ways of making a living are few, form a few simple, direct connections with the land in base areas which are closely restricted, and that the more complex is the culture (that is, the greater is the number of ways of making a living), the greater is the variety of possible connections with the land, the less direct those connections are, and the larger is the base area; (5) that the industrial society is vastly more complex than any previous society, and its base area cannot be less than the whole globe; and that its survival therefore depends on the achievement of some measure of world unity. . . .

*A Geography of Man* makes use of numerous passages from the author's *An Outline of Geography* (Boston: Ginn and Company, 1935), but the present book uses these passages in quite different context from that in the earlier work. Whereas *An Outline of Geography* had as its major objective an understanding of the landscape patterns of the earth, the present book is intended to offer an analysis of the significance of the differences in population density on the earth. In both books the same outline, consisting of eight groups of natural regions, is used—based on the conditions of surface and natural vegetation. These groups are used because they have proved to offer a satisfactory framework for the portrayal of the world's major natural features—features in relation to which man's pattern of distribution is to be described.

## A GEOGRAPHY OF MAN (1959) *

Geography is that field of learning in which the characteristics of particular places on the earth's surface are examined. It is concerned with the arrangement of things and with the associations of things that distinguish one area from another. It is concerned with the connections and movements between areas. The face of the earth is made up of many different kinds of features, each the momentary result of an ongoing process. A process is a sequence of changes, systematically related as in a chain of cause and effect. There are physical and chemical processes developing forms of the land surface, the shapes of the ocean basins, the different characteristics of water and climate. There are biotic processes by which plants and animals spread over the earth in complex areal relation to the physical features and to each other. And there are economic, social, and political processes by which mankind occupies the world's lands.

As a result of all these processes the face of the earth is marked off into distinctive areas: geography seeks to interpret the significance of likenesses and differences among places in terms of causes and consequences.

Since the early nineteenth century, scholars have given more and more attention to systematic studies; that is, to the study of those features that are systematically related to each other because they are the result of a single process. Geography has sometimes been called the mother of sciences, since many fields of learning that started with observations of the actual face of the earth turned to the study of specific processes wherever they might be located.

* Reprinted from *A Geography of Man* (Boston: Ginn and Company, 1951), 2nd ed. pp. iii–vi. Adapted from 1956 edition of *Encyclopaedia Britannica*. Copyright© by *Encyclopaedia Britannica*.

These new disciplines are defined by the subjects they investigate. Some of the processes at work on the surface of the earth, notably the physical and chemical ones, have been reproduced under laboratory conditions where they can be examined in isolation from the environments of particular places. From these studies there has been a great increase in the understanding of cause-and-effect relations, and numerous fundamental principles have been formulated to describe the ideal or theoretical sequence of change. In a similar way the biotic processes have been examined under controlled conditions, and such important concepts have been developed as those of evolution and natural selection. The social sciences, too, have sought to understand the theoretical sequences of economic, social, and political change as these sequences are presumed to go on when isolated from the disturbing circumstances of actual places. Since the so-called cultural processes cannot be isolated in laboratories, they are isolated symbolically by such a phrase as "other things being equal."

Modern geography starts with the understandings provided by the systematic sciences. Unlike these other fields, geography cannot be defined by its subject matter, for anything that is unevenly distributed over the surface of the earth can be examined profitably by geographic methods. Rather, geography is a point of view, a system of procedures. It makes three kinds of contributions to understanding: (1) it extends the findings of the systematic sciences by observing the differences between the theoretical operation of a process and the actual operation as modified by the conditions of the total environment of a particular place; (2) it provides a method for testing the validity of concepts developed by the systematic sciences; and (3) it provides a realistic analysis of the conditions of particular places and so aids in the clarification of the issues involved in all kinds of policy decisions.

*A Geography of Man* deals specifically with those aspects of geography that are concerned with man and his works. It asks such questions as: Where are people located on the earth, and in what densities? What caused these differences in population density to develop as they have? What are the effects of differences of population density, habitat, way of living, and political organization on the conditions of poverty, hunger, insecurity, and conflict? How has man formed connections with the physical land and with the cover of plants and animals that constitute the habitat? What is it that determines the significance to man of the features of the habitat?

The book presents geographic concepts or principles, and illustrates the methods of geographic analysis. It contains an adequate factual content to permit the application of geographic ideas, but the ideas are presumed to be more important than completeness of content. The first two chapters are introductory. First there is a discussion of the meaning of race and culture, and a summary of culture history as a background for an understanding of man on the earth today. Second there is a survey of the major physical characteristics of the earth—its continents, its oceans, and its climates, and an outline of the major groups of natural regions defined in terms of surface features and vegetation cover. The main part of the book is organized around the eight groups of natural regions which constitute the habitats of man. In each group of regions, after a characterization of the physical and biotic features, the experience of man in occupying this kind of habitat is treated with historical perspective. Certain countries are discussed in some detail to illustrate the nature of the problems of man-land relations with which they are faced. The concluding chapter reexamines the population pattern of the earth from three new viewpoints: from that of culture areas, from that of political sovereignty, and from that of the process of population growth itself. . . .

*A Geography of Man* is the successor to the author's *An Outline of Geography* (Boston: Ginn and Company, 1935). The original work was recast around the central theme of population distribution and was published in 1949. This volume is a new and revised edition, incorporating the latest factual information and the newest formulation of geographic ideas. The central theme is an examination of differences of population density from place to place set against the background of eight groups of natural regions defined in terms of surface configuration and original cover of vegetation.

## A GEOGRAPHY OF MAN (1966) *

*A Geography of Man* is designed for an elementary college-level course in world geography. The book is specifically concerned with

---

* Reprinted from *A Geography of Man* (Waltham, Mass.: Blaisdell Publishing Company, 3rd ed., 1966), pp. vii–ix.

the interrelations of man and his natural surroundings. The purpose is to develop geographic concepts and to illustrate the methods of geographic analysis. Adequate factual content is presented to permit the application of geographic ideas, but the ideas are presumed to be more important than completeness of content. Two different kinds of concepts are developed: (1) concepts concerning the character and arrangement over the earth of the major physical-biotic systems that constitute the natural surroundings of man —the human habitats; and (2) concepts regarding the significance to man of these natural surroundings.

A system is made up of interdependent elements so organized that a change in any one element results in changes in all the others. Geography deals with spatial systems—that is, systems that occupy space on the face of the earth. To be sure, the whole surface of the earth, including its animal and human inhabitants, constitutes the only complete system. But the totality of interaction is far too complex for meaningful analysis. It is necessary, therefore, to proceed toward an understanding of the interrelations between man and habitat through the study of subsystems. Geography, as a professional field, deals with many kinds of spatial systems, but for the purposes of this book attention is first directed to the physical-biotic systems that are called habitats.

These physical-biotic systems, or ecosystems, must be simplified to provide a useful conceptual framework for the development of an elementary picture of world geography. This simplification involves the definition of categories of interrelated parts at the same degree of generalization. For the purposes of this book a habitat is considered to be made up of associations of five elements: (1) surface features; (2) climates; (3) water; (4) wild vegetation; and (5) soils.

Nine groups of habitat regions are recognized, and these form the basis of organization for the main part of the text. Each is defined in terms of the association of these five elements in specific segments of earth-space. . . . In previous editions of this book— and of its predecessor, *An Outline of Geography*—eight groups of regions were presented. Continued field studies indicate that the savannas and tropical woodlands (tropical scrub forests) do in fact constitute a system of related parts of special significance to man and therefore merit recognition as a separate group.

These nine habitats are arranged on the earth's land masses in a predictable pattern. The pattern involves the interplay of two principles: (1) that all habitat features causally related to climate are arranged in a regular, repeated pattern in relation to latitude and continental position; and (2) that all habitat features causally related to surface features are irregularly arranged with reference to latitude and continental position. If the earth were all land or all water, the world's climates would form simple latitudinal zones. But the differences between climates over the land and climates over the water modify the simple latitudinal arrangement. The irregular pattern of high mountains on the continents further modifies and distorts the simple climatic patterns as they would develop on flat continents. The actual arrangement of habitats, therefore, is described by the interplay of the principle of climatic regularity and surface irregularity.

Nevertheless, the proper study of the text and its accompanying maps should prepare the student to pass the "thumb test." With his back to a globe the student is asked to indicate with his thumb some part of the earth's surface. He then turns to see what part he has indicated. From looking at the globe he knows two facts about the general area he has indicated: He knows its position in latitude; and he knows whether it is located on the eastern side of an ocean basin, the western side of an ocean basin, the eastern side of a continent, the interior of a continent, or the western side of a continent. With this information he should be able to predict the kind of habitat system he would find in that part of the earth. If a student is unable to say anything about the physical-biotic character of any major part of the earth's surface, he fails the test.

Geography is also concerned with the interrelations between man and habitat. What does the habitat mean to the people who must live and work in it? Is the habitat favorable or unfavorable? In examining these questions we come to one of the core concepts of modern geography: that the significance to man of the physical and biotic features of his habitat is a function of the attitudes, objectives, and technical skills of man himself. The habitat that is favorable to one group of people may prove unfavorable to another. A change in any of the elements of a culture, or way of living of a people, makes necessary the reappraisal of the habitat.

This concept is demonstrated, for selected places within each of the nine groups of regions, by examining the experience of man with the problems of making a living from earth resources. Man's experience with a particular habitat is examined historically. With each change in attitudes or objectives, or especially in technology, the significance of the habitat is reexamined. This is a method of study that the geographers describe as "sequent occupance." For each period during which the culture remains essentially unchanged, the geography of man in relation to habitat is reconstructed. When changes in the culture take place, for whatever reason the differences in the man-habit relations are identified. . . .

# 14

## THE FACE OF THE EARTH

The only living organisms we know are attached to the surface of that otherwise very ordinary planet, the earth. Among its companions in the solar system the earth is neither unusually large, nor unusually small, nor very far from the sun, nor very close to it, nor possessed of any other astronomical features to lend it distinction. Yet the face of the earth is unique in the known universe. Of all the wide range of possible temperatures that exist in nature, from the tremendous heat of the hottest star to the appalling cold of the outer reaches of space, here at the earth's surface are found air temperatures at which water will neither freeze nor boil. The surface of our planet receives its heat from the sun, and, in turn, the thin gaseous envelope we call the atmosphere is heated in its lower portion from the warmed earth. In this environment, in which water can remain a liquid, life has somehow gained a foothold and through great periods of time has evolved those forms now familiar to us. In the narrow zone of contact between the atmosphere and the solid earth the many and varied forms of life have established the most intimate connections, not only with the soil, the water, and the air but also with one another. In this zone the patterns of the organic and the inorganic are tightly interwoven, and from this dynamic combination emerges the everchanging mosaic of forms and colors which is the face of the earth.

And "to man the mystery of mysteries is man." He, of all the forms of life, possesses that remarkable ability to raise his head and look about him, to observe his surroundings and himself, to simplify the confused complexity of the things he sees by arranging

Reprinted from *An Outline of Geography* (Boston: Ginn and Company, 1935), pp. 3–11, 351–57.

and classifying them, to imagine explanations, and to make use of his knowledge, little as it may be, in altering and transforming at least the more plastic parts of his habitat. In fact, as Julian Huxley writes, man has done more in five thousand years to alter the biologic aspect of the planet than has nature in five million years. But much as man has done, most of the basic conditions of life remain beyond his control. He is still a product of the earth and dependent on it—earth-bound.

One of the fields of knowledge into which man divides his observations and experiences is the face of the earth itself. This is the field of geography. To gain a knowledge and understanding of the present-day arrangement of the things organic and inorganic which exist together at the earth's surface is the general objective of geographic study. Of special interest to man are the phases of geography which deal with the forms introduced by man himself in the course of his spread over the earth. From this point of view the alterations of the landscape by mankind are of particular significance. Yet moving about among man-made scenes, as we do, especially those of us who live in cities, we are apt to miss the true proportion of these things as features composing the earth's face. Important as are the forms of human settlement, we must not lose sight of their position as engravings on the older and relatively more enduring background of the physical earth.

### MAJOR LINEAMENTS OF THE FACE OF THE EARTH

Among the major lineaments of this background of the physical earth are the continents and ocean basins. The continents are composed of relatively upstanding masses of the earth's crust, between relatively down-sinking portions which make up the ocean basins. The difference in elevation above the center of the earth of these contrasted parts of its surface averages only about three miles, or less than 1/1300 of the radius. The maximum difference in elevation, or relief, is about twelve miles (between Mt. Everest, about 29,000 feet above sea level, and the ocean deep off the Philippine Islands, about 35,000 feet below sea level). But even this is only about 1/330 of the earth's radius. Small as are these differences of elevation compared with the size of the planet, they nevertheless measure the major relief features of its surface.

Only about 28 percent of this surface, however, stands above the sea. Water fills the ocean basins and, overflowing these, inundates also the margins of the continental masses. As a result the continents are for the most part isolated, while the oceans are relatively continuous. There is more than twice as much land north of the equator as south of it. Except for Antarctica all the continents are broadest in the north, even those in the southern hemisphere. There is an almost complete ring of land around the basin of the Arctic Ocean, while, in contrast, the tapering of the continents toward the south leaves an almost uninterrupted sea in the higher middle latitudes of the southern hemisphere.

All these various continental masses are tied together by more or less continuous chains of high mountains. These mountain ranges, passing from continent to continent or festooned around the oceans in strings of islands, form a framework to which are joined the other major lineaments of the earth's face. Without regard to the complexity of detail at this time, the general distribution pattern of high mountains is one of relative simplicity but profound significance. In a sense the central and southeastern part of Asia is the core of the world's lands, and in the present-day world it is composed of a complex knot of towering mountain ranges. From this core mountain axes extend in three directions: one westward through southern Asia, southern Europe, and northern Africa to the edge of the Atlantic Ocean basin; and one northward and one southward to form, through the American continents and the Pacific margins of the Antarctic continent, a broken ring of mountains around the basin of the Pacific Ocean. The manner in which the several continental masses are joined to this framework gives to each its own peculiar shape. Yet these various lands, when plotted on a polar projection, appear as three peninsulas radiating from the Asiatic core (Figure 1): Europe and Africa, depending from the western limb of the mountain system; the East Indies, Australia, and New Zealand, depending from the southern limb; and the American continents, attached to the limb which starts northward through western Asia and crosses into the western hemisphere through Alaska. The land masses of the world, therefore, are not

Fig. 1. The arrangement of mountains and continents.

symmetrically arranged with reference to the poles and the divisions of latitude and longitude.

All these features would appear as major lineaments of our planet if it were viewed from a distance—let us say by an observer on the moon. The patterns of land and water distribution and the chains of high mountains would probably stand out conspicuously. But, in addition, the land areas outside the mountain regions would probably be divided into a mosaic of lighter and darker patches. The relief of these nonmountainous areas would be inconspicuous, but the cover of natural vegetation would provide great contrast from one region to another. The chief vegetation types—the forests, the grasslands, the deserts, and the tundras—must also be included among the major lineaments.

These vegetation types are the visible reflection of the climates. They are the great climatic emblems. The regions of light rainfall or continuous cold are but scantily covered by plants; the regions of heavy rainfall, on the contrary, are forest-covered; the forests of the hot lands are dense and luxuriant compared with those of the cooler regions; even the rhythm of the seasons finds expression in the changing aspect of the vegetation cover.

The climatic features, unlike the land masses, are systematically distributed over the face of the earth. In a general way latitude is a control of climate, but the simple arrangement of climatic zones parallel to the equator is broken up by the great differences, at the same latitude, between climates developed over the oceans and climates developed over the lands. To the ancient Greeks we owe the concept of *klimata,* or zones based on differences of latitude, and the persistence of the old five-zone division of the climates is a tribute to its simplicity. But the old "torrid, temperate, and frigid zones" represent an oversimplification of the facts of climatic distribution and cannot be given any place in a modern treatment of that subject. Nevertheless, the arrangement of the different kinds of climate is systematically controlled in part by latitude, in part by differences of land and water, and in part by various other influences of lesser importance. Over each continent, therefore, at a given latitude, the arrangement of the climates and of their visible expression in the climatic emblems forms a strikingly similar pattern. Without mountains the similarity would be very great; the actual differences of design which distinguish one continent from another are in large part the result of the mountains.

For the purposes of this book the major lineaments of the earth are divided into eight groups. This classification is, like all classifications, an arbitrary one, for other possible combinations of vegetation and surface form might be argued with as much logic as these. The eight groups include regions of broadly similar landscape: the first seven include nonmountainous surfaces and are based on the vegetation cover; the last group includes all the mountainous regions. The order, as presented in the following list, is a matter of expediency: group I, the dry lands; group II, the tropical forest lands; group III, the mediterranean scrub forest lands; group IV, the mid-latitude mixed forest lands; group V, the grasslands; group VI, the boreal forest lands; group VII, the polar lands; group VIII, the mountain lands.

## Man's Place in the Landscape

Neither man nor the works of man constitute major lineaments of the face of the earth. Viewed in proper perspective, the features wrought on the surface of the land by human beings are only details; intimately, close at hand, the scene has been radically transformed, but the major lineaments of our planet remain essentially unchanged. However, to man himself these details are of the greatest importance and significance, so that in any human study of the earth they must be magnified.

Man, more than any other living creature, has remodeled the details of his habitat and shaped it to his own needs. From a largely indifferent world, he has, in part, created his own environment—an environment "genially civilized." He has removed the cover of natural vegetation or greatly modified it; he has partly replaced the native wild animals with domestic animals; he has plowed up the land and planted crops; he has carried out the exploitation of minerals; and he has erected buildings and laid out highways. His lines of travel now form a complicated web on the face of the earth, with strands frayed out near the frontiers of settlement but with a tightly woven fabric in the more densely populated areas. And all these things have been done in the greatest variety of ways, in accordance with the greatest variety of patterns of arrangement which differ with the traditions and technical abilities of the inhabitants.

These various features can all be mapped and described as a part of the earth. But the interpretation of man's place in the landscape is involved with numerous difficulties. Prejudice, which can be controlled in a study of such features as landforms or types of vegetation, rises unchecked at the first mention of man. To study the various groups of human society, the different nations, the peoples of different races and different cultures, and to remain objective and unprejudiced is an almost superhuman task. We are too close to our subject—too much a part of the things we attempt to describe. Yet if we are to understand man's place on the earth we must attempt to study his problems without national or racial bias, and we must be willing to subject our own cherished traditions and modes of living to the same intimate scrutiny we would give to those of other people. To see our community in its place in the world of communities, to see our nation among nations, to see our race and our civilization in the perspective of their world relationships—these are among the most important objectives of geographic study and among the most difficult.

There are other difficulties, too. Man's behavior is essentially irrational and unpredictable. Because human beings react in one way to a situation at one specific time, there is no reason to predict a similar reaction at another time, even by the same group of people. Very serious errors of interpretation arise from the attempt to explain human behavior as a conscious adjustment to the environment; more often behavior is determined by unconscious habits of thought and action which have been passed down in each human group from generation to generation since the childhood of the race. To attempt to rationalize the human response to a situation —in other words, to explain it as arising from a conscious and intelligent plan of action—is entirely to neglect the place of inherited traditions and deeply ingrained habits.

The influence of the natural environment on human life is chiefly one of limitation and hindrance. The stimulus to such action as will overcome the obstacles resides in man. Nature itself is quite indifferent to human aspirations: it is neither friendly nor unfriendly, except as man has always personified the natural forces about him and given them human attributes. Every now and then, in the long course of human history, groups of people have attempted to establish themselves on the land in accordance with some rational plan. At many other times and places plans have been proposed, but without effect. Up to the present the planned utilization of resources has been carried out only by small groups, in small areas, and for short periods of time. It is notorious that even the so-called advanced civilizations, such as our own, have squandered the resources of their lands stupidly, blindly, and without intelligent plan. One of the world's great tragedies is the contrast between the vision of man on the earth as it lies now within his power to live, and man as he does live, burdened by ignorance, poverty, and warfare. These things are not the result of the world in which we live—they cannot be blamed on an unfriendly nature; they are rather the product of limitations inherent in the human mind.

## THE LANDSCAPE

The geographer's contribution to these various problems consists of a systematic description and interpretation of the present-day distribution of things on the face of the earth. With the aid of maps—the most essential of the geographic techniques—he establishes the position or arrangement of the various material objects which, in complex interrelation, exist together in the landscape. Within the broad limits of this general objective there are many special problems of smaller scope and many different methods of study, all of which contribute some small advance toward the larger goal. Only through the process of education can ignorance and prejudice be dispelled; by portraying the present condition of humanity in its relation to the earth, geography does its bit to aid the painful progress toward a utopia. In the modern world the geographic inventory of the present conditions in an area must form the essential basis for intelligent regional planning.

The various objects which exist together on the surface of the earth combine to form what the geographer calls a "landscape." As defined in the dictionary, this word refers to "that portion of territory which the eye can comprehend in a single view." The geographer, however, redefines the word to mean "that portion of territory which is found to exhibit essentially the same aspect after it has been examined from any necessary number of views." The landscape, in this sense, is composed of a variety of things: some organic, some inorganic, some produced by processes other than human, and some resulting from the presence of man. The following outline suggests the variety of objects which together comprise a landscape. (The outline is modified from Sten de Geer and Jean Brunhes.)

THE CONTENT OF LANDSCAPE

Atmosphere
　　Weather and climate

Lithosphere
　　Geognosy
　　　　Bedrock
　　　　Regolith
　　　　Minerals
　　Landforms

Hydrosphere
　　Surface water

Ground water
Ice
Seas and Oceans
Biosphere
Natural vegetation
Native animals
Man

## THE FORMS INTRODUCED INTO THE LANDSCAPE BY MAN

Buildings
Means of circulation and barriers to circulation (roads and fences)
Crops and forms related to the production of crops (such as irrigation
and drainage)
Domestic animals and pastures
Forms related to recreation
Forms related to the destructive exploitation of plants and animals
Forms related to mineral exploitation

## CONCLUSION

The face of the earth bears the impress of man's successive civilizations. For those who will stop and read, the main outlines of the record are clear. Each culture has set its own peculiar stamp upon the earth, superimposed on the forms and patterns developed by the earlier cultures. In very few instances have groups of people consciously planned their occupance and intelligently carried out their plan. To be sure, a few examples can be found of pioneer communities organized by some great leader whose vision of a better world was successfully translated into action, but such examples are all the more striking because they are rare. Much the greater part of the world's occupance has been guided by traditional habits of thought and action inherent in a culture and more or less unconsciously adopted by the people who have grown up in the environment of that culture. After all, the world's rebels are few. It is not surprising, therefore, that the rise of the machine civilization, with its conquest of so many earlier cultures, has resulted in the elimination of much of the variety in the world's occupance. The individuality of small regions, especially in America, is being to a greater and greater extent submerged by the uniformity in ways of living. Especially is urban life being cast in a standardized mold which is causing all the great cities of the world more and more to resemble one another. Underneath these more recent cultural patterns, however, are the relict forms of earlier modes of living, of earlier civilizations which are survived by their "sticks and stones" and by the furrows which they made in the land.

## Landscapes, Regions, and Groups

Geography and astronomy deal with phenomena which are too far away or too large in relation to the observer to be easily comprehended. Most of the sciences are faced with just the opposite problem: the penetration of the microcosm, or the world of the infinitely small. Whereas the astronomer widens the range of his observations by perfecting the telescope, the geographer cannot make use of this instrument owing to the curved shape of the zone which it is his special province to describe. His intimate knowledge of the face of the earth is limited to his immediate surroundings. Like an ant on the surface of a rug, he may know exactly the nature of the fabric close by, but the general design is beyond his range of vision. In order to reduce the larger patterns of the face of the earth to such proportions that they can be comprehended in a single view, the geographer makes use of the map.

Landscapes are defined by the detailed study of small areas— by topographic studies. Maps are made of the various significant elements which exist together in the area: of the landforms, the soils, the drainage, the plant communities, or the various forms of the occupance. An "essentially similar aspect" is produced by a given combination of these elements, and a different aspect is produced by any significant change in one or more of them. By detailed studies the areas of similar combination, the landscapes, are identified and given exact boundaries. The analysis and interpretation of the distribution patterns which combine to form the landscapes are, then, the primary objectives of topographic studies.

Topographic studies, however, are of only local significance. They may be of practical importance as a basis for planning the proper use of a locality, but their contribution to a knowledge of the earth's surface is small until they are compared with other small areas and until their patterns are generalized into larger areal divisions. A geographic generalization, like all other kinds of generalizations, recognizes broad similarities and neglects detailed differences. To say, for example, that men are taller than women is to recognize a general truth; yet no one expects each individual man to be taller than each individual woman. We may generalize concerning the characteristics of Canadians and Mexicans; but it would be quite incorrect to expect all Canadians to fit the picture of the average Canadian, or all Mexicans to resemble the generalized Mexican. We must follow the same logic with reference to geographic generalizations. The region represents a portion of a continent throughout which the various generalized patterns of the landscape elements are similarly combined. The region differs from a landscape only in that it is formed by a combination of generalized patterns, of patterns drawn on a chorographic scale rather than in topographic detail. To attempt to identify a regional boundary on a topographic scale is as illogical as to expect all Canadians to be cut to a standard form or all men to be taller than all women. Yet the region represents a reality which is no less real than the more specific reality of the landscape. In fact, the region may give meaning to the landscape—the topographic study becomes significant because of its relationship to the larger region of which it is a part.

The groups represent the broadest generalization of the divisions of the face of the earth. The group patterns are based on the arrangement of the major lineaments. Here are the most fundamental of all the geographic patterns, the framework around which our knowledge of the earth can be built. It is perhaps not incorrect to say that the identification and delimitation of the groups is one of the major objectives of geography. The organization used in this book is largely hypothetical, for much of the more detailed work at the topographic and chorographic levels remains to be done. The present classification represents only a workable outline— something to give meaning to the more detailed studies until the time when a better system is devised. . . .

# 15

## THE HABITAT AND CULTURE

### THE HABITAT

Most literate people are aware of the existence of a worldwide population problem. For many decades specialists in the study of population have been warning that mankind is headed for disaster, but during these same decades in the United States food has become more plentiful, and most Americans have improved their living conditions in terms of material comforts. The dimensions of the world population problem, and what it can mean with regard to the capacity of man to support himself from earth resources, are not widely understood even now. Yet among all the complex and disturbing situations that modern man must face, none is more fundamental than that of the increasing pressure of people on the land. This book deals with that problem.

In 1963 the population of the world was 3,180,000,000. In 1950 there were about 2,406,000,000 people in the world. Between 1950 and 1960 the population of the world increased by about 500,000,000. As each minute went by during this decade there were eighty new mouths to feed, and eighty new pairs of hands to employ. Estimates of the world population by the year 2000 offer figures such as five billion.

The population is very unevenly spread over the earth. Vast areas are only very thinly populated, with small concentrations of people separated by many miles of empty country. In southern and eastern Asia, on the other hand, about half of all the people in the world are packed into less than a tenth of the world's habitable area. In Europe a little less than a fifth of mankind occupies an

Reprinted from *A Geography of Man* (Waltham, Mass.: Blaisdell Publishing Company, 3rd ed., 1966), pp. 3–4, 20–23, 25, 37–38, 424.

area that amounts to less than one-twentieth of the habitable world.

Yet to draw the conclusion that a great movement to the empty lands of the earth is about to take place would be quite wrong. People are concentrated in certain parts of the earth's surface as a result of historical processes. These processes are not simple: the fact is that the concentrations of people in Asia took place for very different reasons than those that explain the concentrations in Europe. Furthermore, in this second half of the twentieth century, the tendency is for the densely populated areas to become even more densely populated, and for the thinly populated areas to lose population.

Since all food, clothing, shelter, and other material things that surround civilized man are derived from things produced by the earth, it becomes critical to examine the natural surroundings of man—the human habitat. To understand what the habitats of the earth mean to its human inhabitants requires a long view of how, over the centuries, man has brought the earth resources into use. Furthermore, since man-land relations change through time, and also vary in major ways from place to place at any one time, generalizations about population and resources in the world as a whole are less useful than those that divide the world into distinct areas, in each of which the experience of man in making a living from earth resources has differed. . . .

The habitats of the world are defined in terms of the interaction of . . . various processes, including those of physics, chemistry, and biology, as modified through unplanned human action. There are nine major categories of habitat regions. Each is a recurring areal association of surface features, climate, water, vegetation, and soil. A recurring association is one that is found in essentially similar form in different parts of the earth. The first eight groups of regions are defined in terms of associations of climate, water, vegetation, and soil, and therefore these groups develop a regular pattern over the earth—a pattern that is generalized in Figure 1. Because the arrangement of these eight groups is regular, it is possible to predict the kind of habitat that will be found in any particular part of the earth if one knows the latitude and whether the place is on the western side, the interior, or the eastern side of a continent. The ninth group, on the other hand, includes the high mountains of the

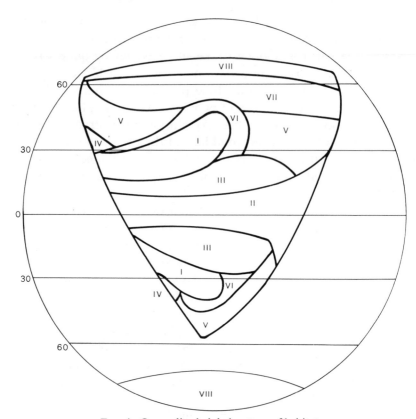

Fig. 1. Generalized global pattern of habitats.

world, and is, therefore, irregular in its arrangement with reference to the poles and the latitudes. The first eight groups are subdivided irregularly by the arrangement of surface features other than high mountains. And the ninth group is subdivided regularly by the vertical arrangement of climate and vegetation. The nine groups are outlined in Tables 1 through 3.

## CULTURE

The nine groups of regions that make up the human habitats have a significance independent of the part they play as natural sur-

TABLE 1 HABITATS

| Groups of Habitat Regions | Climate and Water | | Vegetation | Soil |
|---|---|---|---|---|
| I. Dry Lands | BW | Water deficient at all seasons | Desert | Sierozem |
| II. Tropical Forest Lands | Af, Am, AW | Water adequate at all seasons, or deficient during a dry season | Rainforest and seasonal forest | Laterites |
| III. Tropical Woodlands and Savannas | AW, Bsh | Water deficient during the dry season | Woodlands and savannas, parklands | Laterites |
| IV. Mediterranean Woodlands | Csa, Csb, BShs | Water deficient during a dry season | Evergreen woodlands | Mostly immature soils |
| V. Mid-Latitude Mixed Forest Lands | Cfa, Cfb, Dfa, Dfb | Water adequate at all seasons | Seasonal forests | Podsols, brown forest soils, red and yellow forest soils |
| VI. Mid-Latitude Grasslands | Cfa, Dfa, BSk | Water deficient during a dry season, or adequate at all seasons | Grasslands, parklands | Black prairie soil, chernozem, chestnut-brown soil, brown soil |
| VII. Boreal Forest Lands | Dfc, Dfd, Dw | Water adequate at all seasons, or deficient during a dry season | Seasonal forests, woodlands | Podsols |
| VIII. Polar Lands | E | Water deficient during the cold season, or deficient at all seasons | Tundra, polar desert | Tundra soils |
| IX. Mountain Lands | — | | — | |

*On the World and Its Regions*

TABLE 2

PERCENTAGE OF LAND AREA IN THE NINE GROUPS

|  | North America | South America | Africa | Europe | Asia | Australia New Zealand Philippines East Indies | Antarctica | World |
|---|---|---|---|---|---|---|---|---|
| I | 9 | 8 | 34 | 1 | 24 | 13 | — | 18 |
| II | 3 | 39 | 9 | — | 11 | 8 | — | 10 |
| III | 1 | 31 | 51 | — | 3 | 32 | — | 17 |
| IV | 1 | (T) * | 1 | 6 | (T) | 10 | — | 1 |
| V | 15 | 2 | (T) | 37 | 5 | 9 | — | 7 |
| VI | 11 | 7 | 2 | 19 | 12 | 22 | — | 9 |
| VII | 20 | — | — | 21 | 18 | — | — | 10 |
| VIII | 24 | — | — | 5 | 7 | — | 100 | 16 |
| IX | 16 | 13 | 3 | 11 | 20 | 6 | — | 12 |

* (T) indicates less than one-half of 1 percent.

TABLE 3

PERCENTAGE OF WORLD POPULATION BY GROUPS

AND CONTINENTS ABOUT 1963

|  | North America | South America | Africa | Europe | Asia | Australia New Zealand Philippines East Indies | World |
|---|---|---|---|---|---|---|---|
| I | 3 | 3 | 12 | — | 8 | — | 6 |
| II | 7 | 47 | 19 | — | 38 | 14 | 28 |
| III | 1 | 2 | 42 | — | 1 | 1 | 5 |
| IV | 7 | 5 | 11 | 16 | 0 | 6 | 5 |
| V | 53 | 2 | 1 | 74 | 42 | 75 | 42 |
| VI | 11 | 16 | 5 | 3 | 7 | 3 | 7 |
| VII | 0 | — | — | 1 | 0 | — | (T) * |
| VIII | 0 | — | — | (T) | 0 | — | (T) |
| IX | 18 | 25 | 10 | 6 | 4 | 1 | 7 |

* (T) indicates less than one-half of 1 percent.

roundings of man. In the fields of physical geography, including biogeography, they may be studied as examples of the interaction of physical and biotic processes leading to the differentiation of the surface of the earth into *ecosystems*—that is, areas within which there are associations of interacting natural features. When man enters the scene, either as a user of earth resources or as a creator or modifier of ecosystems, the resulting divisions of the surface of the earth may be described as *habitats*. The nine groups of habitat regions are defined for the purpose of clarifying the changing significance of the habitat to man.

The significance to man of the physical and biotic features of the habitat is a function of the attitudes, objectives, and technical skills of man himself. Attitudes, objectives, and technical skills are traits that form parts of the traditional way of living. Each human group is distinguished by differences in these traditional forms of behavior. Each group has its own peculiar set of beliefs, its own institutions, its customs, its familiar foods, its consecrated system of moral values, and its language in which these things are recorded and communicated. The tendency is to resist change. The aggregate of all these customary forms of thought, communication, and action which characterize a group of people is what may be described as a *"culture."* . . .

In the chapters that follow we shall examine the characteristics of each of the nine groups of habitat regions. These characteristics result from the interplay of surface features, climate, water, vegetation, and soil. Then in each region we shall examine the record of man's experience with the problems of making a living from earth resources. The changing significance of the habitat with changes in the culture is the central theme, the variations of which run as a connecting thread through the whole book. In the final chapter we shall bring together some of the concepts concerning population and resources in an attempt to see more clearly what kind of data are needed to estimate the population capacity of different parts of the earth. . . .

# 16

## WORLD CULTURE REGIONS AND
## REVOLUTIONARY CHANGE

A geographer's view of the state of affairs in the contemporary
world provides a somewhat different perspective from that of other
scholars. The difference is inherent in the structure of his field of
learning. Geographic concepts are generalizations about the development of contrasts and similarities between places on the face of
the earth. The purpose of geographic study is to throw light on the
complex interaction of the processes of change that produce these
contrasts and similarities. Why does one country differ from another? The geographer's approach to such a question makes use of
the same basic information that is used by other students of contemporary conditions. But the geographer arranges this information
in terms of areal association or areal interchange on the face of the
earth. He is concerned with such questions as the significance of
position with reference to other places. He is concerned with the
pattern of movement into and out of areas. He is concerned with
the processes that are interconnected in particular places, and with
the resulting features that are areally associated.

All approaches to learning are essentially descriptive. Explanation in any ultimate sense is beyond the reach of human scholarship. "Explanatory description," the term used by William Morris
Davis many decades ago, consists in adding the time dimension to
mere description. To explain an existing situation, one reconstructs
the geography of a past period and traces the developments or

Reprinted from *One World Divided* (New York: Blaisdell Publishing Company, 1964), pp. vii, 31–32, viii, 33, 421. Text slightly rearranged in order to give the most succinct presentation of the basic concepts of the book.

changes leading to present conditions. Projections into the future based on past trends permit the making of forecasts. But these are only more sophisticated approaches to description.

Description, however, goes beyond the formula, "how much of what is where?" Historical geography, which focuses attention on the recreation of past geographies, and on tracing geographic changes through time, reveals the nature of the processes at work on the face of the earth. Although the specific phenomena observed in any particular place are unique, there are, at the same time, certain uniformities or recurring patterns among the sequences of change. These can be identified and used as the basis for the formulation of general concepts. Where concepts can be formulated in mathematical terms they become models or ideal constructs. But where they can be formulated only in word symbols they still contribute to the theoretical structure of geography.

The purpose of this book is to apply geographic methods and use geographic concepts in the search for meaning in the modern world. Many scholars have described the two sets of revolutionary changes now going on in the world—the technological changes and the many resulting readjustments which we call the Industrial Revolution, and the changes in the status and dignity of the individual which we call the democratic revolution. Social scientists have described the background and antecedents of these revolutions. The special purpose of this book, however, is to note the particular place or places on the earth where these movements originated, to discover the pattern and speed with which they spread, and to observe the results of the impact of change on preexisting societies in particular places. . . .

The two revolutions and the reactions they set up have created a pattern of regional divisions, each characterized by a particular set of economic, social, and political conditions and problems. Each region is a unique segment of the earth's surface, within which there is a unique assortment of resources and habitat conditions, a unique pattern of political organizations, and an arrangement of people and production that is peculiar to the area. Each individual country or state exists in the context of the culture region of which it is a part, and the interactions among countries reveal the nature of international tensions and conflicts. The significance of these tensions and conflicts is related in part to the position of the culture region in its areal relation to other regions.

It is important to understand that no region can be completely uniform, for no two pinpoints on the face of the earth are identical. The "region" is a geographic generalization—analogous to the "period" in history. The characteristics described in each region are most fully developed in the regional cores, and they become less clearly exhibited toward the peripheries. There are areas which are transitional between neighboring culture regions, and share the characteristics of both. Clearly the cores of regions are more important than the peripheral zones. But, because of the convenience of using statistical data and other information, the regions are defined in terms of whole states. Eleven major culture regions (see Figure 1) are defined as follows: European, Soviet, Anglo-American, Latin American, North African–Southwest Asian, South Asian, Southeast Asian, East Asian, African, Australia–New Zealand, and Pacific. . . .

The eleven culture regions presented in this book are, in a sense, a geographic hypothesis. It is assumed that the general picture of the contemporary world offered by this division into culture regions will serve to illuminate rather than obscure the nature of the processes of change that are at work. The regions are defined as contiguous areas because an important part of our analysis deals with the significance of position on the globe. They are defined in terms of political units because a major part of the analysis deals with the viability of states. It is recognized that the characteristics of each region are most clearly developed at the regional core, and that around the margins there are wide zones of transition where the characteristics of neighboring regions are mingled. Regional boundaries, therefore, are less important than regional cores. Regional boundaries are subject to change with increasing knowledge, and with the progress of the processes of revolutionary change over the world. . . .

The purpose is to put the divisions of our one world into perspective. This is done by tracing the geographic changes through time, recognizing that the present geographic division of the world into culture regions is only the most recent such division, and that it is in no sense the end of the series. By understanding the

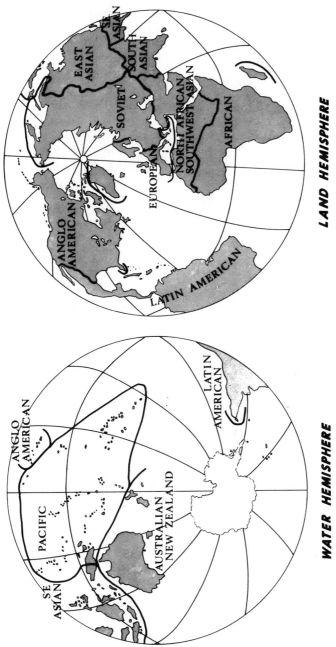

LAND HEMISPHERE

WATER HEMISPHERE

Fig. 1. World culture regions.

causes and consequences of the regional divisions of the earth, a background is created for the study of specific problems, or for the formulation of policies for action. For each of the eleven culture regions which divide our one world into distinctive parts we have considered the areal association and the interactions of four groups of phenomena. These four groups are: (1) the physical and biotic features of the habitat; (2) the density, growth, character, and arrangement of the populations; (3) the nature and stage of economic development in relation to the earth resources; and (4) the political organization and attitudes, and the viability of the states.

Let us follow the sequence of ideas carefully:

1. Our one world is differentiated by variations in the physical and biotic character of habitats, and by variations in the resource base of states.

2. It is differentiated, also, by variations in the population, the economy, and the political conditions.

3. For some two centuries two great processes of fundamental and revolutionary change—the Industrial Revolution and the democratic revolution—have been going on, and have been spreading unevenly from the culture hearth around the North Sea.

4. As the two revolutions spread they also undergo a continuation of the process of development, so that they do not make the same impact today along their advancing fronts as they did a century ago.

5. Distinctive social, economic, and political reactions have been produced by the impact of these revolutionary changes on preexisting societies—the preindustrial and predemocratic societies.

6. In each distinctive culture area, so defined, the significance to man of the features of the habitat changes with changes in the culture, requiring with each change a new evaluation of the resource base.

7. Such reevaluation is aided by grouping the resulting cultures into culture regions, in each of which there is a distinctive association of demographic conditions, economic development, and political expression.

8. This distinctive regional character is most clearly observable in the cores of the regions.

9. Eleven such regions can tentatively be defined; this number

may be subject to change as a result of more precise study or of the continuation of the revolutionary processes.

10. The geographic arrangement of these distinctive regions on the globe has a meaning not found in the separate consideration of the elements that make them up, and this meaning is relevant to the formulation of economic, political, or military policy.

PART IV

# On Teaching

# COMMENTARY

It will be clear from the sections preceding that over the whole of his career Preston James has been primarily a teacher. That he is a research scholar as well, experienced in the library and the field, is to him a simple corollary, for he would insist that the good teacher must perforce be an active investigator. But though necessarily joined, the balance may vary, and the primacy which James has given to teaching is displayed in his books, which are avowed texts rather than research monographs. Those books suggest the range of his academic concern—from the lower grades to the university level—but not the full breadth of his active teaching. For he has taught not only a dozen generations of college students, but in lectures and special programs his university colleagues, school teachers, military officers, other government officials, businessmen, and the general public as well. To all of these his basic theme has been the same: the characteristics of and the necessity for a geographic perspective upon the affairs of mankind.

The papers in this final section represent his special concern for the teaching of geography at pre-college levels. They have been selected from a large body of materials which includes twenty-one articles in the *Journal of Geography,* published by the National Council for Geographic Education (from whom he received the "Distinguished Service Award" in 1964), and nearly as many in various other educational periodicals. Here, too, as at the college level, he has not only discussed objectives and methods; he has demonstrated how it might be done in a series of grade-school texts (co-authored with Gertrude Whipple and Morris Weiss) and a high-school text (co-authored with Nelda Davis).

Two basic and complementary concerns, one "external" the other "internal" to the field of geography, permeate this body of his writings. On the one hand is the concern for geography as a distinctive dimension of knowledge which should not be dissolved into a "social studies" wherein it is likely to become identified only in some spurious form as the "geographic factor." On the other is the need to have the teaching of geography at the elementary levels rest no less firmly than at the higher levels upon a set of concepts which reflect the basic philosophy of the field.

Both of these concerns are clearly expressed in his brief statement to the National Council for the Social Studies in 1940 (article 17). They are elaborated in the next selection, which concludes with a set of five basic concepts which "provide the ideological connections between geographic education and the other subjects dealing with human societies." Article 19 is a still more insistent emphasis upon the critical value of geography to the social studies, and suggests an interesting way in which the student can be taught its basic concepts by "reliving the geographic experience of mankind." Through all of these selections runs the argument that geography, history, and social science represent three complementary but distinct ways of viewing the same phenomena. In arguing for this position, James is of course simply applying to the curriculum at this level the basic definition of geography he has persistently expounded elsewhere, as in the selections of Part I.

The last three papers focus on questions more internal to geography than to its place in relation to social studies, though such matters are of course interdependent. Article 20 summarizes the rationale of the approach he has used in his own very successful textbooks. Article 21 is not only the shortest but the sharpest in this collection, a clear cry of alarm at some trends of the times. It is a concise statement of a critical dispute over principal requirements at the introductory level. Written in 1966, it was prompted quite specifically by what he felt to be a disproportionate emphasis in the work of the High School Geography Project. James was a member of the Steering Committee of that prestigious national program (described in article 22) and worked hard to support a concern for the age-old task of geography to offer "a systematically organized picture of the world."

This same question—"topical or regional"—becomes the grand theme of a subsequent major paper, wherein, typically, he casts the controversy within the history of geography as related to the history of pedagogy. Having reviewed the past he then projects a future in which the "new geography" would be new only as a fresh synthesis of the varied fundamental concerns of the old, a bold attempt to overcome those "false dichotomies" which have recurrently plagued geography over its long history. As a vigorous expression of the concern on the part of an imaginative and influential teacher for the vitality of his chosen field it seems an appropriate conclusion for this entire collection.

# 17

## THE CONTRIBUTION OF GEOGRAPHY
## TO THE SOCIAL STUDIES

The essential elementary aspects of human society are those of time and space. It has long been recognized in theory that these two aspects cannot in reality be separated: that history should be taught geographically, and that geography should be taught historically.

Yet the techniques involved in the search for new truth and in the presentation of the results of this search in either of these fields are such that specialized training is necessary before one can become an effective professional historian or geographer. Similarly, in the teaching of these subjects at any grade level real competence can be gained only by special training—the historian to learn how to teach students to think in terms of the time sequence or in terms of periods; the geographer to learn how to teach students to think in terms of location, or in terms of regions.

In addition to those subjects which treat the fundamental aspects of social science, a number of other fields of advanced study have made their appearance. Economics, sociology, anthropology, political science, and others all make use of both historical and geographical methods in addition to special techniques and procedures of their own. The fact that these other disciplines make use of both historical and geographical methods does not mean that there is no need for special training in the basic subjects. It means the opposite, for such training is all the more important since the historical and geographical methods are so widely used.

Experience in the integration of the social sciences may not be overlooked by those who wish to achieve an integrated social studies program for the schools. In social studies as well as in social sci-

Reprinted from *Social Education*, 5, 5 (May 1941), 334–38.

ences the fundamental aspects are those of time and space, and any program which neglects either of these aspects cannot be other than superficial and, in the long run, unsatisfactory.

### THINKING IN TERMS OF LOCATION

One of the most important skills to be derived from special geographic training is the ability to sense the significance of location. Location is a factor in human affairs which, in our country, has been strangely and perhaps dangerously neglected. In contrast is the close attention given to geographical studies in Germany, especially to the studies in political geography in which the keen estimate of the elements of location has laid the foundation of the present successful German strategy.

Geographic training makes one conscious of the necessity of greater precision in locating things than is commonly required in other disciplines. Economists, for example, seldom show discontent with production figures which are computed for the state as a unit. To be specific, they find sufficient accuracy in figures which show what proportion of the oil and gas of the United States Texas produces. We may hope that a trained geographer, even if no other figures of oil and gas production were available, would insist on pointing out that oil and gas are not produced over the whole of the state of Texas, and that the oil and gas fields overlap the state border into neighboring states.

Training in geography develops consciousness of location—of the position of an isolated fact with reference to the pattern of all those things, physical and human, which combine to differentiate the face of the earth into regions. Training in history develops consciousness of period—of the trends and characteristics of certain divisions of the human time scale, and of the relation of an isolated event to the larger movement of events more or less contemporary.

Studies of location can and should be approached from two directions. There is location with reference to the broader features of the earth's surface, and there is location with reference to one's immediate surroundings. The more adequate the teaching, the closer these two views of location can be brought together. From the wider view, the first need is to treat location with reference to the earth's major lineaments—the great climatic and vegetation divisions, and the major relief features of the earth's surface. The trained geographer, for example, is not content with such a vague climatic location as implied by the obsolete term "Temperate Zone." Long ago the Arab geographers showed that the simple zonal arrangement set forth by the Greeks was an inadequate generalization of the world's climates. The climates are arranged symmetrically with reference to the poles and also with reference to the land masses, so that a similar climate is to be expected at any given latitude on continental west coasts, east coasts, or interiors. Climatic location is simplified and given greater precision by the use of any of the modern classifications of climate.

But climatic location is only one phase of the subject. There is also location with reference to the major pattern of natural vegetation. There is location with reference to the chief soil types. There is location with reference to the larger surface features—the mountains, uplands, and plains—which differentiate the face of the continents. There is location with reference to inhabited parts of the earth, to the centers of human settlement, to the lines of circulation, and to the political divisions which prevail at the moment. Location to a geographer is not a simple matter: it consists in placing the thing to be located in its whole setting, in its relation to the other things which exist together on the face of the earth. A thing so located is then ready to be interpreted.

The other approach to location begins with the individual. Essentially it is the development of the skill of understanding the relative position of one's self and of the territory immediately visible. People who have this by no means common skill are said to have a "bump of location." This means that such people are able to move about, even in a strange locality, without losing the sense of direction—the relative position of things which lie beyond the range of vision. The development of this skill comes only from experience out of doors. It builds a consciousness of the relation of things visible in the foreground to other things which lie beyond the horizon. It leads finally to the ability to visualize the relation of the things in one's immediate surroundings to the larger patterns of the face of the earth.

This consciousness of the position of one thing with relation to other things on the earth's surface is the essence of "thinking geographically." It constitutes the chief difference between the wealth of material gained by a geographer when he travels and the scanty material observed by a nongeographer who passes along the same route.

## Learning to Use Maps

Since the map is the special device used in the study of location, learning to read maps becomes one of the objectives of geographical teaching. The map is to a geographer what a telescope is to an astronomer—it is a device by which vast distances are reduced to a size which human intelligence can comprehend and interpret. Yet if there is any one part of geographical teaching which needs a fundamentally new approach it is in the teaching of maps. The "map illiteracy" of the American people is widespread, and the results, in a democracy, could be disastrous. The map, like the printed page, is a form of symbolism which one must learn to read by carefully considered stages.

Whether because of ineffective geography teaching in the grades, or for other reasons, the fact remains that the average American is illiterate in terms of maps. For example, I was startled last summer by a headline in a southern newspaper: "Germans Drive Forty Miles Below Paris." To many people with whom I have spoken about this headline, the error is not immediately apparent, so common is this way of speaking. The use of the words *up* and *down* with reference to maps leads to complete confusion, for instance in the distinction between the upper Nile and the lower Nile. In fact, it led one college student to insist that the Nile could not possibly flow up to the Mediterranean!

Map illiteracy of this sort is not limited to the nonprofessional public. At least one social studies book I have seen made use of Mercator maps to compare the United States with the Soviet Union. Not long ago I listened as an eminent student of population made the statement that Uruguay was the most densely populated country in South America—a statement which is statistically true, but geographically unimportant. On a population map of South America, Uruguay does not stand out as very densely populated, but it is the one country which includes no unoccupied territory. Statistics by such large political units only obscure the facts of population distribution. The geographer would use greater precision in locating the densely populated parts of a continent.

Another example of map illiteracy appeared last summer at a meeting of Latin American experts at Texas. One of the speakers insisted that there was little excuse for our failure in this country to know Spanish and to understand the Mexicans since Mexico, like Canada, was our next-door neighbor. But to a geographer, Mexico is not like Canada in its proximity to the United States. A country consists of that part which is essentially unoccupied or only scantily occupied. Most of the Canadians live very close to us; most of the Mexicans live hundreds of miles from a border which itself passes mostly through scantily occupied territory. Our contacts with the Mexican people are relatively remote compared with our contacts with the Canadians.

## MAN AND NATURAL ENVIRONMENT

Geography also seeks to develop a valid point of view regarding the relation of people to the physical environment. Yet the achievement of this objective has been retarded by several difficulties. One difficulty, which geographers face along with workers in other social science fields, arises from a false analogy between the so-called natural sciences and the social sciences. It is perhaps unfortunate that so many people insist that each social science must formulate and teach general principles of cause and effect relations, comparable to the principles set forth in chemistry and biology.

The fundamental error in this analogy, I believe, consists in the great difference in the number of cases on which general principles are based. Unbelievable numbers of atoms combine to produce the results covered, for example, by Boyle's Law; even in biology, principles are based on the experience gained over many generations, and individual exceptions are commonplace. Yet in the social sciences we are asked to formulate principles on the basis of such a

relatively small number of cases that close adherence to the generalization is impossible. Yet in how many schools were and are
teachers of social studies asked to formulate general principles of
human behavior and to support these principles with specific examples! To the thinking student, exceptions are so numerous that the
principle and soon the subject itself is discredited.

Geographers, in the days when their training was largely geological, used to be committed to the study of "responses to the
physical environment." The day of uncritical environmental determinism is now happily drawing to a close.

Geographers today think of one of their chief contributions to
social sciences or social studies as essentially an estimate of the factor of location. Any principle or generalization which is not in harmony with the findings of workers in all the social science fields
can not be maintained and should not be taught. This means that
principles derived and supported from the data of any one social
science field are not to be found. It means that geography must
work in close contact and coordination with other social science
fields, and it means that social science cannot advance safely without the contribution of trained geographers, nor can social studies
programs omit sound studies in geography.

Regarding the relation of people to the physical environment,
the point of view which seems most closely to harmonize with the
findings of other social sciences, especially of anthropology, is that
the significance of the elements of the environment is determined
by the nature of the people. A land, therefore, cannot be spoken of
as favorable or unfavorable for human settlement until it has been
made one or the other by a specific group of people. . . . No climate, no soil, no land, then, should be described as inherently favorable or unfavorable except in terms of specific human cultures.

An outstanding example of all this is offered by the story of the
settlement of the mid-latitude grasslands of the world. These regions, now the chief sources of meat and wheat for occidental
peoples, were long considered of little value except for the grazing
of range animals. There could be no care in breeding, no feeding
from planted crops—only extensive pastoral nomadism. A peculiar
sequence of events led to a marked change in the significance to
men of these great grasslands.

With the industrial revolution and the rapid increase in the use of power, great concentrations of urban people became established, and as cities grew it was necessary to bring food to them from greater and greater distances. All sorts of inventions made this movement of commerce possible. Railroads and steamboats cut down the significance of distance. Well-drilling apparatus made it possible to live in regions of scanty surface water. Agricultural machinery made it possible to grow crops over huge areas where the yield per acre was too small for the older hand methods. Barbed wire made it possible to fence the fields, to breed cattle, and to keep the grazing animals out of the growing crops.

As cities grew, a wave of pioneer settlement pressed forward into these grasslands, and as settlement advanced the land values went to even higher figures, thus assuring the financial prosperity of the whole movement. Today all the social scientists can point to the end of an era, and when we reach the end of an era, we must again expect a change in the significance of the factor of location. It is the geographer's business to interpret this changing significance of the land.

The study of the location of man with reference to the land involves a more precise treatment of the land itself than is necessary in other social science fields. The geographer whose interest centers on the distribution of people can not resign his traditional study of the physical aspects of his subject. Among all the social sciences, only geography attempts anything like a precise description of the characteristics of the land—using *land* in the broader sense of the physical environment. This gives rise to a duality in the field of geography—a characteristic which geography shares with anthropology and a characteristic which has long been a source of irritation to the classifiers. In applied geography there is today a very considerable emphasis on the study of the physical processes as they affect and are affected by the use of the land by man. The connecting thread which gives unity to the field is the factor of relative location, just as all the varied content and special approaches of history are tied together by a preoccupation with the time factor.

### DEVELOPING ALERT OBSERVATION

Another of the major objectives of geographical studies is the development of habits of alert and informed observation. The landscape to a geographer is never drab or monotonous, for the habit of picking out significant details reveals the fascinating complexity which underlies apparent uniformity. Even familiar scenes take on new meaning to a person who has been made aware of the significance of the things which lie over the horizon. Any child who has learned to observe the forms and patterns which give character to his own locality quickly identifies the elements which differentiate other localities. He becomes an intelligent traveler who can see his home, his state, or even his nation in the larger perspective; if his traveling must be carried out by means of the printed page, he is nevertheless motivated to seek new adventures in understanding in strange and remote places.

### CONCLUSION

All the social sciences, then, must contribute to the content used in the teaching of social studies. But this does not mean that each of the social disciplines should lose its identity. Especially history and geography, which present the fundamental elementary aspects of time and space, are indispensable for the development of sound principles. And the techniques by which geographers present the factor of location, now perhaps too much neglected in many study programs, must now be overlooked or disregarded. In the hands of teachers not trained as geographers, location becomes the most deadly sort of "place geography." In the hands of teachers trained to appreciate the significance of location and to understand the methods of imparting this significance to students, the geographical contribution to social studies, along with history, provides the solid framework on which important study programs can be erected.

# 18

## UNDERSTANDING THE SIGNIFICANCE
## OF DIFFERENCES
## FROM PLACE TO PLACE

Geography has a role to play in peace which is as fundamentally important as the role it plays in wartime. During two world wars, the demand for more geography and more geographers to instruct everyone from third-grade children to generals and admirals has been notable. But between the wars the decline in attention given to geography in the schools was accompanied by the return to isolationism, the attempt to build a self-sufficient America with a minimum of connections abroad, the denial of responsibility in the international field, and by the erection of barriers to the international exchange of goods. The decline in attention given to geography may have been a result of the same social attitudes which built the spirit of isolationism, but it is not unrealistic to suggest that it may also have been a contributing cause of America's tragic withdrawal.

Geography teaches about the world and the people in it, about the significance of the places where people live, and of the differences from place to place. The study of geography broadens one's horizons and develops an appreciation of the relation of one's own country or locality and the people in it to the other countries and the people of the world. In America this kind of understanding may spell the difference between the waging of another catastrophic war and a gradual relearning of the ways of peace.

There are at least four ways in which the subject matter of ge-

Reprinted from Clyde F. Kohn, ed., *Geographic Approaches to Social Education,* Nineteenth Yearbook of 1948 National Council for the Social Studies (Washington, D.C., 1948), pp. 27–37.

ography sharpens our concept of that rather vague thing called "world understanding," and in these four ways geography makes a contribution which is unique among the social studies: (a) geography presents an effective treatment of the land factor in the study of man-land relations; (b) geography places emphasis on the significance to man of the differences which occur from place to place on the surface of the earth; (c) geography teaches the reading and understanding of the map; and (d) geography develops the capacity of out-of-door observation. Geographers, who, of course, do not do any of these things well enough to be self-satisfied about it, nevertheless bear chief responsibility among the social studies workers for developing these fields. The first two of these contributions are discussed in this chapter. . . .

## THE IMPORTANCE OF THE LAND FACTOR

Geography deals with the earth as the home of man. To the everlasting confusion of people who like to think in terms of inclusive-exclusive categories, geography must always deal with natural phenomena as well as social phenomena. To place its materials among any of the divisions of the academic world is something which can never be done with complete satisfaction because of the fact that geography, like anthropology and psychology, is both a natural and a social science, and may, with equal propriety, be included among the humanities. Geography cuts across conventional categories. To the social studies it contributes a meaningful treatment of the conditions of the physical environment in which human societies operate.

The elements of the physical environment, which geographers sometimes refer to by the single word *land,* include a variety of phenomena. Sten de Geer has suggested the grouping of these phenomena in four overlapping spheres which together form the habitat of man. These are: (a) the lithosphere, or rock crust of the earth with its surface irregularities and its cover of broken rock fragments and its soils; (b) the hydrosphere, the water which fills the hollows of the lithosphere and is in the process of moving from higher toward lower places; (c) the atmosphere, the envelope of gases which surrounds the lithosphere and the hydrosphere; and (d) the biosphere, the earth's cover of natural vegetation and associated groupings of animals. The fifth sphere, the anthroposphere, constitutes an integral part of the earth's landscape, for, as geography informs us, man and the societies of men are as intimately connected with the land as a plant growing "in the sunlight and soil."

### The Understanding of Earth Features

It is important to know much more about the features of the physical earth than the ideas normally included in social studies curriculums by non-geographers. There are, of course, common English words to describe the major kinds of surface features—*plains, hills, plateaus, mountains*. These words are used widely in writings about man, but with little appreciation of the prevailing lack of precise understanding. "What is a mountain?" may seem at first to be an absurdly academic elaboration of something everyone knows about at an early age, but studies indicate that there are many adults, for whom the word itself has become commonplace, who yet associate with it many wholly erroneous ideas. To understand the historical significance of mountains, mountain passes, or mountain peoples, it is necessary to know much more about them than that they are high above sea level and stand out conspicuously on the landscape. For example, there are great differences to be observed in the significance of mountains, like the Rockies, in which the valleys and intermont basins are wide and the summits sharply peaked, and mountains, like the Central Andes, in which the valleys are narrow and deep, and in which there are wide expanses of gently sloping surface at a high elevation. And in the case of plateaus, the human significance of dissected plateaus, like the Allegheny, is fundamentally different from that of plateaus which remain largely undissected, like the Colorado. Even plains differ in significant ways. And with all these major categories and their important subtypes, there are many associated concepts: concepts regarding the cover of vegetation, the soil, the kinds of drainage features, the ways in which different human societies have attached themselves to these features.

Geographic education cannot present the complete understanding of these features all at once. It must build concepts which gradually develop a more penetrating and more profound understanding of the significance of earth features all the way through the elementary and secondary schools, and through the college to advanced graduate work. At some stage after the elementary one, the description of things associated with each natural feature is made more significant by a preliminary discussion of processes. Eventually comes the exciting new understanding that mountains are actually lifted above sea level by movements of the earth's crust, and that rivers, over long periods of time, gradually wear them down again almost to sea level; and as the mountains are worn down they pass through a more or less predictable sequence of landforms, examples of which can be observed among the actual mountains of the present time. Grade by grade, it is only through a knowledge of the varied nature of the earth's features that it is possible to gain an understanding of their importance in human affairs.

The same may be said about the climatic features of the earth. In the search for simplicity in a field not essentially their own, historians, sociologists, economists, and other social scientists have commonly described climatic location in terms of the three traditional zones. Recognizing that climate was of importance in human affairs, they adopted the simple Temperate, Torrid, and Frigid Zones and proceeded to draw conclusions concerning the effect of these climatic zones on human activities. The three zones were first developed by Aristotle, and later discarded by the Arab geographers whose knowledge of the world was greater than that of the founders of Greek science. Yet even today the climate of a place in the middle latitudes of the earth is often described by non-geographers as Temperate. It is now well known that both the world's highest and the world's lowest temperatures have been observed in the "Temperate" Zone; that the "Temperate" Zone has the most varied, changeable, and intemperate of weather; that the only truly temperate climates are in the Tropics; and that there are six or eight major climates within the "Temperate" Zone which range from very wet to very dry, and from very hot to very cold. These significant differences from place to place are well known; yet, it is usually only the geographers who insist on relating these differences to human experience. And why is it important to do so? Because only by treating the land factor with sufficient precision can meaningful relations to human behavior be discovered; unless meaningful relations are shown then the land factor is commonly overlooked. None of the countires with which we must deal can be understood or its problems appreciated simply by a study of its history and its institutions; equally fundamental is a knowledge of the characteristics of its land, presented not in broad meaningless generalities, but in sufficient detail to demonstrate the significance of the land factor.

## The Essential Unity of the Landscape

And the features of the physical earth are important in human affairs. Long ago, John Dewey pointed out that "human nature exists and operates in an environment. And it is not 'in' that environment as coins are in a box, but as a plant is in the sunlight and soil." [1] A landscape is made up of intimately and intricately related features —features which are so mutually dependent on each other that the change of any one feature has far-reaching and often unexpected results on all the others. People in the Great Plains have learned— but not in school—that the killing of certain birds that harmed the chickens also permitted an enormous increase in the gopher population which did much more total damage than would have been done by a loss of the chickens. People in California had to learn the hard way—not in school—that the fig could not be imported from the Old World Mediterranean without bringing certain wild insects to carry on the work of fertilization. People in many parts of the world have not yet learned—even in school—that wasteful and ill-considered agricultural practices are so destructive of the soil that the whole balance of nature is upset, and man, himself, may be unable to support himself in a land which once yielded an abundance. And while farmers on the headwaters permit their farms to be ruined because of their failure to understand natural processes, the people downstream suffer periodic disaster from floods. Human societies are built out of earth resources; human health is to an amazing degree related to the chemical content of the solids in which the food or feed crops are grown; human thoughts reflect the natural conditions of the earth; and human behavior is, in ways still only partially comprehended, closely related to the changing conditions of the atmosphere. If an understanding of man's conflicting ways of living is important, or if it is important to instill in the minds of school children an appreciation of the need for the conservation of resources, then the land factor cannot be neglected or treated with insufficient detail and precision.

### The Meaning of Differences from Place to Place

But to insist that man and his societies are closely connected to the physical features of the land is not to embrace the largely discredited theories of environmental determinism. Of course, it is true that man is biologically enslaved to the earth's physical properties because of his dependence on water in liquid form. And there are parts of the earth's surface which are so cold or so dry or so wet that human life becomes especially difficult there. But the limits of these regions are flexible ones, for men have found the means of occupying even the wettest and driest and coldest places on earth when reasons for doing so were sufficiently pressing.

When geography is studied historically it becomes apparent that the physical characteristics of the different regions of the world have not always had the same significance for the inhabitants of the regions. Large parts of the earth were once considered poor places to live in, but are now generally classified among the world's most favorable habitats. Europe, north of the Alps, was considered by the geographers of antiquity to be fit only for barbarians. . . . The Argentine Humid Pampa for three centuries of occupance by Europeans could only be used for the raising of cattle and mules on the unfenced range. What has happened to change these regions from places considered poor to places considered rich? The land is the same but the way the people live has changed.

The significance to man of the features of the physical land is determined by the attitudes, objectives, and technical abilities of the inhabitants. This does not mean that man is no longer dependent on the earth for his support; but it does mean that with each change in the social or political system, with each new technical device, the significance of the land must be reinterpreted. Even in war, places that once could be great natural bastions for defense are today easily passed, and places that once formed the battlegrounds of conflicting groups today have little significance in this role.

These concepts can be clarified by the consideration of one of the regions previously mentioned—the Argentine Humid Pampa. Here we find the earliest Spanish settlers unable to make a living and forced to abandon their colony. To be sure this was partly the result of the political jealousy of competing groups, but even under the best circumstances the Humid Pampa to the Spaniards of the sixteenth century was a land of low productivity. Even until the nineteenth century the region continued to be important chiefly for the raising of cattle and mules. It was only after the middle of that century that the modern concept of the Humid Pampa as a region of great productivity for grain and meat began to form.

What changed the Humid Pampa from a region of low to a region of high productivity? There was the same deep loess soil, the same regime of rainfall favorable for grain and alfalfa, the same stimulating changes of weather, the same extraordinarily flat plains with very immature drainage. Yet for some three hundred years there was little change in the way the land was used; then, suddenly —in the space of only a couple of decades—the whole significance of these features so far as human inhabitants are concerned, was changed. What happened? Four changes in technology appeared at about the same time: (a) railroads and steamboats for the first time provided low-cost bulk transportation at relatively high speed; (b) the Industrial Revolution in Great Britain and on the Continent brought about the concentration of people in cities which had to be supplied with food from distant places—so, for the first time, there was a market; (c) barbed wire was invented, which made possible the low-cost fencing of grassland pastures and fields; and (d) the steel plow was invented which made possible the turning of the prairie sod. These changes in the objectives and techniques of occidental people changed radically the significance of the Humid Pampa to man.

Even the concept of the Humid Pampa as a natural region is

based on the apparent unity given the area by the pattern of grain farms and cattle ranches in the modern period. If a geographer had described the natural regions of Argentina in 1800 he would certainly have drawn a major regional boundary along the Salado Slough, separating the northern third of what is today the Humid Pampa from the southern two thirds. To argue, then, that this is a natural region discovered and occupied by man as a "response" to natural conditions is to fail to gain the perspective of time in the study of man's experience with the land.

This is an important matter in developing the desirable social attitudes and appreciations which lead to relevant and valid decisions of policy in the modern world. If we accept the theory that people are the creatures of the physical earth and can account for what they do or fail to do in terms of the inevitable consequences of physical geography, then it is easy to develop a feeling of irresponsibility not only with regard to the changing of the economic status of distant countries, but even with regard to the better utilization of our own land. Is the *status quo* not to be changed; is there no hope for the so-called backward parts of the world? Are the present industrial centers solely the result of a combination of natural resources, and are the world's colonial areas which have traditionally supplied the raw materials for industry forever condemned to a colonial status? Are the centrally located states, surrounded by the territory of other states, condemned either to struggle for an outlet to the sea or accept a lesser status in the world? The evidence denies all this. Industrial areas are at present appearing where resources seem to be inadequate, as they once did in New England; colonial countries are asserting their right to industrialize; central states, like Switzerland, play a leading role in world affairs. Close and essential as are the relations between people and the land, the nature of the connections is not predetermined. The differences from place to place on the earth are of critical importance in understanding the economic, political, and social problems of the world, but the significance of these differences at any one time and place is determined by the attitudes, objectives, and technical abilities of the people.

## Occidental Culture

The attitudes, objectives, and technical abilities of a people constitute what social scientists generally describe as a culture, a way of living. The common habits of thought and action in any one society tend to be passed on from parents to children. Only in our own culture, the culture of the industrial society, has the tradition of change become established. But let us see how the industrial society came into being.

The culture of the people of Europe and of the parts of the world settled by Europeans was essentially uniform before the middle of the eighteenth century. There were, of course, local differences of language and custom, but in terms of the attitude toward land as a resource, the objectives of settlement, and especially in terms of the techniques of making a living, there was just one great culture—the occidental culture. The traditional ways of doing things had been derived by a long process of gradual development from the classical cultures of the Mediterranean and its borders.

Since the middle of the eighteenth century one of the greatest revolutions in man's way of living on the earth has made its appearance. In the short span of two centuries the whole relation of man to the earth has been transformed. The invention of the means of using controlled inanimate power have had profound repercussions, and we are living through the period of confusion and turmoil occasioned by so radical a transformation of the basic techniques of living. For the first time people in large numbers could concentrate in cities, and the new means of transportation assured them not only an adequate supply of food, but a far more varied and dependable supply of food than any considerable number of people had ever been able to enjoy before. Industries could produce useful things from the raw materials of the earth in incredible quantities and at much lower cost per unit than ever before. The demand for earth resources increased on an unprecedented scale. And associated with these changes in the technology of living was a rapid increase in the total population not only of the industrialized areas but also of all other areas of the world where Europeans or

Americans brought the new ways of living. The process of change still continues, with the prospect of even greater and more fundamental differences in the relation of man to the earth forecast by the development of atomic power.

But all of the occidental world was not transformed in the same manner. The development of the urban-industrial way of living took place in the nuclear area around the shores of the North Sea. Rapidly it spread over all the parts of the world occupied by English-speaking people. On the continent of Europe, however, the spread was less rapid, and has not yet gone beyond France, Belgium, the Netherlands, parts of the Scandinavian countries, Western Germany, western Czechoslovakia, Austria, and northern Italy. In Latin America the industrial society is making its appearance now in such great cities as São Paulo, Rio de Janeiro, Buenos Aires, and Mexico City. In these places the much greater productivity has built a higher level of living than has ever been possible before, but at the price of international interdependence. For self-sufficiency and economic isolation are a direct contradiction of the global needs of modern industry. The industrial way of living and the great national sovereignties existing in complete independence are incompatible ideas. In the effort to resolve this conflict the industrial society has reached the brink of self-destruction.

Most of the occidental world, however, has been relatively little changed during the past two hundred years. This includes all of Eastern Europe and most parts of Latin America. Here the preindustrial society still flourishes, with its concentration of political power in the hands of the owners of land rather than the owners of capital, and with its large majorities of illiterate farmers rather than literate urban wage earners. And rising in the East is the new Soviet society as a third division of what should be "one world"—a society developed by radical communism out of an essentially preindustrial group.

For each of these three societies into which the once uniform culture of the occident is now divided, geography must be written differently. Any study of present-day society which does not recognize this fundamental point increases the difficulty of understanding the issues involved in world affairs. If we are to broaden the outlook beyond the horizon of the immediate locality we must learn to make relevant judgments concerning distant people, and such judgments cannot be based on a narrow study of our own society. Every society must find ways to utilize earth resources; but the ways that resources are utilized are determined by the economic, political, social, or religious ideas of the people—by their own concepts of value, by their own command of technology. These appreciations are fundamental to our successful emergence from isolation into a world of international responsibility; they are essential even for a clear understanding of the domestic issues in our own varied land.

## THE FIVE BASIC CONCEPTS

Geography, which teaches about the world and the people in it, about the significance of the places where people live, and of the differences from place to place, has certain basic concepts to develop regarding man's relation to the earth. These concepts are derived from all the social sciences, not geography alone; yet they should form the core of geographic education from the elementary grades to the graduate school. Only by stating and restating these concepts, and by illustrating them again and again with important examples, can a proper understanding of the problems of man-land relations and of conflicts between states and societies be gained.

There are at least five such basic concepts, which can be outlined briefly as follows:

1. That all human societies are necessarily forced to establish workable connections with the resources and conditions of the land in order to survive.

2. That simple cultures have a few direct connections with the earth resources of their immediate locality, but that the more complex the culture the greater the variety of connections with the earth resources and the more indirect they become. For this reason they are not so easily perceived, and the principle that connections with the earth resources must in fact exist on a permanently workable basis in order to insure survival is a concept that needs emphatic teaching.

3. That the most complex culture of all—the industrial society —by its essential nature is global in its scope and international in

its needs. If it is to survive it must draw upon all the world's resources, and all the world's people must share its benefits. Our way of living is dependent on the coordinated economic activities of distant people. This is the concept of "One World"—of one community of interdependent peoples, one society of internationally responsible states; it is the exact opposite of international irresponsibility, economic self-sufficiency, and isolationism.

4. That the significance of the features of the physical earth is determined by man and not by nature. That the regions of the world now occupied by the most complex cultures were once considered fit only for barbarians, and that changing technology can again change the whole resource pattern, the significance of the climatic pattern, the basic relation of man to earth. This increases —not decreases—the importance of analyzing the present-day significance of earth features in relation to human societies. It makes geography an adventure in understanding, not an exercise in memory.

5. That the physical and human differences which exist from place to place on the earth are significant to us because the great economic, social, and political issues of our time are in part the direct result of these differences. It is important to know, for example, in what respects the Soviet Union, including its sector of the earth's surface, differs from other countries and places, not because such facts make good discipline for memory training, but because they are essential to the understanding needed in the formulation of our policy in the international world.

These five basic concepts provide the ideological connections between geographic education and the other subjects dealing with human societies. Geography as a social science clarifies and elaborates these concepts in its own unique way: by emphasizing the importance of the land factor in the man-land equation; by analyzing the significance in human affairs of differences from place to place; by teaching the reading and understanding of maps; and by developing the capacity to observe significant differences out-of-doors and to appreciate the essential harmony of man and nature.

NOTE

1. John Dewey, *Human Nature and Conduct* (New York, 1922), p. 296.

# 19

## THE HARD CORE OF
## GEOGRAPHY

Education in America has suffered an impoverishment in those curricula where the hard core of geography has been reduced, diluted, or eliminated. To be useful, geography as well as history must be taught by adequately trained teachers. When it is so taught, along with history, it can provide the kind of perspective in terms of place and period that can give new meaning to the confused events and circumstances of modern life. Unfortunately geography has suffered from relative neglect in the organization of social studies curricula. There are some schools where the remnants of what was once a unified subject are taught by teachers with no training in geography at all. In other schools geography has been weakened by dropping out the more rigorous aspects of the discipline with the plea that the subject matter was "too difficult." This is especially true with regard to training in the understanding of maps. It is time that the hard core of geography be returned to the social studies.

Many centuries ago a teacher had command of almost the whole breadth of human knowledge. Among the ancient Greek scholars there were many who made notable contributions to a wide variety of subjects. Herodotus, for example, is often described as a historian; the anthropologists claim him as one of the first students of man's culture; a reading of his works shows also that he was a competent and skilled geographer. *Geography* was a Greek word, said to have been coined by Eratosthenes, used to identify a field of learning so obvious and so universally understood that no special definition was necessary. *Geography* means, simply, "writ-

Reprinted from *New Viewpoints in Geography,* Twenty-Ninth Yearbook of 1959 National Council for the Social Studies (Washington D.C., 1959), pp. 1–9.

ing about the earth." Herodotus never thought of telling the story of the Egyptians without also telling about Egypt. He did not fail to use historical documents to reconstruct the ancient shorelines of the Mediterranean and so to throw light on the growth of the Nile Delta, nor did he fail to relate the growth of the delta to the load of silt brought down by the Nile. In those days geography and history, place and period, were so intimately tied together that all geography was presented historically, and all history was presented geographically. And both place and period provided the framework in which the institutions of mankind could be described, and the processes of cultural change could be traced.

No one today can embrace universal knowledge. Students of the various fields, each making use of a special set of methods, each requiring specialized training, have diverged into separate and sometimes antagonistic groups. This specialization has made possible extraordinary gains in the understanding of the various processes at work on the surface of the earth. Processes, examined in isolation from their surroundings in any particular place, are now more fully understood than ever was possible before. Yet the more these processes are known, the greater is the need to see how they operate in the real context of place and period. In the training of citizens, as distinct from the training of specialists in the study of particular phenomena, there is pressing need to see the modern world in perspective, to see the United States in its world relationships. The concepts and methods of study developed by geography and history are fully as important in the education of the whole citizen as are the concepts of science or the methods of mathematics.

## FINDING OUT ABOUT THE EARTH

Before people could write about the earth they had to find out what it was like. Mankind has always been curious about the earth. The process of satisfying this curiosity started with the first primitive representatives of *homo sapiens,* and continues to the present. Present-day understandings of the physical character of the human habitat are the result of a long-continued process of exploration and discovery, and are certainly not to be thought of as the final end-product. Along the way many mistakes have been made, many incomplete observations that were considered to be complete, many explanations that failed to explain, many concepts that once seemed to be proved but have had to be modified or discarded. If the earth and man's place on it are presented as if all the problems of understanding had been solved, the result is likely to be dull. If, on the other hand, the study is presented as a great adventure in understanding, with many problems still unsolved, it may well evoke the inborn curiosity about people and places that is a part of human nature.

Primitive men, perhaps even more than the sophisticated city-dwellers of today, were curious about what it was like beyond their horizon. Some were even brave enough to travel and look for themselves. The writings of Homer reflect the stories of travelers who had visited strange places—places where the sun never sets, or where it is always night. "Popular description and travel" is still an important category in libraries, but there was a time when almost all the literary efforts of man were of this kind.

To change an adventure story to geography involves three things. First, the description of what it is like over the horizon has to be made more accurate, more meaningful. Second, when a traveler reaches a new land his description will be of little value unless he can tell how far and in what direction he traveled to reach it. Geographers have long been concerned with the measurement of distance and with the fixing of position on the earth. And third, even the most complete and accurate description, definitely located, leaves the curiosity unsatisfied unless it can show the significance of the things described. Geography must be related to the experiences and interests of American children.

### The Problem of Description

At first the problem of providing accurate and intelligible descriptions posed great difficulties. You cannot easily tell what a place is "like" unless you already possess a fund of knowledge with which to draw comparisons. The method is to set up categories of things, each category carefully defined and represented by word symbols or map symbols. Long before the days of Homer, the Greeks had already enriched their language with word symbols to stand for the familiar earth features, such as river, lake, ocean, mountain, plain, peninsula, island, and many others. It took a long time before people were ready to accept the word symbol to stand for a particular kind of earth feature. Yet today we tend to assume that the child in the primary grades has already somehow learned the *meaning* of *river, lake, ocean, mountain,* and so on, without specific instruction.

The process of using word symbols to stand for things observed on the face of the earth continued throughout the Greek and Roman period. A similar process was going on elsewhere in other languages, but the process in Greece and Rome is of special importance to us because it is from these sources that we derive our language. For example, the Greek geographer Strabo (who wrote at about the time of Christ) reported that "the Meander River (now the Menderes River in Turkey) flows through the Plain of the Meander where its course is so exceedingly winding that everything winding is called 'meandering.' " [1] This is one way the Greeks enriched their language by providing work symbols for a great variety of earth features.

### The Problem of Position

Geographers all through the ages have been concerned with the problem of finding and recording position. The question has been how to measure distance and direction, and how to record distance and direction on a map. The Greeks learned how to do these things in theory, but lack of accurate instruments kept them from making the measurements themselves.

The method of establishing a north-south line was discovered by the Assyrians. They made use of the simple sundial, which is shown technically as a *gnomon*. This consisted of a rod set vertically on a fixed plate. By observing closely the position of the shadow when it was shortest they could establish the moment of noon, and also the exact line of the meridian. The Greek geographer, Thales, made use of the *gnomon* to tell time, to tell the season of the year, to fix the north-south line, and to measure distance along this line. He did the latter by observing that on any given date the shadow at noon was longer the farther he went toward the north. The Greeks, who had no doubt regarding the roundness of the earth, were able to fix position quite accurately in a north-south direction. They could, therefore, tell in what direction they were moving. But the measurement of distance in an east-west direction remained unsolved because of the lack of an instrument for keeping accurate time. Aristotle, the teacher of Alexander the Great, gave his pupil instruction in geographic methods, including the use of the *gnomon,* and the methods of estimating distance on sea and on land. When Alexander led his armies far to the east into India he had a fairly good idea of his position in the north-south dimension, but he greatly exaggerated the east-west distance.

Thales also introduced the basic concepts of geometry to the Greeks. He found Egyptian priests using trigonometry to measure crop areas, and to fix the position of field boundaries covered over by the floods. Much later, using the geometry of lines, Eratosthenes (c. 276–194 B.C.) was able to measure the circumference of the earth, and to arrive at a figure that was almost exactly correct. Hipparchus was the first to divide the circle into 360° and to mark off the face of the round earth with a grid of latitude and longitude lines. Thereafter, in theory at least, any point on the face of the earth could be accurately located with reference to this grid of lines. Unfortunately for the later explorers, notably Columbus, the figure that Eratosthenes had given for the earth's circumference, was disputed by Posidonius, and it was his much smaller figure that was passed on to posterity through the work of Ptolemy.

How can we recapture the atmosphere of excitement that must have existed at Sagres in the early fifteenth century? [2] Here, on a promontory in southern Portugal, Prince Henry the Navigator brought together many of the leading geographers and cartographers of his day. Here was a school for sailors, where the geographical lore of antiquity was collected and studied for the very practical purpose of finding a way around Africa to India.

The whole story is too long to include here. The story of how Mercator devised a way to show the round earth on a flat piece of paper, but only by so distorting the distances on his map that its use for the comparison of areas has led to serious errors by geographically illiterate people. In the modern period many new map projections and new map symbols have been devised. And as the methods of measuring distance and direction have been perfected and as new understandings of the nature of the earth and of man's place on it have been gained, the problem of selecting the fundamental hard core of geography becomes more and more important.

### Distance and Direction in Childhood Experience

But do we often stop to realize that this process of finding out about the earth is a part of every normal child's experience? Every one of us has relived in miniature an important part of the history of geography. As soon as a child learns to walk, the geographic adventure begins. At first, even a peek around the corner of the house is a spine-tingling experience, and the clump of bushes at the back of the family yard is an unexplored jungle. The British author Robert A. Milne has given us the delightful "Pooh" stories (*Winnie The Pooh, The House at Pooh Corners,* and others). These children's books tell vividly of the explorations carried on with a high sense of adventure as the geographic horizons are expanded to include the neighborhood. When Pooh and his friends went on their "expotition" to the North Pole, they were reliving the geographic experience of mankind. Still later, the growing child learns to wander farther from home.

As his geographic horizons widen, however, his sophistication spreads like a shield over his sensitive and curious mind. Unless someone shows him that it is not necessarily "big" to betray no interest in what it is like beyond the horizon, he will learn to shut out this kind of adventure from his life. By the time he gets to geography in the school, if he ever does, it has become something to learn by heart, not something that builds on his own basic experiences.

### GEOGRAPHY AS SEEN BY PROFESSIONAL GEOGRAPHERS

How, then, can geography be made to "come alive" when it is taught in the schools and colleges? How can the inborn curiosity concerning what it is like beyond the horizon be used to stimulate excitement about geographic study? Why has so much geography teaching been described as dull, and lacking an intellectual content? These questions are posed with the clear understanding that over the many centuries since the days of Thales in ancient Greece there have always been scholars devoting themselves to the study and teaching of geography. For these devoted people geography has been a satisfying field of study, and there are many to bear witness that the teaching of geography is not necessarily dull—always and everywhere.

A part of the problem is related to the fact that far too often geography is taught in the United States by untrained teachers. To the teacher unfamiliar with the concepts and methods of geography, the subject can easily become a memory exercise, a listing of things that occur together in an area. It is easy to list the cities of more than 100,000 inhabitants in a country, or the chief products, or the major mountain ranges and the larger rivers. But doing this has no meaning until the causes and consequences of city location are clarified, or until the products are related to the broader aspects of the economic life, or until man's reaction to the mountains and rivers has been introduced. To make an inventory of the things that occur together in an area, without any concept to show why such knowledge is important, is like making a list of the contents of a trash can. As John K. Wright points out, the things that happen to be together in the trash can do not normally justify encyclopedic description. To make the things that occur together within the boundaries of a country meaningful it is necessary to begin with a theme, a concept of wide application regarding the processes that brought these things together. And when the concept is stated, all those features of an area that are irrelevant to the concept are omitted. This is the essence of "thinking geographically."

A geographically trained teacher sees more to the subject than a listing of more or less unrelated facts about a place. Just how the geographers view the field of geography is presented in a book published in 1954: *American Geography: Inventory and Prospect*. The purpose of this book was to define the concepts and the methods of study as accepted by the leading members of the profession. A summary of the ideas contained in this book forms the contents of the second chapter of this Yearbook. This and the other chapters of Part One discuss the field of geography as seen through the eyes of professional geographers. In this part we are offered a picture of the latest trends, the newest concepts, and the most recent suggestions regarding methods of study that characterize American geography today.

There are three major conclusions that emerge from the study of the chapters in Part One of this Yearbook.*

> 1. Physical geography cannot be omitted from any social studies program if that program is to be sound. It is essential, therefore, that teachers follow carefully the history of man's experience in finding out about the earth, the present concepts about the physical character of the earth in historical perspective. Thus Aristotle's brilliant generalization concerning the earth's climatic zones can only be presented as a stage in the learning process, and not as a concept that is valid today.
>
> 2. The old dictum of Herodotus that history must be presented geographically and geography must be presented historically is being given new emphasis in modern geographical studies. Historical geography consists of the recreation of past geographies and the observation of geographical changes through time. The time perspective alone can provide the answer to the question of what processes of change are significant today on the face of the earth.
>
> 3. Cartography is the core technique of geography. Maps are used to record things observed out-of-doors; they are used to analyze the areal relations of things, and to plot the areal spread and the varying intensity of phenomena, and thus to outline the regions which are the basic generalizations of geography. Maps are also used to present the results of geographic study. In the last few decades a rich variety of new kinds of maps have been developed, each useful for a specific purpose.

## Applications to Classroom Instruction

All these findings of the professional geographers should be reflected as promptly as possible in the teaching of geography in

* Part One includes six chapters on the following topics: American Geography at Mid-Century (James), Physical Geography (Clyde Patton), Human Geography (Broek), Economic Geography (Warntz), Regional Geography (Pearson), Cartography (Espenshade)—Ed.

schools and colleges. Inevitably there is a lag between the findings of the more advanced scholars and the materials available for use in classrooms. The social studies teacher should be conscious of this lag, and of the need for making it as short as possible.

When geography and history are treated as the twin aspects of time and place (and not just placed end to end), the study of various social processes is taken out of the isolation of the laboratory and put back in the context of place and period. Social studies curricula are freed from too narrow a concern with political and economic conditions in the United States, and permitted to develop a much-needed world perspective. The citizen of America must not only know and understand his own institutions, but he must also be able to see the United States in relation to the world outside. The improvement of the teaching of world affairs is a vital necessity. This can be done through the use of the framework of space and time as offered by geography and history.

The social studies teacher can incorporate the newest findings of the physical geographers if this aspect of geography is presented as a historical narrative—the narrative of how man found out about the earth, and what his experience has been in the use of the earth. The teacher trained in geography and skillful in the methods of using geography as a teaching vehicle can tie the experiences of the child in exploring the neighborhood to those of mankind in exploring and learning about the earth. If the child learns early enough how to make a map, his inborn curiosity regarding what is over the horizon may be preserved, and his life enriched thereby.

The modern world may seem chaotic and uncertain. It is the responsibility of the social studies teacher to attempt to paint a picture of rapid, but nevertheless orderly, change brought about by the Industrial Revolution and the democratic revolution. The fact that we live in a period of human history when these two major revolutions in living are taking place is a fact of profound importance. The fact that these revolutions are spreading over the earth unevenly, and producing different reactions in different regions of the world, is a part of the world perspective so much needed by all the citizens of a democracy. Teachers of the social studies play a challenging role; for not only are they students of certain subjects, and teachers of certain ideas and methods, but they also are players in the dramatic scenes of modern life. To make vivid the sweep of

the great revolutions of our time, not only in the time perspective
but also in the space perspective which helps to explain the contemporary differences from place to place on the earth, is no simple
undertaking, no task to assign to the untrained person.

It is time that the hard core of geography be returned to the social studies. This is not geography as the list of things contained in
an area, but geography as the analysis of the meaning of place and
position on the earth, as an analysis of the significance of areal associations of things. It is place illuminated by period, and period by
place. It is geography based firmly on the study of the meaning of
word symbols and map symbols, and on an adequate understanding
of the problem of portraying the curved surface of the earth on a
flat piece of paper. It is the geography of the contemporary world
beyond our own immediate horizon made meaningful and alive by
reference to the historical processes that have created the present
out of the past and that will move on to create the future out of the
present. In the education of America's future citizens, the social
studies, organized around the twin dimensions of geography and
history, stand second in importance to no other field.

## NOTES

1. Horace L. Jones, trans. *The Geography of Starbo.* 8 vols. (London: W. Heine-
mann; New York: G. P. Putnam's Sons, 1927), Book 12, Chap. 8.

2. Frank G. Slaughter, *The Mapmaker, A Novel of the Days of Prince Henry
the Navigator* (New York: Doubleday and Co., 1957), p. 320.

# 20

## A CONCEPTUAL STRUCTURE
## FOR GEOGRAPHY

The current ferment of curriculum revision in America provides geographers with both a challenge and an opportunity to formulate appropriate conceptual structures that can be made clear to the fraternity of education. There is no need here to give additional support to the point that facts slip quickly away unless they are relevant to a framework of theory.

The words *concept* and *conceptual structure* have been used in such different contexts and with such varied meanings that they are now dangerously close to becoming meaningless. But if they do become meaningless we shall have to invent new words to refer to the general body of theory that distinguishes our field, and that justifies the place it takes in the curriculum. This paper provides no new theory but only restates in simple language ideas that have been current in the geographic profession for many decades.

First of all it is important to understand that there are just three fundamentally different ways of organizing units of study in a curriculum. One is to build units around concepts that have to do with specific processes or with groups of similar processes. Thus a unit of study in science is built around a physical process or a biotic process, without reference to when the process takes place or where. A unit of study in social sciences is based on concepts of human behavior. This is the *substantive* principle of curriculum organization, and the one on which most curricula are structured. Another way of organizing units of study is around concepts of time sequence. This is the *chronological* principle, most commonly (but not exclusively) associated with history. And the third way of

Reprinted from *Journal of Geography*, 64, 7 (October 1965), 292–98.

organizing units of study is to make use of concepts of areal association and interconnection among things and events of unlike origin, where different kinds of processes interact in particular places.
This is the *chorological* principle, most commonly (but not exclusively) associated with geography.[1] A well-balanced curriculum for
elementary and secondary grades will make use of each of the three
principles of organization at different times.

Geography is that field of learning which undertakes to develop
concepts based on the chorological principle. In this field, therefore, attention is focused on the areal associations of things and
events that result from unlike processes, and on the interconnections among the facts thus associated. Geography is also responsible for developing and teaching the arts of communication and
analysis through the use of maps.

There are three purposes to be served by the teaching of geography. One is to provide a general understanding of the arrangement of things and events over the whole surface of the earth, so
that by the end of the ninth or tenth grades, at least, students
should be able to look at a globe without finding any large areas
about which they are completely uninformed or are unable to predict what kinds of associated features they would be likely to find if
they paid the area a visit. The second purpose to be served is to
teach the pupils to ask geographic questions, and to devise ways of
finding and testing the answers to such questions. The third purpose
is to teach the language of the map. This paper deals only with the
concepts useful for achieving the first of these purposes: namely,
world coverage.

## WHAT IS A GEOGRAPHIC CONCEPT

A concept we may agree, is a mental image of a thing or event. In
this meaning it is opposed to a percept which is the direct observation of a thing or event. Out-of-doors one can look at a specific hill
—this is the percept of a thing—and if the hill is covered with
plants and used in some way by man, it becomes an area, or segment of earth space, within which things of unlike origin are associated and interconnected. But in the classroom one develops a
mental image of "hill" in general. This is a concept. Out-of-doors

one can observe the formation of a gully during a rain. This is the percept of an event. In the classroom we develop a mental image of gullies in general. This is the concept of the event, or sequences of events that result in the formation of gullies. A long list of such concepts can be matched against percepts: valley, river, lake, farm, factory, airfield, or such events as the harvesting of a field of wheat, or even the impact of government on an individual when a census is taken. There are many glossaries of geographic terms, but there is still need for research to identify those concepts that should be taught, and the grade level at which they should be taught.

But geography, because of the nature of the field, must inevitably deal with concepts that can never be matched with percepts. The curved surface of the earth limits the range of vision, even when observations can be made from the moon. The basic instrument of perception is man himself. The things he perceives and the mental images he develops are related to the fact that his eyes are some five feet above the ground and some three inches apart. If the observers were ant-size creatures the mental images of things and events on the face of the earth would be quite different. The ant would not think of a hill as a unit, nor would the process of gully formation come within the field of direct observation. Similarly there are many features of the face of the earth that lie beyond the perception of man. No one has ever directly observed a hilly upland. The mental image of such a general category of surface is based on the observation of many specific hills and valleys. No one has ever perceived the formation of a river system. Geographers must deal with many concepts that lie beyond the range of direct observation: climatic regions, soil associations, types of farming regions, or even the politically organized territory we call a state.

The distinction between concepts that can be matched with percepts and those that cannot is of sufficient importance to merit special terms. This writer describes those features that can be directly observed from a single place as "topographic features," and the mental images of such features are "topographic concepts." [2] Concepts that refer to things and events too widely spread to be observable from one place are described as "chorographic concepts." Concepts that refer to those highly generalized features that occupy the major part of the earth's surface are "global concepts."

It is clear that the only geographic unit is the whole surface of the earth.[3] Like all fields of learning, geography must make a selection of segments of human knowledge sufficiently restricted to be comprehended. Geographers must set off pieces of the whole, or segments of earth-space. Since no two pinpoints on the face of the earth are identical, any segment of earth-space, however small, represents a generalization from which irrelevant details have been eliminated. The segments of earth-space that geographers define as homogeneous are identified by the existence of some kind of areal association of things or events of unlike origin. These are called "regions." [4]

The region, so defined, is one of the core concepts of geography. The word is not to be confused with the popular meaning of *region* as a large, vaguely defined area containing some kind of homogeneity; nor is the regional method to be confused with the compilation of groups of unrelated facts that are summarized within some kind of arbitrary area.

A distinction must be made between "generic regions" and "genetic regions." [5] "Generic regions" are defined as homogeneous in terms of stated criteria—a hilly upland with an associated pattern of land use and settlement, for example. The definition of a "genetic region" requires not only the identification of areal associations, but also of the processes, or sequences of events, that have produced the areal associations.[6] This involves the reconstruction of past geographies (that is, of past areal associations of things or events of unlike origin) and the tracing of geographic change through time. This is called historical geography. The recognition of segments of earth-space within which unlike things and events are interconnected to form systems of related parts is the operative definition of the regional method. Such segments of earth-space may be based on a wide variety of phenomena and processes, and may be defined at very different scales or degrees of generalization, ranging from topographic to global. A conceptual structure is a series of related concepts forming a system.

## AN APPROACH TO GLOBAL GEOGRAPHY

We seek, then, a structure of related concepts to provide an understanding of the causes and consequences of the arrangement and interconnections of the major physical, biotic, and cultural features of the earth. So infinite is the variety of things and events that are interconnected on the earth that many different kinds of conceptual structures could be formulated. The problem is to identify a minimum number of such structures which are useful in providing the framework of a global understanding for Americans. Surely, we may agree that the conceptual structures we want must be relevant to the great contemporary problems: the adequacy of the earth to support the world's rapidly increasing population; the causes and results of the world arrangement of wealth and poverty; the meaning of the conflict between autocracy and democracy. Any conceptual structure that fails to throw new light on these questions may be judged as being poor.

Applying the regional concept on a global scale, we suggest a series of related concept-systems. First, we suggest regions based on "ecosystems" in which the areal associations of things and events resulting from physical and biotic processes, without the intervention of man, are identified. Second, we proceed to regions based on "habitats," wherein man modifies his natural surroundings through interference with physical and biotic processes. And third, we suggest regions based on the interconnections between habitat features and "culture" features, in which changes in the significance of habitats are correlated with the processes of economic, social, and political change in the modern world.

## Ecosystems

Ecosystems are produced by areal associations of interconnected physical and biotic processes, without the interference of man. There are at least five major groups of physical and biotic things and events that are involved in forming these areal associations: surface features, climates, water, biota (wild plants and animals), and soils. Each of these elements forms a subsystem of related parts, and each could be made the subject of a course of systematic study by itself. But it is the interconnected areal associations of all these things and events that form the earth's major ecosystems.

There are two principles involved in the global arrangement of such ecosystems. First, all those things and events that are related to the pattern of surface features and rocks are irregularly distributed with reference to the poles and latitudes. And second, all those things and events that are related to the pattern of climates are regularly distributed over the earth. This basic regularity of climate, and of climatically related phenomena, is the result of the distribution of energy over the earth, and of the mechanisms that tend to equalize energy. The circulation of the atmosphere produces a regular pattern of rainfall and temperature. The distribution of water on the land is related to climate. So also are the patterns of plants and animals. The great soil groups are clearly associated with climate, water, and biota. The circulation of water in the ocean basins is another mechanism for redistributing energy, and this process develops a basic regularity in the movement of water, the temperature, salinity, and other properties of the oceans.

The actual pattern of ecosystems, however, is a compromise between the principle of regularity and the principle of irregularity. For the relatively simple patterns of climatically related features that would exist if the earth were all level land or all water are, in fact, distorted by the irregular disposition of the continents and ocean basins, and by the unique surface configuration of each continent. Yet the underlying climatic pattern is never wholly obscured; rather, the irregularity of surface only distorts the regularity of climate.

As a result it is possible to predict the nature of the ecosystem that would be found in any part of the globe. If one knows the latitude of a place, and whether it is on the eastern, interior, or western part of a continent, or on the eastern or western part of an ocean, and if one recalls the unique surface patterns of seven continents, the basic world patterns fit nicely into place. A pupil who develops this mental image of the world can be expected to pass the so-called thumb test. With eyes closed he places the thumb on a globe. When he sees where his thumb is resting he can predict the physical and biotic character of that part of the world, whether his thumb is on land or water. He fails the test if he cannot make the necessary prediction.

## Habitat

A habitat is an ecosystem that has been modified by human action. For the nearly two million years that the earth has been occupied by the *genus homo,* the ecosystems have been subject to changes introduced by man. The distinguishing characteristic of manmade changes, as opposed to changes resulting from natural processes, is that they are carried out in accordance with a plan of action that extends beyond the immediate. But many changes started by man have spread beyond the range of human plan. Changes introduced at some point in the balance of the ecosystem have repercussions of an unexpected nature throughout the system. Even where primitive man was present in small numbers, his fires, set for the purpose of aiding in the hunt or of clearing the land for crops or pasture, have had a profound and unplanned impact on the original vegetation. In fact, wholly new habitats have been created in certain parts of the pattern of ecosystems—as when grasslands were created where once there was an intermingling of brush and woodland. But these changes of the vegetation took place so long ago that related soils have developed under the new plant cover, and animals adjusted to the new environment have become established. The "natural" surroundings of man are, therefore, partly manmade.

Nevertheless, the global pattern of habitats closely reflects the previous pattern of ecosystems. Furthermore, the principles of regularity and irregularity can also be applied to the prediction of habitat patterns.[7]

## The Concept of Significance

Habitats are significant, not only because they have in part been created by human action, but also because they provide the "natural" surroundings of man's occupancy of the earth. Any human society, if it is to survive for long, must form a workable connection with the earth resources. The habitat is the resource base of man's societies. Answers to many questions regarding wealth and poverty and the capacity of the earth to support the human population must be provided by reference to the habitats with which man is associated. It is of the utmost importance, therefore, to develop a valid concept regarding the significance to man of the features of the habitat.

The dominant concept in American geography until the 1920s was known as "environmental determinism." Many persons not in contact with modern geographical thinking still accept the concept that the nature of man's physical and biotic surroundings either determines, or at least sets limits to man's ways of making a living. Adherents to this concept point out such habitats as the dry lands or the polar lands or the mountain lands are always difficult for human settlement. Oranges, they insist, cannot be grown in the polar lands. No nation can be strong, they say, without coal.

The study of the relations of man to his habitat by the methods of historical geography, however, reveals the inadequacy of the concept of environmental determinism. No land can be properly described as rich or poor, friendly or unfriendly, except in relation to a particular group of people, for the land which may be considered to be richly endowed for people who live by hunting may be considered as poorly endowed for a people who wish to live by farming. Slopes that can be cultivated with the hoe are too steep to cultivate with plows. Soils that are productive for one kind of crop raised with certain farming methods may be quite unproductive for other crops raised by other methods. Even such a resource as coal clearly has a different meaning for people who have the technical skill to make use of it from what it means to people who lack such skill. Climates which the Greeks thought would prohibit the development of civilized living are now occupied by people with high standards of material comfort. The people flocking into Southern California do not think of dry lands as difficult for human settlement.

The cornerstone of the conceptual structure of geography, and the connecting link between habitat and human inhabitants, is the concept of significance. It may be stated as follows: the significance to man of the physical and biotic features of his habitat is a function of the attitudes, objectives, and technical skills of man himself. This is cultural determinism. This concept in no sense eliminates the need for studying man's natural surroundings; nor does it accept the often-repeated idea that as man's technology becomes more advanced, his dependence on the natural resources of the earth decreases. It is not that the habitat ceases to be significant to the people of the industrial society. It is, rather, that its significance changes and becomes more complex. With every change in man's attitudes and objectives, and with every advance in his technical skills, the habitat must be reappraised. This kind of reappraisal is known as "sequent occupance." The concept of sequence occupance is an operational definition of the changing significance of habitat.

## Culture Regions

Attitudes, objectives, and technical skills are included in the idea of a culture. Since the geographic study of habitats has no meaning for man without tracing the interconnections with the culture of the inhabitants, one more step is required to complete the conceptual structure of geography. This is the formulation of some kind of theoretical framework for the definition of culture regions. How can homogeneities of culture be defined so that they are useful in demonstrating the changing significance of habitat, and so that the major divisions of the world in terms of man's ways of living can be identified?

This writer has presented his ideas regarding a framework of theory for the definition of culture regions at a previous meeting of the NCGE.[8] Cultures, or distinctive ways of living, originate in particular places which can be described as culture hearths. From these areas of origin the new way of living spreads, producing conflict and destruction along the advancing front where the new way of living is in contact with the older. In the whole history of *homo sapiens* (who appeared some fifty thousand years ago as the only surviving species of the *genus homo*) there have been only three periods of major culture change, when man's ways of living were fundamentally changed. First was the agricultural revolution, when crops were first planted and animals domesticated. The second great revolution took place when the "Early Civilizations" appeared in six different locations on the earth. And now we are in the midst of the third great period of revolutionary culture change.

The Industrial Revolution and the democratic revolution first appeared about the middle of the eighteenth century around the shores of the North Sea in Europe. The content of these revolutions, and the reasons for the location of these fundamental changes are presented elsewhere.[9] Spreading in somewhat different patterns from the area of origin, each of these revolutions makes contact with preindustrial and predemocratic societies. The first result of this contact is conflict and confusion, as the old ways of living collapse and as reactions against the new are set up by those who resist change. The Industrial Revolution brings economic development, produces the population explosion, changes the relation of human society to the resource base, changes predominantly rural populations into predominantly urban ones, produces the technical skill greatly to increase the food, clothing, and shelter available for man, but requires a fundamental shift of the system of values if the new skills are to be applied effectively. All the world is struggling with the problems posed by the substitution of machines and controlled inanimate power for human and animal muscles.

The democratic revolution is no less profound. The stage is set for the uncompromising struggle between autocracy and democracy, between the idea that the individual has no right but to serve the state and the idea that the state should be erected on the principle of individual dignity and of equality before the law. The reaction against the democratic revolution has been violent, especially where facism or communism are adopted.

The world is now sharply divided as a result of the impact of these two revolutions with preexisting ways of living. The first result of this impact is to increase the contrast between wealth and poverty, between autocracy and democracy. It is possible to define some eleven major regions in each of which the impact of these revolutions with preindustrial and predemocratic societies has produced a distinctive process of culture change. Within each of these eleven regions the present conditions and conflicts are similar, and in each the processes of change follow similar courses.

## A GLOBAL VIEW

The thumb test must include not only an understanding of the eco-systems and habitats based on the principles of regularity and irregularity, but also must include an understanding of the changing significance of habitat. With each change in the culture the meaning of the resource base must be reappraised—and this is a period of profound and revolutionary culture change. The processes of change associated with each of the culture regions bring about changes in the capacity of the earth to support its population, and changes in the meaning of wealth and poverty. The thumb test calls for some understanding of the interconnections among these diverse things and events, and how such interconnections are arranged on the face of the earth.

The student who gains this kind of organized concept of the earth can no longer regard the contemporary conflicts as meaningless. A global picture of change emerges, in which each individual is challenged to play a constructive part. In playing such a role the first step is to understand and appreciate the differences that distinguish one part of the earth from other parts. This is one of the three purposes of teaching geography.

### NOTES

1. Richard Hartshorne, *Perspective on the Nature of Geography* (Chicago, 1959), pp. 173–82.

2. Derwent Whittlesey, "The Regional Concept and the Regional Method," *American Geography: Inventory and Prospect,* ed. P. E. James and C. F. Jones (Syracuse, N.Y.: Syracuse University Press, 1954), p. 61.

3. Hartshorne, pp. 108–145.

4. Whittlesey, pp. 21–22.

5. Edward A. Ackerman, *Geography as a Fundamental Research Discipline,* Research Paper 53, (Chicago, 1958).

6. Preston E. James, "Toward a Further Understanding of the Regional Concept," *Annals of the Association of American Geographers,* XLII (June 1952), 195–222.

7. Preston E. James, *A Geography of Man,* 2nd ed. (New York, 1959), pp. 25–37.

8. Preston E. James, "Geography in an Age of Revolution," *Journal of Geography,* LXII (March 1963), 97–103.

9. Preston E. James and Nelda Davis, *The Wide World* (New York, 1959), and Preston E. James, *One World Divided* (New York, 1964).

# 21

## INTRODUCTORY GEOGRAPHY:
## TOPICAL OR REGIONAL

Introductory courses in geography at the secondary school or college levels are usually structured to reach one of two contrasting objectives. One of these objectives is to introduce the student to geography as a field of learning. The other is to introduce the student to the world as interpreted by geographers.

To approach the first of these two objectives, the student is taught to attack problems the way a geographer does. He is led to ask questions of a geographic nature, and to make use of appropriate methods to find answers. He is exposed to organizing theories which are the conceptual structures around which geographical data are grouped. He finds out about the research clusters that are currently popular. He is taught techniques, methods, and terminology. He finds out what geography is all about. There are many professional geographers today who are strongly in favor of providing rigorous training along these lines in introductory courses. Such courses are usually organized topically, as is the settlement theme course developed by the writers of the High School Geography Project.

To approach the second of these two objectives, the concepts and methods of geographic study are used as a means to develop coherent images of the contemporary world. The idea is to use the geographer's tools and theories to place in perspective the complex events that characterize different segments of the earth. The map of the world's lands and oceans is filled in with systematically organized information, to which meaning is assigned because of the

Reprinted from *Journal of Geography,* 66, 2 (February 1967), 52–53.

framework of concepts to which the information is attached. This is applied geography. This is geography taught not as an end in itself, but as a means for understanding the arrangement of things and events on the face of the earth. Such courses are sometimes called "regional courses" because they seek to illuminate the economic, social, and political conditions and problems of major divisions of the earth.

Each of these kinds of introductory courses can be—and is—vigorously defended by its proponents. The first is currently very popular with many of those geographers who have been active in advancing the "growing edges" of geography through scholarly research. But the sector of learning that is popularly assigned to geography is the second, not the first. The educated adult public assumes that geography is studied in schools and colleges in order to find out where places are and what is important about them. The nonprofessional public is less concerned about what geographers do and more concerned at the appalling geographic illiteracy of most Americans. If geography ceases to introduce students to a systematically organized picture of the world in which we live, some other subject-matter field will be called upon to fill this need.

There is danger in the tendency of many professional geographers to give beginning students a basic pre-professional training. The focus of attention on the concepts and methods of geography itself could develop into a kind of self-contemplation, and could build in student's minds a caricature of the thought structure of the field—a kind of image reflected in its own terms that could become an infinite hall of mirrors, reproducing endlessly things of trivial importance. When geographers are more concerned to use theory to deduce what should be found in particular places than they are to determine what actually is found in these places, there is then some danger that geographic study might become detached from its own universe—the face of the earth. The opposite danger—that geographic study might become an endless list of the contents of earth-space—would seem less immediate.

Let us not forget the overriding importance of using geography to teach people about the world they occupy. And let us not, as

professional geographers, become so entranced with the contempla-
tion of the methods of our field, and of its underlying theory, that
we all forget to face the challenging job of teaching about the
world.

# 22

## THE SIGNIFICANCE OF GEOGRAPHY
## IN AMERICAN EDUCATION

During the thousands of years when something called geography
has been written about, or taught to young people, two quite different objectives have guided the selection of content and method.
One is to provide an introduction to geography as a field of learning. There are, after all, certain kinds of questions concerning the
significance of location on the face of the earth that geographers,
ask, and that differ from the kinds of questions asked by scholars
in other fields of learning. What are these questions? And what are
the methods of finding answers that scholars in this field have
found useful? Ever since the time of Eratosthenes in ancient
Greece, there have been scholars and teachers seeking better ways
to reach this basic objective of introducing geography through an
understanding of its general concepts.

The other objective is to provide a useful image of the contemporary world as interpreted by geographers. Geographic concepts
are used to illuminate the conditions and problems of particular
places on the earth for such practical purposes as making a living,
or seeking the solution of social problems, or guiding the work of
public administrators, or making war. When we talk about educating
young people to become citizens in a democracy, this is the kind of
geography that is needed. In Greece, at about the time of Christ,
the geographer Strabo wrote a voluminous series of books presenting the most reliable information he could find for the use of
Roman administrators.

In American education, these two objectives recur with varying
emphasis since the first schools and colleges were established in the

Reprinted from *Journal of Geography,* 68, 8 (November 1969), 473–83.

colonial period. Unfortunately it has become common to think of them as incompatible—as requiring the selection of one or the other, but not both. The effort to introduce young people to the conditions of the contemporary world has, in fact, led to attempts to stuff too many unrelated facts into young minds. The reaction to this has been the formulation of a "new geography," organized around a new framework of concepts or theory. But after such a new conceptual structure was set forth there were two results: first the teachers found themselves unprepared to teach the new materials; and second the lay public began to press for more effective teaching of facts about places. Both led to a recurrence of rote learning, until the swing of the pendulum produced another new geography. The pendulum used to swing back and forth with intervals of many decades. Now the pendulum is producing a new geography almost every year with thoroughly confusing results.

The two objectives were clearly identified by the seventeenth-century geographer, Bernhardus Varenius. His first books were what he called *special geography*—they were studies of Japan and Siam, written in response to the demand for this kind of practical information among the Dutch traders of Amsterdam.[1] His major work, however, was the *general geography,* in which general concepts about the earth were treated systematically.[2] Varenius, himself, did not think of general and special geography as two incompatible methods of studying the earth as the home of man. Special geography, he insisted, was dependent on the general concepts of the field, but the application of these general concepts to the understanding of particular places made the concepts useful. Unfortunately Varenius died in 1650 at the age of twenty-eight, before he was able to demonstrate the essential unity of the two approaches. Since that time general and special geography (or topical and regional geography) have become competitive rather than complementary.

This paper seeks to put the two objectives into clearer perspective, and asks the question whether a truly "new geography" might not serve both.

### THE INTERPLAY OF TOPICAL AND REGIONAL
### GEOGRAPHY IN THE SCHOOLS

William Warntz's search through the records reveals that geography was regularly taught at the college level in the seventeenth and eighteenth centuries.[3] The widely used text was the general geography of Varenius, usually the Latin editions which had been edited by Isaac Newton. The students were expected to apply the latest theory regarding the effects of gravity on the motions of earth, moon, and other celestial bodies around the sun. All this required the use of mathematics applied to practical problems.

At the same time there was an increasing demand from the lay public that a college education should include some knowledge of where places are in the world, and how one place differs from another. There were books, written in Great Britain, that could be used as texts—books filled with information like gazetteers, books to be committed to memory. Notable were the texts of Patrick Gordon [4] and William Guthrie.[5] These books were used along with Varenius, or with the simplified version of general geography written by Isaac Watts.[6]

After the United States became independent, there was a strong demand for texts that would present geography with an American rather than a British bias. It was to fill this need that the American clergyman, Jedidiah Morse, wrote his books. The Morse geographies were the world's first financially rewarding educational publications. The earliest one, written when Morse was in his early twenties and had just graduated from Yale, was intended for use in the secondary schools.[7] It proved so very successful that Morse decided to write larger and more complete books for mature readers. His *American Geography* and his *American Universal Geography* in two volumes went through numerous revisions between 1789 and 1819. They were widely read for many decades not only in schools and colleges but also in American homes.[8] His books were described as "staunchly American, orthodox in religion, and ultra-conservative in moral tone." [9] It is important that the use of Morse's texts was enthusiastically recommended by the leading educators of that period, including the presidents of Harvard and Yale.

According to Warntz, the replacement of topical geography by the regional gazetteers of Morse resulted in such a decrease of the intellectual content of college courses that the subject was dropped from the curriculums.[10] The colleges continued to require an examination in geography for admission, based on Morse's texts. There were two results. First, geography became a regular part of the secondary school curriculums. And second, after the subject was dropped from the colleges, there were no places where prospective teachers could get training in general geography. Geography lessons, taught by untrained teachers, consisted of recitations from memory of collections of facts organized by political divisions. Teachers experimented with any kind of method that would make such memory work more palatable. Warntz quotes the recollections of a woman who attended school in the mid-nineteenth century.[11] The class, she recalled, would sing:

> Oh Winnipeg, dear Winnipeg, if you
>         will be my bride
> I'll take you down to Athabask, and be
>         your Slave, he sighed.
> This so distressed Miss Winnipeg, she called
>         him a Great Bear,
> And at the Slave she threw the Salt and
>         Toole, and all were there . . .

As each place was mentioned in the song, some one from the class pointed to the location on a map of Canada.

### THE NEW GEOGRAPHY OF CARL RITTER

Meanwhile, events of great importance to the study of geography were taking place in Europe. Jean Jacques Rousseau was leading a revolt against the traditional methods of educating children. In 1762 he outlined a method of teaching that would encourage children to develop their own individual capacities rather than to repeat from memory what their elders thought to be appropriate. The Swiss educator, Johann Pestalozzi, argued that clear thinking was dependent on accurate observation, and that words could have no meaning unless they were related to something perceived by the senses. In Germany, a schoolmaster named Christian G. Salzmann was excited by these radically different teaching methods. To experiment properly, Salzmann sought a child just ready to start through the educational process, who had not been exposed to the traditional methods. The boy he adopted for this purpose in 1784 was the five-year-old Carl Ritter.

Ritter grew up devoted to a career of teaching geography. He was less inclined than his contemporary, Alexander von Humboldt, to ask questions about the earth and man, and to seek answers to these questions. Rather he wanted to present the things he had found in the form of books. His major themes included the essential unity of man and nature, and the concept of a divine plan that would explain the observed facts of man on the earth—much as a carpenter's plan would determine the construction of a house. Ritter insisted that there was a new "scientific" approach to geography in contrast to the traditional "lifeless summary of facts about countries and cities, mingled with all sorts of scientific incongruities." [12] Every detailed observation, said Ritter, must be related to the general laws that govern the operation of processes on the earth. This was the "new geography" in 1817.

Geography in America was greatly influenced by Arnold Guyot, one of Ritter's devoted disciples. Guyot came to Boston from Switzerland in 1848. So exciting were his new ideas about education that he was invited to talk to the Massachusetts Board of Education about his new teaching methods. In 1854 Guyot became professor of physical geography and geology at the College of New Jersey (later Princeton). "Physical geography," he wrote, "is the science of the earth as a great individual organization. . . . Its aim is preeminently the discovery of laws which govern the material body of the earth, the atmosphere, the myriads of plants and animals, and man himself as a part of the life system. To describe these things, without rising to the causes and descending to the consequences, is no more science than merely and simply to relate a fact of which one has been a witness." [13] Guyot's ultimate explanation was given in terms of God's plan, reflecting the teleology of Ritter.

The trend toward increased emphasis on physical geography,

started by Guyot, was greatly strengthened after 1868 by the publication of a series of school texts by Matthew Fontaine Maury.[14] By 1875 his *Manual of Geography* had been adopted by some 60 percent of the states.[15]

## WILLIAM MORRIS DAVIS AND THE COMMITTEE OF TEN

William Morris Davis, however, did more than any other one person to enlarge the significance of geography in American education. Davis was a master at putting the ideas of numerous scholars together in a form easily adaptable for use as texts, and he was a tireless and persuasive salesman of what he had produced. Essentially, Davis went forward with Guyot's explanatory method, but he replaced Guyot's teleology, which was already outmoded by the work of Charles Darwin and Alfred Russel Wallace, with the newer evolutionary concepts. The idea of evolutionary change—as opposed to the notion that after the Creation things remained unchanged—he first applied to the development of landforms through youth, maturity, and old age. Man could be fitted into the same picture by analogy with Darwin's biological concepts. Human society was pictured as resembling an organism, seeking survival by adjusting to the demands of the physical environment. This form of Social Darwinism [16] was derived from the writings of Herbert Spencer. Social Darwinism, or environmental determinism, was taught in schools and colleges, and became the dominant theme of American geography.

It is interesting that both Guyot and Davis continued to support the conceptual structures they had created long after scholars in other fields had found these concepts untenable. The teleology of Ritter and Guyot was abandoned when careful observers like Darwin and Wallace could find no objective evidence of a divine plan. Social Darwinism was already being torn apart by a group of scholars at Harvard during the years when Davis was applying it to geography.[17] Unfortunately, the ideas of environmental determinism have been amazingly persistent, and even today there are examples of teachers who still make uncritical use of the ideas that have been set aside by scholars here and abroad for almost three-quarters of a century.[18]

Davis did insist on the importance of direct field observation. For him geography was an out-of-door subject, and like some of the very successful high school teachers of natural history during the nineteenth century, Davis took his students into the field to go directly to the original source of all geographical knowledge, and to confront the raw and undisturbed phenomena with which geographers must deal.[19]

In 1892 the National Education Association appointed a Committee of Ten, headed by President Eliot of Harvard, to study the related problems of the content of pre-college school programs and of college entrance requirements. The committee organized nine conferences, each to consider a specific field of study, and one of these conferences was asked to review the situation in geography. William Morris Davis, was a member of this conference,[20] and his ideas of the proper nature of geography in schools and colleges dominated the resulting report.[21] Included in what this group called geography were: elementary geography, beginning physical geography, advanced physical geography or physiography, meteorology, and geology. The Committee of Ten, commenting on the conference report, wrote, "considering that geography has been a subject of recognized value in the elementary schools . . . and that a considerable proportion of the whole school time of children has long been devoted to a study called by this name, it is somewhat startling to find that the report of the Conference on Geography . . . exhibits more dissatisfaction with prevailing methods . . . and makes the most revolutionary suggestions." [22]

The conference report was, nevertheless, adopted with its radical proposals to raise geography from pure memory work to the status of a science. Davis himself prepared textbooks and teachers' manuals that presented the new content in form suitable for school use. In many ways these textbooks on physical geography are models of clear writing and logical organization. But in less than ten years the whole effort was recognized as a failure. Why? Basically because Davis was unable to communicate his knowledge and enthusiasm fast enough to a sufficiently large number of teachers. One of the few he was able to reach became an outstanding teacher of teachers. At Ypsilanti Mark Jefferson taught an amazing number of students who later became leaders in the field.[23] But the

great majority of the teachers in secondary schools were quite unprepared to teach physical geography. Most of them could not
identify a landform in the field, and could only ask their pupils to
repeat textbook definitions from memory. In 1910 physical geography was described as a "dry, uninteresting subject."

A variety of new methods was tried in the effort to excite the
pupils. Among the methods suggested were the journey method, the
topical method, the map-drawing and interpretation method, the
problem method, and the type-study method (suggested by Charles
McMurry about 1900). But none of these methods included field
study.[24] The peak enrollment in physical geography was reached in
1896, and thereafter the subject became less and less popular.

## GENERAL SCIENCE AND THE SOCIAL STUDIES

During the first decade of the twentieth century two new developments in American schools greatly affected the significance of geography. One was the appearance of a course of study known as
"general science." This course included some of the ideas of physical geography, but it was much more firmly built on basic physics,
chemistry, and biology, and it included laboratory work rather
than field study. General science, like the present-day earth science,
paid little or no attention to the actual distribution over the earth
of its physical and biotic characteristics. In other words general science cut the ground from under the physical geography without
really satisfying the demand for knowledge about the characteristics of particular places. General science and earth science are now
firmly established in the secondary schools, and for the most part
where geography appears at all it is either as a separate field or as a
part of the social studies.

The concept of the social studies is much older than most geographers realize. It was started, according to Erling H. Hunt,[25] at
Hampton Institute about 1904, where history and some social sciences were grouped in a new division called social studies under the
chairmanship of Thomas Jesse Jones, a sociologist. When the National Education Association undertook still another review of the
secondary school curriculums in 1911, Jones was appointed as

chairman of the subcommittee to deal with this new field. In 1916, when the final report was published, the social studies was defined as including history, civics, economics, geography, and a new course called "problems of democracy." The committee was clearly more concerned with the training of young people to become citizens of a democracy than in meeting the requirements of scholarship—which represented a very great change in point of view since the Committee of Ten. As a result of the 1916 report, the school curriculums were given the following sequence:

> Grade   7: Geography and American History
>         8: American History
>         9: Community and Vocation Civics
>        10: European (or World) History
>        11: American History
>        12: Problems of Democracy

The new courses were to draw facts and concepts from the various social sciences, but without concern about the boundaries that scholars defined between disciplines. The idea was to build a program of study around problems, each of which would cut across subject-matter fields. Even school history, said the report, should follow a sociological orientation "unhampered by chronological or geographical limitations." [26] The kinds of problems that were suggested included nationalism, humanitarianism, imperialism, socialism, internationalism, industrialism, and the need for economic interdependence. Social studies, so conceived, was to become a single field in curriculum planning and in teacher education. As a result in some states where something called geography was included in the social studies, it was taught by teachers who had never been exposed to a single college-level course in geography in their preparation.

In the years immediately following World War I, a group of teachers of social studies led by Harold Rugg undertook to develop new course materials and texts to carry out this program. Recognizing their own lack of background in most fields except history, this group asked for the cooperation of subject-matter specialists. They received help from historians specializing in certain periods and countries, and from sociologists, economists, and others—but not from geographers. The leading geographers of that period who were asked to help in the insertion of "correct" geographical concepts into the social studies, replied that geography was not a social study.[27] For once the professional geographers spoke with one voice. As a result the bits and pieces of geographic ideas that were incorporated in the social studies texts were written by teachers with little understanding of geography. The bits and pieces contained numerous elementary errors, such as the comparison of areas on a Mercator projection, or the conclusion that countries in the Torrid Zone could not expect to achieve much economic development, or the information that Brazil was a major producer of rubber (which it had ceased to be about 1912). Professional geographers who resisted the inclusion of geography in the social studies were even more firmly set against this field as a result of these examples of bad geography. For a long time any professional geographer who cooperated with the social studies teachers was in danger of losing standing in his own field.

Yet some historians and social studies teachers continued to make sincere attempts to improve the geographic content. Daniel C. Knowlton, for instance, tried to give a better definition of the proper items of geographic information to include by using the "essential facts of human geography" proposed by the French geographer Jean Brunhes.[28] Knowlton charged that the geographers themselves were divided about the nature of their field, and that geography attempted to touch on all other fields without having any organizing principle of its own.

In 1926 the American Historical Association appointed another commission to make a new effort to bring unity to the social studies. The commission included historians, political scientists, economists, sociologists, and a geographer. The Carnegie Foundation provided $250,000 to support the undertaking. On this occasion the geographers were represented by Isaiah Bowman, then director of the American Geographical Society, and a former student of Mark Jefferson. Bowman had a long record of cooperation with specialists in other disciplines, for example, his European boundary studies after World War I [29] and his studies of pioneer belts.[30] The report on geography was written by Bowman, and published in 1934.[31] Geography, said Bowman, is only partly "objective science," because it includes also such unpredictable variables as human beings organized in societies. Geography, he insisted, must deal with processes, not with mapping or describing static things alone. He emphasized the importance of recapturing the thrill of discovery, which made the study of science exciting in the first place. The young people must be led to discover facts by deduction from theory and to formulate general concepts from the observation of apparently unrelated facts. This must be a major objective of teaching, he said, quite apart from any immediate social ends that may be served.

## Since World War II

For better or for worse, foreign wars have the effect of calling the attention of the lay public to the prevailing ignorance of Americans concerning place locations. The unfamiliarity of the place names that appear in the news media is blamed on the schools. The lay public was shocked in the 1950s when a survey revealed that less than a third of the college undergraduates interrogated had any useful concept of the location of such places as Laos, or Vietnam, or even Berlin. Articles and editorials in the press called for an improvement in the teaching of geography.

The social studies teachers were expected to do something about this. Geographers have long insisted that no place name should be taught unless it is attached to some information of geographic significance. Yet consider this example of how certain schools undertook to remedy the situation. In some schools near Chicago recently the pupils in a class were supplied with mimeographed lists of places, each list graded for difficulty and labelled "base hit," or "two-base hit," or "three-base hit," or "home run." The class was divided into two teams, and the team in the field threw a place name at the batter—for example, Tierra del Fuego. If the batter could reply that Tierra del Fuego was in South America, this was a home run. For some reason, probably because of its unfamiliarity to the teacher, Tierra del Fuego is considered to be very difficult. If the children could remember that it was located in South America this was enough to expect of them. To expect them to know where in South America it is located, or what is significant about it would be expecting too much. This is the kind of instruction that Pestalozzi attacked in the eighteenth century, or Guyot and Davis attacked in the nineteenth century, and that has been continuously attacked by each of the various commissions and committees in the twentieth century—all without measurable success.

Efforts to improve the social studies after World War II were continued. In the 1950s the American Council of Learned Societies appointed a committee on secondary school curriculums. In 1958 the Panel on the Social Studies arrived at the conclusion that a thoroughgoing reexamination of the objectives and methods of the social studies was needed. It was decided that the social studies should provide insight into the "mainsprings and directions of human behavior, and the resulting interactions among people." It was reported, however, that many teachers found the concepts of the behavioral sciences too abstract to be effectively taught in the secondary schools unless they were placed in the traditional historical framework.

Numerous books were written to wrestle with the problem of what concepts of human behavior should be taught in the secondary schools and how. The National Council for the Social Studies devoted a series of yearbooks first to the social studies as a whole,[32] then in successive years to several individual disciplines, including geography [33] and history.[34] The American Council of Learned Societies and the National Council for the Social Studies jointly appointed a number of subject-matter specialists to prepare a book dealing with the contributions of the several social sciences to the social studies.[35] An abundance of material was thus made available to the curriculum-studies groups which were being organized in school systems all over the United States.

Still a coherent course of studies has yet to be formulated. As Pendleton Herring remarked, the social sciences do not constitute "a single ordered body of fact and theory, operating through an internally consistent and generally accepted methodology." [36] The more specialized each social science discipline becomes the more difficult it is to demonstrate the relevance of its findings to the practical problems of public policy or to the education of citizens who must form opinions on policy. A distinguished political scientist, deploring the increasing fragmentation of the social sciences, made the comment that the public official who turns for advice to the social sciences "risks hearing nothing but noise, or of receiving fractional advice to deal with whole problems." [37]


FINANCIAL AID FROM THE FEDERAL TREASURY

The launching of the first successful earth satellite (Sputnik I) by the Soviet Union in 1957 resulted in the widespread feeling that the American educational system was in need of repair. In 1958 the Congress of the United States passed the first National Defense Education Act. Federal funds were made available to improve the teaching of science, mathematics, and foreign languages.

In 1964 the Congress revised the original act by specifying six additional fields of study that were critically in need of improvement in the interest of national security. These included English, remedial reading, and special education for the disadvantaged. And also three fields usually included in the social studies were named: history, civics, and geography. The social studies, as such, was not included. As a result federal funds were made available for aids to graduate students of geography, for teacher-training institutes, for the appointment of geographers to state education departments, for up-to-date classroom equipment, and other things. A booklet describing geography as a professional field in which students might wish to specialize was published by the Office of Education.[38]

The widespread recognition of the need to improve the teaching of geography also led the National Science Foundation to support two major programs—the High School Geography Project, directed by Nicholas Helburn, and the College Geography Project, directed by John Lounsbury. The new high school course, entitled *Geography in an Urban Age,* was ready for use in schools throughout the nation in 1969–70.[39] This is a topical course which aims to develop general concepts concerning why people live and work where they do and how they adjust to their surroundings, both natural and cultural. Instead of memory exercises the course is built around the inquiry method, helping a student to discover concepts on his own. Teachers who have tried out the various units on an experimental basis have found them intellectually exciting and effective in arousing student interest.

The Commission on College Geography has not developed any one course of undergraduate study. Rather the diversity of offerings in the colleges and universities is described. Numerous pamphlets dealing with college geography have been published.[40]


## What Kind of Geography?

These efforts to define, or redefine, the significance of geography in American education have raised a number of questions not yet answered. Most geographers involved in these efforts recognize the value of promoting diverse approaches rather than adopting one standard course to be urged upon all teachers throughout the United States. It is encouraging to realize that never before have so many professional geographers and so many experienced classroom teachers been involved in the study and improvement of geography courses in schools and colleges. That the significance of geography in American education will be vastly enlarged cannot be doubted.

Yet there is some danger that we may retrace the same futile steps taken by those who have preceded us. It could be that the "new geography" we so loudly proclaim may be just another swing of the pendulum. Unprepared teachers who have never been exposed to geographical concepts could continue to select facts about places and require young people to commit them to memory. There is nothing fundamentally different about singing songs about Miss Winnipeg and identifying Tierra del Fuego as located in South America. On January 8, 1968, the *New York Times* ran a whole column about the "New Geography" which is about to be made available. "Geography, old style," says the article, "is that subject the student bumps into in elementary school in order to learn the capital of Arizona, the annual rainfall in the Amazon Basin, or the duration of the Laotian monsoons. The new geography is much less descriptive than the traditional geography, and much more analytical, theoretical, and mathematical." This could have been written at any time during the past century.

Will the increased use of mathematics improve the teaching of geography? It might—but it has been tried before. We might agree with the person who said, "nowadays everybody thinks that science is mathematics, and that it is only necessary to study mathematics in order to understand everything else." This is not an uncommon complaint among school teachers, or college teachers for that matter. But it is a quotation from Aristotle describing conditions in ancient Greece.[41] There is nothing wrong with the attempt to make wider use of mathematics, in part because it provides the best framework for logical thinking, and in part because mathematics is a language common to all sciences. But it is important to understand that the use of mathematics does not guarantee logical thinking; it only provides a better guide to such thinking. Geographical questions must still be asked in order to get geographical answers. Furthermore there is danger that the effort to make geography more scientific will fail where it failed before—because few teachers of geography are adequately trained in mathematics.

Since the seventeenth century, according to Warntz, we have been swinging back and forth between teaching geography topically, by which he means with major attention to general concepts, and teaching it regionally, by which he means crammed with facts. From Varenius, with his use of applied mathematics, the curriculum makes shifted to Jedidiah Morse, with his uninspiring collections of facts. Since World War II some colleges in the United States have shifted away from regional courses to courses which emphasize theory. Yet it is clearly not true that the topical approach guarantees to the student the "joy of discovery," for there have been numerous examples of topically organized courses that have been described in the public press as "dry and uninteresting." And regional courses are not necessarily crammed with unrelated facts. There are some examples of such courses that provide a challenging interpretation of the conditions and problems of particular places in the world, which is one of the contributions people expect geography to provide.

## ANOTHER NEW GEOGRAPHY

Another kind of "new geography" might be developed by making a serious attempt to study regions topically. It is quite possible to lead students to discover general concepts concerning the major regional divisions of the contemporary world, thus not only introducing young people to the kinds of questions geographers ask, but also satisfying the public demand that geography should fill in the map with some kind of useful information about the significance of location.

We can agree that the period in which we live is one of rapid and fundamental change, not only in technology, but also in social attitudes and economic objectives. Too long have these changes been taught only by historians, or by specialists in different aspects of human behavior. Change also has a geography, and the geographical pattern of change is all too often overlooked. Yet there is an excellent body of theory regarding the spread of innovation.[42] Every innovation begins somewhere on the earth, in some definable "culture hearth." It spreads from the place of origin, faster in some directions, more slowly in others. Innovation sweeping into a receiving region also sets up resistance and reaction, which can be expected to appear in certain kinds of location. Innovation moves along lines of maximum accessibility; yet the places most exposed to innovation may develop as centers of reaction.

The northern part of America in the contemporary world is a major area of culture innovation. Technology in this region is far advanced over the rest of the world, so that Europeans now feel the impact of culture radiation coming from across the ocean—a kind of return current affecting the older culture hearth around the North Sea where the modern revolutionary movements began. In northern America, also, an open society is in the process of redefining its purposes and attitudes to the accompaniment of much noise and conflict. It is in this part of America that the future is being shaped for all mankind. Changes of this sort have been discussed by historians and behavioral scientists. They should also be discussed by geographers, because the patterns of innovation create geographical differences from place to place, which it is the unique responsibility of geography to analyze.

For example, consider briefly the geographical situation of Latin America as a culture region. No other major part of the underdeveloped world is receiving such massive doses of culture radiation as is Latin America. Here is rare opportunity to observe the developing patterns of change, and to seek valid ways of interpreting the patterns of change in terms of general concepts of geography. Here is a rare laboratory in which to measure the essential elements of accessibility. And in the parts of Latin America most directly exposed to innovation radiating from northern America we find the strongest reactions against innovation—in Mexico in 1910 and in Cuba in 1959. Only slowly are the innovations transformed into the kinds of change that are domestically acceptable.

A study of this and other culture regions of the modern world provides for both inductive and deductive reasoning, and also gives the student experience in distinguishing between information that is relevant to a geographical question and information that must be discarded as irrelevant. This is also a part of the scientific method, and a part that is often neglected when the student receives only data that are pre-selected for their relevance to a general concept. Such a regional study of the modern world would serve to develop geography as a challenging and useful field of learning, yet it would not neglect the responsibility for filling in the map with organized knowledge about places. It would provide a demonstration that the supposed dichotomy between topical and regional methods is a false dichotomy. And it would enrich the curriculums of schools and colleges with a highly significant "new geography."

## NOTES

1. Bernhardus Varenius (Bernhard Varen), *Descriptio Regni Japoniae et Siam* (Amsterdam, 1649).

2. Bernhardus Varenius (Bernhard Varen), *Geographia Generalis, in qua affectiones generalis Tellusir Explicantur* (Amsterdam, 1650). Later editions in Latin in 1664, 1671, and 1672. Isaac Newton edited two Latin editions published in Cambridge in 1672 and 1681; English translations in 1693 and 1712.

3. William Warntz, *Geography Now and Then*, Research Series No. 25 (New York: American Geographical Society, 1964).

4. Patrick Gordon, *Geography Anatomized, or the Geographical Grammar, being a short and exact analysis of the whole body of modern geography after a new and curious method* (London, 1693). There were some twenty revised editions, of which the latest was in 1728.

5. William Guthrie, *A New System of Modern Geography* (London, 1770). There were many revised editions of which the latest appeared in 1843. See also W. Gordon East, "An Eighteenth Century Geographer: William Guthrie," *Scottish Geographical Magazine,* 72 (1956), 32–37.

6. Isaac Watts, *The Knowledge of the Heavens and Earth Made Easy* (London, 1728).

7. Jedidiah Morse, *Geography Made Easy* (Boston, 1784).

8. Jedidiah Morse, *The American Geography* (Elizabethtown, N.J., 1789); *The American Universal Geography* (Boston, 1793). Later editions of the latter two-volume work appeared in 1796, 1802, 1805, 1812, and 1819. It was also published in London, Edinburgh, and Dublin, and in French and Dutch translations. After Morse's death in 1826, his son, Sidney Morse, continued to produce Morse geographies for many years.

9. Ralph H. Brown, "The American Geographies of Jedidiah Morse," *Annals* of the Association of American Geographers, 31 (1941), 145–217.

10. Warntz, *Geography Now and Then.* Geography was dropped from college curriculums at the following dates: Dartmouth, 1811; Harvard, 1816; Columbia, 1825; Yale, 1825; Brown, 1827; Princeton, 1829; Pennsylvania, 1831; Rutgers, 1861.

11. *Ibid.,* p. 139.

12. H. Bogekamp, "An Account of Prof. Ritter's Geographical Labors," in W. L. Gage, *Geographical Studies by the Late Professor Carl Ritter of Berlin* (Boston, 1863), pp. 33–51; reference p. 37.

13. Arnold Guyot, *Physical Geography* (New York, 1873).

14. M. F. Maury, *Manual of Geography* (New York, 1870, 1887, 1892).

15. William L. Mayo, *The Development and Status of Secondary School Geography in the United States and Canada* (Ann Arbor, Mich.: University Publishers, 1965), p. 16.

16. Jurgen Herbst, "Social Darwinism and American Geography," *Proceedings* of the American Philosophical Society, 105 (1961), 538–44.

17. John Leighly, "What Has Happened to Physical Geography?" *Annals* of the Association of American Geographers, 45 (1955), 309–18.

18. Preston E. James, "On the Origin and Persistence of Error in Geography," *Annals* of the Association of American Geographers, 57 (1967), 1–24.

19. Robert S. Platt, *Field Study in American Geography,* Research Paper No. 61 (Chicago: Dept. of Geography, University of Chicago, 1959).

20. The members of the Conference on Geography included: T. C. Chamberlin, chairman, Chicago; G. C. Collie, Beloit; W. M. Davis, Harvard; D. A. Hamlin, Rice Training School, Boston; M. V. Harrington, U.S. Weather Bureau; E. J. Houston, Philadelphia; C. F. King, Dearborn School, Boston; F. W. Parker, County Normal School, Chicago; I. C. Russell, University of Michigan.

21. I. C. Russell, "Reports of a Conference on Geography, 1892," *Journal of the American Geographical Society of New York,* 27 (1895), 30–41. One member, E. J. Houston, wrote a minority report omitting meteorology and geology.

22. National Education Association, *Report of the Committee of Ten on Secondary School Studies* (New York: American Book Co., 1894), pp. 32–33.

23. Geoffrey J. Martin, *Mark Jefferson, Geographer* (Ypsilanti, Mich.: Eastern Michigan University Press, 1968).

24. R. H. Whitbeck, "Thirty Years of Geography in the United States," *Journal of Geography*, 20 (1921), 121–28; Charles Redway Dryer, "A Century of Geographic Education in the United States," *Annals* of the Association of American Geographers, 14 (1924), 117–49.

25. Erling H. Hunt, "Changing Perspectives in the Social Studies," *High School Social Studies Perspectives* (New York: Houghton Mifflin Co., 1962), pp. 3–28.

26. James Harvey Robinson, *The New History* (New York: Macmillan, 1912).

27. Harlan H. Barrows, "Geography as Human Ecology," *Annals* of the Association of American Geographers, 13 (1923), 1–14.

28. Daniel C. Knowlton, "The Relation of Geography to the Social Studies Curriculum," *Journal of Geography*, 20 (1921), 225–34.

29. Isaiah Bowman, *The New World: Problems in Political Geography* (New York: World Book Co., 1921).

30. Isaiah Bowman, *The Pioneer Fringe* (New York: American Geographical Society, 1931).

31. Isaiah Bowman, *Geography in Relation to the Social Sciences*, Report of the Commission on the Social Studies, Part V, American Historical Association (New York: Charles Scribner's Sons, 1934).

32. Roy A. Price, ed., *New Viewpoints in the Social Sciences*, 28th Yearbook of the National Council for the Social Studies (Washington, D.C., 1958).

33. Preston E. James, ed., *New Viewpoints in Geography*, 29th Yearbook of the National Council for the Social Studies (Washington, D.C., 1959).

34. William H. Cartwright and Richard L. Watson, Jr., eds., *Interpreting and Teaching American History*, 31st Yearbook of the National Council for the Social Studies (Washington, D.C., 1961).

35. Gordon B. Turner, ed., *The Social Studies and the Social Sciences* (New York: Harcourt, Brace and World, 1962).

36. Pendleton Herring, "Toward an Understanding of Man," in Price, ed., *New Viewpoints in the Social Sciences*, pp. 1–19.

37. From an editorial in the *New York Times* for September 9, 1968.

38. Preston E. James and Lorrin Kennamer, eds., *Geography as a Professional Field* (Washington, D.C.; Office of Education, 1966); reprinted by the Association of American Geographers, 1969.

39. Published by the Macmillan Company.

40. (1) *Geography in Undergraduate Liberal Education*, 1965; (2) *A Basic Geographical Library*; (3) *A Selected and Annotated Book List for American Geography*, 1966; (4) *New Approaches in Introductory College Geography Courses*, 1967; (5) *Introductory Geography; Viewpoints and Themes*, 1967, (6) *Undergraduate Major Programs in American Geography*, 1968; (7) *Climatology: An Interdisciplinary Approach*, 1968; (8) *A Systems Analytic Approach to Economic Geography*, 1969. Resource Papers: (1) *Theories of Urban Location*, 1968; (2) *Air Pollution*, 1968. Technical Paper: *Field Training in Geography*, 1968. Available at the Central Office, Association of American Geographers.

41. Aristotle, *Metaphysica,* trans. E. Gershenson and D. A. Greenberg (New York: Blaisdell, 1963): reference in Book I, p. 51.

42. Peter Haggett, *Locational Analysis in Human Geography* (New York: St. Martin's Press, 1966), pp. 56–70.

# BIBLIOGRAPHY

A Chronological List of the Writings and Major
Addresses of Preston E. James, 1922–1971

ARTICLES AND ADDRESSES

"Köppen's Classification of Climates: A Review." *Monthly Weather Review* (February 1922), 69–72.

"The Geographic Setting of the Tacna-Arica Dispute." *Journal of Geography*, 21, 9 (1922), 339–48.

"Geographic Factors in the Development of Trans-Andean Communications." *Bulletin of the Geographical Society of Philadelphia*, 21, 3 (1923), 74–83; reprinted in *Bulletin of the Pan American Union*, (November 1923) and "Las Communicaciones Transandinas entre Argentina y Chile; Factores Geograficos del Desarrollo," *Boletin de la Union Panamericana* (Julio 1924), 700–13.

"The Upper Parana Lowland: A Problem in South American Railroad Development." Address: American Association for the Advancement of Science, Boston Meeting (December, 1922); *Journal of Geography*, 22 (1923), 245–56; reprinted in *Pan American Bulletin* (March, 1924).

"The Transportation Problem of Highland Colombia." *Journal of Geography*, 22 (1923), 346–54.

"Feats of Railroading in the Andes." *Popular Mechanics Magazine* (April, 1924), 538–42.

"The Possibilities of Cattle Production in Venezuela." *Bulletin of the Geographical Society of Philadelphia*, 22, 2 (April, 1924), 45–46.

"Geographic Principles and Their Application to the Teaching of Geography." Address, Michigan Schoolmasters Club (April, 1924); *Journal of Geography*, 23, 4 (April 1924), 136–41.

"Outline for a Course on the Principles of Geography." Mimeographed by Edwards Brothers, 1924, with R. Burnett Hall.

"A Suggested Outline for the Treatment of a Geographic Region." Address, Michigan State Teachers Association (October 1924); *Journal of Geography*, 23 (October 1924), 288–91, with R. Burnett Hall.

"The Climate of Trinidad." *Monthly Weather Review*, 53, (February 1925), 71–75.

"Geographic Factors in the Development of Transportation in South America." *Economic Geography*, 1 (1925), 247–61.

"The Pitch Lake, Trinidad." *Journal of Geography,* 24 (September 1925), 212–20.

"Geographic Factors in the Trinidad Coconut Industry." *Economic Geography,* 2, 1 (January 1926), 108–25.

"Some Geographic Relations in Trinidad." *The Scottish Geographical Magazine,* 42 (March 1926), 84–93.

"L'Isola Di Trinidad." *Le Vie D'Italia e Dell 'America Latina,* 32 (November 1926), 1231–36.

"A Geographic Reconnaissance of Trinidad." *Economic Geography,* 3, 1 (January 1927), 87–109.

"Notes on the Geography of Trinidad." *Journal of Geography,* 25, 4 (April 1927), 130–42.

"Iquique and the Atacama Desert." *The Scottish Geographical Magazine,* 43 (July 1927), 203–15.

"Regional Geography." *A Chorographical Study of the World,* 2 vols. (June 1929), mimeographed by Edwards Brothers.

"The Blackstone Valley: A Study in Chorography in Southern New England." *Annals* of the Association of American Geographers, 19 (June 1929), 67–109.

"Filling in the Map: The Freshman Work in Geography at the University of Michigan." *Journal of Geography,* 29 (1930), 199–202.

"The Tapajoz and Xingu Valleys of Brazil: A Type Study in the Evolution of Amazon Landscape." *Bulletin of the Geographical Society of Philadelphia,* 28 (April 1930), 63–77.

"The Shari Plain." *Journal of Geography,* 29 (1930), 319–30.

"Vicksburg: A Study in Urban Geography." *Geographical Review,* 21 (April 1931), 234–43.

"The Coffee Lands of Southeastern Brazil." *Geographical Review,* 22 (1932), 225–44.

"Bello Horizonte and Ouro Preto: A Comparative Study of Two Brazilian Cities." *Papers, Michigan Academy of Science, Arts and Letters,* 18 (1932; published 1933), 239–58.

"The Higher Crystalline Plateau of Southeastern Brazil." *Proceedings of the National Academy of Sciences of the U.S.A.,* 19 (January 1933), 126–30.

"Notes on a Journey up the Valley of the Rio Doce, Brazil." *Journal of Geography,* 32 (March 1933), 98–107.

"Rio de Janeiro and São Paulo." *Geographical Review,* 23 (April 1933), 271–98.

"The Surface Configuration of Southeastern Brazil." *Annals* of the Association of American Geographers, 23 (September 1933), 165–93.

"A Specialized Rice District in the Middle Parahyba Valley of Brazil." *Papers, Michigan Academy of Science, Arts and Letters,* 19 (1933; published 1934), 349–58.

"The Terminology of Regional Description." First of a series on

"Conventionalizing Geographic Investigation and Presentation." *Annals* of the Association of American Geographers, 24 (1934), 78–86.

"Industrial Development in São Paulo State, Brazil." *Economic Geography*, 11 (1935), 258–66.

"A Quantitative Comparison of Methods of Measuring Land Use." *Papers, Michigan Academy of Science, Arts and Letters*, 21 (1935; published 1936), 355–57.

"Regional Planning in the Jackson Hole Country" *Geographical Review*, 26 (1936), 439–53.

"The Geography of the Oceans: A Review of the Work of Gerhard Schott." *Ibid.*, 664–69.

"The Surface Configuration of South America." *Papers, Michigan Academy of Science, Arts and Letters*, 22 (published 1937), 369–72.

"On the Treatment of Surface Features in Regional Studies." *Annals* of the Association of American Geographers, 27 (1937), 213–28.

"The Distribution of People in South America." In C. C. Colby, ed. *Geographic Aspects of International Relations*, (Chicago: University of Chicago Press, 1938), Harris Foundation Lectures, 1927; pp. 217–40.

"The Changing Patterns of Population in São Paulo State, Brazil." *Geographical Review*, 28 (1938), 353–63.

"Air Masses and Fronts in South America." *Ibid.*, 29 (January 1939), 132–34.

"Itabira Iron." *Quarterly Journal of Inter-American Relations*, 1 (April 1939), 37–48.

"Forces for Union and Disunion in Brazil." *Journal of Geography*, 38, 7 (October 1939), 260–66.

"O problema da colonizacao permanente no sul do Brasil." *Revista Brasileira de Geografia* (Outubro 1939), 70–81; paper presented before the Associacao dos Geografos Brasileiros.

"The Problem of Foreign Immigration in Brazil." *Papers, Michigan Academy of Science, Arts and Letters*, 25 (1939, published 1940), 385–95.

"The Expanding Settlements of Southern Brazil." *Geographical Review*, 30, 4 (April 1941), 121–37.

"The Process of Pastoral and Agricultural Settlement on the Argentine Humid Pampa." *Journal of Geography*, 40, 4 (April 1941), 121–37.

"The Contribution of Geography to the Social Studies." *Social Education*, 5, 5 (May 1941), 334–38.

"Expanding Frontiers of Settlement in Latin America—A Project for Future Study." *The Hispanic American Historical Review*, 21, 2 (May 1941), 183–95.

"Geopolitical Structures in Latin America." *Papers, Michigan Academy of Science, Arts and Letters*, 27 (1941, published 1942).

"Water Power Resources in Brazil." *Economic Geography*, 18 (1942), 13–16.

"The Surface Features of Southeastern Brazil: A Review." *Geographical Review*, 33 (1943), 135–39.

"As Terras Cafeeiras do Brasil Sudeste." *Boletim Geografico* (Brasil), 3 (Agosto 1945), 701–16.

"Western Solidarity." *Land Policy Review*, 4, 8 (October 1941), 41–44.

"Differences from Place to Place." *Journal of Geography*, 45, 7 (October 1946), 279–85.

"A Configuracao da Superficie do Sudeste do Brasil." *Boletim Geografico* (Inst. Brasileiro de Geografia e Estadistica), Ano. IV, 45, (Dezembro de 1946), 1104–21.

"The Service of Geography in Government." *Our First Twenty-Five Years* (Worcester, Mass.: The Clark Graduate School of Geography, 1946), pp. 47–52.

"Belo Horizonte e Ouro Preto, Estudo Comparativode Duas Cidades Brasileiras." *Boletim Geografico* (Inst. Brasileiro de Geografia e Estadistica), Ano. IV, 48 (Março de 1947), 1598–1609.

"Instructing Pupils in Map Reading." *Social Education*, XI, 5 (May 1947), 205–208, with Gertrude Whipple.

"A Expansao das Colonias do Brasil Meridional." *Boletim Geografico* (Inst. Brasileiro de Geografia e Estadistica), Ano. V, 49 (Abril de 1947), 21–34.

"Developments in the Field of Geography and Their Implications for the Geography Curriculum." *Journal of Geography*, 46, 6 (September 1947), 221–26.

"Teaching Geographic Understanding." *The American School and University, 1947–48* (19th annual edition), pp. 194–98, with Gertrude Whipple.

"Geography." *Encyclopaedia Britannica—Ten Eventful Years*, 2, 450–53.

"Objectives of Geography." *Ontario Educational Association Year Book and Proceedings*, 1947, pp. 44–46.

"Trends in the Teaching of Geography." *Cram's Classroom Classics*, 3, 2 (1948), 1–5.

"The São Francisco Basin: A Brazilian Sertao." *Geographical Review*, 38, 4 (October 1948), 658–61.

"Formulating Objectives of Geographic Research." *Annals* of the Association of American Geographers, 38, 4 (December 1948), 271–76.

"Understanding the Significance of Differences from Place to Place." In Clyde F. Kohn, ed., *Geographic Approaches to Social Education* (Washington, D.C.: 19th Yearbook of the National Council for the Social Studies, 1948), pp. 27–37.

"On the Treatment of Controversial Topics of Geography." *Journal of Geography*, 48 (February 1949), 45–58.

"The Significance of Industrialization in Latin America." *Economic Geography*, 26 (July 1950), 159–61.

"Programa para Un Relevamiento Geografico de America," Ministerio de

Educacion, Universidad de Buenos Aires, Facultad de Filosofia Y Letras, Instituto de Geografia, Serie A, 15 (1950).

"An Assessment of the Role of the Habitat as a Factor in Differential Economic Development." *Papers and Proceedings, American Economic Review,* 41 (May 1951), 229–38.

"The Cultural Regions of Brazil." In T. Lynn Smith and Alexander Marchant, *Brazil, Portrait of Half a Continent* (New York, 1951), pp. 86–103.

"Observations on the Physical Geography of Northeast Brazil." *Annals* of the Association of American Geographers, 42, 2 (June 1952), 153–76.

"Toward a Further Understanding of the Regional Concept" (Presidential Address, AAG, 1952). *Annals* of the Association of American Geographers, 42, 3 (September 1952), 195–222.

"A Program for an Exploratory Survey of the Americas." *Revista Geografica,* 9 & 10 (1952), 61–79.

"Mapping at Chorographic Scales." *Proceedings, VIIIth General Assembly —XVIIth Congress,* (Washington, D.C.: International Geographical Union, 1952).

"Patterns of Land Use in Northeast Brazil." *Annals* of the Association of American Geographers, 43 (1953), 98–126.

"Trends in Brazilian Agricultural Development." *Geographical Review,* 43 (1953), 301–28.

"Latin America." In Howard R. Anderson, ed., *Approaches to an Understanding of World Affairs* (Washington, D.C.: 25th Yearbook of the National Council for the Social Studies, 1954), 102–17.

"Conditions of Economic Development." *Encyclopaedia Britannica Book of the Year, 1955,* pp. 29–30.

"Brazilian Agricultural Development." In S. Kuznets, W. E. Moore, and J. J. Spengler, eds., *Economic Growth: Brazil, India, Japan* (Durham, N.C.: Duke University Press, 1955), pp. 78–102.

Geography and Responsible Freedom in the Americas." In Angel del Rio, ed., *Responsible Freedom in the Americas* (New York: Columbia University, Bicentennial Conference Series, 1955), pp. 180–87.

"Geography." *Encyclopaedia Britannica* (1956), 10, 139–53.

"The Problem of Brazil's Capital City." *Geographical Review,* 46 (1956), 301–17, with Speridiao Faissol.

"Latin America: State Patterns and Boundary Problems"; "Latin America: Economic and Demographic Problems"; "Latin America: Four Case Studies." In W. G. East and A. E. Moodie, eds., *The Changing World* (London: Harrap; New York: World Book Co., 1957), pp. 881–941.

"Man's Role in Changing the Face of the Earth." *Economic Geography,* 33 (1957), 267–74.

"Changes in the Geography of Trinidad." *Scottish Geographical Magazine,* 73, (1957), 158–66.

"Man-Land Relations in the Caribbean Area." In Vera Rubin, ed., *Carib-*

*bean Studies: A Symposium* (Kingston, Jamaica: Institute of Social and Economic Research, University College of the West Indies, 1957), pp. 14–21.

"Four Basic Trends in the Postwar World." In C. F. Kohn, ed., *The United States and the World Today* (Chicago: Rand McNally, 1957), pp. 2–17.

"New Viewpoints in Geography." In National Council for the Social Studies *Yearbook,* (1958), pp. 39–64.

"The Nations of North'America." In *The Romance of North America,* (Boston: Houghton Mifflin, 1958), pp. 7–39.

"The Core and Boundaries of Regional Science." *Papers and Proceedings of the Regional Science Association,* 4 (1958), 23–26.

"The Geomorphology of Eastern Brazil as Interpreted by Lester O. King." *Geographical Review,* 49 (April 1959). 240–46.

"Recent Developments in Latin America." *Journal of Geography,* 58 (April 1959), 167–74.

"American Geography at Mid-Century." In National Council for the Social Studies *Yearbook* (1959), pp. 10–18.

"The Hard Core of Geography." *Ibid.,* pp. 1–9.

"The Use of Culture Areas as a Frame of Organization for the Social Studies." *Ibid.,* 162–76.

"Remarks on the Presentation of Papers." *The Professional Geographer,* XI, 5 (September 1959), 6–8.

"The Dissertation Requirement." Based on an address before the ninth annual Deans and Directors Pinebrook Conference, September, 1959, Syracuse University. *School and Society* (March 26, 1960), 147–48.

"Prepodavanie Geografii v Coedinennykh Shtataxh Ameriki" (The Teaching of Geography in the United States of America). *Geography in the School,* 6 (1959), 52–58, with Jack Fisher.

"Santo Domingo de Los Colorados—A New Pioneer Zone in Ecuador." *Economic Geography,* 36 (1960), 221–30, with Al L. Burt, C. B. Hitchcock, C. F. Jones, and C. W. Minkel.

"Implications of the Race Between Economics and Population in Latin America." *The Annals of the American Academy of Political and Social Science,* 330, (July 1960), 95–102.

"New Perspectives on Teaching Geography." *Current Issues in Higher Education* (1962), p. 3.

"The Region as a Concept." *Geographical Review,* 42 (1962), 127–29.

"Geography." In Gordon Turner, ed., *The Social Studies and the Social Sciences* (New York: American Council of Learned Societies and National Council for the Social Studies, 1962), pp. 42–87.

"Geography in an Age of Revolution." *Journal of Geography,* 62 (1963), 97–103.

"Dynamics of National Power." *Military Review,* 43 (1963), 17–26.

"A New Look at Latin America—How Bright the Future." *U.S. News and World Report*, 15, 2 (July 8, 1963), 72–83.

"George Babcock Cressey, 1896–1963." *Geographical Review*, 54 (1964), 254–57.

"A New Concept of Atmospheric Circulation." *Journal of Geography*, 63 (1964), 245–50.

"Some Attributes of the Regional Concept." Paper presented at the 20th International Geographical Congress, London (1964).

"A Conceptual Structure for Geography." *Journal of Geography*, 64 (1965), 292–93.

"Estructura Conceptual de la Geografia." *Revista Geografica*, 34 (1965), 5–28.

"Recent Developments in Latin America." *Journal of Geography*, 65 (1966), 260–65.

"Resources for the Future." *Social Education*, 30 (1966), 614–17.

"Careers in Geography." *Bulletin of the National Association of Secondary-School Principals*, 50 (1967), 49–52.

"Introductory Geography: Topical or Regional." *Journal of Geography*, 66 (1967), 52–53.

"On the Origin and Persistence of Error in Geography" (Honorary Presidential Address, 62nd Annual Meeting of the AAG, Toronto, 1966). *Annals* of the Association of American Geographers, 57 (1967), 1–24.

"Hunger and Communism in the Developing World" (Address at Honors Convocation, Eastern Michigan University, May, 1967). Published Eastern Michigan University Press (July 1967).

"Continuity and Change in American Geographic Thought." In S. B. Cohen, ed., *Problems and Trends in American Geography* (New York, 1967), pp. 3–14.

"Some Fundamental Elements in the Analysis of the Viability of States." In Charles A. Fisher, ed., *Essays in Political Geography*, London: Methuen & Co., 1968, pp. 33–37.

"Changing Patterns of Population and Settlement in Latin America." In S. P. Chatterjee, ed., *Developing Countries of the World* (Calcutta: 21st International Geographical Congress, 1968), pp. 89–92.

"Geography in the Secondary Schools." *Encyclopedia of Education.*

"The Significance of Geography in American Education." *Journal of Geography*, 68 (1969), 473–83.

"Geographic Factors and National Strength." *Perspectives in Defense Management* (Industrial College of the Armed Services) (December 1969), 21–30.

"World Population in Historical Perspective." In Paul F. Griffin, ed., *Geography of Population*, 1970 Yearbook of the National Council for Geographic Education (Palo Alto: Fearon, 1969), pp. 15–26.

"Epilog." *The East Lakes Geographer* (special edition on Latin America), 6 (1970), 90–94.

BOOKS

*An Outline of Geography.* Boston: Ginn and Company, 1935.
*Latin America.* New York: Odyssey Press, 1942; second edition, 1950; third edition, 1959; fourth edition, 1969.
*Brazil.* New York: Odyssey Press, 1946.
*A Geography of Man.* Boston: Blaisdell, 1949; revised, 1959; third edition, 1966.
*American Geography, Inventory and Prospect.* Ed. with Clarence F. Jones. Syracuse: published by Syracuse University Press for the Association of American Geographers, 1954.
With Gertrude Whipple: New York: Macmillan Company: *Our Earth,* 1947, 1954; *Using Our Earth,* 1947, 1954; *Living on Our Earth,* 1948, 1955; *At Home on Our Earth,* 1949, 1955; *Neighbors on Our Earth,* 1950, 1955; *Our Earth and Man,* 1951, 1955; *Our Changing Earth,* 1954; *Como Vivimos en la Tierra,* 1959.
*Man on the Earth.* With Gertrude Whipple and Morris Weiss. New York: Macmillan Company, 1971.
*The Wide World, a Geography.* With Nelda Davis. New York: Macmillan, 1959, 1967.
*New Viewpoints in Geography.* Editor, National Council for the Social Studies Yearbook, 1959.
*One World Divided.* Boston: Blaisdell, 1964.
*One World Perspective.* Boston: Blaisdell, 1964.
*Introduction to Latin America.* New York: Odyssey Press, 1964.
*Geography as a Professional Field.* Editor, with Lorrin Kennamer. Washington, D.C.: Office of Education, H.E.W., 1966; reprinted by the Association of American Geographers and the National Council for Geographic Education, 1969.
*All Possible Worlds, A History of Geographical Ideas.* Indianapolis: Bobbs-Merrill, forthcoming.

# INDEX

Ackerman, E. A., 82
Aerial photography: 17; and large surveys, 23–24
Africa: explorations of Ibn Batutah, 11; resource survey, 23; vegetation and soil maps, 96
Agassiz, Louis, 54, 198
Agriculture: American Indian, 138; Blackstone Valley, 138, 140, 142–44, 148, 150, 163–73; Brazil, 268–69; Jackson Hole area, 185–87, 192–95; land-use surveys, 203; origins and dispersal, 204; Trinidad, 212–21, 225–32
Agricultural development: 337–39; Brazil, 261, 270–71; Planalto Central of Brazil, 263–64
Agricultural regions, 96
Al-Baladhuri, 11
Al-Biruni, 11
Alexander the Great, 10, 349
American Council of Learned Societies, 381
American Geographical Society: 51; Latin American research, 198–201; Millionth Map Project, 201
American Historical Association, 379
Anaximander, 8
Anthroposphere, 335
Apianus, Petrus, 12–13
Arab geographers: 11, 336; and climate zones, 327
Arctic explorations, 51
Area, definition, 35
Area differentiation, 85, 288
Area studies. See Regionalism
Argentina: Humid Pampa, 338–40; railroad surveys, 202–203
Aristotle: 68, 336, 349; sphericity of earth, 8
Ashmead, Percy H., 200
Asia: Humboldt's travels, 15

Association of American Geographers, xi–xii, 3–4
Astronomy, 306
Atlantis, 50
Atmosphere, 334–35
Atmospheric movement, 61–63
Atwood, Wallace W., 26
Avicenna, 53

Bacon, Roger, 11
Baker, O. E., xiv
Barbacena, Brazil, 252
Barbed wire, 339
Barents, Willem, 51
Barnes, Torbern, 12
Baulig, Henri, 20
Belém, Brazil, 258
Belo Horizonte (Bello Horizonte), Brazil, 233–53, 260, 270
Bergman, Torbern, 12
Bienewitz, Peter. See Apianus, Petrus
Bingham, Hiram, 198
Biosphere, 335
Blackstone Canal, 145–46
Blackstone Valley, 132–80
Blumenbach, J. F., 13
Bolton, H. E., 207
Boundaries, regional, 307
Boundary problems: Europe, World War I, 200; Guatemala-Honduras, 200
Bowman, Isaiah, 198–201, 288, 379–80
Brand, Donald, 208
Brazil: 20, 99, 120; Belo Horizonte and Ouro Preto, 233–53; capital city plans, 254–72; field research, 207; Planalto Central, 262–64
Brazilian Highlands, 56
British Land Utilization Survey, 23
Brunhes, Jean, 19, 287–88, 304, 379
Buache, Philippe, 12, 16
Bucher, August Leopold, 79

399

Railroads: Belo Horizonte, Brazil, 246–47; Blackstone Valley, 146–47

Rank-size theory of cities, 45, 59

Ratzel, Friedrich, 20, 25, 27

Reclus, Élisée, 19

Region: area differentiation, 84–91; definition, 31, 35–36, 307; inexact use of word, 43; parallel systems, as defined by different processes, 90; *see also* Culture regions

Regional boundaries, Argentine Humid Pampa, 340

Regional concept in geography: 78ff, 127–28, 293, 358; research objectives, 95ff

Regional geography, 323, 367–69; French tradition, 19–21; James's perspective, 280–81; Ritter, 16; Varenius, 371; and topical geography, dichotomy between, 66–67

Regional planning: Jackson Hole area, 181–96

Regionalism, 4, 294

Regionality, 83

Research, geographic: 123ff; definition, 125; exploratory studies, 125–28; genetic studies, 128–29; Latin America, 197ff; regional approach to geography, 95ff; remedial studies, 129–31

Relationships, geography as study of, 24–27

Remote sensing, 31

Residential areas, Belo Horizonte, Brazil, 250

Resource utilization, 343–44

Revolutionary change. *See* Social change

Richthofen, Ferdinand von, 18

Rio de Janeiro, 233, 242–43, 247, 257–62, 266, 272

Rio Doce, Brazil, 247

Ritter, Carl: 14–17, 61, 373–74; as regional geographer, 67

Rousseau, Jean Jacques, 373

Rugg, Harold, 378

Russell, R. J., 281

Russia, soil geography of, 21

St. Brandan's Island, 50

Salvador, Brazil, 256

Salzmann, Christian G., 374

São Paulo, Brazil, 242–43, 257–59, 265–66

Sauer, Carl O.: xiii–xiv, 22, 27, 207–208, 281, 288; land-use surveys, 203; Latin American research, 203–204; revolt against Social Darwinism, 58

Scale: chorographic, 101–105; of field maps, 101; geographic, 102; global, 102–103; intermediate, 99; large-scale studies, 97–99; mapping at different scales, 100–101; and regional patterns, 91–95; small-scale studies, 96–97; topographic, 101–103

Schlüter, Otto, 27

Scientific knowledge: 6–7, 285–86, 291–92; developments in 16th–19th centuries, 11–17; and the social sciences, 329–30

Semple, Ellen C.: 26; Social Darwinism, 58

Sequent occupance: xiv, 119, 127, 296, 305–306, 363; Blackstone Valley, 132, 137–50; Jackson Hole area, 183, 185–87

Settlement patterns: 331; Blackstone Valley, 137–45, Brazil, 254–57, 261, 270; Jackson Hole area, 183, 185–87; Latin America, 275; Mexico, 204; Minas Gerais state, Brazil, 252; Trinidad, 223–26

Shantz, H. L., 96

Significance and concept formulation, 38–40

Site selection: capital city of Brazil, 265–72; criteria for, 268

Slavery, Trinidad, 215, 224, 226

Smith, William, 12–13

Social area analysis, Belo Horizonte, Brazil, 243–51

Social change: 314ff, 353, 364; Latin America, 273–74

Social class, Brazil, 254–55

Social Darwinism, 57–58, 69, 375

Social processes, 292

Social sciences: and geography, 6; integration of in education, 325–26; intuitive judgment in, 88–89; and